Sport and Society

Series Editors

Benjamin G. Rader

Randy Roberts

A list of books in the series appears at the end of this volume.

Sport and Exercise Science

Sport and Exercise Science

Essays in the History of Sports Medicine

Edited by

Jack W. Berryman and Roberta J. Park

University of Illinois Press
Urbana and Chicago

© 1992 by the Board of Trustees of the University of Illinois
Manufactured in the United States of America
1 2 3 4 5 C P 5 4 3 2 1

This book is printed on acid-free paper.

Library of Congress Cataloging-in-Publication Data

Sport and exercise science : essays in the history of sports medicine
  / edited by Jack W. Berryman and Roberta J. Park.
        p.   cm. — (Sport and society)
    Includes bibliographical references and index.
    ISBN 0–252–01896–6 (cl : alk. paper). — ISBN 0–252–06242–6 (pbk. :
alk. paper)
    1. Sports medicine—History.   I. Berryman, Jack W.   II. Park,
Roberta J.   III. Series.
RC1210.S638   1992
617.1′027′09—dc20   91–27220
                                                                                          CIP

Contents

Acknowledgments

We would like to thank the North American Society for Sport History for permission to reprint the following essays (with slight editorial modifications) from the *Journal of Sport History:* Whorton, "'Athlete's Heart': The Medical Debate over Athleticism, 1870–1920" (9:1 [Spring 1982]); Park, "Physiologists, Physicians, and Physical Educators: Nineteenth-Century Biology and Exercise, *Hygienic* and *Educative*" (14:1 [Spring 1987]); Vertinsky, "Exercise, Physical Capability, and the Eternally Wounded Woman in Late Nineteenth-Century North America" (14:1 [Spring 1987]); J. Todd, "Bernarr Macfadden: Reformer of Feminine Form" (14:1 [Spring 1987]); Mrozek, "The Scientific Quest for Physical Culture and the Persistent Appeal of Quackery" (14:1 [Spring 1987]); Whorton, "Muscular Vegetarianism: The Debate over Diet and Athletic Performance in the Progressive Era" (8:2 [Summer 1981]); and T. Todd, "A History of Anabolic Steroids in Sport" (published as "Anabolic Steroids: The Gremlins of Sport," 14:1 [Spring 1987]).

Appreciation is also extended to the American College of Sports Medicine for allowing us to include a revised version of Berryman's essay, "Exercise and the Medical Tradition from Hippocrates through Antebellum America: A Review Essay," which originally appeared in *Exercise and Sport Sciences Reviews* (17 [1989]).

We also wish to thank Larry Malley for showing an initial interest in this book, Benjamin Rader and Randy Roberts for their early encouragement and support, and Dick Wentworth for his persistence in convincing us to finish the manuscript.

Jack W. Berryman

Roberta J. Park

Jack W. Berryman and Roberta J. Park

Introduction

In 1976, a contributor to a feature article in *The Physician and Sports-medicine* prophesied that "by 2001, there will be a bona fide specialty in sport medicine."[1] Responding to influences similar to those that led to the founding of the American College of Sports Medicine (ACSM) in 1954, various local, national, and international organizations expressed an interest in "sports medicine" and/or "exercise and sports sciences." In 1960, Warren R. Johnson, editor of *Science and Medicine of Exercise and Sports,* observed that although "in recent years great progress has been made in the scientific study of exercise and sports," the interests of researchers and the ways in which they approached these topics had remained so diverse across different areas of specialization that the "entire research field associated with exercise and sports" remained diffuse and even bewildering.[2] Three decades later, Allan J. Ryan, former team physician for the University of Wisconsin and past editor of *The Physician and Sportsmedicine,* offered a similar opinion when he declared that "the strict definition of areas of medical practice is made difficult by the fact that many designations are historically rather than logically developed." He noted that this was also the case for "sports medicine," which had "developed gradually, though sporadically, over a period of 2500 years."[3]

The Greeks, as we know, honored the body, elevating it to aesthetic realms expressed statically in bas-reliefs and statues and dynamically in the athletic contest. They also developed a systematic approach to the body that upheld a close connection between exercise and medicine. Exercise, both as part of hygiene and for harmonious all-round development, was advocated for the average citizen. Specific training regimens—and specialists who possessed detailed knowledge of the body and its functions (*gymnastes*)—were devised for athletes. The Middle Ages, by contrast, was singularly unconcerned with such interests. In the nineteenth century, in substantial measure in response to the resurrection of "the athletic impulse," both medical and physiological interest again began to be directed at ways to clinically and scientifically understand and work with elite performers. These endeavors might appropriately be characterized as the distant and embryonic outlines of modern "sports medicine."

If we are to come to grips with these early antecedents, we must be willing to cast a rather large net, including in our investigations interests and events that, at first glance might appear too removed. But a closer inspection of contemporary sources and Dr. Ryan's recent analysis of the subject should serve to keep us on course. First, sports medicine today continues to draw "upon many scientific and nonscientific areas of inquiry and practice."[4] Moreover, the practice of "sports medicine" is not confined to physicians alone.[5] If this was the case in 1989, it was all the more so in the nineteenth and early twentieth centuries.

The January 1991 issue of *The Physician and Sportsmedicine* listed eighty-two groups that considered themselves involved in some manner with "sports medicine." In addition to organizations like the ACSM and the American Academy of Orthopaedic Surgeons, the list included groups such as the Association for Fitness in Business, National Athletic Trainers Association, Amateur Athletic Union, President's Council on Physical Fitness and Sports, and the Women's Sports Foundation. The array included nutritionists, health care professionals, physicians, researchers in the psychosocial as well as biological sciences, teachers, coaches, and entrepreneurs—to cite only some of the types of individuals interested in exercise, fitness, recreational sports, physical education, and/or elite athletics who feel, in some manner, a relationship to "sports medicine."[6] At the very least, the following areas are generally perceived to be embraced, at least conceptually, under the modern rubric "sports medicine": (1) medical supervision of the athlete; (2) special, or adapted, physical education; (3) therapeutic exercise; and (4) the role of exercise in the prevention of chronic degenerative diseases.[7] These four tend to be considerably expanded in the popular mind to include a vast assortment of exercise and "fitness" activities, many of dubious worth, as any quick glance at the magazine section of the local supermarket will attest.

The quest for "scientific" sports medicine has a lengthy history. The myriad issues, concerns, controversies, and downright myths that surround current debates about physical activity, athletics, and personal health have their roots in the nineteenth and earlier centuries. Indeed, the essays that comprise this volume clearly attest to the lengthy history of numerous ideas and practices that we believe are our own modern creations. Many of our conceptions, in fact, still bear traces of their Greco-Roman origins. While the precursors of our post—World War II search for a scientific understanding of the exercising body may have been present by the last decades of the nineteenth century, the ghosts of Hippocrates and Galen still linger in many popular ideas and practices.

By the 1870s, a few physiologists and scientifically oriented physicians, along with a handful of physical educators, began to undertake experimental investigations of the exercising body. An early and continuing interest centered upon the heart and circulation. Efforts were also made to study the dietary intake and the influence of metabolism on athletic performance. Such studies were pursued in Britain, the United States, France, and elsewhere. But it was in Germany, the home of modern *experimental* science, that "sports medicine" first became an identifiable field of study.

By the1890s and early 1900s, many athletic teams in the United States had a "team surgeon." Yet "sports medicine" did not become a formally identified area of endeavor in this country until the founding of the American College of Sports Medicine in 1954. Since the 1960s, a burgeoning interest in the scientific study of human performance has resulted in the formation of numerous specialized societies and journals (e.g., sport biomechanics and sport psychology). Exercise physiology and exercise biochemistry are now wellestablished research specialties. And the team physician and highly qualified athletic trainers are now an integral part of intercollegiate as well as professional sport. These developments, and much more, attest to the fact that sport, fitness, exercise, and the body are major industries in modern society. Similarly, the scholarly study of these phenomena has expanded dramatically in the last three decades. One such area has been the history of sport and exercise.

This volume offers a historical perspective on the growing field of sports medicine and the scientific study of exercise, sport, and physical education. Because, historically, attempts to understand the body and its responses to increased physical activity (whether in calisthenics, out-of-door pursuits, or competitive athletics) have attracted a great amount of fanciful theorizing, attention is also directed to the persistence of "pseudoscience." A special edition of the *Journal of Sport History* devoted to "Sport, Exercise, and American Medicine" was published in 1987. Shortly thereafter, we began to think about the development of a work such as this. Although the *JSH* special issue forms the core of this volume, the present volume also draws from other published works. Moreover, it includes new essays that have never been published.

We believe that these essays will be of interest to scholars working in several fields (e.g., history, American studies, sociology, anthropology, medical history, and women's studies). Given its timeliness, it is likely that the volume will also be of interest to the general reader. Most contemporary practitioners, athletes, coaches, and sports officials now fully realize the value of modern "scientific" sports medicine and exercise science. Yet the opportunity to examine the historical antecedents of these and such related topics as nutrition, metabolism, athletic training, school-based physical education, and social constructions of human performance potentials and limitations has been limited.

All-inclusiveness has not been our objective. Indeed, the field is still too broad to attempt any encyclopedic approach. Instead, we look at what we believe are important traditions, trends, and ideas. Each author is already known for having made valuable contributions to the history of exercise, sport, the body, and so forth. The contributors also represent a range of academic backgrounds—history, medical history, exercise science, American studies, physical education, and Germanic languages.

In the opening chapter, Jack Berryman examines the long-standing association between exercise and medicine, beginning with the Hippocratic and Galenic tradition and continuing through the mid-nineteenth century. As part of the doctrine of the "six things non-natural," exercise in sufficient quantity and intensity was recommended by physicians for a healthy life-style. The importance of exercise was carried into the nineteenth century via the broader concepts of the "laws of health" and the hygiene movement and was finally embodied in the term "physical education."

In chapter 2, Roberta Park looks at both persistence and change in the ways athletes were trained in Britain and America between 1800 and World War I. The emergence of a new "amateur" ethos in the mid-1800s dislodged earlier perceptions and ultimately resulted in altered ideas about how one should prepare for a major competition. By the turn of the century, a growing number of investigators were examining the physiological effects of intense muscular effort. Nevertheless, trainers continued to rely predominantly on "experience," and rarely on much that was more "scientific."

The effect of strenuous athletic participation on the heart and circulation attracted extensive interest and concern among athletes, coaches, and the medical community in the decades between 1870 and the 1920s. In chapter 3, James Whorton documents the debate in the medical literature during the late nineteenth and early twentieth centuries. By the early 1900s, it was increasingly acknowledged that the "athletic heart" was not a "diseased organ" but a "superior pump." For decades, however, the "hypertrophied" heart was the source of debate within athletic circles.

By the late 1800s, some physiologists and physicians had joined with the growing field of physical education in advocating carefully designed school and college programs directed by well-trained professionals. Female as well as male physicians contributed to the formation in 1885 of the Association for the Advancement of Physical Education. Those who had studied physical training in Europe were convinced that the German and Swedish systems were considerably more "scientific" than anything to be found in America. The nineteenth-century interest in the nervous system, brain, and "mind" (especially strong in English-speaking coutries) also formed an important part of the emergent "theories" of physical education. With the ascendancy in the early 1900s of "play" as an important development and evolutionary process, games and sports became an official part of the physical education curriculum. Roberta Park examines these issues in chapter 4.

In chapter 5, Patricia Vertinsky analyzes the Victorian contention that women were "eternally wounded" as a consequence of the menses and their reproductive functions. Too much study, it was widely believed, would lead to "mental strain," uterine complaints, and even complete breakdown. A somewhat convoluted logic held that academic study for women was a threat to the future of "the race." Carefully controlled exercise and participation in sport were invoked to enable women to attain a modicum of strength (which would allow them to undertake limited intellectual pursuits) and sometimes as an effective agent of social control.

Not everyone, however, fully subscribed to the prevailing Victorian and Edwardian views of women. As Jan Todd makes clear in chapter 6, early twentieth-century physique contests staged by physical culturist Bernarr Macfadden stressed vitality, strength, and body proportion. He considered these to be as valuable for women as for men. And his "perfectly developed woman" earned her title through a combination of bodily form and moderate proficiency in athletic events. Although censured by Anthony Comstock and others, Mac-fadden, through his contests and publications, presented an alternate model to the woman who was "inferior," "weak," and "eternally wounded."

In the early 1900s, the desire to achieve understanding and rational control of the individual and society intensified. In chapter 7, John Hoberman describes the emergence of "sports medicine" in Germany and its development as a recognized field by the 1920s. German physicians, physiologists, and psychologists focused especially upon efforts to understand high level sport performance. The first Sportartz (sport physician's) congress took place in September 1912. By 1924 the German Association of Physicians for the Promotion of Physical Culture had initiated the world's first sports medicine journal. Interest in "constitutional theory" and an "athletic type" (popularized in the 1920s by Ernst Kretschmer) was used by Nazi theorists to buttress their arguments about variations in human performance among different populations and races.

The quest for an "ideal" body and for understanding human performance attracted the interest of investigators in several countries in the late 1800s and early 1900s. The borders between "science and quackery," however, were, and are, difficult to maintain. In chapter 8, Donald Mrozek discusses ambiguities and tensions occasioned by the desire to scientifically study fitness and the body and persistent appeals to "quackery." Much as unqualified "experts" still purvey their "systems" and "theories" of exercise and fitness today, nineteenth-century charlatans were ever ready to foist their views on the American public.

The final two chapters deal with issues of current national concern—nutrition and drugs. They also return our attention to fundamental questions of health, hygiene, and bodily function, which are as old as the ideas of Hippocrates. What constitutes the best diet? How does increased physical activity affect the body's needs? What are the social and moral—as well as physiological—effects of the use of ergogenic aids?

In chapter 9, James Whorton surveys the literature relating to diet and athletic achievement, looking specifically at claims made by vegetarians during the first half of the twentieth century. John Harvey Kellogg ("father of the pre-cooked breakfast cereal industry") was a leading critic of meat, presumed to be a major cause of "autointoxication" caused by putrefying bacteria in the intestinal tract. Yale professor of physiological chemistry Russell Chittenden, likewise, eschewed the consumption of large quantities of meat protein. Terry

Todd follows in the final chapter with an historical survey of the use of anabolic steroids by athletes and strength seekers to enhance performance. This paper offers a compelling perspective from which to reconsider debates about steroids, an issue that is currently engaging the attention of the educational, legal, and medical communities.

Notes

1. "Gameplan: Athletes and Sports—Bigger and Better in 2001?" *The Physician and Sportsmedicine*, 4 (1976), 27.

2. Warren R. Johnson, ed., *Science and Medicine of Exercise and Sports* (New York: Harper & Brothers, 1960), xiii–xiv.

3. Allan J. Ryan and Fred L. Allman, *Sports Medicine*, 2nd ed. (San Diego: Academic Press, Inc., 1989), 3.

4. Ibid.

5. Ibid.

6. "Sportsmedicine Groups in 1991," *The Physician and Sportsmedicine*, 19 (1991), 105–18.

7. Ryan and Allman, *Sports Medicine*, 12.

1 *Jack W. Berryman*

Exercise and the Medical Tradition from Hippocrates through Antebellum America: A Review Essay

Cary Kimble has shown that since the 1960s we have seen a revival of "interest among many Americans in 'lifestyle' health care: jogging and bicycling, health foods, special diets, sports and exercise, yoga and meditation, health spas, reformed smoking and drinking habits."[1] Kimble noted that Robert Rodale's *Prevention* magazine, with a circulation of 2,225,000 in 1980, was the fastest growing U.S. magazine except for *People*. In addition, books such as *Better Homes and Gardens Family Medical Guide,* Fixx's *Complete Running Book*, Eshleman and Winston's *American Heart Association Cookbook*, and Morehouse and Gross's *Total Fitness in 30 Minutes a Week*, dominated the *New York Times* best-seller list during the 1970s. These have been replaced by Jane Fonda's *Workout*, Pearson and Shaw's *Life Extension: A Practical Scientific Approach*, among numerous others, and a multitude of diet books in the 1980s. John Naisbitt in his own best-seller *Megatrends*, published in 1982, believed that the recent trend of individuals promoting and improving their own health was the "triumph of the new paradigm of wellness, preventive medicine, and wholistic care over the old model of illness, drugs, surgery, and treating symptoms rather than the whole person."[2] He substantiated his point with statistics of millions of exercising Americans, changing diets, health foods, and fitness equipment sales.

More recently, in 1988, at a regional hearing to provide input for improving public health by the year 2000, organized by the U.S. Public Health Service and the National Academy of Sciences' Institute of Medicine, Dr. Mark Oberle from the Centers for Disease Control in Atlanta testified that "we could be pushing ahead with high-tech medicine when the dollars would be better put to use in a preventive strategy that reduces the burden of illness on society." Additional testimony by Dr. Peter Pulrang, medical consultant for Washington State's Department of Social and Health Services' Bureau of Parent and Child Health, suggested that "the idea is to figure out how to prevent things from happening rather than just treating them after the fact."[3]

These few examples of America's changing health care system, as well as the thoughts of health care professionals, are only the tip of the iceberg when it comes to providing examples of the "new era" in medicine. No one living in American society during the 1980s could avoid noticing the increased interest in popularizing a preventive form of health behavior. Much like the lessons taught during the time of Hippocrates and Galen, we are told to breathe fresh air, eat proper foods, drink the right beverages, exercise, get adequate sleep, have a bowel movement a day, and take into account the emotions when analyzing our overall well-being. These "laws of health," which are presently so effectively disseminated throughout the population via a system of public and private schools as well as through an elaborate media network of published materials, tapes, films, videos, television, and radio, were usually referred to as the "six things non-natural" before the mid-nineteenth century. While we have benefited immensely from technological advances in the communications process during the twentieth century, the primary method of health popularization from the ancient period through the 1850s was the published book. Accordingly, the primary objective of this chapter is to review the book literature pertaining to the "six things non-natural" and to explain their critical role in hygiene education before 1860.

Today, research has shown quite convincingly that exercise is good for one's health and that insufficient exercise can be detrimental to overall bodily functioning. Although adequate data to support these conclusions are fairly recent in historical terms, the recognition of the necessity for sufficient exercise for healthy living dates back to at least Hippocrates (460–370 B.C.) and Galen (129–210 A.D.). The concept of medicine as articulated by these two ancient physicians became known as the "humoral theory" and up through the eighteenth century was often referred to as "Galenic medical theory."

Galen, who borrowed much from Hippocrates, structured his "theory" around the naturals (of, or with nature—physiology), the non-naturals (things not innate—hygiene), and the contra-naturals (against nature—pathology). Central to this theory were the six non-naturals: (1) air, (2) food and drink, (3) motion and rest, (4) sleep and wake, (5) excretions and retentions, (6) passions of the mind.[4] The non-naturals needed to be utilized in moderation as to quantity, quality, time, and order; for if taken in excess or put into an imbalance, disease would result. Regulation of the six non-naturals could also influence the naturals, especially the qualities (hot, cold, moist, and dry) and the humors (blood—hot and moist; phlegm—cold and moist; yellow bile—hot and dry; and black bile—cold and dry). Therefore, along with drugs and surgery, the non-naturals were critical therapy for a variety of disease states. Exercise then, as part of motion and rest in the non-natural tradition, was incorporated in much of the early regimen, hygiene, and preventive medicine literature, and, to a lesser extent, the literature of therapeutic medicine. While exercise was recommended as therapy for a variety of ailments and as a cure for those suffering from gout, dyspepsia, and consumption among others, the focus of this chapter is on exercise and prophylaxis rather than exercise as treatment.

Classical Greek preventive hygiene was part of formal medical training through the eighteenth century and continued on in the American health reform literature of the first half of the nineteenth century. During the latter period, an effort was made to popularize the "laws of health" as the non-naturals came to be known. Their maintenance and balance was something that each individual had to be responsible for. Accordingly, "self-help," "self-regulation," "self-management," "health behavior," and "personal health" were all popular terms used in the preventive medicine literature of the nineteenth century.[5]

Before getting to the most important books of the non-natural tradition, there is a section devoted to an explanation of the "six things non-natural" and the history of the term. This is followed by a review of some recent historical studies utilizing the non-natural concept. Then, since our major focus within the non-naturals is exercise, an analysis of the historical literature pertaining to exercise is included.

The remainder of the chapter is developed chronologically with an emphasis on the key authors and their books representing the non-natural theme. These primary sources are supplemented by appropriate secondary literature. The book coverage begins with the origins of the non-naturals in the ancient period, resumes in the sixteenth and seventeenth centuries in western Europe with the revival of the theme during the Renaissance, and continues through the eighteenth century Enlightenment when the non-natural tradition was expanded. Beginning with the nineteenth century, books by American physicians and American editions of European publications are surveyed. These publications, all dealing with preventive medicine and hygiene, are divided into two groups representing thirty-year time periods. The first group of books was published between 1800 and 1830 and the second group between 1831 and 1860. This section is followed by a final cluster of books, also published between 1830 and 1860. They represent a literature that began using the term "physical education," which at the time embodied the non-natural tradition.

In each of these books from the ancient period through antebellum America, it is shown that much of the contents, structure, and message was attributable to the non-natural tradition. Consequently, numerous medical books had entire sections or chapters devoted to exercise. In addition, just as physicians decided to write individual works on air, diet, sleep, evacuations, or passions of the mind, several physicians published treatises on exercise.

The "Six Things Non-natural" and the History of the Term

As explained in the introduction, the non-natural tradition is inherent to humoral theory and Galenic medicine. Historian Edward Withington provided a detailed analysis of the naturals, non-naturals, and contra-naturals and presented the complicated material in a clear manner. The role of exercise and rest in the "theory" related to its effects on the qualities and humors in particular. It was believed that excessive rest would increase cold and moisture, whereas excessive exercise would at first heat the body and then be followed by cold and dryness. Moderate exercise would maintain warmth. Various baths were also part of this division. Baths of different temperatures and contents (sweet, salt, bitter, etc.) were recommended for their coolness, dryness, or heating capabilities. Since causes for disease were thought to be due to heat, cold, dryness, or moisture, exercise and the other non-naturals played important roles in therapy. Regulating the six non-naturals along with drug prescription and surgery were all within the physicians' realm. However, the non-naturals also played a significant role in hygiene. Those liable to illness or those wishing to maintain their healthfulness were given a regimen whereby the six non-naturals were regulated to provide a proper balance.[6]

It was medical historian L. J. Rather, in his book on Jerome Gaub (1705–80) in 1965, who first began exploring the origins, meaning, and use of the term "non-naturals." In his discussion of two of Gaub's essays published in 1747 and 1763, Rather noted that "physicians of Gaub's day still held to some aspects of the Galenical tradition of medical treatment with great persistence. Down to the end of the eighteenth century they continued to write books, monographs, and dissertations on the six non-naturals."[7] Later in the book, Rather explained that "the conception of the non-naturals is especially set forth by Galen, although he does not use the term."[8] Curious about the term, Rather then provided some additional information in his footnotes. Gaub himself believed that "the term indicates their position midway between things in accord with nature *(secundum naturam)* and against nature *(contra naturam)*."[9] Galen's *Ars medica* also contained some relevant passages. Rather explained that the "conserving causes *(phylaktika aitia)* of health and disease include both necessary and non-necessary factors, the former being those which cannot be avoided and therefore the more important. They are numbered by Galen as follows: (1) air, (2) motion and rest, (3) sleeping and waking, (4) that which is taken in, (5) that which is excreted or retained, (6) the emotions or passions. Whether they are good or bad for the health depends on their various relations with other things."[10] Finally, Rather suggested that Levinus Lemnius (1505–68), in reference to a passage in Galen's *Ars medica,* provided another explanation of the term. Lemnius noted, "Galen's conserving causes are termed non-naturals by later physicians not because they are praeternatural but because they are things external rather than within us."[11]

His interest piqued by the non-natural dilemma that surfaced in his book on Gaub, Rather published an article on the subject in which he investigated "the origins and fate of a doctrine and a phrase." He explained that the concept or doctrine referred to the "six categories of factors that operatively determine health or disease, depending on the circumstances of their use or abuse, to which human beings are unavoidably exposed in the cause of daily life. Management of the regimen of the patient, that is, of his involvement with these six sets of factors, was for centuries the physician's most important task."[12] Rather also noted that the "*phrase* 'six things non-natural' makes its debut early in the history of Western European medicine. It plays an important role for six centuries or more. Then, early in the nineteenth century, it bows out, departs from the scene, and is forgotten."[13] Although the term itself was not used, Rather was clear to point out that "medical involvement with the factors designated by the phrase remains as active as ever, but they are now subsumed under the rubric of physical and moral (or mental) hygiene."[14] He concluded that "the term and phrase were introduced into the Western European medical vocabulary in Latin translations of Arabic works largely based on Galen."[15]

After Rather's initial article in *Clio Medica* in 1968, several other historians of medicine began researching and writing about the term in the medical history literature of the early 1970s. Jarcho's essay appeared in the *Bulletin of the History of Medicine* in 1970. Here, like Rather, he traced the concept to Galen's *Ars medica*.[16] The following year, the same issue of the *Bulletin* included articles on the non-naturals by Niebyl and Bylebyl. Both authors attributed their interest in the topic to Rather and Jarcho. Niebyl suggested that Joannitius, a translator of Galen's works into Arabic, obtained the non-naturals term from Galen's pulse books "rather than from an imperfect recollection of the list of necessary causes in the *Ars medica,* as suggested by Rather."[17] And, important for the purposes of this chapter, Niebyl asserted that "although the humoral aspect of ancient doctrine gradually disappeared, the regimen of the non-naturals continued to play a dominant role in medicine, especially in the more popular hygiene literature."[18] Bylebyl, through further reading of Galen's works on the pulse, discovered that Galen had in fact written, "First is change of [the pulse] according to nature. Second is [change] which is neither according to nature, nor entirely against nature. Third is [change] which is against nature." In a later discussion, Bylebyl said, "Galen referred to the second category several times as non-natural causes."[19] Bylebyl also noted that "from the kinds of things he placed in these three categories it also appears that the non-naturals are activities which are more or less optional and not harmful in themselves, as distinct from unavoidable circumstances and activities which are either essential for life (the naturals) or intrinsically pathological (the praeternaturals)."[20] Temkin's book on Galenism as a medical philosophy also devoted some attention to the non-natural tradition and its origins.[21]

The final article published in the 1970s was by Burns. He referred to the earlier work of Rather, Jarcho, Niebyl, and Temkin and called the non-naturals "a paradox in the western concept of health."[22] Burns noted that in the Galenic tradition, "physicians were needed by those suffering from praeternatural conditions. As prognosticators and therapists, they were expected to discern the nature of the imbalance among the naturals or between the naturals and non-naturals."[23] Also, as hygienists, "physicians were expected to protect their patients from harm by attending especially to the non-naturals. Prescribing a proper regimen of non-naturals would secure a group of healthy clients attuned to the beneficent purposes of nature."[24] The paradox, as Burns saw it, resided in the fact that since the latter decades of the nineteenth century when physicians devoted themselves to disease rather than health, "the traditional obligation of physicians to act as hygienists" disappeared along with the idea of the non-naturals.[25]

Recent Historical Studies Utilizing the Non-natural Concept

On the basis of the previous section, it is not surprising to learn that medical historians did not begin to include the non-naturals in their research until the early 1970s. Once the term, its origins, and its significance were better understood, however, it did not take long for historians to begin to produce some important publications. Burnham, in his recent book, explained why historians were attracted to the topic:

> Implicit in the historians' interest in the non-naturals was the striking and amusing fact that the specific content in the modern obsession with the health of body and mind closely resembled those ancient teachings about the non-natural elements essential to life. In the late twentieth century and in Roman times both, health writers believed that health was profoundly determined by those elements: air, food and drink, movement and rest, evacuation and retention, and harmonious "passions of the soul." The continuities were perfectly explicit. . . . By the 1980s only the term had disappeared from much of the health advice popularizers were still passing on.[26]

While historians like Rather,[27] Riley,[28] and Jackson[29] acknowledged the existence of the non-naturals, or the "laws of health" like Verbrugge,[30] others have done significant research on the non-natural tradition or its individual components.

Coleman's work on the *Encyclopedie* explained the origins of the modern hygiene movement in eighteenth-century France and the non-naturals were central to this research. At the outset, he explained that "during the eighteenth century both conception and action with regard to the health of the individual were identified with the use of the Galenic-Arabic 'six things non-natural.' The use of the non-naturals was essential to the definition of health advocated by Enlightenment authors, notably Arnulfe d'Aumont writing in the *Encyclopedie*."[31] In fact, in his essay on "Hygiene," Aumont stated, "These conditions are essentially defined by the proper use of the *six things* which we call, following the ancients, *non-natural*. They become natural when our use of them benefits health and contra-natural when their use is harmful to the animal economy. . . . The rules which must be stated regarding their good and bad effects constitute practical medicine, that is, hygiene."[32] Lawrence's article included a discussion of the non-naturals as used in Buchan's *Domestic Medicine* and Burnham devoted considerable attention to the role of the non-naturals in the popular health literature in the United States.[34] Smith explained how the non-naturals were incorporated into the self-help literature of late eighteenth-century England;[35] Dannenfeldt published an article on the theory and practice of sleep as one of the non-naturals during the late Renaissance;[36] and Lomax discussed the non-naturals as the basis for instruction in health and human physiology in the American school system during the 19th century.[37]

Exercise and the Non-naturals in the Historical Literature

Although numerous books and articles have been written about the history of exercise, medical gymnastics, and physical education, one is struck by the paucity of information concerning the relationship between exercise, medicine, and good health. Not until Haley's book in 1978 did any historian studying exercise even mention the non-naturals. Haley referred to "natural law" and the "laws of nature" and then noted that "physicians increasingly turned to hygiene and to the *res non-naturales*—air, water, food, sleep—as the basis of their therapeutics."[38] Finney, writing in 1966 about medical theories of vocal exercise, referred to Galen's "six eminently sensible rules" and listed the traditional six. While she did not use the non-naturals as a term, it is clear she was aware of the concept.[39] Whorton's *Crusaders for Fitness,* published in 1982, included the best description and analysis of the non-naturals and their role in American health reform during the first half of the nineteenth century.[40] While not yet published, Virginia Smith's essay on "regimenical literature in Britain from 1700–1850, with special reference to exercise," examined the household book literature on regimen and exercise within the context of the non-naturals.[41]

At least two authors writing about the history of exercise included the term "non-naturals" in their articles, but only because it was mentioned in a book they were quoting. Fletcher quoted Giorgio Baglivi (1669–1707) who referred to "the six nonnatural things." Then in a note Fletcher said that "in medieval medicine, the six 'nonnatural' things (things which caused health or disease and were not actual parts of the human parts) were meat and drink, retention and evacuation, air, exercise, sleep and waking, and passions of the mind."[42] Licht noted that "Rhazes was the first Arab physician to write a book on hygiene" and it stated "health is preserved by a just measure of exercise and the other non-naturals."[43]

Most of the remaining literature reviewed in this section is devoted to the history of physical education and the key individuals and important developments that assisted in the profession's growth. Exercise in one form or another is their major focus, but invariably most of the authors look toward educational literature rather than medical history for information. There has been commendable work done listing what exercises people performed, explaining systems of exercise, and identifying major proponents of exercise, but very little research into the origins of the medical rationale for exercise. Most historians have looked to the "humanistic educators" of the Renaissance as a source of interest in the body rather than to the role exercise played in the non-natural medical tradition. Even those who have looked at the influence of medicine seem surprised that the topic of exercise would be discussed by a physician or appear in a medical publication. In reality, most of the interest in exercise came from the non-natural tradition and those educators espousing exercise were doing so as a result of medicine's influence.

Leonard and Affleck did not mention Hippocrates or Galen but referred to Cardano (1501–76) and Mercurialis (1530–1606). They wrote about "physical training advocated by writers on education" and devoted an entire chapter to Locke and Rousseau. In the same chapter, they also noted that "a number of medical writers had been directing attention to the importance of bodily exercise in the restoration and preservation of health" and devoted some space to Friedrich Hoffmann (1660–1742) and Joseph-Clement Tissot (1750–1826).[44] Joseph's four articles published in 1949 are filled with valuable information on exercise in both education and medicine. He utilized many original works and dealt with most of the leading individuals from the sixteenth to the eighteenth centuries. The four-article series is one of the most important cursory views of the topic.[45] Hackensmith briefly referred to Galen and Mercurialis but included very little else on medical writers and their influence on physical education.[46] Brailsford had a chapter entitled "Exercise, Education and Social Attitudes, 1600–1650" and one on "The Motion of Limbs." A major section of the latter chapter was devoted to "Medicine and Exercise." Here he gave considerable attention to Robert Burton, Francis Fuller, and John Locke. Brailsford's analysis was excellent and he did a good job with the medicine and exercise relationship.[47] Finally, Van Dalen and Bennett noted that Galen "devoted considerable attention to the influence of exercise and diet upon health."[48] Later, in their discussion of the Enlightenment, they stated "medical men began to study anatomy and physiology, and a number of treatises appeared concerning exercises and their influence on health."[49]

Some of the best work to be done on exercise, health, and medicine was authored by John Betts and Roberta Park. While neither dealt directly with the role of exercise in the non-natural tradition, both were keenly aware of the significant role played by medicine in the popularization of exercise. Betts's 1968 article on "Mind and Body in Early American Thought" was quite inclusive and mentioned most of the major medical works and their authors during the first fifty years of the nineteenth century. While we now know that a medical rationale for exercise was developed before the nineteenth century, or the Enlightenment for that matter, Betts was still not wrong when he said, "In the quarter century between 1820 and 1845 educators, physicians, and reformers had begun to develop a philosophical rationale concerning the relationship of physical to mental and spiritual benefits derived from exercise, games, and sports. From the diffusion of ideas developed by the medical profession under the influence of the Enlightenment and by educators and reformers affected by the romantic spirit, Americans were alerted to the threat against their physical and mental powers that came from the confinements of the home and school and the more sedentary habits of the city."[50] Betts's article, "American Medical Thought on Exercise as the Road to Health, 1820–1860," also quite inclusive and informative, concluded in much the same way as his earlier article: "A scientific and medical rationale for the movement toward health reform, physical education, field sports, athletics, and exercise for the masses had nonetheless been laid by scores of conscientious, observant, and informed physicians in the decades prior to the Civil War."[51] Again, while Betts was not really wrong, the rationale being promulgated was nothing more than a continuation of the value of exercise for good hygiene as stipulated by the non-natural tradition.

Roberta Park has written more authoritatively about the history of health and exercise than any other individual. Although she has written more, only six of her articles are dealt with here. The first reviewed is the most important one for our purposes since she dealt with the writings of eighteenth-century physicians and informed laypersons on health and exercise. Here, although she did not refer to the term or concept of the non-naturals, Park summarized her research in a sound and accurate manner:

> During the 1700s a substantial number of works were written by physicians and informed laymen who expressed concern for the maintenance and restoration of health and/or for hygiene and the role of exercise and active recreations in the growth and development of children. The publication of popular medical texts in the vernacular, rather than the traditional Latin,

and the translation of several of these works into other languages enabled an increasingly literate citizenry to become acquainted with the ideas presented. Those who read such works could hardly escape their message—active physical exercise, along with proper diet, rest, and similar care, could be a powerful means for achieving, preserving, and even restoring, health."[52]

Park also wrote about New England Transcendentalists and their attitudes toward health and exercise, concerns for health and exercise in the English educational reform movement of 1640 to 1660, and the concern for the physical education of American women during the antebellum period.[53] A major part of the latter research dealt with "various medical and quasi-medical contributions" and in that section Park made reference to "the laws of health."[54] While not dealing with the reasons why, Park said that "both doctors and laymen authored books and pamphlets on the general subject of health, many of which devoted considerable attention to matters of hygiene and physical education."[55] Additional articles by Park dealt with the "healthful regimens" of the sixteenth- and seventeenth-century Utopian authors and the American hygienic and educative interests in athletics and physical education between 1865 and 1906.[56]

Eleanor English has also written meaningfully about exercise, health, and the influence of a few key Renaissance physicians. She discussed the writings of Girolamo Cardano (1501–76) and Thomas Elyot (1490–1546) in her 1982 article[57] and added Christobal Mendez (1500–61) and Hieronymus Mercurialis (1530–1606) to her 1984 essay.[58] In analyzing the writings of the four physicians, it is clear that English was not aware of the non-natural tradition or the role exercise played in it. She credited "the Italian humanists who advocated an educational curriculum *(studia humanitatis)* which brought forth the harmonious development of the whole man *(l'uomo universale)*— intellectually, morally, and physically" for introducing "the concept of exercise as being necessary for physical and mental development."[59] Later, in the same article referring to Cardano's *Care of Health* (1560) and the appearance of materials on exercise, English suggested that "by this inclusion of a treatise on exercise in a medical work, an unusual occurrence, exercise was given status among medical concerns."[60]

Two recent books provide an informed treatment of exercise, health, and the American medical community. Whorton, already mentioned, wrote eruditely and convincingly about the antebellum health reform movement and was fully aware of the role and importance of the non-natural tradition. Early in his book, in reference to

Jacksonian "hygienic optimism," Whorton explained that "as modern as that optimism was, it borrowed heavily from ancient ideas about health." He went on to say that the "rules of healthful living" were

> formally codified as part of medical thought by Galen. . . . Galenic answers to virtually all medical questions dominated theory and practice into the 1600s, but while most features of Galenism were cast aside during that century, the code of hygiene retained its hold. It was, after all, solidly founded on experience, ordered around the individual's careful regulation of those factors of existence over which he had control: air, food and drink, sleep and wake, motion and rest, evacuation and repletion, and passions of the mind. Attention to these "six non-naturals," as they had come to be confusingly called, had been urged by medical writers throughout the late Middle Ages and Renaissance, but the matter seemed to assume new importance during the mid-1700s.[61]

Lastly, Harvey Green's *Fit for America: Health, Fitness, Sport, and American Society* covered the century between the 1830s and the 1930s and offered insights into a variety of topics like diet, dress, sanitation, nervousness, ventilation, exercise, sport, and therapies utilizing water and electricity.[62]

Origins of the Non-natural Tradition with the Ancient Physicians

Historians are in agreement that the close connection between exercise and medicine dates back to three ancient physicians: Herodicus (ca. 480–? B.C.), Hippocrates (460–370 B.C.), and Galen (129–210 A.D.). The first to study "therapeutic gymnastics," or "gymnastic medicine" as it was often called, was the Greek physician and former *paidotribes*, Herodicus. As a wrestling and boxing instructor, he realized that his weakest students could be made strong through exercise.[63] Blundell noted that Herodicus believed that it was "just as important to provide against diseases in the healthy man as to cure him who was already attacked." In the mind of Herodicus, physicians "recognized bodily exercise as part of their duties under the designation of 'Conservative Medicine' or 'Hygiene.' "[64] The anonymous author of a biographical sketch of Herodicus in *Rees' Encyclopaedia* in 1819 reported that he was "a master of a school of exercise, or *gymnasium*" and that he devoted his career to "gymnastic medicine" whereby he set out to "ascertain the regulations of it most conducive to its proper end, according to the difference of age, constitution, and disorder of the patient, and to the climate, season, & c."[65] Cyriax blamed Herodicus for causing a feud between physicians and gymnasts because "the physicians accused the gymnasts of usurping the functions of medical men."[66]

Most historians credit the interest of Hippocrates in exercise and diet to the influence of Herodicus. Hippocrates has been universally honored as "the father of scientific medicine" and physicians still take the "Hippocratic oath." He is given credit as the chief compiler of some eighty-seven treatises on Greek medicine known as the "Corpus Hippocraticum."[67] In addition, the humoral theory of medicine, mentioned earlier in the chapter, is attributable to Hippocrates.[68]

It appears that Hippocrates authored two separate works on regimen—*Regimen in Health,* with nine very short chapters, and *Regimen,* composed of four long sections or books. The first seven chapters of *Regimen in Health* offered advice on the preservation of health and were directed to "the layman." Advice was given on what to drink and eat at certain times of the year. Hippocrates also suggested rapid walking in winter and slow in summer, recommended emetics and clysters for the bowels, and devoted a chapter to "athletes in training."[69]

Regimen, the longer of his two works, was probably written sometime around 400 B.C. Once it is read, it becomes clear why Hippocrates has been called "the father of preventive medicine."[70] In book 1, we are told,

> eating alone will not keep a man well; he must also take exercise. For food and exercise, while possessing opposite qualities, yet work together to produce health. For it is the nature of exercise to use up material, but of food and drink to make good deficiencies. And it is necessary, as it appears, to discern the power of various exercises, both natural exercises and artificial, to know which of them tends to increase flesh and which to lessen it; and not only this, but also to proportion exercise to bulk of food, to the constitution of the patient, to the age of the individual, to the season of the year, to the changes in the winds, to the situation of the region in which the patient resides, and to the constitution of the year.[71]

Instructions were given to "take sharp runs so that the body may be emptied of moisture" and to take walks after dinner.[72] Much of book 2 was devoted to exercise and training. Hippocrates classified exercises as natural (sight, hearing, voice, thought, and walking) and violent (running, wrestling, sparring, and ball games, among others). He also discussed the value of "running in a cloak" to increase body heat, swinging the arms while running, and how to avoid "fatigue pains" for "men out of training."[73] In book 3, Hippocrates explained his invention of prevention of disease: ". . . the discovery that I have made is how to diagnose what is the overpowering element in the body, whether exercises overpower food or food overpowers exercises; how to cure each excess, and to insure good health so as to prevent the approach of disease, unless very serious and many blunders be made."[74] Later in the same book he elaborated: "This discovery reflects glory on myself its discoverer, and is useful to those who have learnt it. . . . It comprises prognosis before illness and diagnosis of what is the matter with the body, whether food overpowers exercise, whether exercise overpowers food, or whether the two are duly proportioned. For it is from the overpowering of one or the other that diseases arise, while from their being evenly balanced comes good health."[75] Much of the remainder of book 3 was devoted to the proper food and exercises for each of the four seasons.

Just as Herodicus influenced Hippocrates, Hippocrates was a major influence on the career of Claudius Galenus or Galen, a physician in Rome during the second century A.D. Galen authored numerous works of great importance to medical history, but for our purposes *On Hygiene* is of most interest. Galen was the dominating authority in the field of medicine at least through the Renaissance and his works were widely read among physicians and educated laypersons alike.[76] Galen followed Hippocrates and borrowed from him the concepts of the four cardinal humors and the elementary qualities. As a hygienist, Galen the physician tried to maintain normal equilibrium by prescribing various orderings of the non-naturals, among other preventives and therapies. Until the age of twenty-eight, Galen suffered from a variety of illnesses. But, after that, he discovered that there was "an art of health."[77] Overall, Galen regarded exercise as one branch of hygiene and hygiene as part of the science of medicine.

On Hygiene provides the best collection of Galen's views on exercise and health. The book, called *Hygieina* in Greek and *De sanitate tuenda* in Latin, was translated into French by Thomas Linacre in 1517.[78] It was not translated into English until Robert M. Green did so in 1951.[79] Probably written around 180 A.D., *On Hygiene* was not directed to physicians but toward the educated layman. The medical historian Henry Sigerest has observed, "It was a scientific work intended for educated people who were studying medicine as amateurs, to be sure, without the intention of ever practising the art."[80] The work was divided into six books. Galen did not include the non-naturals as a term in *On Hygiene* but did subject the inevitable causal factors of disease to a fourfold classification: (1) things taken (food, drink, drugs), (2) things eliminated (bodily secretions and excretions),

(3) things done (massage, walking, riding, exercise, sleep, watch, and coitus), and (4) things happening from without.[81]

Most of the material on exercise is to be found in the first three books. Book 1, "The Art of Preserving Health," was composed of fifteen chapters. Chapter 8 was entitled "The Use and Value of Exercise" and dealt mainly with the need for motion in all ages. Whether by sailing, riding on horseback, driving, or via cradles, swings, and arms, everyone, even infants, Galen said, needed exercise.[82] Other chapters commented on bathing and massage, fresh air, beverages and evacuations. "Exercise and Massage," the title of book 2, comprised twelve chapters. Chapter 2, "Purposes, Time, and Methods of Exercise and Massage," included some very important material on the role exercise played in Galen's conception of hygiene. In reference to the type and definition of exercise, Galen said, "To me it does not seem that all movement is exercise, but only when it is vigorous. But since vigor is relative, the same movement might be exercise for one and not for another. The criterion of vigorousness is change of respiration; those movements which do not alter the respiration are not called exercise. But if anyone is compelled by any movement to breathe more or less or faster, that movement becomes exercise for him. This therefore is what is commonly called exercise or gymnastics."[83] The benefits that Galen attributed to exercise conform quite well to those that modern science has proven:

> The uses of exercise, I think, are twofold, one for the evacuation of the excrements, the other for the production of good condition of the firm parts of the body. For since vigorous motion is exercise, it must needs be that only these three things result from it in the exercising body—hardness of the organs from mutual attrition, increase of the intrinsic warmth, and accelerated movement of respiration. These are followed by all the other individual benefits which accrue to the body from exercise; from hardness of the organs, both insensitivity and strength for function; from warmth, both strong attraction for things to be eliminated, readier metabolism, and better nutrition and diffusion of all substances, whereby it results that solids are softened, liquids diluted, and ducts dilated. And from the vigorous movements of respiration the ducts must be purged and the excrements evacuated.[84]

He also provided extensive discussions regarding the proper time for exercise, factors to consider before exercise, the varieties of exercise, the different qualities of exercises, and the places for exercise. Book 3, entitled "Apotherapy, Bathing, and Fatique," has a chapter on "Bathing after Exercise" and one on "Exercise after Sex Relations." In all,

Galen's *On Hygiene* was a masterful and perceptive document with far-reaching ramifications.

Renaissance Medicine and a Revival of the Non-naturals in Sixteenth- and Seventeenth-Century Europe

"Orthodox Greek hygiene" as Smith called it, or the "regimen of the non-naturals," flourished as part of the revival of Galenic medicine as early as the thirteenth century.[85] The leading medical schools of the world, Italy's Salerno, Padua, and Bologna, taught hygiene to their students as part of general instruction in the theory and practice of medicine. The works of Hippocrates and Galen dominated a system whereby "the ultimate goal was to be able to practise medicine in the manner of the ancient physicians."[86] In fact, Galen's influence had become so strong that Bylebyl referred to the sixteenth century as "the golden age of Galenism." He noted that "thanks to the work of the scholars, translators and book publishers, Galen's works were more widely available, and in more complete and accurate form, than previously, and thanks to the dedication of his followers they were also more highly admired, more thoroughly studied, and probably better understood, than at any time before or since."[87] Padua, for example, was so dedicated to the classical tradition, that the school continued to teach medical theory from the works of Hippocrates and Galen through the mid-1700s.[88]

At the same time that physicians were learning about the non-naturals in their medical education, the early stirrings of the "self-help" movement were beginning in Western Europe. Classical medicine also informed physicians and the lay public alike that responsibility for disease and health was not the province of the gods. Each individual, either independently or in counsel with a physician, had a moral responsibility for the preservation and attainment of health. As the sixteenth century progressed, "laws of bodily health were expressed as value prescriptions."[89] Accordingly, as Paul Slack concluded in his study of medical literature in Tudor England, "regimens, textbooks and collections of remedies dominated the list of medical best-sellers between 1485 and 1604."[90] In reference to the same literature, which she aptly called "medical advice books," Smith noted "for individuals who sought some means of rational and prudential control for reasons of simple survival or personal enlightenment, there were the medical advice books. These vernacular works were written ostensibly for the lay individual. . . . For a large number of people they could well have been a far more familiar source of information than the personal advice of the trained physician. . . . One of the most obvious facts relating to the medical advice books is that they are published in English, and were on the face of it accessible to all those who could actually read—not just those who could read Latin."[91] In a very real sense then, non-natural regimen, the major component of the "advice book," became more and more important in one's management of the body and in the ideas of proper health behavior. In addition, all aspects of the non-natural tradition began to enter into the common language of life itself.

Regimen also became important during the Renaissance in a literature identified as "prolongevity hygiene." Gruman defined it as "the attempt to attain a markedly increased longevity by means of reforms in one's way of life."[92] Central to the writings on longevity was the belief that any individual who decided to live a temperate life, especially with reforms in their habits of diet and exercise, could extend their longevity in a significant manner. Beginning with the writing of Cornaro in 1558, the non-natural tradition received increasing attention from those wishing to live longer and more healthy lives.

Thomas Elyot's (1490–1546) *The Castel of Helthe*, published in the 1530s—most likely in 1539, was the "originator and chief representative" of the genre of publications dealing with regimen as part of the new sixteenth-century medical advice literature.[93] Its contents and style, built on the Galenic traditional regimen and the *Regimen Sanitatis Salernitanum* (to be discussed later), served as a model for additional advice books for at least another century. Elyot's work was the first manual of popular or "domestic" medicine in the vernacular designed to provide the poor with simple instructions on how to keep well.

Although not a physician, Elyot had studied medicine with Thomas Linacre, England's most eminent physician at that time, who himself had trained at Padua and translated Galen's *On Hygiene* in 1517. In his preface, Elyot explained he "was not all ignorante in phisycke" since the physician to Henry VIII (Linacre) had read "unto me the workes of Galene. . . ."[94] Elyot, like Galen before him, and like others writing about the non-naturals after him, improved his own poor health with proper attention to regimen. Toward the end of his book when discussing certain "grievous diseases," Elyot said, "I my selfe was by the space of foure years continually in this discrasy, . . . at the last felynge my selfe very feeble, and lacking appetite and slepe, as I happned to reade the bokes of Galene. . . . I perceyved that I had ben longe in an errour."[95]

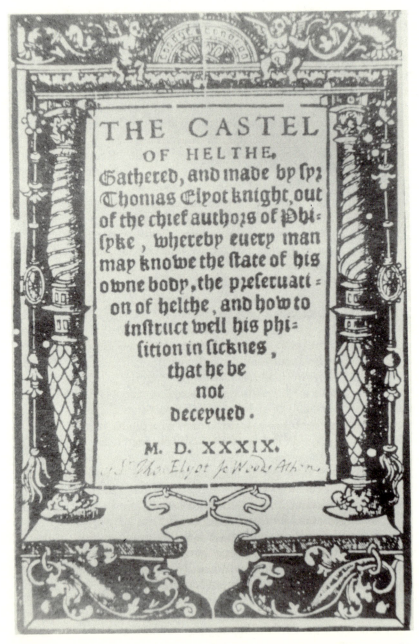

Figure 1.1 Title page from Sir Thomas Elyot, *The Castel of Helthe* (London, 1539).

Elyot intended his book to be a fortress against disease, thus the title of *The Castel of Helthe*. The content was devoted almost entirely to the "thynges naturall, thynges not naturall, and thynges against nature."[96] The "thynges not Naturall be soo called, by cause they be no portion of a naturall body, as they be which be called Naturall things: but yet by the temperance of them, the body beinge in healthe, is therin preservyd."[97] After sections on "Of meate and drinke" and "Of sleape and watche," Elyot included a part on "The commoditie of exercise, and the tyme when it should be used." Galen's influence was obvious when Elyot stated, "Every meuving is not an exercise, but only that whiche is vehement, thence wherof is alteration of the breath or mynde of a man. Of exercise do procede two commodities, evacuation of excrements, and also good habite of the body, for Exercise beinge a vehement motion, therof nedes must ensue hardness of the members."[98] He also included material on friction and rubbing before exercise, the diversities of exercises, and the use of the voice as a form of exercise. *The Castel of Helthe* went through at least fifteen editions by 1610 and far surpassed Elyot's earlier work, *The Boke Named The Governour*, in popularity. This latter work, written in 1531, also included a substantial amount of information and advice on exercise.[99]

Christobal Mendez (1500–61), who received his medical training at the University of Salamanca, was the first physician to write a printed book devoted to exercise. A resident of the city of Jaen in Spain and later Seville, Mendez published his *Libro del Exercicio Corporal, or Book of Bodily Exercise,* in 1553. Much of the contents seems to be based upon his own experience and those of his acquaintances; however, Mendez does refer to Aristotle, Celsus, Galen, and Pliny, among other ancient authors. His debt to Galen is obvious since he made reference to him twice in the first three pages and identified Galen's three parts of medicine as "prevention, restoration and preservation." In regard to the latter, Mendez said, "The last group we may say is healthy, and to preserve health must do our exercises."[100] Although *Book of Bodily Exercise* does not appear to have had a very wide readership, Mendez's ideas on the subject of exercise were novel and preceded developments in exercise physiology and sports medicine thought to be unique to the early twentieth century.

The book was divided into four treatises, each with several chapters. The first treatise dealt with exercise and its benefits; the second showed the divisions of exercise, including which is best; the third explained the common exercises and the advantages of each; and the fourth pertained to the best time for exercise. In chapter 3 of the first

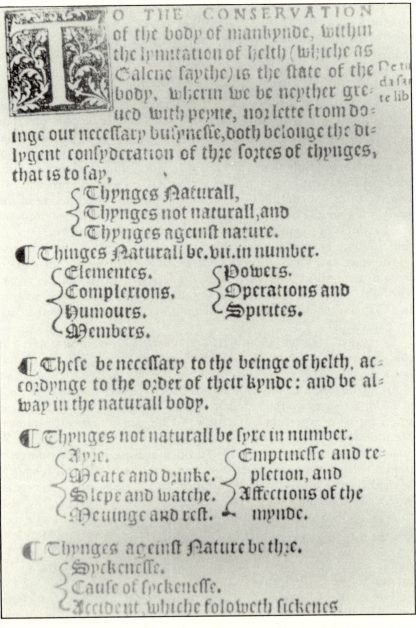

Figure 1.2 First page from Sir Thomas Elyot, *The Castel of Helthe* (1539), illustrating the importance of Galenic medicine and the "non-natural" tradition.

treatise, "Exercise Is the Easiest Way to Preserve Health," Mendez, in keeping with the non-natural tradition, said, "The physician must organize his patient's life and the things called un-natural such as eating and drinking, evacuation and retention, sleep and vigil, movement and rest, and the passions of the soul and the alteration of the air."[101] Also in the first treatise in chapter 10, believing as the humoral theorists did that the physician had to clear away excess moisture in the body, Mendez wrote of the popularity of vomiting, bloodletting, purging, sweating, and urination. Then, after explaining the ill effects of each method, he noted, "Having considered this, we realize that exercise was invented and used to clean the body when it was too full of harmful things. It cleans without any of the above-mentioned inconvenience and is accompanied by pleasure and joy (as we will say). If we use exercise under the conditions which we will describe, it deserves lofty praise as a blessed medicine that must be kept in high esteem."[102] In the remaining three treatises, some of the subjects Mendez addressed were exercises for women, walking as the most beneficial exercise, exercises for youth, injuries from exercise, and exercise for the handicapped.

As noted earlier, Luigi Cornaro (1467–1565), a non-physician resident of Padua, was the most influential proponent of prolongevity hygiene. Cornaro discovered that he was in very poor health when he was in his late thirties and, through his knowledge of Galenic medical theory, blamed his condition on eating and drinking to excess as he lived in the fashion of the nobility during the early years of the sixteenth century in Italy. He reformed his life-style and adopted the regimen of a "sober life" whereby he avoided intemperance, preserved health and happiness, and attained a ripe and enjoyable old age.[103] Putting his habits into words at the age of eighty-three, Cornaro published *Trattato della Vita Sobria (Treatise on a Sober Life)* in 1558 which was followed three years later by *Compendio della Vita Sobria (Compendium of a Sober Life)*.

In *Treatise on a Sober Life*, Cornaro recommended moderation in everything with more emphasis on diet than the other non-naturals. Since the book was written by a layman, who "practiced what he preached," for laypersons, it had a certain appeal and persuasive power lacking in other books of the period. It was translated and published in French, Dutch, and German, although the English editions were the most popular. The first English edition was published in 1634 and the first American edition was published in Philadelphia in 1793. The 1826 London edition was listed as the thirty-sixth.[104]

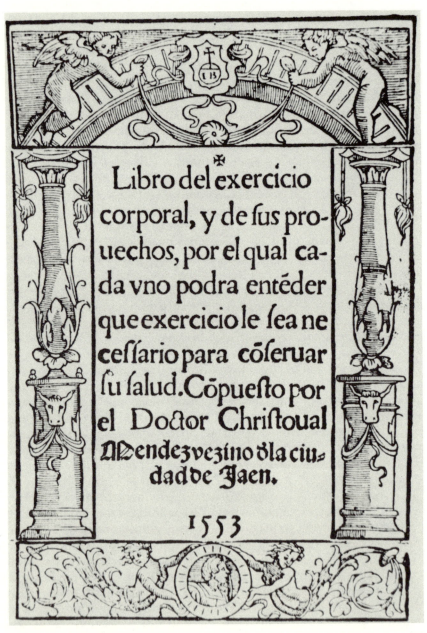

Figure 1.3 Title page from Christobal Mendez, *Book of Bodily Exercise,* . . .
(Jaen, 1553).

Another Italian physician and graduate of Padua, Girolamo Cardano (1501–1576), published *De sanitate tuenda (Care of Health)* in Rome in 1560. Since it had the same title as Galen's earlier work, which was translated as *On Hygiene*, others have referred to Cardano's book as *On Safeguarding the Health*. And while he admitted that Galen, "whose very high position and virtue have been conspicuous, has necessarily had great influence with me," Cardano said Galen's treatise was "too pedantic" and "wanders from the point, goes far afield and lingers on irrelevancies" when it came to his discussion of massage and exercise.[105] The book was written in Latin with two editions appearing in 1580 and 1582.

Care of Health was composed of six volumes with the material on exercise in volume 4 on "Old Age." In this section Cardano discussed exercise as a factor in "quickening the spirits," the value of exercise for increasing the appetite, aiding digestion, and resisting illness and disease, and different physical activities for various age groups. We also learn from his autobiography *De Vita Propria Liber (The Book of My Life)* published in 1575, that he had been ill for much of his early life and exercised himself with swords and shields, running, jumping, and walking while fully armed.[106] Exercise, combined with the other parts of the non-natural tradition, assisted in his recovery. In "Manner of Life," chapter 8 of his autobiography, Cardano reported, "There are seven principal genera of things: air, sleep, exercise, food, drink, medication, and preservative."[107] Although not identical to the original list of the "six things non-natural," it is clear Cardano's philosophy of regimen and hygiene was based upon them.

The third Italian physician to write about exercise was Hieronymus Mercurialis (1530–1606) or Girolamo Mercuriale, as his name is sometimes written. Mercuriale's book, *De arte gymnastica aput ancientes (The Art of Gymnastics among the Ancients),* was published in Venice in 1569 and went through numerous editions. Although the book never moved beyond its original Latin, it was still an effective transmitter of Galenic doctrine. Mercuriale quoted Galen relentlessly throughout the book and really provided more of a descriptive compilation of ancient material than an original work. Most of book 1 was devoted to the gymnasia and thermae in Greece and Rome; book 2 included dancing, Roman ball games, and Olympic events; book 3 dealt with more recreative activities like fishing, swimming, and hunting; in book 4 Mercuriale examined the pros and cons of exercise while surveying the opinions of past notables; and books 5 and 6 provided information on the effects of different exercises, when they ought to be done, and who should do them. Again, much of this was taken directly from Galen.[108]

Mercuriale was educated at Padua and taught medicine at Padua, Bologna, and Pisa while writing extensively in the field of medicine on subjects ranging from dermatology and pediatrics to gynecology. He had acquired such a reputation that he was called to Vienna to attend Emperor Maximilian II in 1573. In all, Mercuriale used nearly two hundred works from Greek and Roman authors in his *Art of Gymnastics* and, in so doing, helped further the non-natural tradition. That a physician of his stature wrote what appears to be the first illustrated book on exercise and medicine has had extensive ramifications. Joseph, in his article on medical gymnastics, wrote, "In reality, all the books on gymnastics of the next centuries are based on this standard work."[109]

English physician Thomas Cogan authored *The Haven of Health*, which was first published in London in 1584. Cogan directed his epistle to students whom, because of their sedentary ways, he believed were susceptible to sickness. He based his work on that of Elyot and the School of Salerno, but it was the non-natural tradition of Hippocrates and Galen that formed the real basis of his work. In his opening message, "To the Reader," Cogan wrote, "But wise Englishmen I trust will use the old English fashion still: and follow the rule of Hip. approved by Galen, and by common experience in mens bodies found most wholesome: Such as have written of the preservation of health before me, for the most part have followed the divisio of Galen of things not natural, which be six in number."[110] He then divided his chapters into (1) "Labour or Exercise," (2) "Meate," (3) "Drinke," (4) "Sleep," and (5) "Venus."

Cogan particularly liked "Tenise" as an exercise for students because it exercised "all parts of the body alike, as the legges, armes, neck, head, eyes, backe and loynes, and delighteth greatly the minde, making it lusty and cheerful." He went on to praise colleges for erecting "Tenis-courts for the exercise of their Schollers. . . ."[111] He also emphasized that "exercise must be used in a good and wholesome aire. . . . faire and cleare . . . lightsome and open . . . not stinking or corrupted. . . ."[112] Almost at the end of the book, Cogan left a message to the student to "practice in your life, this short lesson":

> Ayre, labour, food, repletion,
> Sleepe, and Passions of the minde,
> Both much and little, hurt a like,
> Best is the meane to finde.[113]

Cogan's book, like that of Elyot, was not directed toward physicians. It was a major representative of the medical advice literature of sixteenth-century England.

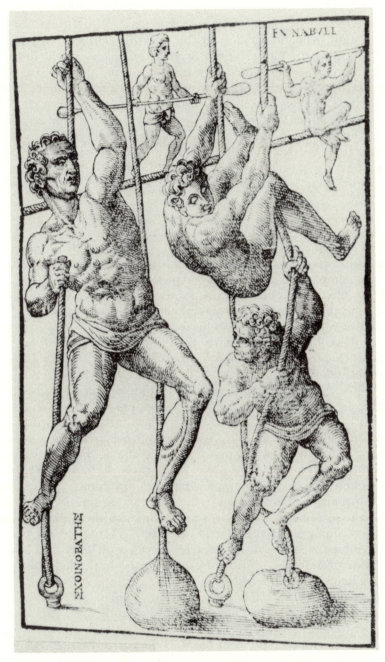

Figure 1.4 Illustration of gymnasts climbing ropes from Hieronymus Mercurialis, *The Art of Gymnastics among the Ancients*
(Venice, 1569).

Although probably written in the late thirteenth or early fourteenth century, the Latin *Regimen Sanitatis Salernitanum* is included in the seventeenth-century literature since it was not popularized until John Harington (1561–1612) translated it into English in 1607. Under the title *The Englishmans Doctor. Or the Schoole of Salerne. Or Physicall observations for the perfect Preserving of the body of Man in continuall health,* the book is thought to be an accumulation of all the hygienic wisdom from Salerno's medical school.[114] Clearly based on Galen's physiology, it was widely read. It was reprinted repeatedly and Sigerist claimed that "never has there been a more successful medical book."[115]

Beside the fact that the contents were addressed to the physician and laypersons alike, the book was also very popular because it was written in verse. Early editions had over 360 verses while more recent editions have included additional ones accumulated over the years. It included simple and commonsense rules applying to sleep, rest and exercise, effects of foods and drinks, as well as the "foure humors" and "foure Elements."[116] For several centuries, the *Regimen Sanitatis Salernitanum* provided rules on personal hygiene in a very attractive and readable form modeled after the old non-natural tradition.

In his chapter on "Pathology at Mid-Century" in Debus's *Medicine in Seventeenth-Century England,* L. J. Rather called Robert Burton's (1577–1640) "entertaining discussion of the six non-naturals in the *Anatomy of Melancholy* . . . the best treatment of the subject in English."[117] Burton, without formal medical credentials, wrote this very popular treatise in 1621. For Burton, melancholy was used to signify the disease known by many as "melancholia," but he also made use of the term to refer to the melancholy humor (black bile). Throughout the book, he emphasized the importance of rectifying any disturbances or imbalances in the "six non-natural things."[118] Accordingly, sections of the book were devoted to the topics of "passions," "sleeping and waking," and "exercise." A large section, part 2, sec. 2, memb. 4, was called "Exercise rectified of Body and Mind." Here Burton referred to numerous authorities in the field but used Galen's writings most heavily.[119]

First published in 1564, Ambroise Pare's (1510–90) classic work *Surgery* did not appear in English translation until 1634. Pare (sometimes written as Parey) was a famous surgeon and served as the court physician for the two different kings in his native France. His book does not contain as much on exercise as the others reviewed, but it is included as an example of how powerful and popular the non-natural tradition was in the medical community. Part 1, "An Introduction or

THE HAVEN

OF HEALTH,

Chiefly made for the comfort of Students, and
consequently for all those that haue a care of their health,
amplified vpon fiue wordes of *Hippocrates,* written
Epid.6. *Labour, Meate, Drinke, Sleepe, Venus:*
By *Thomas Cogan* Maister of Artes, and Bacheler
of Phisicke : And now of late corrected
and augmented.

*Hereunto is added a Preseruation from the Pestilence :
With a short Censure of the late sicknesse at Oxford.*

Ecclesiasticus, Cap. 37. 30.
By surfet haue many perished : but he that dyeteth
himselfe prolongeth his life.

Imprinted at London by Richard Field
for *Bonham Norton.* 1 5 9 6.

Figure 1.5 Title page from Thomas Cogan's *The Haven of Health . . .*
(London, 1596).

Compendious Way to Chirurgery" was divided into several chapters pertaining to the medical theory of the period. Beginning with chapter 12, which was devoted to "Of Things Not Naturale," and continuing through several more chapters, Pare elaborated on each of the non-naturals and how they contributed to good health. Chapter 15 was entitled "Of Motion and Rest" and included information on the uses of exercise, the best time for exercise, the qualities of exercise, and "what discommodities proceed from idleness."[120] Pare also used the common form for listing the non-naturals whereby each was preceded by "of," as popularized by Elyot in his *Castel of Helthe.*

The final book to be covered in this section is Friedrich Hoffmann's (1660–1742) *Fundamenta Medicinae,* which he published in 1695. A distinguished German physician, Hoffmann was appointed the first professor of medicine at Halle University around 1694. Although Hoffmann wrote on such diverse medical topics as personal hygiene, physiology, pathology, pediatrics, and medical ethics, *Fundamenta Medicinae* was his most distinguished work. It combined "the old and the new, Galenic teachings and new mechanical philosophy," directed toward students. Hoffmann organized the small book along the lines of the tradition of "Institutes," which involved relatively succinct instruction in a compendium form. The "Institutes" normally covered physiology, pathology, semeiology, hygiene, and therapeutics.[121] The fourth section, "Medical Hygiene," included chapters devoted to (1) "Of the general rules for maintaining health," (2) "Of the various uses and abuses of the six non-naturals," and (3) "Of special rules to be observed in diets."[122] Later in his career, Hoffmann wrote several essays on bodily exercise and the preservation of health. Johann C. F. GutsMuths (1759–1839) referred to the work of Hoffmann several times in his classic work on *Gymnastics for the Young,* published in 1793 in Germany.[123]

Enlightenment Medicine and the Expansion of the Non-natural Theme in Eighteenth-Century Europe

Although Galenism and the humoral theory of medicine were affected by new ideas from the fields of anatomy and physiology in particular, the non-natural tradition in the form of hygiene and regimen continued to flourish in eighteenth-century Europe. Individual treatises continued to be written focusing on health preservation via "self-help" and on living long. In some instances, specific books focussed on exercise as a therapy for certain diseases. Generally using the term "medical gymnastics," the authors looked to exercise as a cure as well as for the rehabilitation of body parts, particularly the limbs. Also, some physicians during the eighteenth century began to look at exercise and the other non-naturals as viable alternatives to the heroic therapeutic practices of bleeding, purging, and drugging. Realizing that the "cure" could be worse than the disease, some physicians advocated non-intervention tactics, which revolved around guiding and monitoring health behavior.

Books on health for the layperson generally fell into two broad categories through the end of the eighteenth century. The first group comprised regimen and long life and were written for the educated and leisured classes. The non-natural message was directed to wealthy and sedentary city dwellers, generally aristocratic and professional men who tended to overeat and overdrink. Regimen was presented as a way to counteract the "diseases of civilization" where excess, intemperance, and inactivity abounded. In most instances, this literature was sort of a "religio-medical" prescription for regularity and sober living. And since those individuals to whom the literature was directed could afford physicians and regular medical attention, very little in the way of therapy or the description of specific diseases was included. These were books to read and contemplate.

The second group of books were health manuals generally consisting of material on health preservation as well as information on diseases and their cure. They included the typical non-natural guidance but also included "recipes" or lists of medicines and their applications for home or self-treatment. This literature was more directed to the middle classes rather than the idle rich or working poor, and the physicians that authored these handbooks often spoke out against drugging and the use of medical men. Instead, they recommended using one's own intuition, relying more on nature, and a proper ordering and balancing of the six non-naturals. Skepticism of the heroic healers combined with a commitment to self-sufficiency and a concern for the family group led the authors of this literature to value prevention in the form of hygiene and regimen over treatments by physicians. Because of this basic philosophy and their prospective audience, terms like "easy and natural," "prevention," and "domestic" were incorporated in their titles.

Three important books were written during this time that advocated the use of exercise or "medical gymnastics" as a cure. This new form of therapy would continue on into the nineteenth century and, in some instances, beyond. Francis Fuller's (1670–1706) *Medicina Gymnastica: or, a Treatise Concerning the Power of Exercise* was published in London in 1704 and had gone into nine editions by 1777. Not a physician himself, Fuller based many of his ideas on his own experiences as well as on the influence of Thomas Sydenham, one of Britain's most famous physicians.[124] Joseph-Clement Tissot's (1747–1826) *Medicinal and Surgical Gymnastics* was first published in Paris in 1780 and was translated into several other languages by the 1790s.[125] The third book was written by John Pugh (dates unknown) in London in 1794 and was titled *A Physiological, Theoretic and Practical Treatise on the Utility of the Science of Muscular Action for Restoring the Power of the Limbs.* Pugh was an anatomist and included a chapter "On the necessity and importance of exercise" in which he quoted several individuals, including Hippocrates, Galen, and Cornaro.[126]

The first division of health literature for the layperson devoted to regimen and long life is represented by five publications: *The Ladies Library*, George Cheyne's *An Essay of Health and Long Life*, John Armstrong's *The Art of Preserving Health*, the *Encyclopedie*, and James Mackenzie's *The History of Health, and the Art of Preserving It. The Ladies Library*, "written by a Lady," published in three volumes in London in 1714, was a compilation of material both earlier and contemporary on all aspects of the proper life of the eighteenth-century woman. Major chapters were entitled "Employment," "Recreation," "The Wife," "The Mother," and "The Mistress." It went through eight editions in English and two in French and was translated into Dutch before 1772. The influence of the non-natural tradition was clearly evident when the author summarized the hygienic recommendations of the work as a "few and easie observable Rules; Plenty of *open* Air, *Exercise* and *Sleep*, plain *Diet*, no *Wine* or *strong Drink*, and very little or no *Physick.*"[127]

George Cheyne's (1671–1743) *An Essay of Health and Long Life* was published in London in 1724 and by 1745 had gone through ten editions and translations in French, Dutch, Latin, and German. Cheyne himself turned to regimen after he had grown to 445 pounds. The author of numerous medical works, Cheyne was a respected physician, a member of the Royal Society, and included John Wesley among his elite patients.[128] His message was directed to the London affluent and the health problems of intellectuals, professional men, and the aristocracy. *An Essay of Health and Long Life* followed the Galenic doctrine very closely and in his introduction Cheyne said, "And that I might write with some Order and Connexion, I have chosen to make some Observations and Reflections on the *Non-naturals. . . .* they seem to me, the best general Heads for bringing in those *Observations* and *Reflections* I am to make in the following Pages."[129] Not surprising then, chapter 1 is entitled "Of Air," chapter 2 "Of Meat and

Drink," chapter 3 "Of Sleeping and Watching," and chapter 4 "Of Exercise and Quiet." In the latter chapter, Cheyne recommended walking as the "most natural" and "most useful" exercise while riding was the "most manly" and "most healthy."[130] He also advocated exercises in the open air like tennis and dancing and recommended cold baths and the use of the "flesh brush" to promote perspiration and improve circulation.

The *Art of Preserving Health* by John Armstrong (1709–79), was first published in London in 1744 and by 1757 had been reprinted five times, including a United States edition in Philadelphia in 1745. By 1830, it had been reprinted thirteen times. The work was divided into four books, one devoted to "Air," one to "Diet," one to "Exercise," and one on "Passions." Like the *Regimen Sanitatis Salernitanum*, Armstrong presented his rules for health in verse form. Book 3 on "Exercise" offered

> Toil, and be strong. By toil the flaccid nerves
> Grow firm, and gain a more compacted tone;
> The greener juices are by toil subdu'd,
> Mellow'd, and subtiliz'd; the vapid old
> Expell'd, and all the rancour of the blood.[131]

Armstrong also wrote about the joys of nature and the healthfulness of hunting and fishing. As the chapters indicated, Armstrong was continuing the non-natural tradition in his guide to the preservation of health.

The *Encyclopedie,* a dictionary of the sciences and arts, was directed by the philosopher Diderot and the mathematician D'Alembert in collaboration with the most prominent scientists of the mid-eighteenth century. Historian William Coleman called the entries on "health," "hygiene," and the "non-naturals" "a medical doctrine for the bourgeoisie" and viewed the *Encyclopedie* as a true representative of Enlightenment thought.[132] Originally published in 1751 in Paris, it went through several editions. Arnulfe D'Aumont, a graduate of Montpellier and a professor at the medical school in Valence, authored the articles noted above. Jean Noel Halle, a member of the medical faculty at Paris, authored the entry on "hygiene" in editions of the *Encyclopedie* after 1780. In this section, Halle identified the substance of hygiene as "the things which mankind uses or handles, improperly called non-natural, and their influence on our constitution and organs."[133] Halle also identified "public hygiene" compared to "private hygiene" and said hygiene can vary "depending on whether one attends to man collectively or in a society or whether he is viewed as an individual."[134] The *Encyclopedie,* like the other literature in this classification, went primarily into the hands of the educated members of the bourgeoisie and nobility. Yet as Coleman so aptly explained in reference to Enlightenment thought, "the doctrine of the non-naturals as a guide to correct hygienic practice was wholly consonant with this striking reorientation of Western thought."[135]

James Mackenzie's (1680–1761) book *The History of Health, and the Art of Preserving It* was published in Edinburgh in 1758. Mackenzie was a Fellow of the Royal College of Physicians in Edinburgh and wrote a book that was designed to be casual and relaxed reading for an educated elite. His book was a history and review of the rules related to the preservation of health and thus devoted a considerable amount of space to the non-naturals. In chapter 6 on Hippocrates, Mackenzie noted, "I shall endeavor, *first,* to range in order all his precepts and remarks on the *six articles necessary to life,* vulgarly called the Non-Naturals."[136] Other major portions of the book were devoted to "Motion and Rest" and "Of Exercise." In his introduction, Mackenzie credited Galen with originating the term "non-naturals" and explained that in their "proper use and regulation of which the art of preserving health principally consists."[137]

The second division of health literature for the layperson usually consisted of information on the preservation of health but also included lists of diseases and medicines for them. More directed to the middle classes and designed to be used rather than studied and contemplated, this literature is also represented by five publications: John Wesley's *Primitive Physic,* William Buchan's *Domestic Medicine,* Bryan Cornwell's *The Domestic Physician, or Guardian of Health,* Bernard Faust's *Catechism of Health,* and *The Art of Preventing Diseases, and Restoring Health* by George Wallis.

John Wesley's (1703–91) *Primitive Physic,* first published in 1747, was influenced to a large degree by George Cheyne, and as Turner suggested, "There was an obvious attraction between Wesley's religious asceticism and Cheyne's view of the Christian importance of maintaining the body in good health through sober living, regular hours, exercise and temperance."[138] However, through Wesley's book, Cheyne's ideas probably reached a much wider audience. In his preface Wesley noted, "The power of exercise, both to preserve and restore health, is greater than can well be conceived; especially in those who add temperance thereto."[139] Later in the preface, Wesley reported, "For the sake of those who desire, through the blessing of God, to retain the health which they have recovered, I have added a few plain, easy rules, chiefly transcribed from Dr. Cheyne."[140] Wesley then proceeded to discuss each of the six non-naturals, including two pages devoted to exercise. The second part of *Primitive Physic* was devoted to "A Collection of Recipes" for a multitude of ailments since Wesley believed "simple remedies are in general the most safe for simple disorders, and sometimes do wonders under the blessing of God."[141] Through an American edition published as early as 1793 and through numerous English editions, Wesley's faith in the non-natural tradition was spread from chapel to chapel and throughout the congregation of Methodism in Western Europe and the United States.

Domestic Medicine by William Buchan (1729–1805) was the classic of classics. Aimed at individual and family improvement via proper regimen, Buchan's book contained rules for the healthy as well as the sick. It was written for the layperson as a substitute for the deficiencies of medical care and was so popular that it achieved a life span of 144 years. First published in 1769 in Edinburgh where Buchan was educated, *Domestic Medicine* appeared in new editions and reprints every few years in Britain through 1846. The first American edition appeared in Philadelphia in 1771. The book was translated into French, Spanish, Italian, German, Russian, and Swedish. The last edition appeared in Boston in 1913.[142]

While Buchan did not use the term non-naturals, he acknowledged his debt to Cheyne and divided his book into the six classical headings. For example, chapter 4 was "Of Air," chapter 5 "Of Exercise," chapter 6 "Of Sleep," and chapter 10 "Of the Passions." Chapter 1, "Of Children," included a portion devoted to"Of the Exercise of Children" in which Buchan said, "Of all the causes which conspire to render the life of man short and miserable, none have greater influence than the want of proper Exercise. . . . Sufficient exercise will make up for several defects in nursing; but nothing can supply the want of it. It is absolutely necessary to the health, the growth, and the strength of children."[143] In chapter 5 Buchan exclaimed, "Inactivity never fails to induce a universal relaxation of the solids, which disposes the body to innumerable diseases. When the solids are relaxed neither the digestion nor any of the secretions can be duly performed. . . . Weak nerves are the constant companions of inactivity. Nothing but exercise and open air can brace and strengthen the nerves, or prevent the endless train of diseases which proceed from a relaxed state of these organs."[144] Other portions of *Domestic Medicine*, like *Primitive Physick,* dealt with numerous remedies for ills ranging from "dropsy" to rheumatism. In the realm of therapy, Buchan was particularly against the use of drugs and, where possible, advocated herbal medicines. Before the term was popular, Buchan seemed to be practicing "holistic medicine."[145]

Bryan M. L. Cornwell (dates unknown) followed the Wesley and Buchan models in his book *The Domestic Physician, or Guardian of Health,* published in London in 1788. In his preface, Cornwell quoted Galen's definition of medicine as "the art of preserving present health, and of retrieving it when lost."[146] Also in the preface, Cornwell explained that medicine was "divided into five principal branches" and said that "the fourth branch considers the remedies, and their use, whereby life may be preserved; whence it is called hygiene; its objects are what we strictly call non-natural."[147] Part 1 of the book, "On the Causes of Diseases," had chapters entitled "Of Air," "Of Exercise," "Of Sleep," and "Of the Passions." Part 2 was devoted to "Of the Knowledge and Cure of Diseases."

German physician Bernard Christoph Faust (1755–1842) wrote *Catechism of Health for the Use of Schools, and for Domestic Instruction* in 1794. It was a small booklet of ninety-two pages designed to teach the elements of hygiene to children. More than 150,000 copies were sold in a few years and it was translated into several different languages. An edition "Published for the use of the Citizens of the United States" was printed in New York in 1798.[148] *Catechism of Health* was divided into two major parts, "Of Health" and "Of Disease." The first part incorporated the usual non-natural divisions, with chapters on "Of Air," "Of Food," "Of Exercise and Rest," and "Of Sleep." Each of the chapters was arranged with a question-and-answer format.[149]

The first popular text devoted solely to preventive medicine to be published in the United States was written by London physician George Wallis (1740–1802). *The Art of Preventing Diseases, and Restoring Health* was published in New York in 1793 with a second edition in 1794. In the style of Buchan, the book was directed to a wider audience than those manuals discussed in the first classification. Wallis quoted Hippocrates, Galen, Hoffmann, and Cornaro, among others, and wrote of the "non-naturals" in his "Explanatory Preface." Section 3 was devoted to "Of the Non-Naturals" and spanned some twenty-four pages with two on "Exercise and Rest." Wallis concluded his "Non-Naturals" section almost apologetically by saying, "What we have here delivered, perhaps may be by some thought of too trivial consequence; and is by many too much, even in the practice of medicine, neglected—still will be found, on experience, worthy of very close attention: for the knowledge from thence to be collected, and properly, as we shall soon have occasion to shew, forms one part of medicine, comprehending that which is stiled—prophylactic or preventive."[150] Regarding exercise in particular, Wallis emphasized the importance of activities that incorporated the mind because when "the mind is exhilarated" it "will communicate agreeable sensations, and give firmness to the moving parts."[151]

American Editions and United States Physicians: The Non-naturals in Antebellum America

Nineteenth-century America was fertile ground for both the non-natural tradition and the general hygiene movement, which were finding their way into the United States via American editions of Western European medical treatises or through books on hygiene written by American physicians. The United States between 1800 and 1860 was a rapidly changing land with a large percentage of its inhabitants residing in the northeastern cities. While Americans still looked to Europe for guidance in several realms, including medical practice, the young country was also trying to stand on its own merits and demonstrate "independence" in all walks of life.

Part of this latter trend was the concern for the physical degeneracy of the American people, particularly city dwellers. Comparisons with their European counterparts, especially England, generally showed that urbanites were in poor health and lacked the basic rudiments of proper hygiene. Health of the new nation became part of a general reform movement with nationalism as a primary motivator.

The "self-help" era was also in full bloom during antebellum America. Individual reform writers wrote about "self-improvement," "self-regulation," the "responsibility for personal health," and "self-management." It was suggested that the responsibility for disease resided with each individual and that if one got sick, it was his or her own fault. Personal health, the reformers claimed, could be improved and disease prevented by obeying the "natural laws." If one ate too much, slept too long, or did not get enough exercise, then they could only blame themselves for illness. By the same token, they could also dictate their own good health.[152]

Others took the doctrine of "natural laws" further when they suggested that morality resulted from individual hygienic improvements. These Christian reformers saw "natural law" as the dictate of God and healthfulness and Godliness going hand-in-hand. If one chose to violate the "laws," then illness or death would follow. For those who obeyed and followed the principles of health, they would be rewarded by God with a long and wholesome life under His watchful eye.[153]

Prevention literature and hygiene instruction were also popular in American medical practice before 1860 because there still were not many known cures. It was an era when many laypersons and physicians alike still had much faith in nature. In fact, the term "natural" was used in the medical literature to signify a state of well-being. As such, improvements in public health measures, a reliance on and trusting of nature, and plans for educating the public on living habits each received attention in the medical literature.[154]

Medical literature was a blend of newer discoveries in the biological sciences and traditional hygienic instructions. It also contained recommendations for individual aspects of the non-natural tradition as part of an opposition to "heroic" healing practices. Drugging, bleeding, and purging were often viewed as being more dangerous than the disease they were enlisted to cure. Sleep, diet, exercise, herbs, and water, among others, were recommended either individually or wholly as alternative medicines.[155]

Numerous health care books were written for the layperson during the antebellum period. These may be conveniently grouped under publication dates between 1800 and 1830 and 1831 and 1860. Six representative books are covered in this section. They include A. F. M. Willich's *Lectures on Diet and Regimen*, Shadrach Ricketson's *Means of Preserving Health, and Preventing Diseases*, James Thacher's *American Modern Practice: Or, A Simple Method of Prevention and Cure of Diseases*, James Ewell's *The Medical Companion, or Family Physician*, John Gunn's *Domestic Medicine*, and Edward Hitchcock's *Dyspepsy Forestalled and Resisted*.

Willich's (dates unknown) book, directed to "the most rational means of preserving health and prolonging life," was designed "for the use of families" and was first published in London in 1799. Two editions were sold out that first year and in 1800 it went into its third edition. The first New York edition appeared the next year in 1801. It was simple enough for families to use, yet formal enough for physicians. As the title suggests, Willich's lectures in England during the winter of 1798 made up the bulk of the contents. He indicated his intent in the "Postscript": ". . . my design, in these Lectures, has not been to lay down particular rules for the distinction and treatment of diseases, but rather for their prevention, and, consequently, for the preservation of health."[156] Also in his "Postscript," Willich indicated his reliance on the non-naturals, saying that "we cannot effect a favorable change in the nature and progress of a disease, whether chronic or acute, without due attention to food, drink, air, sleep, exercise, or rest, & c."[157]

The chapter arrangement included the typical non-natural topics. Chapter 1 dealt with "On the Means of Preserving Health and Prolonging Life" and some of the other chapters were as follows: "Of Air and Weather," "Of Food," "Of Exercise and Rest," "Of Evacuations," and "Of the Passions and Affections of the Mind." Willich's chapter on exercise began with the idea of the necessity of motion: "Motion, or bodily exercise, is necessary to the preservation of health, which is promoted, while the bounds of moderation are not exceeded. Too violent exercise, or a total want of it, are attended with equal disadvantages."[158] He included information on specific kinds of exercises (active and passive), the time for exercise, and the duration of exercise. The essential advantages of exercise included increased bodily strength and improved circulation of the blood and all other fluids. It aided in necessary secretions and excretions and helped in clearing and refining the blood and in the removal of obstructions. In all, the chapter spanned twenty pages.

Shadrach Ricketson (1768–1839), a New York physician, is credited with writing "the first American text on hygiene and preventive medicine."[159] Published in 1806, Ricketson's book was titled *Means of Preserving Health, and Preventing Diseases: Founded Principally on an Attention to Air and Climate, Drink, Food, Sleep, Exercise, Clothing, Passions of the Mind, and Retentions and Excretions.* His dependence on the non-natural tradition is obvious from the title. The book was well received by other physicians and contained material from his own experiences as well as quotations from other medical writers.

Like most of the other books examined, Ricketson's chapter structure followed each of the non-naturals. Chapter 5 was devoted to "Exercise" and, like Willich's, covered about twenty pages. Ricketson quoted from Cheyne's *Essay on Health* as well as various encyclopedias. In his opening statement, he explained, "A certain proportion of exercise is not much less essential to a healthy or vigorous constitution, than drink, food, and sleep; for we see, that people, whose inclination, situation, or employment does not admit of exercise, soon become pale, feeble, and disordered."[160] Ricketson went on to say that "exercise promotes the circulation of the blood, assists digestion, and encourages perspiration."[161] He also warned of the destructiveness of "high living and strong drink" and noted that "idleness and luxury create more diseases than labour and industry."[162]

James Thacher (1754–1844), a Boston physician and author of *The American New Dispensatory* and *Observations on Hydrophobia,* published *American Modern Practice* in Boston in 1817. Thacher's ability and knowledge of American medicine was illustrated in his introduction,

LECTURES

ON

DIET AND REGIMEN:

BEING

A SYSTEMATIC INQUIRY

INTO THE MOST RATIONAL MEANS OF PRESERVING HEALTH
AND PROLONGING LIFE:

TOGETHER WITH

PHYSIOLOGICAL AND CHEMICAL EXPLANATIONS,

CALCULATED CHIEFLY

FOR THE USE OF FAMILIES,

IN ORDER TO BANISH THE PREVAILING ABUSES AND PREJUDICES IN MEDICINE.

By A. F. M. WILLICH, M. D.

Qui ftomachum regem totius corporis effe
Contendunt, vera niti ratione videntur;
Hujus enim tenor validus firmat omnia membra;
At contrà ejufdem franguntur cuncta dolore.
SERENI SAMMONICI, *de Medicina Præcepta faluberrima.*

THE FIRST NEW YORK, FROM THE THIRD LONDON, EDITION.

NEW-YORK:

Printed by T. and J. SWORDS, Printers to the Faculty of Phyfic
of Columbia College, No. 99 Pearl-ftreet.

1801.

Figure 1.6 Title page from A. F. M. Willich, *Lectures on Diet and Regimen . . .* (New York, 1801).

titled "Historical Sketch of Medical Science, and the Sources and Means of Medical Instruction in the United States." This sixty-five page survey was then followed by four books. The first book dealt with the means of preserving health and obtaining longevity, with chapters including "Of the Nonnaturals," "Of Air or Atmosphere," "Exercise," "Of the Passions," and "Of Sleep," among others. The other three books pertained to diseases, with the second focusing on children. A small portion of it dealt with "Of the Exercise of Children."

Thacher credited Willich's book for information on the "nonnaturals." In chapter 2 on "Exercise," he made reference to Galen and Sydenham and said that "the position is universally established, that exercise should be ranked as among the most agents which we can employ, for the preservation of life and health."[163] He recommended walking, running, leaping, riding, swimming, and fencing as active exercises and referred to "friction" as "a kind of exercise that remarkably contributes to the health of sedentary persons."[164] In his concluding statement, Thacher warned of the old non-natural theme of balance and moderation for all aspects of regimen, including exercise: "Although bodily exercise is an essential requisite for the preservation of health, this should not exceed the bounds of moderation; as too violent exercise, and to a total want of it, are attended with equal disadvantges."[165]

The Medical Companion, or Family Physician by James Ewell (1773–1832) was written in the best tradition of Buchan, Wesley, Cornwell and others since part of the book dealt with the preservation of health and the remainder addressed specific ailments and offered advice for treatment. Ewell practiced medicine in Savannah, Georgia, and then moved to Washington, D.C., when he wrote the book. Originally published in 1822, *The Medical Companion* had reached its eighth edition by 1834.

The first major section, "On Hygiene; Or the Art of Preserving Health," was divided into parts devoted to each of the non-naturals. In a brief introduction Ewell said, "I shall now show, that by due attention to the 'Non-naturals,' *air, food, exercise, sleep, evacuations, and passions,* we may go far to preserve this fabric in good health from the cradle to the grave. Nay, so wonderful is the body and its resources, its powers of renovation; and so sovereign are the virtues of the Non-naturals, that thousands are the instances of persons who, after having their health apparently ruined by an *abuse* of them, have on returning to a wise and temperate use, entirely recovered their health, and attained to a most active and happy old age."[166] The section "Of Exercise" included warnings about inactivity and the power of "daily exercise in the open air." Also included was material on the value of exercise in cold climates and the ability of the body's physiological system to resist cold.

Like Buchan's *Domestic Medicine,* John C. Gunn's (1800–63) *Gunn's Domestic Medicine, Or Poor Man's Friend* was a classic. Written and originally published in Knoxville in 1830, the book went through many editions until it was revised and enlarged in 1857. By 1876, the book had reached 160 editions, and by the time the last recorded edition was issued in 1920, it had achieved 234 printings. Gunn dedicated the book to President Andrew Jackson and directed much of the book to a southwestern population, mainly residents of Tennessee. Part of the text dealt with prevention and part dwelled on diseases and a "Dispensatory, or Classification of Medicines" for the "home doctors" he was writing for. Evidently, the book also was used quite frequently as a book of basic reference for physicians on the frontier, which increased Gunn's popularity throughout much of the West.[167]

It was clear that Gunn adhered to the non-natural tradition when he noted in his introduction that, "The greatest number of diseases and infirmities are of our own begetting; because we have infringed the healthy laws of nature."[168] This was followed by a lengthy section called "Of the Passions." Gunn's part on "Exercise" recommended temperance, exercise, and rest and valued nature's way over traditional medical treatment. "Exercise, for the purpose of producing perspiration, and throwing off the excrementitious or bad matter from the system, is much better than any merely medical means; not only because it is the means which nature herself prescribes, but because, unlike medical drugs generally, it strengthens instead of weakening the system."[169] He also recommended exercise for women and claimed that all of the "diseases of delicate women" like "hysterics and hypochondria, arise from want of due exercise in the open, mild, and pure air."[170] Finally, in an interesting statement for the 1830s, if not the 1980s, Gunn recommended a training system for all: "The advantages of the *training system,* are not confined to pedestrians or walkers—or to pugilists or boxers alone; or to horses which are trained for the chase and the race track; they extend to man in all conditions; and were training introduced into the United States, and made use of by physicians in many cases instead of medical drugs, the beneficial consequences in the cure of many diseases would be very great indeed."[171]

The final book to be reviewed as one of the six representational health care books published between 1800 and 1830 is Edward Hitchcock's (1793–1864) *Dyspepsy Forestalled and Resisted: Or Lectures on Diet, Regimen, and Employment; Delivered to the Students of Amherst College, Spring Term, 1830.* Much like Willich's *Lectures on Diet and Regimen,* Hitchcock divided his book into nine different "lectures."[172] A second edition was published in nearby Northampton in 1831 by the Amherst College professor of chemistry and natural history. Hitchcock later became president of the college and was the father of the first president of the Association for the Advancement of Physical Education, Edward Hitchcock, Jr.

Whereas books by Gunn and others were directed to the general populace, Hitchcock directed his "lectures" to college students who did not understand good health practices. As D. F. Allmendinger, Jr., has noted, "The student lived without family restraints or collegiate custom, a potential victum of his own ignorance or intemperance."[173] Accordingly, Hitchcock provided guidance in "self-regulation" with information on alcohol, narcotic substances, study time, recreation, rules for diet, and the physical and mental effects of dyspepsy. He quoted Galen, Cheyne, Cornaro, and Wallis and devoted two lectures in part 2 on "Regimen" to the various non-naturals. Lecture 6 was totally given to exercise and spanned some thirty pages. Lecture 7 included advice on air, clothing, cleanliness, evacuations, sleep, manners, and the imagination and passions. Hitchcock was particularly fond of "physical education" and included the transcript of an "Address on the Physical Culture Adapted to the Times Delivered before the Mechanical Association in Andover Theological Seminary, September 21, 1830" as the final portion of the book.

Four books are representative of the health care literature published in the United States between 1831 and 1860. Although many more existed, the four chosen are some of the more important ones and appeared at different times throughout the period. These are Andrew Combe's *The Principles of Physiology Applied to the Preservation of Health,* Robley Dunglison's *On the Influence of Atmosphere and Locality . . . Exercise, Sleep . . . On Human Health . . . ,* Sylvester Graham's *Lectures on the Science of Human Life,* and John King's *The American Family Physician: or Domestic Guide to Health.*

Andrew Combe's (1797–1847) *The Principles of Physiology Applied to the Preservation of Health, and to the Improvement of Physical and Mental Education* was another classic work with far-reaching ramifications. One scholar, in commenting on Combe's book, said American health reformers cited it "as theologians cited the Bible." It was originally published in Edinburgh in 1834 where Combe served as personal physician to the Queen of Scotland. There was a New York edition that same year and, by the 1843 New York edition, it was in its seventh Edinburgh edition. It was included in the Harper Brothers Home Library series selling for fifty cents, which increased its availability considerably. Combe's book was designed to help people help themselves live a comfortable and healthy life. As Cooter said, "Combe's works were eminently sensible and readable, offering cogent discussion on the structures and functions of the body and the rational regimen necessary for maintaining health."[174]

There was much on the value of exercise spread through several of Combe's eleven chapters, but chapter 4 on the "Nature of the Muscular System" and chapter 5 on the "Effects of, And Rules For, Muscular Exercise" contained the most important information on the topic. After discussing the physiological effects of muscular exercise on the human body, Combe elaborated on the best time for exercise and the different kinds of exercise. He recommended walking, riding, dancing, gymnastics and "callisthenic exercises," fencing, shuttlecock, and reading aloud. Combe particularly disapproved of the different exercises often prescribed for the two sexes and suggested that the exercises for women should not differ that radically from men. In this regard he suggested "club exercise" for women.[175]

Robley Dunglison (1798–1869) was a professor of hygiene and medical jurisprudence at the University of Maryland and is credited with writing "the first American textbook on preventive medicine prepared for use by medical students."[176] His book *On the Influence of Atmosphere and Locality; Change of Air and Climate; Seasons; Food; Clothing; Bathing; Exercise; Sleep; Corporeal and Intellectual Pursuits, & c. on Human Health; Constituting Elements of Hygiene* was a testimony to Dunglison's strong belief in the importance of the non-naturals. He paid tribute to Combe and his book and noted in the preface that: "Hygiene is, therefore, a part of *practical* medicine. It teaches the course to be adopted in the way of prophylaxis or preservation."[177] Chapter 5 was called "Exercise" and Dunglison's opening statement was, "There is no hygienic agency of more importance than the due exercise of the body."[178] He discussed the topic for the next eighteen pages in considerable detail.

The life and contributions of Sylvester Graham (1794–1851) are widely known as a result of the fine work of Shryock,[179] Nissenbaum,[180] and Whorton.[181] Graham argued for self-improvement and asked each individual to become "a healthy animal." His message of a "physiology of subsistence" was directed primarily to the middle classes.[182] Graham published several books, including his lengthy *Lectures on the Science of Human Life* in 1839. As a Presbyterian minister rather than a physician, Graham's impact on American health reform was impressive.

Volume 2 of Graham's *Lectures* included a major portion devoted to diet in which he compared vegetables and flesh, gave the proper times for eating and the frequency, and discussed quantities of food along with what to drink. This material encompassed more than six hundred pages. The remaining fifty pages dealt with the other non-naturals of sleep, air, exercise, and evacuations. For exercise, Graham said, "Indeed, exercise may truly be considered the most important natural *tonic* of the body." Later, Graham noted that "exercise in order to be most beneficial, must be enjoyed."[183] He also discussed the benefits of walking, running, leaping, dancing, swimming, and riding on horseback.

The final book is included because of its lateness chronologically and the fact that it maintained a style of health care first popularized by Buchan. John King (1813–93), a professor at the Eclectic College of Medicine in Cincinnati, published *The American Family Physician; Or Domestic Guide to Health* in 1860. Like other books of this type, King structured the contents around chapters devoted to each of the non-naturals. Intended for "the most uneducated," King presented "the greatest amount of useful information, in *plain* and *familiar* language, free from the mysterious and incomprehensible *medical terms*, in which physicians endeavor to hide their art."[184] Chapter 9 was devoted to exercise and included information on the rules for exercise, sailing, walking, running, dancing, swimming, friction, and gymnastics. Like so many before him, King divided exercises into passive and active.

Learning the "Laws of Health": The Non-naturals Embodied in the Term "Physical Education"

The basic rudiments of the hygiene movement, or the non-natural tradition itself, found further expression in antebellum America through a new literature devoted to "physical education." In the early nineteenth century, a number of physicians began to use the term "physical education" in journal articles, speeches, and book titles to represent the task of teaching children the "laws of health." As Willich explained in 1801, "by *physical education* is meant the bodily treatment of children; the term *physical* being applied in opposition to *moral.*" He continued in his section "On the Physical Education of Children" to discuss stomach ailments, bathing, fresh air, exercise, dress, and diseases of the skin among various other topics.[185] Similarly, Dr. John

G. Coffin's editorship of the *Boston Medical Intelligencer, Devoted to the Cause of Physical Education and to the Means of Preventing and of Curing Diseases*, from 1826 to 1828, represented a definition of "physical education" much broader than exercise or gymnastics. "Physical education," then, implied educating about one's *physical* body rather than exercising the body in a gymnasium or elsewhere. Knowledge about one's physical body was deemed crucial to a well-educated and healthy individual by several physicians who, as Whorton has suggested, "dedicated their careers to birthing the modern physical education movement."[186]

The writings on "physical education" by four of these physicians are reviewed as representatives of this antebellum American trend. These include Charles Caldwell's *Thoughts on Physical Education*, John C. Warren's *Physical Education and the Preservation of Health*, Miles M. Rodgers's *Physical Education and Medical Management of Children*, and Elizabeth Blackwell's *The Laws of Life, with Special Reference to the Physical Education of Girls*.

A former student of the well-known physician Benjamin Rush, Charles Caldwell (1772–1853) held a prominent position in Lexington's Transylvania University Medical Department. Although he wrote on a variety of medical topics, his *Thoughts on Physical Education* gained him national recognition. Originally a speech delivered to a teacher's convention in his hometown in 1833, *Thoughts on Physical Education* was published as a book the following year by Marsh, Capen and Lyon of Boston. It was later published in Edinburgh in 1836 and again in 1844.

Caldwell explained the relationship of physical education to moral and intellectual education and reminded his audience that "physical education is far more important than is commonly imagined. Without a due regard to it . . . man cannot attain the perfection of his nature."[187] Later in the book, Caldwell defined "physical education" as: "that scheme of training, which contributes most effectually to the development, health, and perfection of living matter.—As applied to man, it is that scheme which raises his whole system to its summit of perfection. . . . Physical education, then, in its philosophy and practice, is of great compass. If complete, it would be tantamount to an entire system of Hygeiene. It would embrace every thing, that, by bearing in any way on the human body, might injure or benefit it in its health, vigor, and fitness for action."[188] As an example of this "scheme of training" for maximum health, Caldwell said a sound nursery education for children should consist of "the judicious management of diet, cleanliness, clothing, atmospherical temperature, respiration, muscular exercise, sleep, and animal passions."[189]

John C. Warren (1778–1856) was a professor of anatomy and surgery at Harvard University and was quite interested in exercise and health from the 1820s on. He gave several addresses on the topic of "physical education," one of which was published in 1845 as *Physical Education and the Preservation of Health.* A second edition appeared in 1846. The book was divided into several sections focusing on such topics as digestion, exercise, sleep, ventilation, and the external use of water. Warren's adherence to the non-natural tradition and its philosophy of the individual's duty to obey the "laws of nature" is exhibited by his concluding advice: "When, by the combined influence of nature and education, the constitution has become developed in its full power and stength, it depends on the individual to retain health and avoid disease. In other words, it may be considered as a general law, that health may be preserved to a late period of life by the use of those things, which are friendly, and the avoidance of those which are noxious. Most diseases are the consequences of violations of the laws of nature, sometimes the result of ignorance, more frequently of inattention."[190] That Warren's definition of "physical education" included more than just physical development became clear when he noted, "Exercise is so material to physical education, that it has sometimes been used synonymously, though it really constitutes only a part of it."[191]

Physical Education and Medical Management of Children. For the Use of Families and Teachers, published in 1848 by Upstate New York physician Miles M. Rodgers (dates unknown), showed through its title that "physical education" was part of the overall "medical management of children." In his introduction, Rodgers lamented the fact that "a general knowledge of the laws of life and health form[ed] no part of a popular system of education."[192] He went on to say, "The study of our own natures is perhaps the most elevating and ennobling subject which can engage the mind."[193] The non-natural tradition was also evident in Rodgers's book, since he devoted sections of chapter 2 to "Air," "Sleep," "Exercise," "Diet," and "Drinks."

Elizabeth Blackwell's (1821–1910) treatise on *The Laws of Life, with Special Reference to the Physical Education of Girls* was published in 1852 and serves as a final example of the idea that "physical education" as a term embodied the basic components of the non-natural tradition. While Blackwell was the first woman in the United States to graduate from medical school, she also had an impact on history through a variety of publications and lectures devoted to hygiene. As was common for the 1850s, physicians who wrote about "physical education" based much of their analysis on anatomy and physiology. Blackwell was no exception and discussed the "law of exercise" and how movement was

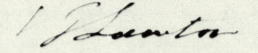

THOUGHTS

ON

PHYSICAL EDUCATION:

BEING

A DISCOURSE

DELIVERED TO A

CONVENTION OF TEACHERS

IN LEXINGTON, KY.

ON THE 6TH & 7TH OF NOV. 1833.

By CHARLES CALDWELL, M. D.

BOSTON:
MARSH, CAPEN & LYON.
1834.

Figure 1.7 Title page from Charles Caldwell, *Thoughts on Physical Education* . . . (Boston, 1834).

important for blood flow, organ health, and muscle tone. She blamed a lack of understanding of the laws of health for the impaired health of American girls and actively campaigned for physical education instruction in schools and colleges.[194]

Postscript

After this review of the literature of the non-naturals, their place in the history of medicine, and the dominant position exercise had in that structure, it should be evident that the contemporary discussions of wellness, preventive medicine, and exercise prescription are simply the latest flowering of a tradition dating to antiquity. The cordial and growing relationship between exercise and medicine during the 1980s and into the 1990s is neither new nor unique. We are simply rekindling a practice once popular but abandoned.

Notes

1. C. Kimble, "In Pursuit of Well-Being," *Wilson Quarterly* 4 (1980): 72–73.
2. J. Naisbitt, *Megatrends: Ten New Directions Transforming Our Lives* (New York: Warner Books, 1984), 147.
3. *Seattle Post Intelligencer* (December 4, 1988): B-3.
4. E. T. Withington, *Medical History from the Earliest Times: A Popular History of the Healing Art* (London: Scientific Press, 1894).
5. S. J. Reiser, "Responsibility for Personal Health: A Historical Perspective," *Journal of Medicine and Philosophy* 10 (1985): 7–17.
6. Withington, *Medical History*.
7. L. J. Rather, *Mind and Body in Eighteenth Century Medicine: A Study Based on Jerome Gaub's* De regimine mentis (Berkeley: University of California Press, 1965), 16–17.
8. Ibid., 82.
9. Ibid.
10. Ibid., 212.
11. Ibid., 213.
12. L. J. Rather, "The 'Six Things Non-natural': A Note on the Origins and Fate of a Doctrine and a Phrase," *Clio Medica* 3 (1968): 337.
13. Ibid.
14. Ibid.
15. Ibid., 341.
16. S. Jarcho, "Galen's Six Non-naturals: A Bibliographic Note and Translation," *Bulletin of the History of Medicine* 44 (1970): 372–77.
17. P. H. Niebyl, "The Non-naturals," *Bulletin of the History of Medicine* 45 (1971): 488.

18. Ibid., 491.

19. J. J. Bylebyl, "Galen on the Non-natural Causes of Variation in the Pulse," *Bulletin of the History of Medicine* 45 (1971): 483.

20. Ibid., 484.

21. O. Temkin, *Galenism: Rise and Decline of a Medical Philosophy* (Ithaca: Cornell University Press, 1973).

22. C. R. Burns, "The Nonnaturals: A Paradox in the Western Concept of Health," *Journal of Medicine & Philosophy* 1 (1976); 202.

23. Ibid., 203.

24. Ibid., 204.

25. Ibid., 210.

26. J. C. Burnham, *How Superstition Won and Science Lost: Popularizing Science and Health in the United States* (New Brunswick, N.J.: Rutgers University Press, 1987), 46.

27. L. J. Rather, "Pathology at Mid-Century: A Reassessment of Thomas Willis and Thomas Sydenham," in *Medicine in Seventeenth-Century England*, ed. A. G. Debus (Berkeley: University of California Press, 1974), 71–112.

28. J. C. Riley, "The Medicine of the Environment in Eighteenth-Century Germany," *Clio Medica* 18 (1983): 167–178 and *The Eighteenth-Century Campaign to Avoid Disease* (New York: St. Martin's Press, 1987).

29. S. W. Jackson, *Melancholia and Depression: From Hippocratic Times to Modern Times* (New Haven, Conn.: Yale University Press, 1986).

30. M. H. Verbrugge, "The Social Meaning of Personal Health: The Ladies' Physiological Institute of Boston and Vicinity in the 1850s," in *Health Care in America: Essays in Social History*, ed. S. Reverby and D. Rosner (Philadelphia: Temple University Press, 1979).

31. W. Coleman, "Health and Hygiene in the *Encyclopedie:* A Medical Doctrine for the Bourgeoisie," *Journal of the History of Medicine and Allied Sciences* 29 (1974): 399.

32. Ibid., 405.

33. C. J. Lawrence, "William Buchan: Medicine Laid Open," *Medical History* 19 (1975): 20–35.

34. J. C. Burnham, "Change in the Popularization of Health in the United States," *Bulletin of the History of Medicine* 58 (1984): 183–197.

35. G. Smith, "Prescribing the Rules of Health: Self-help and Advice in the Late Eighteenth Century," in *Patients and Practitioners: Lay Perceptions of Medicine in Pre-Industrial Society*, ed. R. Porter (Cambridge: Cambridge University Press, 1985), 249–82.

36. K. H. Dannenfeldt, "Sleep: Theory and Practice in the Late Renaissance," *Journal of the History of Medicine and the Allied Sciences* 41 (1986): 415–41.

37. E. R. Lomax, "The Introduction into the School Curriculum of Instruction in Health and Human Physiology," ms., 1987.

38. B. Haley, *The Healthy Body and Victorian Culture* (Cambridge, Mass.: Harvard University Press, 1978), 15–17.

39. G. Finney, "Medical Theories of Vocal Exercise and Health," *Bulletin of the History of Medicine* 50 (1966): 395–406.

40. J. C. Whorton, *Crusaders for Fitness: The History of American Health Reformers* (Princeton, N.J.: Princeton University Press, 1982).

41. V. Smith, "Household Books: Regimenical Literature in Britain 1700–1850, with Special Reference to Exercise," ms., (Cambridge: Wellcome Unit for the History of Medicine, 1987).

42. G. F. Fletcher, "The History of Exercise in the Practice of Medicine," *Journal of the Medical Association of Georgia* 72 (1983): 38.

43. S. Licht, "History [of Therapeutic Exercise], in *Therapeutic Exercise*, ed. J. V. Basmajian, 4th ed. (Baltimore: Williams & Wilkins, 1984), 9.

44. F. E. Leonard and G. B. Affleck, *A Guide to the History of Physical Education*, 3rd ed. (Philadelphia: Lea & Febiger, 1947), 64.

45. L. H. Joseph, "Physical Education in the Early Middle Ages," *Ciba Symposia* 10 (1949): 1030–33; "Gymnastics during the Renaissance as a Part of the Humanistic Educational Program," Ibid.: 1034–40; "Medical Gymnastics in the Sixteenth and Seventeenth Centuries," Ibid.: 1041–53; and "Gymnastics in the Pre-revolutionary Eighteenth Century," Ibid.: 1054–60.

46. C. W. Hackensmith, *History of Physical Education* (New York: Harper & Row, 1966).

47. D. Brailsford, *Sport and Society. Elizabeth to Anne* (London: Routledge & Kegan Paul, 1969).

48. D. B. Van Dalen and B. L. Bennett, *A World History of Physical Education: Cultural, Philosophical, Comparative* (Englewood Cliffs, N.J.: Prentice Hall, 1971), 77.

49. Ibid., 187.

50. J. R. Betts, "Mind and Body in Early American Thought," *Journal of American History* 54 (1968): 805.

51. J. R. Betts, "American Medical Thought on Exercise as the Road to Health, 1820–1860," *Bulletin of the History of Medicine* 45 (1971): 152.

52. R. J. Park, "Concern for Health and Exercise as Expressed in the Writings of 18th-Century Physicians and Informed Laymen (England, France, Switzerland)," *Research Quarterly* 47 (1976): 763.

53. R. J. Park, "The Attitudes of Leading New England Transcendentalists toward Healthful Exercise, Active Recreations, and Proper Care of the Body: 1830–1860," *Journal of Sport History* 4 (1977): 34–50; "The Advancement of Learning: Expressions of Concern for Health and Exercise in English Proposals for Educational Reform—1640–1660," *Canadian Journal of History of Sport and Physical Education* 8 (1977): 51–61, and "Embodied Selves: The Rise and Development of Concern for Physical Education, Active Games, and Recreation for American Women, 1776–1865," *Journal of Sport History* 5 (1978): 5–41.

54. Park, "Embodied Selves," 23.

55. Ibid., 24.

56. R. J. Park, "Strong Bodies, Healthful Regimens, and Playful Recreations as Viewed by Utopian Authors of the 16th and 17th Centuries," *Research Quarterly* 49 (1978): 498–511; and "Physiologists, Physicians, and Physical Educators: Nineteenth-Century Biology and Exercise, *Hygienic* and *Educative*," *Journal of Sport History* 14 (1987): 28–60.

57. E. B. English, "Girolamo Cardano and *De sanitate tuenda:* A Renaissance Physician's Perspective on Exercise," *Research Quarterly for Exercise and Sport* 53 (1982): 282–90.

58. E. B. English, "Sport, the Blessed Medicine of the Renaissance," Paper presented at the North American Society for Sport History conference, Louisville, Ky., 1984.

59. English, "Girolamo Cardano," 283.

60. Ibid., 288.

61. Whorton, *Crusaders for Fitness*, 14–15.

62. H. Green, *Fit for America: Health, Fitness, Sport, and American Society* (New York: Pantheon Books, 1986).

63. V. Olivova, "Scientific and Professional Gymnastics," in V. Olivova, ed., *Sports and Games in the Ancient World* (New York: St. Martin's Press, 1984), 135–44 and S. Licht, "History [of Therapeutic Exercise]," 1–44.

64. J. W. F. Blundell, *The Muscles and Their Story, from the Earliest Times; Including the Whole Text of Mercurialis, and the Opinions of Other Writers Ancient and Modern, on Mental and Bodily Development* (London: Chapman & Hall, 1864), 32.

65. A. Rees et al. *The Encyclopaedia; Or, Universal Dictionary of Arts, Sciences, and Literature* (London: Longman, Hurst, Rees, Orme & Brown, 1819), vol. 17.

66. R. J. Cyriax, "A Short History of Mechano-Therapeutics in Europe until the Time of Ling," *Janus* 19 (1914): 181.

67. J. Precope, *Hippocrates on Diet and Hygiene* (London: Williams, Lea & Co., 1952); Cyriax, "A Short History;" Licht, "History [Of Therapeutic Exercise];" and Olivova, "Scientific and Professional Gymnastics."

68. L. Ackerman, *Health and Hygiene. A Comprehensive Study of Disease Prevention and Health Promotion* (New York: Ronald Press, 1943).

69. Hippocrates. *Regimen.* trans. by W. H. S. Jones (Cambridge, Mass.: Harvard University Press, 1967), 45–59.

70. Ibid., 1.

71. Ibid., 229.

72. Ibid., 283.

73. Ibid., 353–59.

74. Ibid., 367.

75. Ibid., 383.

76. E. H. Ackerknecht, "Aspects of the History of Therapeutics," *Bulletin of the History of Medicine* 36 (1962): 389–419.

77. A. J. Brock, (trans. and annot.) *Greek Medicine: Being Extracts Illustrative of Medical Writers from Hippocrates to Galen* (London: J. M. Dent & Sons, 1929), 230.

78. H. E. Sigerist, *Landmarks in the History of Hygiene* (London: Oxford University Press, 1956).

79. R. M. Green, *A Translation of Galen's Hygiene (De sanitate tuenda)* (Springfield, Mo.: Charles C. Thomas, 1951).

80. Sigerist, *Landmarks*, 6.

81. Rather, "The 'Six Things Non-natural,' " 341.

82. Green, *A Translation of Galen's Hygiene*, 25.

83. Ibid., 53–54.

84. Ibid., 54.

85. G. Smith, "Prescribing the Rules of Health: Self-help and Advice in the Late Eighteenth Century," in *Patients and Practitioners: Lay Perceptions of Medicine in Pre-Industrial Society*, ed. R. Porter (Cambridge: Cambridge University Press, 1985), 249–82.

86. J. J. Bylebyl, "The School of Padua: Humanistic Medicine in the Sixteenth Century," in *Health, Medicine and Mortality in the Sixteenth Century*, ed. C. Webster (Cambridge: Cambridge University Press, 1979), 341.

87. Ibid., 340.

88. Ibid.

89. Burns, "The Nonnaturals," 208.

90. P. Slack, "Mirrors of Health and Treasures of Poor Men: The Uses of the Vernacular Medical Literature of Tudor England," in *Health, Medicine and Mortality in the Sixteenth Century*, ed. C. Webster (Cambridge: Cambridge University Press, 1979), 247.

91. Smith, "Prescribing the Rules," 250–51.

92. G. J. Gruman, "The Rise and Fall of Prolongevity Hygiene: 1558–1873," *Bulletin of the History of Medicine* 35 (1961): 221.

93. Slack, "Mirrors of Health," 250.

94. T. Elyot, *The Castel of Helthe*. Together with the Title Page and Preface of the Edition of 1539. With an Introduction by Samuel A. Tannenbaum (New York: Scholar's Facsimiles & Reprints, 1937), 4.

95. Ibid., 79.

96. Ibid., 1.

97. Ibid., 13.

98. Ibid., 43–44.

99. Brailsford, *Sport and Society*, 17–22.

100. C. Mendez, *Book of Bodily Exercise*, trans., F. Guerra; ed., F. G. Kilgour (New Haven, Conn.: Elizabeth Licht, 1960), 3.

101. Ibid., 6–7.

102. Ibid., 22.

103. W. B. Walker, "Luigi Cornaro, A Renaissance Writer on Personal Hygiene," *Bulletin of the History of Medicine* 28 (1954): 525–34.

104. L. Cornaro, *The Art of Living Long. A New and Improved English Version of the Treatise By the Celebrated Venetian Centenarian Louis Cornaro with Essays by Joseph Addison, Lord Bacon, and Sir William Temple* (Milwaukee: William F. Butler, 1905).

105. J. Cardan [Cardano], *The Book of My Life,* trans., J. Stoner (New York: E. P. Dutton & Co., 1930), 234–35.

106. Ibid., 26–27.

107. Ibid., 31.

108. P. C. McIntosh, "Hieronymus Mercurialis 'De Arte Gymnastica': Classification and Dogma in Physical Education in the Sixteenth Century," ms., 1980.

109. Joseph, "Medical Gymnastics in the Sixteenth Century," 1045.

110. T. Cogan, *The Haven of Health, Chiefly made for the comfort of Students, and consequently for all those that have a care for their health, amplified upon fine wordes of Hippocrates, written Epid. 6. Labour, Meate, Drinke, Sleepe, Venus* (London: Bonham Norton, 1596), iii.

111. Ibid., 4.

112. Ibid., 7.

113. Ibid., 265.

114. J. Harington, trans. *The School of Salernum. Regimen Sanitatis Salernitanum. The English Version* (New York: Paul B. Hoeber, 1920).

115. Sigerist, *Landmarks,* 22.

116. Ibid., 30–31.

117. Rather, "Pathology at Mid-Century," 102.

118. Jackson, *Melancholia and Depression,* 95–97.

119. R. Burton, *The Anatomy of Melancholy* (New York: A. C. Armstrong and Son, 1885), 336–56.

120. A. Pare, *The Collected Works of Ambroise Pare.* Trans. by T. Johnson (Pound Ridge, N.Y.: Milford House, 1968), 34–35.

121. F. H. Hoffmann, *Fundamenta Medicinae.* Trans. and an Introduction by L. S. King (New York: American Elsevier, 1971), ix–xi.

122. Ibid., 103–13.

123. F. E. Leonard, "The Beginnings of Modern Physical Training in Europe," *American Physical Education Review* 9 (1904): 89–110.

124. F. Fuller, *Medicina Gymnastica: or, A Treatise Concerning the Power of Exercise, With Respect to the Animal Oeconomy; And the Great Necessity of it, in the Cure of Several Distempers* (London: John Matthews, 1705).

125. E. and S. Licht, *A Translation of Joseph-Clement Tissot's Gymnastique Medicinale et Chirurgicale with a facsimile of the Original French and facsimiles of eighteenth-century translations into German, Italian, and Swedish* (New Haven, Conn.: Elizabeth Licht, 1964).

126. J. Pugh, *A Physiological, Theoretic and Practical Treatise on the Utility of the Science of Muscular Action for Restoring the Power of the Limbs* (London: C. Dilly, 1794).

127. R. F. McCoy, "Hygienic Recommendations of the *Ladies Library,*" *Bulletin of the History of Medicine* 4 (1936): 372.

128. H. R. Viets, "George Cheyne, 1673–1743," *Bulletin of the History of Medicine* 23 (1949): 435–52; and T. McCrae, "George Cheyne, An Old London and Bath Physician (1671–1743)," *Johns Hopkins Hospital Bulletin* 15 (1904): 84–94.

129. G. Cheyne, *An Essay of Health and Long Life* (New York: Edward Gillespy, 1813), 3.

130. Ibid., 94.

131. J. Armstrong, *The Art of Preserving Health* (London: T. Cadell and W. Davies, 1795), 89.

132. Coleman, "Health and Hygiene in the *Encyclopedie*"; "The People's Health; Medical Themes in Eighteenth-Century French Popular Literature," *Bulletin of the History of Medicine* 51 (1977): 55–74.

133. L. J. Jordanova, "Earth Science and Environmental Medicine: The Synthesis of the Late Enlightenment," in *Images of the Earth: Essays in the History of the Environmental Sciences,* ed. L. J. Jordanova and R. S. Porter (Bucks, England: British Society of the History of Science, 1979), 124.

134. Coleman, "Health and Hygiene in the *Encyclopedie*," 414.

135. Ibid., 419.

136. J. Mackenzie, *The History of Health, and the Art of Preserving It: Or, An Account of all that has been Recommended by Physicians and Philosophers, towards the Preservation of Health, from the Most Remote Antiquity to this Time* (Edinburgh: William Gordon, 1759), 81.

137. Ibid., 4–5.

138. B. S. Turner, "The Government of the Body: Medical Regimens and the Rationalization of Diet," *British Journal of Sociology* 33 (1982): 265.

139. J. Wesley, *Primitive Physic: Or, an Easy and Natural Method of Curing Most Diseases* (Philadelphia: Parry Hall, 1793), iv.

140. Ibid., vii.

141. Ibid., xi.

142. Lawrence, "William Buchan"; J. B. Blake, "From Buchan to Fishbein: The Literature of Domestic Medicine," in *Medicine without Doctors: Home Health Care in American History,* ed. G. B. Risse, R. T. Numbers, and J. W. Leavitt (New York: Science History Publications, 1977), 11–30.

143. W. Buchan, *Domestic Medicine: or, A Treatise on the Prevention and Cure of Diseases, By Regimen and Simple Medicines. With an Appendix, A Dispensatory for the Use of Private Practitioners. To Which are Added, Observations on Diet; Recommending A Method of Living Less Expensive, and More Conducive to Health, Then the Present. Also, Advice to Mothers, On the Subject of their Own Health; and of the Means of Promoting the Health, Strength and Beauty of Their Offspring* (Boston: Joseph Bumstead, 1813), 43.

144. Ibid., 85–86.

145. C. E. Rosenberg, "Medical Text and Social Context: Explaining William Buchan's *Domestic Medicine*," *Bulletin of the History of Medicine* 57 (1983): 22–42.

146. B. Cornwell, *The Domestic Physician, or Guardian of Health* (London: Printed for the Author, 1788), v.

147. Ibid., viii–ix.

148. H. E. Sigerist, "Faust in America," *Medical Life* 41 (1934): 192–207.

149. B. C. Faust, *Catechism of Health for the Use of Schools, and for Domestic Instruction.* Trans. by J. H. Basse (Dublin: C. Dilly, 1794).

150. G. Wallis, *The Art of Preventing Diseases, and Restoring Health, Founded on Rational Principles, and Adapted to Persons of Every Capacity* (New York: Samuel Campbell, 1794), 88–89.

151. Ibid., 76.

152. M. H. Verbrugge, "Healthy Animals and Civic Life: Sylvester Graham's Physiology of Subsistence," *Reviews in American History* 9 (1981): 359–64; R. M. Morantz, "Making Women Modern: Middle-Class Women and Health Reform in 19th-Century America," in *Women and Health in America: Historical Readings*, ed. J. W. Leavitt (Madison: University of Wisconsin Press, 1984), 346–58; J. H. Cassedy, "Why Self-help? Americans Alone with Their Diseases, 1800–1850," in *Medicine without Doctors: Home Health Care in American History*, ed. G. B. Risse, R. L. Numbers, and J. W. Leavitt (New York: Science History Publications, 1977), 31–48; and, R. L. Numbers, "Do-It-Yourself the Sectarian Way," in *Medicine without Doctors*, 49–72.

153. J. C. Whorton, "Christian Physiology: William Alcott's Prescription for the Millenium," *Bulletin of the History of Medicine* 49 (1975): 466–81.

154. J. H. Warner, *The Therapeutic Perspective: Medical Practice, Knowledge, and Identity in America, 1820–1885* (Cambridge: Harvard University Press, 1986).

155. J. C. Whorton, "The First Holistic Revolution: Alternative Medicine in the Nineteenth Century," in *Examining Holistic Medicine*, ed. D. Stalker and C. Glymour (New York: Prometheus Books, 1985), 29–48; C. E. Rosenberg, "The Therapeutic Revolution: Medicine, Meaning, and Social Change in Nineteenth-Century America," in *The Therapeutic Revolution: Essays in the Social History of American Medicine*, ed. M. J. Vogel and C. E. Rosenberg (Philadelphia: University of Pennsylvania Press, 1979), 3–25.

156. A. F. M. Willich, *Lectures on Diet and Regimen: Being a Systematic Inquiry into the Most Rational Means of Preserving Health and Prolonging Life: Together with Physiological and Chemical Explanations, Calculated Chiefly for the Use of Families, in Order to Banish the Prevailing Abuses and Prejudices in Medicine* (New York: T. and J. Swords, 1801), 454.

157. Ibid., 455.

158. Ibid., 303.

159. F. B. Rogers, "Shadrach Ricketson, (1768–1839): Quaker Hygienist," *Journal of the History of Medicine* 20 (1965): 140.

160. S. Ricketson, *Means of Preserving Health, and Preventing Diseases: Founded Principally on an Attention to Air and Climate, Drink, Food, Sleep, Exercise, Clothing, Passions of the Mind, and Retentions and Excretions* (New York: Collins, Perkins, and Co., 1806), 152.

161. Ibid.

162. Ibid., 153.

163. J. Thacher, *American Modern Practice; Or, A Simple Method of Prevention and Cure of Diseases, According to the Latest Improvements and Discoveries, Comprising a Practical System Adapted to the Use of Medical Practitioners of the United States* (Boston: Ezra Read, 1817), 77.

164. Ibid., 80.

165. Ibid.

166. J. Ewell, *The Medical Companion, or Family Physician;. . . . An Essay on Hygiene, or the Art of Preserving Health, Without the Aid of Medicine . . .* (Philadelphia: Carey, Lea & Blanchard, 1834), 65.

167. B. H. McClary, "Introducing a Classic: *Gunn's Domestic Medicine*," *Tennessee Historical Quarterly* 45 (1986): 210–16.

168. J. C. Gunn, *Gunn's Domestic Medicine.* A Facsimile of the First Edition with an Introduction by Charles E. Rosenberg (Knoxville: University of Tennessee Press, 1986), 13.

169. Ibid., 108.

170. Ibid., 109.

171. Ibid., 113.

172. E. Hitchcock, *Dyspepsy Forestalled and Resisted: or Lectures on Diet, Regimen and Employment; Delivered to the Students of Amherst College, Spring Term, 1830* (Amherst, Mass.: J. S. & C. Adams, 1831).

173. D. F. Allmendinger, Jr., *Paupers and Scholars: The Transformation of Student Life in Nineteenth-Century New England* (New York: St. Martin's Press, 1975), 105.

174. R. Cooter, "The Power of the Body: The Early Nineteenth Century," in *Natural Order: Historical Studies of Scientific Culture,* ed. B. Barnes and S. Shapin (London: Sage Publications, 1979), 75.

175. A. Combe, *The Principles of Physiology Applied to the Preservation of Health, and to the Improvement of Physical and Mental Education* (New York: Harper & Brothers, 1843), 131–54.

176. Rogers, "Shadrach Ricketson," 147.

177. R. Dunglison, *On the Influence of Atmosphere and Locality; Change of Air and Climate; Seasons; Food; Clothing; Bathing; Exercise; Sleep; Corporeal and Intellectual Pursuits, & c. on Human Health; Constituting Elements of Hygiene* (Philadelphia: Carey, Lea & Blanchard, 1835), iii.

178. Ibid., 425.

179. R. H. Shryock, "Sylvester Graham and the Popular Health Movement, 1830–1870," *Mississippi Valley Historical Review* 18 (1931): 172–83.

180. S. Nissenbaum, *Sex, Diet, and Debility in Jacksonian America: Sylvester Graham and Health Reform* (Westport, Conn.: Greenwood Press, 1980).

181. Whorton, *Crusaders for Fitness.*

182. Verbrugge, "Healthy Animals and Civic Life."

183. S. Graham, *Lectures on the Science of Human Life.* 2 vols. (Boston: March, Capen, Lyon and Webb, 1839), 652, 655.

184. J. King, *The American Family Physician: or Domestic Guide to Health, Prepared Expressly for the Use of Families, In Language Adapted to the Understanding of the People* (Indianapolis: Streight & Adams, 1860), iii.

185. Willich, *Lectures on Diet and Regimen,* 60, 60–73.

186. Whorton, *Crusaders for Fitness,* 282.

187. C. Caldwell, *Thoughts on Physical Education: Being a Discourse Delivered to a Convention of Teachers in Lexington, Ky., on the 6th and 7th of Nov. 1833* (Boston: Marsh, Capen & Lyon, 1834), 26.

188. Ibid., 28–29.

189. Ibid., 34.

190. J. C. Warren, *Physical Education and the Preservation of Health* (Boston: William D. Ticknor Co., 1846), 90.

191. Ibid., 33.

192. M. M. Rodgers, *Physical Education and Medical Management of Children. For the Use of Families and Teachers* (Rochester, N.Y.: Erastus Darrow, 1848), 10.

193. Ibid.

194. E. Blackwell, *The Laws of Life, with Special Reference to the Physical Education of Girls* (New York: George P. Putnam, 1852).

2 *Roberta J. Park*

Athletes and Their Training in Britain and America, 1800–1914

In 1831, Horatio Smith lamented: "The Olympic Games, with their emblazoned glories and massive monuments, have passed away like a sun-illusioned vapor." The ancient Panhellenic festivals had honored the human body. Athletes were required to swear that they had "regularly exercised for ten months" and to exhibit their strength and skill before the judges for thirty days preceding the contests. Before entering the stadium, contestants declared that they had prepared themselves "in a manner suitable to the dignity of the Olympic Games."[1] Celebrated in ode and legend, by steles and statues, victorious athletes might be accorded the status of "heroes"—superior to other men; inferior to the gods.[2]

In nineteenth-century Britain, the *icon* of the athlete again assumed "heroic" proportions. The *ideal* Victorian athlete "embodied" strength, fortitude, tenacity, courage, and something tantamount to moral rectitude. In portrait, poem, novel, and sermon, classical athleticism, medieval chivalry, and middle-class concepts of "manliness" were celebrated and endlessly proclaimed. The athlete, it was repeatedly said, possessed qualities that were needed to extend and protect an Empire. The athlete represented the future of the "race."[3]

Horatio Smith was not the only early nineteenth-century commentator to mourn the passing of both the athletics of Antiquity and what he referred to as "traditional" British sports and pastimes. Introducing a review of Charles Beck's 1828 English translation of *Die Deutsche Turnkunst* (1816), the *American Quarterly Review* declared the Olympian, Isthmian, and Nemean Games to have been "the animating spirit" of the Greek love for "strength, beauty, and religion."[4] Three years later, the *North American Review* devoted twenty-five pages to a review of a new edition of Joseph Strutt's monumental *Sports and Pastimes of the People of England,* asserting that traditional recreations and sports had been instrumental in making Britain great.[5] At mid-century the Unitarian clergyman A. A. Livermore effusively praised Greek athletics while denouncing what he saw as an American neglect of health, exercise, and vigorous manhood.[6] Livermore's contemporaries Oliver Wendell Holmes and Thomas Wentworth Higginson did likewise. Higginson, often called "the American muscular Christian," declared that his countrymen should be guided by the views of Thomas Arnold, Charles Kingsley, and *Tom Brown's School Days at Rugby* as they devised their own unique system of physical education.[7]

Thomas Hughes's enormously popular 1857 fictionalized account of life at Rugby School in the early 1800s fostered (although it did not initiate) the vigorous, "manly," athletic ethos which swept first Britain and then the United States in the second half of the nineteenth century. *Fraser's Magazine* in 1855 had proclaimed: "We are the stronger, the more vigorous, and the more healthy people; we fight as men conscious rather of massive strength than of suppleness and agility."[8] The following year, the *Westminster Review* asked the reader to consider the importance of games in forming the strength of character of the English. Ranging broadly from the Olympic and Pythian Games to Apollo ("as the model of manly strength and grace"), to medieval chivalry and sixteenth-century English pastimes, the writer asserted: "A manly vigor from the earliest time has been perceptible in the recreations of the English nation." Echoing Horatio Smith, he called upon the State to provide for exercises and pastimes to promote "strength and health of the body and cheerfulness of spirit."[9] In 1858, *The Edinburgh Review* found the football matches in *Tom Brown's School Days* to be "described in the style of a Homeric battle . . . with a certain combination of zest and solemnity" for which the only appropriate word was *agon*—"something between a battle and a sacrifice."[10]

Fascination with the classical world and with agonistic athletics increased during the Victorian period, especially within the orbit of Oxford, Cambridge, and the elite public schools. The *ideals* around which Arnold's Rugby revolved, Richard Jenkyns has written, were "Greek *and* cricket."[11] *Realities,* however, were closer to James Mangan's assessment: "Manliness . . . embraced antithetical values"—"success and ruthlessness tempered by a certain amount of courtesy and an ethos which held that victory must be attained within the rules."[12] These were the values of a rising class of "gentleman amateurs" who increasingly came to use the athletic contest as a major arena in which to act out, quite literally, statements about their own perceived status and values.

In democratic and "egalitarian" America, athletes were frequently compared with frontiersmen or portrayed as possessing the same qualities as military heroes or "captains of industry." Everyone who recognizes "the importance of robust, physical manhood in a modern commonwealth," John Bingham wrote in 1897, must acknowledge the absolute value of athletics.[13] The realities of preparing for the contest—that is *training*—were much more mundane.

Grafted onto what were largely classical conceptions of the body, nineteenth-century training regimens initially drew much of their rationales and practices from Galen and other ancient authorities.[14] Around mid-century, as competitive contests began to assume new proportions—and an "amateur" ethos burgeoned—new ideas began to erode the earlier "professional" orientation. The French historian Hippolyte Taine declared of England in the 1870s: "There are . . . gentlemen in this country whose ambition and regimen are those of the Greek athlete: they adopt a special diet . . . and follow a careful system of training. As soon as they are ready they set out to obtain the prize for rowing or cricket at all the principal athletic games meetings in England."[15] To accommodate the needs of such men, a new type of training manual began to appear—first in England, then in the United States and on the Continent.

English Sporting Pastimes in the Early 1800s

Although Smith had not acknowledged the fact when he called for a revival of "wholesome traditional sports," an extensive "sporting calendar" already existed. *Bell's Life in London and Sporting Chronicle,* the *Sporting Magazine,* and other early nineteenth-century sources reported an almost unending cycle of pedestrian, boxing, rowing, and cricket matches. In addition, there was wrestling, coursing, pigeon shooting, singlestick, trap-ball, cock fighting, and the ubiquitous "turf" (horse racing). Widely popular, illegal, and beset by cheating, pugilism cut across class lines.[16] Pierce Egan asserted that boxing exemplified such "British" traits as manliness, strength, and vigor. It had the support of "Dukes, Lords, and Honourables"; and had been brought to "the rank of a science" by Jack Broughton in the mid-1700s.[17] Significantly, Egan dedicated his *Boxiana; or Sketches of Ancient and Modern Pugilism* to the noted pedestrian Captain Barclay, whom he called "that distinguished patron of the old English sports."[18]

According to contemporaries, no late eighteenth- or early nineteenth-century pedestrian eclipsed the fame that Captain Barclay (Allardice) had attained by the 1810s. His best-known feat was walking 1,000 miles in 1,000 hours. Competitors like Peter Jackson attracted large crowds and sizeable wagers in the 1820s. Interest in pedestrianism waned somewhat, but revived in the 1850s when "the amateurs began to turn out again and make matches with each other or with the [professional] pedestrians."[19] Sculling, rowing, and sailing were also popular during the first half of the nineteenth century, with scores of amateur as well as professional contests on the Thames and the Tyne. The Doggett's Coat and Badge Race (established in 1715 for professional watermen) had attracted annual attention by the 1790s; and wagers on races between "gentlemen amateurs" often exceeded those placed for avowedly "professional" events. *Bell's Life* for August 2, 1829, for example, reported a rowing match for 100 sovereigns a side between Eton and Westminster scholars.[20]

The most popular sport was pugilism, a favorite among all ranks of society. The funeral of the sports-loving George IV in 1830 was not sufficient cause to interrupt announcements of the latest odds at St. Leger or forthcoming cricket, aquatic, and boxing contests.[21] Fighters like Thomas Cribb, Thomas Molineaux, and Jem Ward attracted huge crowds. The 1500 guineas allegedly wagered on a "mill" between Ned Neal and Young Dutch Sam in December 1829 was a pittance when compared to the £10,000 the Duke of Cumberland lost in 1750 or the £100,000 stakes in the early 1800s that Brailsford has reported.[22]

The 1829 University Boat Race between Oxford and Cambridge initiated a new era in rowing and, ultimately, the beginnings of a newly defined "amateur" ethos in sport. Reporting on the "match between nine Collegians of the Cambridge and nine of the Oxford Universities, for 500 guineas," *Bell's Life* observed that so much excitement had been aroused that "scarcely a bed was to be had for love or money." When it was learned that the Oxonians had left "nothing untried in the way of training," the heavy betting turned from the Cambridge to the Oxford crew.[23]

Devotees of sporting activities in the 1820s, 1830s and 1840s, then, had ample from which to choose. Taken together, the annual "chronicles" of pedestrianism, wrestling, and pugilism alone reported in *Bell's Life* for the year 1840 list upwards of 600 contests.[24] To prepare themselves for these, men were frequently subjected to Draconian training measures.

Early Nineteenth-Century Concepts of Training

Although it is often said that Walter Thom's *Pedestrianism* (1813) was the first modern treatise on *athletic training*,[25] it was neither "modern" nor the first sustained account. Sir John Sinclair's massive four-volume *Code of Health and Longevity; or Concise View of the Principles Calculated for the Preservation of Health and the Attainment of Long Life* (1807) had already discussed training for pedestrianism and pugilism. The Earl of Cathness drew upon ancient sources (e.g., Herodicus, Asclepiades, Celsus, Galen), Sir Francis Bacon, contemporary physicians A. P. Bucan and Bryan Robinson, and a small tract entitled *The Manual of Defense, or a System of Boxing* (1789). He also solicited information from Thomas Parkyns (a noted contemporary trainer of wrestlers), John Hall (trainer of pugilists), and the pedestrian Peter Jackson.[26]

As Peter Radford has observed, it was no easy matter in the early 1800s to obtain information from the hundreds of trainers currently practicing their arts as "their training methods were their livelihood, with the details often kept within a family. . . ." Such men were usually poorly educated; their "theories" derived from observation, experience, and word-of-mouth. Many of their ideas were distillations of practices used in the training of racehorses and gamecocks.[27] Because existing practices relied upon an oral tradition, the information provided by Sinclair and Thom offers valuable insights into what were probably widely accepted ideas regarding athletic training in the early 1800s.

At the beginning of the nineteenth century the "non-naturals,"[28] classical therapeutics, and traditional theories of hygiene still exerted a major influence on concepts of health and disease. Galen remained the standard authority. Proper diet, exercise, and evacuations (along with cleanliness and adequate sleep) formed the basis for both the hygienic practices advocated for the average man and the training regimens for athletes. Whereas the average man was encouraged to practice *moderation* (which in Georgian parlance might mean two or three pints of wine a day), athletes needed nourishment sufficient to replenish a body subjected to extraordinary exertions. The athlete had particular need to reduce fat and build muscle. Therefore, the Georgian pugilist and pedestrian was advised to eat large quantities of lean, red meat (which most resembled muscle, the flesh it was supposed to build).[29]

Describing the British experience of sickness and health between

PEDESTRIANISM;

OR,

AN ACCOUNT

OF

The Performances of celebrated Pedestrians

DURING

THE LAST AND PRESENT CENTURY;

WITH A FULL NARRATIVE OF

Captain Barclay's

PUBLIC AND PRIVATE MATCHES;

AND

AN ESSAY ON TRAINING.

———

BY THE

AUTHOR OF THE HISTORY OF ABERDEEN,

&c. &c. &c.

———

ABERDEEN:

Printed by D. Chalmers and Co.

FOR A. BROWN, AND F. FROST, ABERDEEN; CONSTABLE AND CO.
AND GREIG, HIGH-STREET, EDINBURGH; LONGMAN AND
CO. PATERNOSTER-ROW; FORSYTH, 114, LEADEN-
HALL-STREET; AND RICE, 28, BERKELEY-
SQUARE, LONDON.

———

1813.

Figure 2.1 Title page from Captain Barclay, *Pedestrianism . . .*
(Aberdeen, 1813).

1650 to 1850, Roy and Dorothy Porter have shown how the older humoral theory persisted alongside newer explanations of how the body functioned. Such conjunctions were evident in nineteenth-century ideas about *training*. Georgians relied upon external symptoms, from which they inferred functions. "The active body obviously needed nourishment to provide strength and warmth. . . . Hence, health consciousness fixed upon the stomach, . . . the 'grand Monarque' of the Constitution." The best "body-building" foods were those thought to be rich and invigorating (e.g., roasted beef and wine, a fluid that resembled the blood).[30]

Classical theories of alimentation, which classified foods according to purgative, weakening, and strengthening, held that the body must first be prepared to receive food; imbalances could lead to "peccant humours" (toxic fluids). When these built up, illness and loss of strength ensued. Purging, vomiting, and bleeding (often not advised for athletes, who needed all their strength) were the standard means to help rid the body of noxious material. According to Sinclair, Thom, and those who followed their advice, the particular "constitution" of each individual was of some consequence. However, the core of all training regimens was: purging, puking, sweating, diet, and exercise. (Substantially the same concepts were applied to training racehorses and gamecocks.)[31] Whether for running or for boxing, the major aim of training was "to increase the muscular strength, and to improve the free action of the lungs, or *wind*"[21] (i.e., strengthen the skeletomuscular system and improve cardiorespiratory function).

First, the trainer must attend to the state of the athlete's bowels, administering a series of three physics (preferably Glauber's salt),[33] spaced four days apart. (If at any time the "stomach seem[ed] foul" or the athlete flagged, an emetic was to be given.) After the physicking, regular exercise began, gradually increasing in intensity as the athlete progressed toward the day of competition. Regularity was deemed essential since both the mind and the body must be disciplined. The trainer was enjoined to keep a watchful vigil to insure that the athlete did not deviate from the prescribed regimen, relieving monotony with cricket, bowles, throwing quoits, and other distracting exercises.[34]

Thom's 1813 pedestrian was to arise at 5:00 A.M., run a half mile at top speed, then walk for six miles. A 7:00 A.M. breakfast consisted of "under-done beefsteaks or mutton-chops with a little stale bread and old beer." Another six-mile walk at a moderate pace followed breakfast. At noon the athlete rested for a half hour without clothes, then walked four miles. Dinner, at 4:00 P.M., was the same as breakfast. "Immediately after dinner," the pedestrian resumed exercise, running half a mile at top speed followed by a six-mile walk at a moderate pace. No further exertions were allowed before bed at 8:00 P.M.. These same procedures were to be repeated with monotonous regularity for two to three months, building up to twenty to twenty-four miles a day.[35]

Three or four weeks after training commenced, the pedestrian also began a sweating regime, the purpose of which was to "reduce fat." After running four miles at top speed dressed in flannels, the man was given one English pint of "hot sweating liquor" (caraway seed, coriander, root liquorice, and sugar candy boiled together with two bottles of cider until the preparation reduced to half its original volume). He was then put to bed and warmly covered for thirty minutes. Upon rising, his body was rubbed dry and wrapped in a great coat; he was walked out gently, returning for breakfast—this time of roasted fowl. Such weekly "sweats" continued until shortly before the competition. Similar procedures were advocated for pugilists.[36] It was claimed, for example, that the boxer Tom Cribb reduced his weight "in a course of five weeks, from sixteen stone to fourteen and nine pounds" by diet, sweating, and increasing his walks to eighteen or twenty miles a day.[37]

According to Thom, Sinclair, and others, the diet of a man in training was to consist largely of meat, especially lean beef (deemed most nourishing) and mutton (thought easy to digest). Broiling was considered better than roasting or boiling; the legs of fowls were recommended as sources of energy. Fish was considered to be "watery." Most trainers avoided veal and lamb (both young animals); but a few advocated several small meals a day of veal stew and sherry wine. Pork—a meat included in classical training programs—was uniformly rejected. Only stale bread was allowed as new bread was thought to be spongy and to expand in the stomach. Turnips, carrots, and potatoes were considered watery, difficult to digest, and apt to produce flatulence. Butter was indigestible; cheese turned rancid on the stomach. Spices and seasonings (except vinegar) were prohibited, as were eggs (although a raw egg might be given in the morning). Milk curdled on the stomach; broths and any warm and relaxing drink weakened the stomach. All liquids were to be taken cold and water was to be avoided as much as possible.[38]

Sinclair maintained that although the Ancients had allowed water, modern trainers permitted only small quantities since "too much liquor" swelled the belly, was "bad for the wind," took up space needed for solid food, and promoted "soft unhealthy flesh." Sinclair also advised against tea—which some trainers permitted. Old, home-brewed, unbottled beer was widely held to be most nourishing; boxers might have up to three pints a day—runners, up to four. Up to a half a pint of red wine could be given after dinner, but "ardent" spirits were strictly forbidden.[39] (Beer, a malted beverage in which cereal starches are converted into sugar, long remained a staple of British regimen. As late as 1914 some writers would remark with surprise about its absence in the typical American training diet.)

It is not known how scrupulously pedestrians, boxers, or oarsmen followed the prescribed procedures. However, since backers were likely to have made heavy investments in both training costs and wagers, it behooved the trainer to ensure that his man was prepared for the match. Pierce Egan contrasted the colored boxer Tom Molineaux, who without a patron indulged in excesses and had no "regular *training*," with Tom Cribb, Champion of England, who had been "placed under the immediate direction of Capt. Barclay, and secluded from the world at the estate of that gentleman" for *his* training.[40] In 1830, *Bell's Life in London* attributed Jem Ward's failure to attain the Championship of England to "his own imprudence rather than to any natural defect of stamina,"[41] *Pugilistica,* Henry Downes Miles's history of British boxing, refers to boxers whose dissipations shortened their athletic careers. The general belief was that a man in training was quite fit. It was overindulgence *after* the contest that ruined an athlete's health.[42]

The Emergence of a New Athletic Ethos, 1850s–1870s

Attitudes regarding athletic sport underwent significant changes around the middle of the nineteenth century, leading to altered views of training.[43] Much of this centered around university sport—notably rowing and track and field ("athletics" in British usage). Eric Halladay has pointed to the importance "of a group of clubs characterized by their proficiency in rowing and by their links with the two universities whose values they had come to share."[44] The author of *Principles of Rowing, by an Oarsman* (1846) observed: "No national amusement, perhaps, has so much advanced in the last ten years as Rowing," largely due to an increased interest among gentlemen that emerged after the Oxford-Cambridge Boat Race of 1829. The *British Rowing Almanack and Oarsman's Companion* for 1867 listed clubs under four headings: gentlemen; professional; tradesmen; watermen. However, "no club outside the Thames was to be found in the first group other than Oxford and Cambridge."[45]

Figure 2.2 Thomas Cribb, from Henry Downes Miles, *Pugilistica: The History of British Boxing* (Edinburgh: John Grant, 1906), vol. 1, facing p. 242.

The emergence of these new attitudes was noted by Americans. Following the June 1857 race between the Volant and the Herron on the Charles River, for example, there had been calls for "stricter training among the college oarsmen." *Tom Brown's School Days* and *Tom Brown at Oxford* (1861) were warmly received in the United States, as were visits such as that of the "Eleven of All England" (Cricket), which *Harper's Weekly* reported in 1859.[46] It would not be until the 1890s, however, that American athletic achievements would challenge British supremacy.

T. S. Egan objected to the "extravagance . . . enveloped in a proportionate degree of mystery," which was so often imparted to amateur crews by professional watermen. *Gentlemen* needed moderation in sleeping, eating, and drinking (avoiding liquors, which tended to produce "internal fat"), not the fanciful practices used when preparing *professsional* crews.[47] To assist the "amateur gentleman," authors like John Henry Walsh ("Stonehenge") began to include information about training regimens in their sporting manuals in the 1850s and 1860s. Reporting that the Oxonians had easily outdistanced a "professional" crew that it had engaged for practice—rowing "as throughout their training with great power" (up to forty-four strokes per minute)—*The Times* declared that betting on the 1866 Boat Race with Cambridge had risen to "5 and 6 to 4 on Oxford."[48]

The popularity of the annual Boat Race fostered the growth of "athletics" (track). John Tyler, editor of *The Rowing Almanac*, noted that the principle rowing clubs in the London area had been offering prize competitions in running since 1861 as a means of conditioning oarsmen and "ensuring their interest" during the non-rowing season.[49] The two universities held their first "Inter-Varsity" meeting at Oxford's Christ Church Cricket Ground in 1864. Looking back from the vantage point of the 1890s, H. H. Griffin declared: "When the Universities took up athletics, and inaugurated a contest, foot racing became a matter of real interest, and it became possible for gentlemen of refined taste and ladies to look on with pleasure."[50] The 1867 races were open to: (1) members of recognized rowing and athletic clubs; (2) Oxford, Cambridge, and other universities; (3) the public schools; (4) members of the Civil Service; and (5) officers of the army, navy, and volunteers.[51] These designations clearly excluded professional pedestrians.

The *Contemporary Review* declared in 1866: "It would be difficult to point to any part of daily life in which the last half-century has brought about a greater change than in out-of-door exercise." In the early 1800s, the author observed, the principal sporting

Figure 2.3 "The Oxford and Cambridge Athletic Sports in the Christ Church Meadows, Oxford: The Two-Mile Race," from *The Illustrated London News*, supplement, March 24, 1866.

preoccupations had been cock fights, racing, four-in-hand driving, boxing, and pigeon matches, with "boating scarcely known beyond the Thames or Tyne" and athletics (track) "pretty nearly unheard of, except in the Highlands of Scotland." Now the annual contests between Oxford and Cambridge were considered major events.[52] The same year, *Blackwood's Magazine* acknowledged: "The development of 'muscular' education both at our public schools and universities is a fact which is beginning to attract a good deal of attention." *Sketches by a Don*, the writer observed, now provided athletic views of Cambridge in much the same way as *Verdant Green* and *Tom Brown at Oxford* did for rival Oxford.[53]

The London Athletic Club held its first regular meeting at Beaufort House on March 23, 1866, the same year that the Amateur Athletic Club (A.A.C.) was formed by former University and Club athletes to "supply the want of an established ground upon which competitions in amateur athletic sports might take place . . . without being compelled to mix with professional runners."[54] The emphasis on "gentlemen amateurs" is significant. Although professional pedestrianism remained popular (W. G. George, "World's One Mile Record Holder," established a sporting goods business in the late 1800s much as did Albert Spalding in the United States), efforts were increasingly made to distinguish between the "amateur" and the "professional." The A.A.C. added the *mechanic's* clause in 1867 to its definition of an amateur, effectively eliminating anyone who was "by trade or employment a mechanic, artisan, or laborer."[55]

A comparable situation existed in rowing. The three major rowing clubs on the River Tyne in the 1860s were: Tyne Amateur Rowing Club; Northern Rowing Club (made up of "both landsmen and watermen alike on an equal footing"); and Albion Club (made up mainly of men who worked on land as opposed to water). Harry Clasper ("Hero of the North") was the most notable of the northern professional oarsmen, holder of numerous championships, and designer of the modern outrigger boat. In 1845, he and his brothers had been victorious over a crew of Thames watermen, until then considered the "undisputed champions of the World." For many years, Clasper was an acknowledged authority on "training"; and many amateurs as well as professional oarsmen adopted his theories.[56]

Clasper devoted more attention to the condition of each man than did many contemporaries. The oarsman should rise between 6:00 A.M. and 7:00 A.M., walk four or five miles, then breakfast on a mutton chop or a couple of eggs and a cup of tea. Following a rest, he then completed a row on the river. Broiled beef or mutton, ale or wine, and a light farinaceous or egg pudding with currants formed the mid-day meal. A hard row on the river followed another rest; then tea with sparsely buttered toast and an egg. If supper (not recommended) was taken, it should consist of "new milk and bread, or gruel, with raisins and currants and a glass of port wine with it."[57] (Clasper's emphasis on currants and raisins is not encountered in most other earlier training diets.)

Those who sought to foster "amateur" sports—notably track—frequently complained about the persistence of wagering and other hallmarks of "professionalism." Reviewing the precipitous growth of these contests, *Baily's Magazine of Sports and Pastimes* in 1870 summarized the views of those who reveled in the new sporting ethos and those who railed against "excessive athleticism in the Universities and public schools." The giving of silver trophies, watches, and other expensive awards (which "amateurs" actually received in abundance) was denounced while high praise was given to the physical and mental benefits which *training* was thought to offer. Initially, the writer asserted, training for track competitions had been as "irrational" as it was for boating; however, of late athletes had begun to train "with great judgment, and in many cases their method is based upon considerable knowledge of the human frame and hygienic laws."[58]

It is not clear precisely what the writer meant by "knowledge of the human frame," but by the 1860s, chemists like Justus von Liebig and physiologists like Claude Bernard were advancing new concepts regarding metabolism. Other investigators were exploring the nervous system and the role of red corpuscles in carrying oxygen to the cells.[59] It requires a major shift in thinking, however, to transform the results of laboratory experiments into information that is useful to the practicing athlete. Although the term "scientific training" appeared with increasing frequency from 1870 onwards, most training methods continued to rely heavily upon the *accumulated experience* of successful athletes and trainers.

American Involvement in Athletics 1820s–1870s

American ideas and practice have been deeply, if selectively, influenced by British—and especially English—sport. Before the Civil War, pedestrianism, pugilism, and especially horse racing enjoyed a considerable following. Amateur rowing clubs had been founded in New York and Detroit by the 1830s; Harvard College organized a boat club in 1844. The quintessential "American" game of baseball evolved from English "rounders" in the late 1830s and 1840s, taking on its own distinctive features by the 1850s. In 1844, *The Spirit of the Times* reported that a purse of several thousand dollars would be awarded to the winner of a "footrace between England and America." The most famous of America's pedestrians, Edward Payson Weston, drew large audiences in Britain as well as at home. In 1868, the New York Athletic Club organized the nation's first indoor track meet to pit its representatives against those of the Scottish Caledonian Club of New York. Three years later, the N.Y.A.C. constructed the first cinder track in the United States at Mott Haven and opened its games to amateur athletes. Intercollegiate regattas facilitated the growth of American track in somewhat the same manner that the annual Oxford-Cambridge Boat Race had benefitted that sport in England. The first intercollegiate track meet was held in conjunction with the 1874 rowing contests at Saratoga.[60]

The Nation had asserted in 1869, "the taste for athletic sports in America is not over fifteen years old."[61] By the late 1870s, however, Benjamin Dwight and others could comfortably comment upon a "zeal for physical development and prowess." This was manifested in intercollegiate regattas, hurdle races, and "prize-contests" in walking and swimming. Noting the "pale and exhausted" winner of the one-mile run at the 1875 Saratoga regatta, Dwight compared the "irregular hours of eating and sleeping . . . almost universal use of narcotics (tobacco)," and mental slothfulness of young collegians to the "methodological and rigid training" that was necessary for success in muscular contests. He hoped, however, that American collegians would not imitate the "noisy physicality," drunken revelries, and other objectionable features of British and European college life as they took up with ever greater enthusiasm the competitions that had already become the rage in English public schools and universities.[62]

Dwight might have had in mind the boisterous celebrations that followed the 1868 Harvard-Yale boat race; twenty students were jailed for disorderly conduct. Flush with victory, Harvard sought to arrange matches on English waters. After considerable negotiations, a Harvard four-plus-coxswain set sail from New York.[63] The 1869 Harvard-Oxford race from Putney to Mortlake, which received extensive publicity on both sides of the Atlantic, contributed to the growing sporting fervor in the United States. It also engendered criticisms of American training practices. Upon arrival in Britain, the American crew had declined an invitation to stay with the Liverpool and Chester Boat Clubs, citing the need to concentrate on training. (Harvard alumnus William Blaikie expressed amazement that the Oxford oarsmen were doing only "twenty-five minutes of hard work each day" and taking days off.) The intensity of the losing American crew's training methods, its rowing technique, and what was seen as a single-minded emphasis on winning were all criticized by the British press. The *New York Times*, however, contended that local professional rowers (who reputedly disliked elite English amateur attitudes and "valued the end result rather than the means") had supported Harvard rather than Oxford.[64]

The entrepreneurial Albert G. Spalding became the arbiter of American "amateur" sport, establishing the *Spalding Library of American Sports* in 1885 to provide up-to-date information on training methods, techniques, and "records"—as well as to advertise his expanding equipment business.[65] By the beginning of the twentieth century, the firm issued approximately three hundred "separate publications on sport and physical activity." Spalding called upon newspapermen, physical educators, athletes, coaches, luminaries like the A.A.U.'s James E. Sullivan, and trainers like the University of Pennsylvania's Michael C. Murphy to write for and give status to his publications.[66]

The Emergence of "New" Attitudes toward Training

In the same article in which it had registered enthusiasm for the new forms of "gentlemanly" athletic competitions, the 1866 *Contemporary Review* had commented on a "modern method of training" written by Charles Westhall, the professional "pedestrian champion of England."[67] Westhall's (alias Hall) small book was but one of a growing number of such publications that appeared between 1855 and the mid-1870s.

In his introduction to *Athletics* (1891), H. Hewitt Griffin declared John Henry Walsh's 1855 *Manual of British Rural Sports Comprising Shooting, Hunting, Coursing, Fishing, Hawking, Racing, Boating, and Pedestrianism* to be the first of its kind and "a sure sign that sport was making headway."[68] Walsh included a section entitled "The Training of Man for Pedestrian Exercise." The information was reprinted in his handbook *Athletic Sports and Manly Exercises* (1864). In the Preface to the twelfth edition of the larger work, Walsh declared: "Amateur Pedestrianism and the various forms of Athletic amusements have developed in a marvelous manner." The fourteenth edition, published in 1878, contained an extensive compilation of the best amateur and professional races dating from Captain Barclay's famous walk of "1,000 miles in 1,000 consecutive hours."[69]

MANUAL

OF

BRITISH RURAL SPORTS:

COMPRISING

SHOOTING, HUNTING, COURSING, FISHING, HAWKING,
RACING, BOATING, PEDESTRIANISM,

AND

THE VARIOUS RURAL GAMES AND AMUSEMENTS OF
GREAT BRITAIN.

BY STONEHENGE,

AUTHOR OF "THE GREYHOUND," "THE SHOT-GUN AND SPORTING RIFLE."

ILLUSTRATED BY NUMEROUS ENGRAVINGS ON WOOD, BY MESSRS. DALZIEL AND HODGKIN,
FROM DRAWINGS BY WELLS, HARVEY, AND HIND.

Fifth Edition.

ENTIRELY REVISED, WITH ADDITIONS.

LONDON:

ROUTLEDGE, WARNE, AND ROUTLEDGE,

FARRINGDON STREET;

AND 56, WALKER STREET, NEW YORK.

1851.

Figure 2.4 Title page from Stonehenge, *Manual of British Rural Sports* . . . , 5th ed. (London, 1851).

Walsh compared men whom he called active and indolent "free liv-
ers" with the "over-studious" man. The former first must be weaned
from alcohol by substituting ammonia mixtures for the customary alcoholic drinks. Since alcohol "stimulated kidneys and skin to secrete a
greater quantity than was natural," these men would experience considerable thirst; this could be slaked by "claret and soda-water"—or
better, "porter or bitter beer mixed with soda-water." Such men
needed to be purged with caution (e.g., a half-ounce of sweet essence
of senna and salts or rhubarb pills rather than Glauber's salt). Yellow
or brown faeces indicated that the liver was working well; clay-colored
faeces called for "blue-pill"; loose bowels called for laudanum or sul-
furic acid. Over-studious men, on the other hand, tended to have impaired nervous systems due to excessive "strain upon the mind." They
must give up smoking, green tea and coffee, except at meals.[70]

Walsh—and others by the 1860s—usually distinguished between
gentlemen's sons and men from the "lower ranks." Because the
former had been "generously brought up," they could achieve good
condition in a relatively short time. The "lower ranks," brought up on
an "abstemious fare" with "no hunting or cricket to take up [their]
attention," were more likely to overindulge in tobacco and liquor.
These men required "much more careful treatment to get . . . into a
state of health fit for [athletic] exertion than the Oxonian or the
Cantab."[71] The class-biased attribution of bodily function conformed
to generally held contemporary views about the physical *and* "moral"
differences among classes.

Walsh recommended *natural* as well as *artifical* sweating along the
lines of the plan of the Silesian hydropath Vincent Priessnitz. The use
of *sweating liquors* he rejected. His diet included oatmeal porridge,
meat and table beer for breakfast; beef or mutton (occasionally
roasted fowls or partridges) with modest amounts of potatoes and
vegetables, beer, sherry, or claret for the midday meal; and porridge,
a chop, an egg and sherry at supper. "Red rags" (i.e., grossly under-
done meat) he deemed unpalatable; the athlete's meat should be adequately cooked.[72]

In 1863 Charles Westhall compared the "old method" (i.e., physicking and sweating) with "new rules of training." Since no two men
were alike, considerable variation in diet was acceptable. Westhall also
anticipated modern views regarding *specificity* in training, maintaining
that "the same amount of work and strict regimen is not requisite for
the sharp burst of a hundred yards or so, that it is . . . in preparation
for the more arduous struggle of a mile's duration." Rather than one
general formula, trainers should adjust the intensity and the duration

of the exercise bout for the distance to be run; it was not adequate to run at full speed for only one hundred yards if the race was longer.[73]

Westhall advised beginning with "gentle purgative medicines . . . to cleanse the stomach, bowels, and tissues from extraneous matter." When "the internal portion of the man's frame" was healthy (that is, properly evacuated), training proper commenced. Westhall's "modern" athlete was to arise at 6:00 A.M., bathe or shower, then walk at a slow pace for an hour before breakfast. (Those who needed nourishment could take a new-laid egg beaten in a cup of tea.) If the weather was inclement, dumbbell work, rope skipping, the swinging trapeze, and the vaulting bar were to be substituted for the walk. He advised *against* malted beverages early in the morning and recommended for breakfast a mutton chop or cutlet, dry bread or toast, and a cup or two of tea with as little milk as possible.[74] After rest to allow digestion, exercise to "reduce the mass of fat" commenced. In the beginning, a brisk walk and a run home would be sufficient; pace and distance increased as training progressed. Six to eight weeks (rather than the customary three or four) were needed to get a man into condition. Dinner at 1:00 P.M. was to consist of a joint of beef or mutton, stale bread or toast, and "good sound old ale." Recently, he noted, small portions of fresh vegetables or potatoes—and even a light pudding—had been permitted in the pedestrian's diet.[75]

After eating, the athlete rested for an hour then strolled about for another hour or two before putting on his racing shoes and gear. He then practiced his distance against the watch. At this stage, the advice of the trainer—"the only person capable of knowing how far towards success the trained man has progressed"—was of the utmost importance. If the athlete was not up to par, he should be stopped and his energies saved for another day. "Tea" (the evening meal) consisted of stale bread or toast and tea, with a new-laid egg. A gentle walk, followed by a rubdown, preceded early retiring.[76]

By the 1860s, Westhall and others were paying considerable attention to over-training or "training off." This could be recognized by "flaccid and sunken" muscles, patches of red in different portions of the body, and a continual and unquenchable thirst. When this occurred, the pedestrian must be rested and allowed variation in his diet rather than, as formerly, given another dosing with purgative or emetics.[77] Indeed, the whole matter of a transition from violent evacuating to milder forms of physicking seems to have been connected as much with the emergence of the gentleman "amateur" as with any altered concepts of physiological function.

An Embryonic "Science" of Athletic Training versus the "Persistence of Tradition"

Were there any exercise or training authorities who drew from the more detailed and exact understandings of human physiology which had begun to emerge around mid-century? Scottish-born Archibald Maclaren, who opened a gymnasium in 1855, had studied fencing, gymnastics, and medicine in Paris. By 1858, he was well on the way to becoming a widely recognized authority on the "scientific study of physical education."[78] In 1865, Macmillan and Company published his *A System of Physical Education* and in 1866 his *Training in Theory and Practice*. Although the focus was rowing, Maclaren noted that the same principles applied to training for other sports.

Maclaren found fault with almost every training system currently in vogue. Why was it necessary to evacuate the stomach and scour the intestines? Acknowledging that it was increasingly the tendency to administer purgatives only at the commencement of training, he declared all medicines to be "virtually poisons since they were calculated to change normal functions." Dosages were still too harsh for "feats of pedestrianism" and for boxers (who often were given "one grain of tartar emetic and twenty grains of ipecacuanha worked off with camomile tea"—and sometimes bled). It was remarkable, he asserted, that men were able to stand up to continual purging, vomiting, forced sweatings, restricted liquid, and semi-raw flesh. It was these practices—not exercise—which caused "training off" (or what he considered a better term, "falling to pieces"). In the preface to a second and enlarged edition of *Training in Theory and Practice* (1874), Maclaren stated: "The mischievous habit of amateur physicking is being abandoned, and the dangerous custom of forced perspiration, undertaken to exorcise the demons of 'internal fat' and 'loose flesh,' may be said to be discarded."[79]

Drawing upon what happened to a roasting joint of meat, for decades trainers had advocated "forced sweating." Exercising while wearing layers of heavy clothing, Maclaren pointed out, could reduce *weight* through perspiration, but it did not effect *fatty tissue*. Changes in the tissues was an *internal* process, dependent upon changes in respiration, "quickened circulation," and increased "demands upon the upstored fuel of the body." Running longer distances wearing light clothing was more effective than running "two miles in flannel encumbrances." Warm, not cold, water was needed after exercise to keep the pores open and allow "the deepest cutaneous deposits to be reached and removed." (Soap should be used to remove "matter exuded by the oil ducts.") A cold bath upon rising, however, could be refreshing and was permissible.[80]

If he was critical of forced sweating, Maclaren objected even more vociferously to the long-standing belief that athletes should be denied water. Quite the contrary! They should drink as much water as they pleased since fluid lost in perspiration and exhalations had to be replaced. He maintained that he had "never been able to comprehend how the idea of restricting this natural demand of the body for fluid arose" until he had chanced upon the "internal fat" theory. This, Maclaren speculated, may have gained support in connection with professional watermen, who were thought to overindulge in alcohol. He distinguished *general thirst* (a demand for liquid experienced by the entire body) from *local thirst* (which involved the mucous linings of mouth, throat, and air passages). The latter was occasioned by dust, heat, and other irritants. For this, rinsing the mouth or sucking a lemon or pebble was the remedy, not water (which unduly filled the stomach). Like most British writers, Maclaren considered beer to be a "wholesome beverage," useful for quenching thirst but apt to put on fat if consumed in large quantities. Port or sherry (which have high alcohol contents) should be used sparingly. "Continental wines" were good as stimulants; but distilled drinks did not belong "on a young man's table." Tea, coffee, and chocolate were refreshing unless taken too strong, hot, or in too great quantities.[81]

By the 1860s, researchers in France and Germany had begun to elucidate the body's metabolic processes. It is probable that Maclaren was familiar with some of this work although he did not cite it. He did include, however, tables of the chemical composition of various foods drawn from Dr. Horace Dobell's *A Manual of Diet and Regimen* (1863). The organic compounds, Maclaren noted, had been divided into three groups: *albuminous* (substances resembling in chemical composition animal tissues), *saccharine*, and *oleaginous* (oily). He deemed a diet consisting of animal food, "with a due admixture of farinaceous and vegetable food," the best combination, although he acknowledged that the role of vegetables in nutrition was not yet clearly understood. He criticized trainers for permitting men to eat the yolk ("little more than a ball of oil") but not the whites of eggs ("an article of almost pure albumen, the special pablum of the muscular tissue"). Spinach, sea kale, asparagus, turnip tops, beetroot, and French beans, as well as meat, pudding, bread, plain jellies, biscuits, dried fruits, and beer or wine should be consumed by athletes. (In winter, the diet should include more heat-producing foods, but fewer vegetables and less water.) Although he considered tobacco to be inimical to health,

Maclaren felt that men addicted to it could not immediately cease. Therefore, a pipe after dinner was permitted. A glass of wine or two helped promote sleep and could be a "restorative from depression"; but he found "fanciful" such formulas as those which recommended wine for pedestrians and sherry for boxers.[82]

Of all the "agents of health" (diet, sleep, air, clothing, exercise), Maclaren considered the proper regulation of *exercise* to be most crucial for athletes. Training must begin slowly; the typical three weeks preparation for a race was insufficient. Since oarsmen needed both muscular and respiratory power, they should have three hours of rowing a day as well as running to strengthen the legs, "the chief agents in rowing." He and others (as for example, William Blaikie, who drew upon Maclaren for his own *How to Get Strong* [1879]) considered chest *girth* to be important because there must be sufficient room to permit proper action of the vital organs. A man's chest, therefore, should be at least thirty-six inches before he put "his hand on an oar."[83]

Given Maclaren's advanced views, his standing as an authority on exercise, and his prestigious Oxford clientele, it is surprising that his writings did not do more to dislodge many of the traditional ideas which enjoyed considerable persistence into the twentieth century. There was—and still is—a certain mystique associated with athletic training. Traditional views of the body have persevered in matters of health; why should we expect, then, much to be different with regard to training?[84] Throughout the last quarter of the nineteenth century, training manuals reflected, in varying mixtures, vestiges of Thom's *Pedestrianism* and newer concepts of the functional processes of the body.

Walter Bradford Woodgate, a graduate of Brasenose College, winner of the Wingfield Sculls, and a noted rowing authority, published *"Oars and Sculls," and How to Use Them* (1875) for coaches of novice oarsmen. The small volume, clearly intended for "amateur gentlemen" of Oxford, Cambridge, and similar establishments, represents a kind of "intermediary" work. More modern in his views than "Stonehenge" or Westhall, Woodgate's treatment of diet and exercise was not quite as comprehensive as Maclaren's. Endurance, Woodgate stipulated, must be developed largely by means of running; rowing practice should concentrate on *technique*. He advocated "greens" (i.e., watercress and lettuce), peaches, gooseberries, strawberries, grapes, asparagus, kidney beans, cauliflower, and young green peas. He, too, considered it to be great folly to stint "a man in his liquid," although the stomach should not be distended with drink. Rather than have a man forced by some "relic of barbarism" to avoid a glass of water at bedtime, Woodgate (like Maclaren) held that a man should take a half pint of water gruel before bedtime to quench the thirst, soothe digestion, and prevent "coppers."[85]

Since he was dealing with the sons of gentlemen, Woodgate believed that "if a trainer can trust his men" they might take a morning plunge; however, no swimming was allowed. When the weather was hot, it was better for a man to sleep late and do his rowing practice in the evening. A cup of "strong beef tea in the evening" was permitted a man who "suffers from thirst"—even though "university trainers and oarsmen of past years" still believed that such liquid hampered the "wind." Men who could not lose weight should be prohibited from using sugar in their tea.[86]

Age, physical condition at the commencement of training, the length of the course to be rowed, and the time available to the athlete were all important considerations. While *skill* might enable a crew to win a *short* race, training (i.e., replacement of fatty with muscular tissue) was imperative for longer races. Woodgate provided specific information about the pace of rowing, suggesting lighter work on "bye" days, anticipating modern views of "interval training." He also offered recommendations on dressing blisters and boils—two frequent complaints of oarsmen. "Painting" a boil with iodine alone was not sufficient; the blood had to be purified. To do this, a teaspoon of yeast or syrup of iodide of iron in a glass of water after a meal was useful—as was port wine. Diarrhea could be checked by three or four tablespoonsful of raw arrowroot in a tumbler of water, or by a "confection of opium, and brandy, and water."[87]

In 1888, Longman's, Green and Company published an extended version of *"Oars and Sculls"* entitled *Boating* as one of its Badminton Library of Sports and Pastimes series. Here Woodgate compared earlier notions of training prize fighters and watermen with practices that had become more widely accepted. He considered the older system to have been analogous to the principle of giving "physic balls" to "a hunter on being taken up from grass." This might be appropriate "for men of mature years, who had probably been leading a life of self-indulgence," but it was quite inappropriate for young gentlemen. An even more emphatic class distinction was driven home in *Cycling* (1896), written by the Earl of Albermarle and G. Lacy Hillier. Until comparatively recently, the authors stated, only men who made sport a profession had trained seriously. As a consequence, "most of the training lore that has come down to us is . . . the outcome of much hard and sharp experience, largely diluted with ignorance and absurdity." When athletes had been from "among the lowest class," it had been necessary for backers to use harsh methods. Young men, "eager for every word," had turned to "rules and regulations laid down orally by these athletic fossils." However, cyclists now followed practices dictated by modern concepts: moderation, slow preparation, and due consideration to the needs of each man.[88]

These assertions were not entirely correct for Westhall had already referred to differences between "sturdier and hardier watermen" and amateurs.[89] His training recommendations for pugilists were substantially those that he offered for pedestrians. A short run would indicate the state of the boxer's lungs. Weight loss must be gradual; therefore, the boxer's diet should consist largely of meat. Wine, especially good old port, was permitted for men who were in good condition. "Modern" pugilists, "Hall" observed, strengthened their arms, loins, and shoulders by hitting a straw-filled sack, rope skipping, and the use of dumbbells.[90]

It is not clear exactly what Westhall meant by "modern" pugilists. However, the thirty-seven-round fight between English champion Tom Sayers and American John Heenan ("The Benicia Boy") in 1860 had intensified criticisms of the British prize ring. New rules were developed in 1867 under the patronage of the Marquess of Queensberry. In the preface to *British Sports and Pastimes* (1868), Anthony Trollope declared that prizefighting had "so fallen in general interest, that we do not doubt but that we shall be thought to have shown a proper discretion in excluding it from our little volume." This assertion was premature, for developments that followed upon the Queensberry rules gave the sport a new life. The 1885 *New Book of Sports* identified four "species of encounter," attempting to make acceptable demarcations between "sparring" and boxing or fighting.[91] Describing the transition for the Badminton Library, E. B. Michell credited the use of padded gloves, the efforts of the Amateur Athletic Club, and the contributions of the new Queensberry rules with transforming the old forms of pugilism into "modern boxing" or *sparring*.[92] Whereas *sparring*—usually referred to as "the manly art of self-defense"—continued to be included in manuals aimed at the amateur, commentaries on *professional* forms of boxing were typically given cursory treatment wherein the writer's frank admiration of the physical prowess of such men was hedged with terms like "pernicious influences," "venomous element," and the "perplexing question" of the negro boxer.[93]

These views influenced authors of American sporting manuals. John Boyle O'Reilly's *Athletics and Manly Sport* (1890) insisted that the use of padded gloves had turned brutal mauls into a sport of "inestimable value" for training and discipline. The training systems used at American and English universities (notably Oxford), he believed, were the best. In his descriptions, O'Reilly drew upon Westhall, Woodgate, Maclaren, and the Boston physician Francis A. Harris (demonstrator of medico-legal examinations at Harvard University).[94] A decade later, W. W. Naughton (self-proclaimed as "America's Best-Known Sporting Authority") spoke of a growing "tolerance in regard to professional pugilism" as well as " the amateur or physical culture phase" of boxing. Educators, he maintained, now accepted amateur boxing as a healthful form of exercise for strengthening the body and imbuing "feelings of chivalry" better even than could the immensely popular game of football.[95]

Naughton's *Kings of the Queensberry Realm: An Account of Every Heavy-Weight Championship Contest Held in America under the Queensberry Rules* (1902) resonates with panegyrics to contemporary professional boxers. A common mistake, Naughton declared, was the assumption that all boxers still pursued identical conditioning regimens. Quite the contrary! Modern pugilists followed their own "fads" and insisted upon having considerable say in their conditioning. The use of pulleys and wrist machines, stationary rowing machines, bicycles, skipping ropes, the medicine ball, and "shadow fighting"—as well as running and sparring—were all part of modern training. All this, Naughton held, differed markedly from the Deaf Burke era (1823–1843) when a man was "compelled to jog mile after mile while holding on to the rear of a swiftly moving cart," fell from sheer exhaustion, was driven back to the tavern which served as his training headquarters, "soused in cold water, rubbed and scrubbed, and then fed on rare beef, stale bread and old ale."[96]

Having claimed all this, Naughton acknowledged that because fighters still tended to indulge their appetites when not in training, it was customary to commence with a "physic in sufficient quantities to free [the] system from bilious accumulations and eliminate the lingering effects of rich viands and seductive liquids from [the] blood." Fattening foods were to be avoided since it was vital for a boxer to "reduce himself to his fighting weight." Water, which increased the weight and destroyed hours of hard exercise, was a "nemesis." Boxers should "chew gum" or gargle a "fevered throat and palate" instead.[97]

Some authors (as for example Ralph Henry Barbour) advised school and college athletes against chewing gum or taking any water at exercise time. After a few days, the athlete would become accustomed to doing without: "Never take water, save to rinse the mouth out, from the time you dress for play until you are once more in street clothes." As did many Americans, Barbour forbade all alcoholic drinks unless prescribed by a physician. Beef, mutton, chicken, and turkey were his preferred meats, with fish occasionally added for variety. He considered cereals, boiled rice, and potatoes to be valuable, as were fresh vegetables and dried fruits, which could be eaten freely.[98]

Although his *Book of School and College Sports* (1904) included information about baseball, track, lacrosse, ice hockey, and tennis, Barbour addressed his comments substantially to football. During the first two or three weeks, the coach must avoid "overtraining." If this occurred, the player must rest, stay away from the training table, and "keep his mind away from football." Similar advice had been offered a decade earlier in books like Amos Alonzo Stagg and Henry L. Williams's *A Scientific and Practical Treatise on American Football for Schools and Colleges* (1894), Walter Camp and Lorin F. Deland's *Football* (1896), and Camp's *American Football* (1891). The last named included a thirty-one-page chapter on "training" in which the Yale mentor presented his own views. These, he claimed, were an amalgam of: the Oxford and Cambridge Systems; Torpid Races; Clasper's System; Westhall's System; Maclaren's System (which Camp considered to be the most comprehensive); Stonehenge's System; those of Jackson, Goodbar, J. B. O'Reilly, and what Camp described as "A Common Sense System."[99]

Rather than the "raw beef" and limited fare of "the fifties and sixties," Camp and Deland maintained, the modern collegiate "training table" included garden vegetables, fruits, rice, bread puddings, cereals, potatoes, roast beef, lamb chops, broiled chicken, and plenty of pure drinking water. Such a menu made the college athlete "an object of envy" to his classmates. The still prevalent belief that varsity football players consumed large chunks of raw beef was false; athletes frequently had "skittish" appetites. Regularity of habits, ample sleep, cleanliness (hot and cold showers, but not long hot baths), graded exercise bouts, and regular practice sessions—not Draconian measures—were now recognized as the basis for forging successful intercollegiate teams.[100]

International Competitions, the Olympic Games, and the Decline of British Athletic Prowess, 1890–1914

Britain long had been acknowledged as the world's preeminent "sporting nation" and authoritative source for information about the conduct of athletic competitions. By the last decades of the nineteenth century, however, athletes in other countries were rapidly developing. George Kolb's *Beiträge zur Physiologie maximaler Muskelarbeit besonders des modernen Sports (1887)* was prompted by examinations the German physician had made of members of the Berliner Ruder Club. American athletes were also collectively flexing their muscles, anxious to extend their influence beyond the continental United States. In 1894, W. H. Grenfell summarized the results of the "first intentional intercollegiate" track meet (between Oxford and Yale) for the *Fortnightly Review*. The visit of the losing American team, Grenfell maintained, had done much to "draw two great portions of the Anglo-Saxon race closer together." Most Americans, however, were not disposed to place common ancestral origins (real or assumed) ahead of contest victory.[101]

In 1895, athletes representing the London Athletic Club were soundly beaten by those of the New York Athletic Club. The victorious Americans responded with great enthusiasm; the British sporting fraternity was stunned. The Americans, trained by Yale's Michael Murphy, had won all eleven events. Writing for the *Badminton Magazine of Sports and Pastimes*, Montague Shearman cited hot weather and the "superior system of training and coaching which is in vogue at Yale [and] . . . other leading University and athletic centers," as reasons for the embarrassing defeats. Americans used too many officials, supported their "amateur" athletes with "the pyrtaneum at the public expense" (by which he meant "training tables"), and used cadres of paid professional coaches. Shearman hoped that the "scientific" coaches and training tables of American athletics would never be introduced into England.[102]

That same year, Cornell University sent an eight-oared crew to the Henley Regatta. Intent upon demonstrating their superiority, the Americans employed practices that they used at home. Charles "Pop" Courtney, their paid (and "professional") coach, was criticized for keeping the American oarsmen away from other competitors and holding secretive and work-like training sessions. A dispute over an improper start, resulting in the defeat of the Leander crew, intensified the agitations. Dissatisfaction with "Yankee" attitudes became so intense in 1901 following the visit of a University of Pennsylvania crew that stewards served notice that henceforth Americans wishing to compete at Henley would be obliged to leave their salaried instructors at home. Responding to allegations that American collegians preferred to venture abroad only when they believed victory to be certain, Ralph Paine observed: "Our army of professional coaches and trainers, and the most incredible cost of intercollegiate sport, have helped feed the suspicions of the British onlooker."[103]

Figure 2.5 "Finish of the Inter-Varsity 100 Yards, 1890," from H. Hewitt Griffin, *Athletics* (London: George Bell and Sons, 189?). This was one of the "All-England Series."

The *Quarterly Review* in 1904 expressed growing alarm that tainted streams of professionalism were emerging in one of the "ancient strongholds of fair-play" (Oxford) in the form of Rhodes Scholars. American athletes had already "proved their value as undergraduates at the Queen's Club meeting." At age twenty-two or twenty-three, such seasoned men represented attitudes that were "foreign" to the gentlemanly Oxbridge ethos. Even worse, the author hinted, the athletic prowess of the Americans could become a factor in victories for Oxford over rival Cambridge.[104]

Those who were candid acknowledged that the vaunted British "amateur" ethos was less pristine than contemporaries were wont to proclaim. What was particularly objectionable was the blatancy of the Americans and the intensity with which they pursued athletic victories. A. B. George, writing a chapter entitled, "American Methods" for his brother's *Training for Athletics and Kindred Sports* (1902), stated: "The American does the thing thoroughly, and devotes all his energy toward the end in view. We take the thing more easily and do not look on the winning of a certain race as a life and death matter."[105] It is possible that George had in mind the 1895 defeat of the London Athletic Club as well as what he referred to as "remarkable performances by American athletes in England during recent years." Recent American victories, he asserted, had "induced the rank-and-file of British sportsmen" (especially younger ones) to display an interest in their training methods. As athletes representing the United States repeated their successes in international competitions in the early 1900s, coaches and trainers in other countries would also become increasingly interested in American training methods.[106]

Hans Langenfeld and John Hoberman have analyzed the beginnings of sports medicine in Germany in the late 1800s and early 1900s; and Dietrich Quanz had recently detailed the growing German interest in American athletics following the 1896 Olympic Games. Kolb's *Beiträge zur Physiologie maximaler Muskelarbeit* was translated into English in 1893 as *Physiology of Sport*. Medical student and Olympic contender Martin Brustmann compared athletic techniques in *Olympischer Sport, Theorie, Technik, Training und Taktik der olympischen Sportzweige* (1910), finding American methods superior to those of the British. In 1914, Otto Herschmann arranged for decathelte Alexander Copeland to visit Vienna; and Carl Diem brought American Olympic 1900 gold-medalist Alvin Kreanzlein to Berlin to give short-term "training courses" to aspirants for the 1916 Games. Since Kreanzlein was of German parentage, it was believed that his victories had been due to superior training methods, not any "racial superiority" on the part of the Americans.[107]

In our own era, the quadrennial Olympic Games have come to be viewed as the international sporting extravaganza par excellence. Their tenuous start at Athens in 1896, however, did little to portend the influence these Games would ultimately exert on both sport and the training of elite competitors. In spite of herculean efforts, Coubertin had difficulty convincing others of the merits of reviving the great athletic festivals of the ancient world. In addition to the host Greeks, only Hungary, Denmark, Germany, France, England, and the United States were represented. Not one American who had competed in the 1895 L.A.C.–N.Y.A.C. track meeting competed at Athens.[108] Nevertheless, the United States won nine of the twelve events. Americans were scarcely more interested in the confused 1900 Paris Olympics. Yet in what he declared to be a clear athletic ascendancy for the United States since 1876, A.A.U. President James E. Sullivan boasted that Americans had won all the significant prizes at Paris.[109]

Overcoming the near disasters of Paris in 1900 and St. Louis in 1904, the 1908 London Olympic Games were successfully carried out in spite of recurring disputes over officiating.[110] Reporting on these, the London *Times* observed: "[W]e of the United Kingdom have learnt that in speed and strength we are far behind the Americans." Even a hope that "the older nation was endowed with greater powers of endurance" had been dashed since British long-distance runners had been seriously outclassed by both Americans and "other countries whose devotion to athletic sports [was] more recent and less wide-spread that [was] the case of the Anglo-Saxon nations."[111] The *Saturday Review* commented upon differences between the ancient and the modern Olympics and answered its own question, "do international games serve to promote international amity?" with a decisive *no!* An ill-informed public placed too much emphasis on national superiority; "managers and trainers considered concord [to be] a small thing in comparison with the victory of their own team." This, the author asserted, destroyed the "true" purpose of sport.[112]

J. Astley Cooper, writing for *The Nineteenth Century*, went farther, reasserting his declaration that the British Olympic Association should abandon these aberrant games and implement instead his "Pan-Britannic" ideal as a "great Racial Festival." Quoting the contemporary "all-round amateur" sportsman C. B. Frey, Cooper proclaimed with nationalistic pride that bordered on raw arrogance: "A revival of the Olympic Games has small chance of being successful anywhere except in Britain, or in one of the greater British colonies, or in the United States of America; for nowhere else in the world are the athletic 'events' which form the program, and the necessary organization and administration, sufficiently understood."[113]

He was not the only one who expressed alarm that other countries that had failed to fully embrace the "amateur spirit" were achieving standards of training that could ensure victory over British athletes. Indeed, it is not entirely clear which Cooper and his contemporaries lamented most—the absence of an "amateur" spirit or the athletic decline of the nation that had "taught the world to play." A. B. George had implied this six years earlier when he observed shortly after the 1895 defeat of the L.A.C. that the famous American trainer "Mike" Murphy had stated "that if he could train the English team for six months they would reverse the verdict." The American achievements, George had concluded, were due to "attention to detail . . . and advice and assistance of experts . . . not to any inherent superiority."[114]

Smarting from even more devastating defeats at the 1912 Stockholm Games and again anguishing over "lost leadership," the *Saturday Review* complained that although Britain had taught the world to "play games . . . for fun," other nations (now the Americans were the greatest culprits) had made "a business of pleasure." Resisting the "cowardly wish" to train a band of professionals just once, see British athletes victorious in Berlin in 1916, and then "retire once and for all," the writer concluded that it was England's role to "teach the world the proper attitude toward games."[115] In the United States, sportswriters enthused over victories, lauded "America's Olympic Argonauts," and referred to a "British Athletic Slump." A correspondent for the *London Times,* the *Literary Digest* claimed, had praised the discipline and training of the American athletes and decried the lack of same among British athletes.[116]

At Stockholm, Finland placed first in the discus, the 5,000 meter, 10,000 meter, and cross-country runs. Sweden won the javelin and decathlon, and swept the triple jump. The only victories British athletes could achieve were the 1,500-meter race and the 400-meter relay. Considerable credit for the Swedish successes was given to E. W. Hjertberg, who had returned from a career as athlete and coach in the United States to prepare the 1912 team. Introducing Hjertberg's *Athletics in Theory and Practice* (1914) for a British audience, S. S. Abrahams (member of the 1912 British Olympic Team and Cambridge University Club) declared: "It is now agreed on all sides that if the undoubted fine athletic material here [Britain] is to hold its own with the flower of the world the same scientific application as is given to rowing and cricket must be bestowed on upon athletics."[117] With a population smaller than that of London, Sweden had become "a formidable factor in international contests," substantially due to the training practices that Hjertberg had instituted. It was encouraging, Abrahams continued, that in a "spirit of athletic reform in England . . . a number of *amateurs* [had] indicated their willingness to advise others" (emphasis added).[118]

A different solution was proposed by S. A. Mussabini, author of *The Complete Athletic Trainer* (1914). Mussabini maintained that in spite of recent successes by French, German, Italian, Swedish, and American athletes, Britain remained "rich in raw material." The average athlete, however, could spare only an hour or so in the early mornings or evenings for training while in other countries much more time was devoted. Most qualified trainers had gone out of business, moved to America, or found employment with professional football teams. It had been *professional* pedestrians (men like W. G. George and George Littlewood) and those "amateurs" who had adopted the techniques of the *professional* who had established British supremacy in footracing in the 1880s. *Their* training methods would be required if future athletic successes were to be secured.[119] A similar opinion was expressed by Harold Wade, who noted that the "gentleman amateur" could no longer expect to be a champion unless he was "prepared to devote the whole of his leisure time to training."[120]

The United States, with a population far larger than Sweden— or Britain—was in an unequalled position to develop a pool from which athletic talent could be drawn. A vast reservoir existed in the intercollegiate programs. These were supported by cadres of semi-professional coaches, trainers, and managers—and well-equipped, even lavish, training equipment and facilities. So extensive had such programs become by 1890 that faculty and administrators were nearly powerless to combat "commercialism" and other excesses that critics claimed plagued school sports. Although they were ostensibly "amateur," intercollegiate athletics were frequently as elaborate— and often better endowed—than were avowedly "professional" sports like baseball.[121]

Looking back at the development of these programs between 1877 and 1910, Ellery H. Clark, "All-Around Athletic Champion of America" (1897 and 1903) and victor in the broad jump and high jump at the 1896 Olympics, remarked that the rapid growth of "specialized and systematized" training had dramatically changed the nature of American athletics. There were now men who "threatened not to compete at all, unless prizes of a certain value were promised them."[122] Clark's depiction of the newer approach to athletics as "specialized and systematized" was probably a more accurate characterization than were claims that training had become "scientific." The typical trainer relied much more upon experience, traditional authorities, and *specialized* knowledge gathered through observations than upon facts obtained through carefully designed and controlled experiments. Nevertheless, in the late nineteenth century, athletic training increasingly became a matter of *scientific* interest.

Efforts to Scientifically Study Athletes and Their Training: 1870–1914

The term "scientific" has a powerful appeal, suggesting rational control over nature, predictive certainties, and other features that resonate with modernity. Around the middle of the nineteenth century, the Hippocratic belief that there was "a universal nutrient substance" present in all foods (extracted during digestion) had begun to be overturned. Gmelin first used the term *stoffwechsel* (metabolism) in 1836 for chemical transformations of food. In *Animal Chemistry* (1842), Liebig advanced the view that exercise was always attended

with an increased activity in the destruction "of the nitrogenized substance of the muscular tissue; and that this could be measured by the
amount of urea excreted." Fick and Wislicensus hypothesized that either "fats or hydrates of carbon"—not albuminous substances—provided the source of muscular power. In 1870, Carl Voit reviewed the
literature on both sides of the argument.[123] Although the question of
"the origin of muscular power" remained unsettled, this and other
physiological issues pertaining to *training* attracted the attention of increasing numbers of investigators.

Traditionally believed to be the source of innate heat, intelligence,
and such essential functions as warming the body, the heart had interested medical men for centuries. Its rhythmicity continued to be a
source of curiosity and speculation. Increasing attention was directed
to "irritable heart" (a condition said to be found among soldiers who
had been subjected to sudden and/or continued overwork) and to the
influence of prolonged exertions on the hearts of oarsmen. In 1867,
the London *Times* reported that the surgeon F. C. Skey contended
that, even if they were not immediately apparent, "calamities with
over-exertion in athletic sports" were likely to appear later in life.[124]

John Morgan (physician to the Manchester Royal Infirmary, and a
former oarsman at Shrewsbury and at University College, Oxford) set
out to investigate this question, publishing *University Oars, Being a
Critical Enquiry into the After Health of the Men Who Rowed in the Oxford
and Cambridge Boat-Race from the Year 1829 to 1869, Based on the Personal Experiences of the Rowers Themselves* (1873). The evidence submitted by the men he had contacted, Morgan insisted, was quite contrary
to Dr. Skey's allegations. The vast majority believed that rowing had
caused no ill effects; and many believed that the training had been
beneficial. *Nature* immediately printed Archibald Maclaren's three-
part review of Morgan's book.[125]

Concerned about excessive athleticism in the public schools and
universities, the Clinical Society took up the discussion, looking into
reports of "severe injury to the heart from over strain" and hypertrophy among professional pedestrians and mountain climbers. The
British Medical Journal reported that "Over strain of the Heart and
Aorta" had been a major topic at the 1873 meetings, and noted "the
barrenness of medical literature" with regard to scientific works dealing with exercise and "training for the guidance of athletes."[126] Dr.
Robert J. Lee's, *Exercise and Training, Their Effects upon Health* (1873)
called for more study of the effects of training on the "musculo-
cardiac" and "pneumo-cardiac" functions and of the whole "vexed
question of diet." An anonymous reviewer took exception to what he

called Lee's intimation that the Oxford and Cambridge "varsity" man was the center of the athletic universe, but agreed that the lecturer on pathology at Westminster Hospital had provided a useful compilation of heretofore "scattered physiological and pathological truths bearing on athletics."[127]

"The vexed question" of what constituted the best diet for athletes had been examined in 1870 by New York physician Austin Flint, Jr., who analyzed urine collected from the celebrated pedestrian Edward Payson Weston during a 100-mile walk. Weston subsequently agreed to permit Flint and others to study the food and liquid he consumed (and urine and faeces excreted) during a five-day 400-mile walk. To obtain baseline data, chemical and statistical analyses were made for five days preceding and following the event. Of the tentative conclusions that Flint advanced, the one that created the greatest controversy was: "the muscular system may consume its own substance by exercise, even when the individual takes all the food required by his appetite."[128]

Dr. F. W. Pavy, Fellow of the Royal College of Physicians, disputed Flint's idea that food contained force in a "latent state" that was "liberated" in muscular (or nervous) action. He conducted his own investigations when Weston appeared for an endurance walk in Britain in 1876 and published these in *The Lancet*. Rejecting Pavy's "conservation of force" analogy as inconsistent with established fact, Flint insisted that much more attention needed to be directed to the whole question of whether food is used repairing muscular tissue consumed in work "or in the direct production of work itself."[129]

Physiologists, physicians, and physical educators in several countries sought to extend scientific understandings of the effects of extreme muscular exertions on the body. A sportsman as well as physician, Kolb insisted that only those who had both athletic experience and medical training were qualified to conduct the necessary investigations. Medical men, he believed, could not fully comprehend the enormous strain of a race unless they had experienced it; and athletes typically ignored the discoveries of physiologists, who they thought approached men in training as they would laboratory specimens.[130] When Eustace Miles (Amateur Champion of the World at Tennis; Winner of the Open Competition in Rackets in 1896 and 1899; author of *Muscle, Brain and Diet,* etc.) prepared an English translation of F. A. Schmidt's book on training, he added information derived from both his own experiences and recent research that had been conducted in the United States. Like many of his contemporaries, Miles believed that "lessening the water in the body" eased the

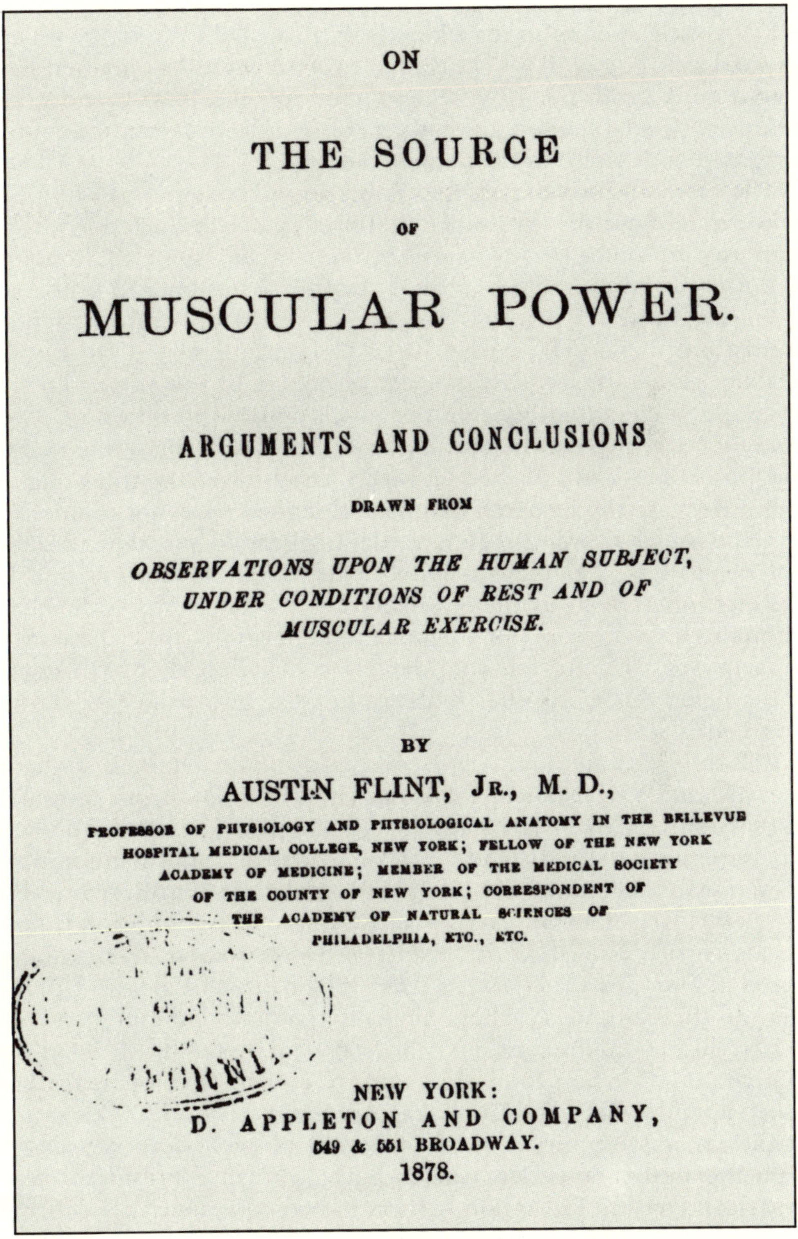

ON

THE SOURCE

OF

MUSCULAR POWER.

ARGUMENTS AND CONCLUSIONS

DRAWN FROM

*OBSERVATIONS UPON THE HUMAN SUBJECT,
UNDER CONDITIONS OF REST AND OF
MUSCULAR EXERCISE.*

BY

AUSTIN FLINT, JR., M.D.,

PROFESSOR OF PHYSIOLOGY AND PHYSIOLOGICAL ANATOMY IN THE BELLEVUE
HOSPITAL MEDICAL COLLEGE, NEW YORK; FELLOW OF THE NEW YORK
ACADEMY OF MEDICINE; MEMBER OF THE MEDICAL SOCIETY
OF THE COUNTY OF NEW YORK; CORRESPONDENT OF
THE ACADEMY OF NATURAL SCIENCES OF
PHILADELPHIA, ETC., ETC.

NEW YORK:
D. APPLETON AND COMPANY,
549 & 551 BROADWAY.
1878.

Figure 2.6 Title page from Austin Flint, Jr., *On the Source of Muscular Power* . . . (New York, 1878).

action of the heart, enabling each beat to deliver a larger number of red corpuscles per volume of blood. With regard to food, he recommended avoiding *all* flesh. Adequate protein could be obtained from cheese, milk products, Hovis bread, gluten, peas, lentils, and grain-products. Vegetables and a great deal of fruit were permitted; but he disagreed with Kolb on the value of sugar.[131]

The German physiologist Leo Zuntz studied oxygen consumption in horses and cyclists. In France, Phillipe Tissié conducted investigations on endurance performances by the bicycle champion Stephane. The famous English surgeon Sir T. Lauder Brunton and others experimented with the effects of resistance exercise on local and general circulation.[132] The Harvard Athletic Committee invited Dr. Eugene Darling to investigate physiological responses of the varsity crew in the hope of shedding light on the much-debated question of "over-training." Darling conducted metabolic studies of the crew in May and June 1899—and of the Harvard football team the following autumn. Because the research had been designed so as not to interfere with the men's training regimens, data collection was difficult. Normal weight loss, Darling concluded, had produced no ill effects. He also attempted to study the effects of severe exercise upon the heart. Although his data were not adequate to help resolve the debate about hypertrophy, Darling felt comfortable concluding that with regard to the heart, "as with other muscles, not size but quality tells in the long run."[133]

Wilbur O. Atwater and A. P. Bryant undertook metabolic studies of Harvard and Yale crews in 1898—and analyzed data from several dietary studies for *University Boat Crews* (1900). Drs. J. B. Blake and R. C. Larrabee reported they could find no evidence of permanent injury in men who had run in the 1900, 1901, and 1902 Boston marathons. In 1904, George Meylan, M.D., director of physical training at Columbia University, published the results of his analyses of men who had rowed in Harvard varsity crews from 1852 to 1892. He found, as had Morgan three decades earlier, that oarsmen did not die prematurely; in fact, they lived "longer than healthy men accepted by life insurance companies."[134] When John Hayes won the 1908 Olympic marathon, American interest in endurance races increased. The 1909 Pittsburgh marathon was organized so as to obtain physiological information from the participants. Dr. Watson Savage (former President of the American Physical Education Association) and his associates collected extensive data in the form of pulse rates, blood pressures, temperatures, and urine samples, publishing their findings in the *American Physical Education Review*.[135]

Doubtless, those coaches and trainers who were qualified to do so utilized relevant information from studies such as these. Most training "theories," however, continued to rely heavily upon observations of successful athletes and little that was more "scientifically" exact. In the introduction to Michael Murphy's *Athletic Training* (1914), Edward R. Bushnell stated that Murphy (widely acknowledged as America's preeminent trainer) had spent thirty years developing "track and field athletics as a science."[136] A qualified athlete before he became trainer of Yale's teams in 1887, Murphy ended his career as track and football coach at the University of Pennsylvania. He had also coached for the Detroit and New York Athletic Clubs and trained American athletes who defeated the London Athletic Club in 1895 and the men who participated in the 1900 Paris Olympics. He was selected by the American Olympic Committee to coach the 1908 and 1912 teams. For his many successes, Murphy earned the appellation "the foremost authority in the world on all kinds of athletic training."[137]

Murphy had enrolled in a two-year medical course at the University of Pennsylvania; it was said that he understood the human body as well as did any physician. He claimed, however, that his methods were based on observing athletes at home and abroad. In his "Author's Introduction" to *Athletic Training,* the mortally ill Murphy stated that a major reason why Americans had become so successful was the enormous popularity that competitive sports had attained since the 1870s. Hundreds of thousands of school, college, and club competitors provided an enormous pool of talent. The majority of men who became "intercollegiate, Olympic, and the world's champions"[138] had begun serious training at about the age of eighteen. Younger boys, seeking to emulate their heroes, often started athletic activities in their early teens.

Similar reasons for America's ascendancy were noted by Paul Withington, M.D., in the preface to his *Book of Athletics* (1914). A multi-sport athlete at Harvard University, Withington had won the New England Wrestling Championship (1909) and the Boston Metropolitan Championships in single sculls (1912 and 1913). His five-hundred page treatise, intended as an updated version of Norman Bingham's *Book of Athletics* (1895), drew upon more than two dozen experts to present the latest information on training regimens and techniques for thirteen sports. (Murphy contributed to the sections on "Track Athletics" and "Football.") There were, Withington maintained, "dozens of men skilled in coaching scattered all over the country" who could be called upon to accommodate the "ever-increasing desire and demand for the expert's view."[139]

Figure 2.7 Michael C. Murphy, from Murphy, *Athletic Training,* ed. Edward R. Bushnell (New York: Charles Scribner's Sons, 1920). Originally published in 1914.

Neither Murphy nor Withington, both of whom had medical train-ing, made direct reference to any experimental studies that had been conducted on athletes between 1870 and 1914. Although "sports medicine" would emerge—albeit slowly—as an increasingly system-atic specialty after 1920,[140] before World War I such information re-mained largely in medical and physiological journals (e.g., *Boston Medical and Surgical Journal, American Journal of Medical Sciences, American Journal of Physiology*), not in manuals prepared by or for trainers or coaches. A few of the books designed for the emerging field of physical education, such as R. Tait McKenzie's *Exercise in*

Education and Medicine (1910), contained brief references to experimental studies. A graduate of McGill University Medical School, McKenzie dedicated this work to physical educators, teachers, and physicians, drawing upon metabolic, cardiovascular, and anthropometric studies, as well as his own urinary studies of athletes at the 1904 St. Louis Olympics.[141]

For McKenzie, director of the department of physical education at the University of Pennsylvania, Luther Halsey Gulick, M.D., director of physical training at Springfield College, and many other turn-of-the century physical educators, athletics had far-ranging purposes that went well beyond a concern for the body. "Educational athletics" stressed sportsmanship and character as well as physical performance.[142] Just how attentive a coach or trainer could (or can) be to "character development" when preparing a man for an important match is questionable. Yet the litany that pervaded the literature held that athletics benefitted a man mentally and morally even more than physically. "Sand," "pluck," and "courage" are words that continued to appear repeatedly in the early twentieth-century English-language sporting press.

Fielding Yost, football coach at the University of Michigan, proclaimed: "Along with the mental benefits of football comes the moral development, of which the most evident characteristic is courage."[143] Walter Camp, like scores of his contemporaries, maintained that the moral benefits of football outweighed the physical benefits, even if "the playing of important games in great cities [had] led to all forms of disorder" and excess. Even so, Camp optimistically asserted: "There is apparently no reason why our great games should not be converted into functions similar to the Eton-Harrow cricket match in England." He then resorted to various circumlocutions to explain why it had been necessary to introduce the forward pass and enact "the Rules of 1910" to lessen "the danger of playing exhausted players too long."[144]

In spite of whatever excesses might occur, American sports enthusiasts were convinced that the benefits of school-boy athletics far outweighed their evils. Much as Tom Brown's youthful heroisms were acted out at Rugby, the hero of Ralph Henry Barbour's *For the Honor of the School* (1900) called upon reserves of *both* physical and moral courage to cross the finish line ahead of the rival St. Eustice runner.[145]

What athletics might do for the boy and man, they could also do for the nation—and even for the world! Or so the litany ran. The patina of middle-class Victorian expressions of the "amateur" ethos had been firmly fused upon the mundane realities of physically preparing for the athletic encounter. In words that might have warmed the hearts of Horatio Smith and Pierre de Coubertin—even if the author of the 1912 *Saturday Review* article "England and the Olympic Games" would have remained skeptical—McKenzie declared in his dedication to his colleague Murphy's *Athletic Training:* "The national conscience is but the sum of that of its citizens, and from the value of athletics to the nation it is but a step to their international importance. The place of the great Greek athletic festivals in promoting peace throughout the ancient world has been a text on which the modern Olympic idea has been preached."[146] From the isolation and comparative safety of a continent separated from the rest of the sporting world by vast stretches of ocean, McKenzie ironically proclaimed shortly before the outbreak of World War I: "Each Olympiad shows a better understanding of the principles of sportsmanship by more nations."[147]

Notes

This is a greatly elaborated version of my 1988 NASSH presentation "Science, Medicine, Exercise and Sport, 1870–1910: The Body as Object and Icon" and my 1988 International Olympic Congress paper "Athletes and Their Training: 1870–1914." Grateful thanks are extended to James Whorton for helpful comments regarding nineteenth-century physiology and chemistry.

1. Horatio Smith, *Festivals, Games and Amusements. Ancient and Modern* (New York: Harper and Brothers, 1842), chaps. 5, 6, and especially pp. 60, 74. The American edition contains an "appendix," written by Samuel Woodworth that describes festivals, games, and amusements of American Indians, New England, the middle and the southern states. In this, "games" included: cricket, base, cat, football, trapball, quoits, billiards, ninepins, and shovelboard. Cock-fighting and "other cruel amusements," Woodworth claimed, were not practiced, except in the South, where these and the turf (horse racing) were "indulged with avidity" (pp. 330, 351).

2. See, for example, Stephen G. Miller, *Arete: Ancient Writers, Papyri, and Inscriptions on the History and Ideals of Greek Athletics and Games* (Chicago: Ares Publishers, 1979), 58–65; C. Kerenyi, *The Heroes of the Greeks* (New York: Thames and Hudson, 1978), 142; David Sansone, *Greek Athletics and the Genesis of Sport* (Berkeley: University of California Press, 1988).

3. See, for example, Mark Girouard, *The Return to Camelot: Chivalry and the English Gentleman* (New Haven: Yale University Press, 1981), especially chap. 11 and 14; James A. Mangan and James Walvin (Eds.), *Manliness and Morality: Middle-Class Masculinity in Britain and America, 1800–1940* (New York: St. Martin's Press, 1987).

4. "Gymnastics," *American Quarterly Review* 3 (1828), 126–50.

5. "Article III. Popular Sports and Festivals. The Sports and Pastimes of the People of England. By Joseph Strutt. A New Edition, with a Copious Index. By William Hone," *North American Review* 33 (1831), 191–225.

6. A[bel] A. Livermore, "Gymnastics," *North American Review* 169 (1855), 65–69.

7. Oliver Wendell Holmes, *The Autocrat of the Breakfast Table* (Boston: Phillips, Sampson and Co., 1859); Thomas Wentworth Higginson, "Barbarism and Civilization," *Atlantic Monthly* 7 (1861), 51–61; Higginson, "Gymnastics," ibid., 283–302.

8. "Military Hospitals a Century Ago," *Fraser's Magazine* 51 (1855), 400. The January issue had included a panegyric to "sport," the light cavalry brigade at Balaclava, and all British forces in the Crimean.

9. "Popular Amusements," *Westminster Review* 10, n.s. (1856). 163, 184–88.

10. "Tom Brown's School Days, By An Old Boy," *Edinburgh Review* 107 (1858), 173.

11. Richard Jenkyns, *The Victorians and Ancient Greece* (Cambridge, Mass.: Harvard University Press, 1980), 214.

12. James A. Mangan, *Athleticism in the Victorian and Edwardian Public School: The Emergence and Consolidation of an Educational Ideology* (Cambridge: Cambridge University Press, 1981), 135–36, passim.

13. John Bingham, "This Foot-Ball Question," *DePaw Palladium* 1 (1897). (Reprint of article; Greencastle, Ind.: Press of Democrat, n.d., 1–7).

14. John Sinclair, *The Code of Health and Longevity; or, a Concise View of the Principles Calculated for the Preservation of Health and the Attainment of Long Life* (Edinburgh: Arch. Constable and Co., 1807), especially pp. 39–150 and the lengthy Appendix which contains some eighty pages devoted to exercises and training methods for pugilists, wrestlers, runners, jockeys, racehorses, and game cocks. On horse racing, see Wray Vamplew, *The Turf: A Social and Economic History of Horse Racing* (London: Allen Lane, 1976), especially chap. 10. Vamplew notes that many of the poorly educated early nineteenth-century trainers "ruined horses whose delicate constitutions could not stand up to a regimen of drenches, sweats, purges, and in some cases even bleeding" (p. 176).

15. Quoted in Jenkyns, *Victorians and Ancient Greece*, 215. See also, John J. MacAloon, *This Great Symbol: Pierre de Coubertin and the Origins of the Modern Olympic Games* (Chicago: University of Chicago Press, 1981), 45–48, passim.

16. See, for example, Robert W. Malcomson, *Popular Recreations in English Society, 1700–1850* (Cambridge: Cambridge University Press, 1973); Dennis Brailsford, "1781: An Eighteenth-Century Sporting Year," *Research Quarterly for Exercise and Sport* 55 (1984), 217–230.

17. Pierce Egan, *Boxiana; Or Sketches of Ancient and Modern Pugilism, From the Days of the Renowned Broughton and Slack, to the Heroes of the Present Milling Era* (London: G. Smeeton, 1812), 7–16.

18. Ibid.

19. "Pedestrianism," *Bell's Life in London and Sporting Chronicle*, 13 January 1828; "Pedestrianism," *Bell's Life*, 18 January 1828; Montague Shearman, *Athletics and Football* (London: Longmans, Green and Co., 1887), 36–41.

20. W[alter] B[radford] Woodgate, *Boating* (London: Longmans, Green and Co., 1888), 26, 303–4; see also, Robert F. Kelley, *American Rowing: Its Background and Traditions* (New York: G. P. Putnam's Sons, 1932), 3–13; "Rowing Match Between Eton and Westminster Scholars, for 100 Sovs. A-Side," *Bell's Life in London and Sporting Chronicle*, 2 August 1829.

21. "Biographical Sketch of the Life and Reign of George the Fourth," *Bell's Life in London and Sporting Chronicle*, 4 July 1830; "Funeral of His Late Majesty," *Bell's Life*, 18 July 1830.

22. "Ned Neal and Young Dutch Sam, or, the Fancy in an Uproar," *Bell's Life in London and Sporting Chronicle*, 6 December 1829; Dennis Brailsford, "Morals and Maulers: The Ethics of Early Pugilism," *Journal of Sport History* 12 (1985), 126–42.

23. Woodgate, *Boating*, 30–44; *Bells's Life in London and Sporting Chronicle*, 14 June 1829.

24. See Delabere P. Blaine, *An Encyclopedia of Rural Sports; or, A Complete Account, Historical, Practical, and Descriptive of Hunting, Shooting, Fishing, Racing, and Other Field Sports and Athletic Amusements of the Present Day* (London: Longman, Orme, Brown, Green and Longmans, 1840) 1213–18; "Vindication of the Prize-Ring," *Bell's Life in London and Sporting Chronicle*, 29 August 1830. Another author, describing himself as "One of the Old School," fulminated against "white-livered scribes" who had railed against the results of a contest between Simon Byrne and Sandy M'Kay, declaring, "Strip, then, Englishmen of their habit of boxing" and you reduce them to "a set of maudlin milksops—to a race of canting curs" ("British Boxing and Its Enemies," *Bell's Life in London and Sporting Chronicle*, 20 June 1830).

25. W[alter] Thom, *Pedestrianism, or An Account of the Performances of Celebrated Pedestrians during the Last and Present Century: With A Full Narrative of Captain Barclay's Public and Private Matches, and an Essay on Training* (Aberdeen: D. Chalmers and Co., 1813). Thom indicated that he had originally intended to confine his treatise to Captain Barclay's performances, but decided to include other pedestrians. He also wished to draw the public's attention to the importance of strengthening the "capacities," especially when "the conflicts of war" called for "the physical energies of many of our countrymen" (p. iii). Thom made numerous references to Dr. Churchill's *Genuine Guide to Health*, to Dr. Willich's *Lectures on Diet and Regimen*, to Sinclair's *Code of Health*, and to classical authors.

26. Sinclair, *The Code of Health and Longevity*, appendix, pp. 39–150.

27. Peter F. Radford, "From Oral Tradition to Printed Record: British Sports Science in Transition, 1805–1807," *Stadion* 12/13 (1986/87), 295–304. Radford notes that Sinclair's *Code of Health* was circulating in Britain, Europe, and America and had been translated into French, German, and Italian within five years of the 1807 publication (p. 295); idem., "The Art and Sci-

ence of Training and Coaching Athletes in Late Eighteenth and Early Nineteenth Century Britain," in J. A. Mangan (ed.), *Proceedings of the 1985 HISPA Congress, Glasgow,* 80–83.

28. See Jack W. Berryman, "The Tradition of the 'Six Things Non-Natural': Exercise and Medicine from Hippocrates Through Ante-Bellum America," in Kent B. Pandolf (ed.), *Exercise and Sport Sciences Reviews,* vol. 17 (Baltimore: Williams and Wilkins, 1989), 515–59. [See revised version as chapter 1]. Until well into the early nineteenth century hygiene was typically taught under the headings of the six "non-naturals": air; motion and rest of the body and its parts [exercise]; sleep and wakefulness; food; excretion and retention; the passions of the soul. See Owsei Temkin, *Galenism: Rise and Decline of a Medical Philosophy* (Ithaca: Cornell University Press, 1973), 102.

29. See Owsei Temkin, *The Double Face of Janus and Other Essays in the History of Medicine* (Baltimore: The Johns Hopkins University Press, 1977), 154–61, passim.

30. Roy Porter and Dorothy Porter, *In Sickness and in Health: The British Experience, 1650–1850* (New York: Basil Blackwell, 1988), 47.

31. See Radford, "From Oral Tradition to Printed Record," 299, and Vamplew, *The Turf,* chap. 10.

32. Thom, *Pedestrianism,* 225.

33. Colorless crystalline sulfate of sodium used as a cathartic. Named for the German chemist Johann Glauber.

34. Thom, *Pedestrianism,* 228, 231.

35. Ibid., 229.

36. Ibid., 230–31.

37. Henry Downes Miles, *Pugilistica: The History of British Boxing* (Edinburgh: John Grant, 1906), vol. 1, 259.

38. Thom, *Pedestrianism,* 233–35, passim; Sinclair, *Code of Health,* Appendix.

39. Sinclair, *Code of Health,* Appendix. Also, John Sinclair, *Code of Health and Longevity; or, General View of the Rules and Principles Calculated for the Preservation of Health, and the Attainment of Long Life,* 4th ed. (London: Printed for the Author, 1818), Appendix, 33–36.

40. Egan, *Boxiana,* 368.

41. "Jem Ward—His Merits and Defects," *Bell's Life in London and Sporting Chronicle,* 28 November 1830.

42. Jem Belcher, for example, was said to have died of "an enlargement of the liver." Tom Belcher, who was known to become *bacchi plenis* at sporting dinners, got into rows outside the ring. Jack Scroggins became a "hanger-on at pothouses," and so forth. Miles, *Pugilistica,* vol. 1, 152, 165–66, 433 passim. For a more recent example of the often extravagant living of a boxer, see Michael T. Isenberg, *John L. Sullivan and His America* (Urbana: University of Illinois Press, 1988).

43. See, for example, H. Hewitt Griffin, *Athletics* (London: George Bell and Sons, 189[?]), 5–20. (By 1892, there were twenty-four of these small

"All-England Series" volumes, with another three listed as in preparation.)
W[alter] B. Woodgate, *Rowing and Sculling* (London: George Bell and Sons,
1892), passim; George G. T. Treherne and J. H. D. Goldie, *Record of the University Boat Race, 1869–1880 and of the Commemoration Dinner 1881* (London:
Bickers and Son, 1883), passim.

44. Eric Halladay, "Of Pride and Prejudice: The Amateur Question in English Nineteenth Century Rowing," *International Journal of the History of Sport*
4 (1987), 44; idem, *Rowing in England* (Manchester: Manchester University
Press, 1990).

45. John Tyler (ed.), *The Rowing Almanac for 1867* (London: Dean and
Son, 1867), 190.

46. James D'Wolf Lovett, *Old Boston Boys and the Games They Played* (Boston: Privately Printed at the Riverside Press, 1907), 211; Christian K. Messenger, *Sport and the Spirit of Play in American Fiction: Hawthorne to Faulkner*
(New York: Columbia University Press, 1981), 159; "The Cricket Mania,"
Harper's Weekly, 15 October, 1859, 658.

47. [T. S. Egan], *Principles of Rowing by an Oarsman* (London: F. C. Westley,
1846), 3, 16, 21–22.

48. *The Times*, 23 March 1866 and 24 March 1866; "The Oxford and Cambridge University Boat Race," *Illustrated London News*, 31 March 1866.

49. Tyler, *Rowing Almanac for 1867*, 190.

50. Griffin, *Athletics*, 5–20; see also, Casper W. Whitney, *A Sporting Pilgrimage: Riding to the Hounds, Golf, Rowing, Football, Club and University Athletics.
Studies in English Sport, Past and Present* (New York: Harper and Brothers,
1895), 229–31.

51. Tyler, *Rowing Almanac for 1867*, 190.

52. "Athletics," *Contemporary Review* 3 (1866), 374.

53. "Light and Dark Blue," *Blackwood's Edinburgh Magazine*, 100 (1866),
446–60. Leslie Stephen had published *Sketches from Cambridge by a Don* in
1865. For an analysis of the hero worship of Victorian athletes and critics of
same, see Mangan, *Athleticism in the Victorian and Edwardian Public School*, especially chap. 8; idem, "Oars and the Man: Pleasure and Purpose in Victorian and Edwardian Cambridge," *British [International] Journal of the History of
Sports* 1 (1984), 245–71; *The Rowing Almanac and Oarsman's Companion for
1866* (London: Dean and Son, 1866), 176.

54. Quoted in Shearman, *Athletics and Football*, 52–53.

55. See, for example, Wray Vamplew, *Pay Up and Play the Game: Professional Sport in Britain, 1875–1914* (Cambridge: Cambridge University Press,
1988), 187; "Argonaut" (ed.), *The Rowing Almanac and Oarsman's Companion for
1886* (London: Horace Cox, 1886), 178; Shearman, *Athletics and Football*,
chap. 8.

56. David Clasper, *Harry Clasper: Hero of the North* (Gateshead: Gateshead
Books, 1990), 6.

57. Ibid., 24–29.

58. "The Present Aspect of Athletics," *Baily's Magazine of Sports and Pastimes* 18 (1870), 197–204.

59. See for example, John E. Lesch, *Science and Medicine in France: The Emergence of Experimental Physiology, 1790–1855* (Harvard: Harvard University Press, 1984); William Coleman and Frederic L. Holmes (eds.), *The Investigative Enterprise: Experimental Physiology in Nineteenth Century Medicine* (Berkeley: University of California Press, 1988); Edwin Clarke and L. S. Jacyna *Nineteenth Century Origins of Neuroscientific Concepts* (Berkeley: University of California Press, 1987); Gerald L. Geison, *Michael Foster and the Cambridge School of Physiology: The Scientific Enterprise in Late Victorian Society* (Princeton: Princeton University Press, 1978), especially chap. 1–3.

60. See for example, John R. Betts, *America's Sporting Heritage: 1850–1950* (Reading, Mass.: Addison-Wesley Publishing Co., 1974), passim; Kelley, *American Rowing*, chap. 2 and 3; John A. Lucas and Ronald A. Smith, *Saga of American Sport* (Philadelphia: Lea and Febiger, 1978), 97–98, 107–8; [Edward P. Weston]. *The Pedestrian's Adventures, While on His Walk From Boston to Washington, in Fulfillment of An Election Wager, Performed in Ten Consecutive Days, Between February 22 and March 4th, 1861* (New York: Printed for Edward Payson Weston, 1862.)

61. "The Boat Race," *The Nation*, 2 September 1869, 187–89.

62. Benjamin Dwight, "Intercollegiate Regattas, Hurdle-Races and Prize Contests," *The New Englander* 35 (1876), 257, 271–72.

63. Guy M. Lewis, "America's First Intercollegiate Sport: The Regattas from 1852–1875," *Research Quarterly* 38 (1967), 637–48; *A History of American College Regattas, Containing Names of All Competing Crews, Time, Location, etc.* (Boston: Wilson and Co., 1875), 7–8; Kelley, *American Rowing*, chap. 5–7.

64. See William G. Durick, "The Gentleman's Race: An Examination of the 1869 Harvard-Oxford Boat Race," *Journal of Sport History* 15 (1988), 55–56; William Blaikie, "The University Rowing Match," *Harper's New Monthly Magazine* 40 (December 1869); *History of American College Regattas*, 23–30.

65. Bob Considine and Fred G. Jarvis, *The First Hundred Years: A Portrait of the N.Y.A.C.* (London: The Macmillan Co., 1969); Richard Wetten and Joe Willis, "Effect of New York's Elite Athletic Clubs on American Amateur Athletic Governance—1870–1915," *Research Quarterly* 47 (1976), 499–505; Lucas and Smith, *Saga of American Sports*, 154–58; Benjamin G. Rader, *American Sports: From the Age of Folk Games to the Age of Televised Sports*, 2d ed. (Englewood Cliffs, N.J.: Prentice Hall, 1990), 86–88.

66. Peter Levine, *A. G. Spalding and the Rise of Baseball: The Promise of American Sport* (New York: Oxford University Press, 1985); Michael C. Murphy, *College Athletics—Training: Spalding's Athletic Library* (New York: American Sports Publishing Company, 1895), 71. At this time, Murphy was athletic director at Yale University.

67. "Athletics," *Contemporary Review*, 382–89.

68. Griffin, *Athletics*, 6.

69. John Henry Walsh ("Stonehenge"), *Manual of British Rural Sports: Comprising Shooting, Hunting, Coursing, Fishing, Hawking, Racing, Boating, Pedestrianism, and the Various Rural Games and Amusements of Great Britain*, 5th ed. (London: Routledge, Warne, and Routledge, 1861); idem, *Athletic Sports and*

Manly Exercises (London: George Routledge and Sons, 1864); idem., *British Rural Sports: Comprising Shooting, Hunting, Coursing, Fishing, Hawking, Racing, Boating, Pedestrianism. With All Rural Games and Amusements* 14th ed. (London: Frederick Warne and Co., 1878).

70. Walsh, *Manual of British Rural Sports*, 582–603.

71. Ibid., 445–49; Walsh, *Athletic Sports and Manly Exercises*, 432–65.

72. Ibid.

73. Charles Westhall, *The Modern Method of Training for Running, Walking, Rowing, and Boxing, Including Hints on Exercise, Diet, Clothing, and Advice to Trainers*, 7th ed. (London: Ward, Lock, and Tyler, 1863), 21–43.

74. Ibid., 28–29.

75. Ibid., 29–31.

76. Ibld., 32–34.

77. Ibid.

78. See Peter C. McIntosh, *Physical Education in England Since 1800* (London: G. Bell and Sons, 1952), 90–96.

79. Archibald Maclaren, *A System of Physical Education, Theoretical and Practical* (Oxford: The Clarendon Press, 1865); idem., *Training in Theory and Practice* (London: Macmillan and Co., 1866), 149–52; idem., *Training in Theory and Practice*, 2nd and enlarged ed. (London: Macmillan and Co., 1874), iii–iv.

80. Maclaren, *Training* (1866), 132–40.

81. Ibid., 74–79, 87–101, 106–12, passim.

82. Ibid., 63–66, 104–112, passim.

83. Ibid., part 3, passim.

84. As recently as November 1989, *The Journal of the American Dietetic Association* (89:11) concluded that athletes often still do not follow sound nutritional practices. Dietary supplements are popular among marathoners in spite of the fact that there is evidence that additional vitamins and minerals do not improve performance by "supercharging the metabolic processes of the body" (1619). David C. Nieman et al., "Supplementation Patterns in Marathon Runners" (1615–19); also Diane R. Green, "An Evaluation of Dietary Intakes of Triathletes: Are RDAs Being Met?" (1653–54).

85. Walter Bradford Woodgate, *"Oars and Sculls," and How to Use Them* (London: George Bell and Sons, 1875), 1–2, 124–40.

86. Ibid.

87. Ibid.

88. Woodgate, *Boating*, 153–72; The Earl of Albermarle and G. Lacy Hillier, *Cycling* (London: Longmans, Green and Co., 1896), 172–81.

89. Westhall, *Modern Method of Training*, 44–47.

90. Ibid., 48–51.

91. Anthony Trollope (ed.), *British Sports and Pastimes* (London: Virtue, Spalding, and Co., 1868), 2; *A New Book of Sports* (London: Richard Bentley and Son, 1885), 126–36.

92. Walter H. Pollock, C. F. Grove, and Camille Prevost, *Fencing;* E. B. Michell, *Boxing,* and Walter Armstrong, *Wrestling,* 2d ed. (London: Long-

mans, Green and Co., 1890), 135–47; John Arlott (ed.), *The Oxford Companion to World Sports and Games* (London: Oxford University Press, 1975), 803.

93. For example, J. G. Bohun Lynch, *The Complete Boxer* (New York: Frederick A. Stokes Co., 1914), chap. 13. Written for a British audience, it concludes with appendices detailing such things as "Rules of the Amateur Boxing Association" and "Conditions for Public School Boxing."

94. John Boyle O'Reilly, *Athletics and Manly Sports* (Boston: Pilot Publishing Co., 1890), 82–99; 101–18.

95. W. W. Naughton, *Kings of the Queensberry Realm* (Chicago: The Continental Publishing Co., 1902), 10.

96. Ibid., 20–28.

97. Ibid., 32–33.

98. Ralph Henry Barbour, *The Book of School and College Sports* (New York: D. Appleton and Co., 1904), 32–41.

99. A. Alonzo Stagg and Henry L. Williams, *A Scientific and Practical Treatise on American Football for Schools and Colleges* (New York: D. Appleton, 1894), 12–17; Walter Camp and Lorin Deland, *Football* (Boston: Houghton, Mifflin and Co., 1896), 273, 308, 316. Walter Camp, *American Football* (New York: Harper and Brothers, 1892), 133–64.

100. Camp and Deland, *Football,* 77–83.

101. W. H. Grenfell, "Oxford v. Yale," *The Fortnightly Review* 56 (1894), 368–82.

102. Considine and Jarvis, *First Hundred Years,* 34–41; Montague Shearman, "International Athletics," *Badminton Magazine* 1 (1895), 573–92.

103. Ralph D. Paine, "The Spirit of School and College Sport: American and English Rowing," *The Century Magazine* 70 (1905), 483–503.

104. "Some Tendencies in Modern Sport," *The Quarterly Review* 149 (1904), 127–52.

105. George, *Training for Athletics,* 75.

106. Ibid., 73.

107. Hans Langenfeld, "Auf dem Weg zur Sportwissenschaft: Mediziner und Leibesübungen im 19. Jahrhundert," *Stadion,* 14 (1988), 125–48; John Hoberman, "The Early Development of Sports Medicine in Germany," [included herein as chap. 7]; Dietrich Quanz, "The Impact of North American Sport on European Sport and the Olympic Movement," paper presented at the International Symposium—Sport . . . The Third Millennium, May 21–25, 1990, Quebec City, Canada.

108. The origins of the modern Games—and the motivations of their creator—have been masterfully analyzed by John MacAloon in *This Great Symbol.* Allegheny College's Professor William A. Elliot, "The New Olympic Games," *Chautauquan* 23 (1896), wrote: "When first proposed the plan was regarded as the airy project of unpractical enthusiasts or the pedantical effort of worshipers of the past to bring forth from antiquity's grave an institution long since dead. Now that success seems certain, carpings have given place to murmurs of expectant interest. . . . It is the purpose of this new movement to revive the

genuine old spirit of Olympia, adding to athletics in all nations real elements of life and interest. It is hoped to stem the tide that has been setting so strongly of late toward professionalism and turn it back in the direction of legitimate amateur sport. We here in America especially need such an influence. . . . Every one of our out-of-door sports has been debased to the service of the professional athlete, whose object is to develop not a symmetrical and healthy man, but a distorted animal machine fitted by long training for the performance of this or that particular feat or skill" (pp. 47–51).

109. James E. Sullivan, "Athletics and the Stadium," *Cosmopolitan* 31 (1901), 501–8.

110. See Bill Henry, *An Approved History of the Olympic Games* (New York: G. P. Putman's Sons, 1948), chap. 5–8; John Kiernan and Arthur Daley, *The Story of the Olympic Games, 776 b.c.–1960 a.d.* (Philadelphia: J. B. Lippincott, 1961), chap. 3, 4, 6. Although the London *Times* gave considerable attention to the Paris Exhibition of 1900, little was said of "the Olympic games which are to be held in Paris," *Times,* 16 April 1900. The 1908 London Games, not surprisingly, received sustained attention in the British press. Reporting on their closing, the 27 July 1908 issue of the *Times* declared: "These Olympic Games, with their surprises and their heart-burnings and their series of athletic records, are built upon a healthy as well as manly spirit. . . . The games have not been all plain-sailing. The perfect harmony which every one wished for has been marred by certain regrettable disputes and protests and objections to the judges' rulings. In many newspapers, the world over, national feeling has run riot, and accusation, and counteraccusations have been freely bandied about." Nonetheless, the writer continued, the twenty nations that had competed had received many valuable lessons and had parted friends.

111. *Times,* 27 July 1908.

112. "The New Olympics," *Saturday Review,* 25 July 1908, 104–6.

113. J. Astley Cooper, "Olympic Games: What Has Been Done and What Remains to Be Done," *The Nineteenth Century* 68 (1908), 1011–21. For the background to Cooper's "Pan-Britannic Festival," see Katharine Moore, "The Pan-Britannic Festival: A Tangible but Forlorn Expression of Imperial Unity," in J. A. Mangan (ed.), *Pleasure, Profit, Proselytism: British Culture and Sport at Home and Abroad, 1700–1914* (London: Frank Cass, 1988), 144–62.

114. Cooper, *Olympic Games,* 1013; George, *Training for Athletics,* 73–77.

115. "The New Olympics," *Saturday Review,* 104; "England and the Olympics Games," *Saturday Review,* 17 August 1912, 195–96. (The switch from "British" to "English" occurs in the original, and is not entirely insignificant.)

116. E. B. Moss, "America's Olympic Argonauts," *Harper's Weekly* 56 (1912), 11–12; "British Athletic Slump," *Literary Digest* 47 (1912), 13.

117. S. S. Abrahams, Introduction, in E. W. Hjertberg, *Athletics in Theory and Practice* (New York: G. P. Putnam's Son's, 1914), v–viii.

118. Ibid., vi

119. S. A. Mussabini, *The Complete Athletic Trainer* (London: Methuen and Co., 1913), v–viii.

120. Harold Wade, "Cross-Country Running," in *The Encyclopedia of Sports and Games*, The Earl of Suffolk and Berkshire (Ed.), vol. 1 (New York: J. .B. Lippincott Co., 1911), 98.

121. See, for example, Clarence Deming, "Athletics in College Life: The Money Power in College Athletics." *Outlook* 80 (1905), 569–72. A Yale University alumnus, Deming accused his alma mater of being a leader among those colleges where athletic programs were inordinately costly. Ralph D. Paine, "The Spirit of School and College Sport, II. English and American Football," *Century Magazine* 71 (1905), 99–116; Henry Beach Needham, "The College Athlete: How Commercialism Is Making Him a Professional"—Part I, "Recruiting and Subsidizing," *McClure's Magazine*, 25 (1905), 115–28; idem, "The College Athlete: His Amateur Code: Its Evasion and Administration"—Part II, *McClure's Magazine* 25 (1905), 260–73.

122. Ellery H. Clark, *Reminiscences of An Athlete: Twenty Years in Track and Field* (Boston: Houghton Mifflin Co., 1911), 17–21, 52, chap. 6.

123. E. V. McCollum, Elsa Orent-Keiles, and Harry G. Day, *The Newer Knowledge of Nutrition*, 5th ed. (New York: Macmillan Co., 1939), 6–13. Austin Flint, Jr., *On the Physiological Effects of Severe and Protracted Muscular Exercise; With Special Reference to Its Influence Upon the Excretion of Nitrogen* (New York: D. Appleton and Co., 1871), 7–10. See also, Roberta J. Park, "Tradition and Science in the Training of Athletes, 1870–1914," paper presented at the International Symposium—Sport . . . The Third Millennium, May 21–25, 1990, Quebec City, Canada.

124. Cited in John Edward Morgan, *University Oars, Being a Critical Enquiry into the After Health of the Men Who Rowed in the Oxford and Cambridge Boat-Race from the Year 1829 to 1869, Based on the Personal Experiences of the Rowers Themselves* (London: Macmillan and Co., 1873), xiii–xv.

125. Ibid.; Archibald Maclaren, "University Oars," *Nature*, 27 March 1873, 397–99; ibid., 3 April 1873, 418–21; ibid., 17 April 1873, 458–60. For a detailed discussion of this issue, see James C. Whorton, "Athlete's Heart: The Medical Debate Over Athleticism, 1870–1920," *Journal of Sport History* 9 (1982), 30–52 (see chap. 3).

126. "Review and Notices," *The British Medical Journal*, 24 May 1873, 589. The two books reviewed were: Samuel Haughten, *Principles of Animal Mechanics*, and R. J. Lee, *Exercise and Training: Their Effects upon Health*.

127. R[obert] J. Lee, *Exercise and Training: Their Effects Upon Health* (London: Smith, Elder and Co., 1873), chap. 1. Lee referred several times to Maclaren. He defined the physiology of exercise as "chiefly the mechanical effects which muscular contraction produces on the structures of the human body. . . . There are two conditions necessary for sustaining muscular activity—one which relates to the muscles themselves, which we may call local; the other to the organs chiefly of circulation and respiration, which we may term general or constitutional." Lee also made the important observation: "The development of the muscles has usually been regarded as far more important than attention to the condition of the constitution; but this is to be attributed

to the fact that we can estimate by its size the power of a muscle, while the proof of constitutional condition (the evidence of which comes out in a race) is not so easily obtained" (pp. 10–11).

128. Flint, *On the Physiological Effects of Severe and Protracted Muscular Exercise*, 1–6, 63, passim.

129. Austin Flint, Jr., *On the Source of Muscular Power. Arguments and Conclusions Drawn from Observations upon the Human Subject, under Conditions of Rest and of Muscular Exercise* (New York: D. Appleton and Co., 1878), 9–11, 83–103. Flint was obviously well acquainted with Carl Voit's work on metabolism, with Fick and Wislicensus, *On the Origin of Muscular Power* (1866), with Liebig's *The Source of Muscular Power* (1870), and with such general physiology texts as William Carpenter's *Principles of Human Physiology* (1876 Philadelphia edition). In his 1876 *A Text-Book of Human Physiology: Designed for the Use of Practitioners and Students of Medicine* (New York: D. Appleton), Flint included a brief section on "Development of Power and Endurance by Exercise and Diet," in which he observed: "A fully-grown, well-developed man, in perfect health, may be trained so as to be brought to what is technically called fine condition, and he will present at that time all the animal functions in their perfection. . . . The argument that professional pugilists are short-lived is fallacious; for it is well known that almost all of them, after training for and passing through an encounter, immediately relapse into a course of life in which all physiological laws are habitually violated" (p. 499); William F. Pavy published a series of articles in *The Lancet*. See also James C. Whorton, "Muscular Vegetarianism: The Debate over Diet and Athletic Performance in the Progressive Era," *Journal of Sport History* 8 (1981), 58–75 for an interesting discussion (see chap. 9).

130. George Kolb, *Physiology of Sport: Contributions Toward the Physiology of Maximum Muscular Exertion, Especially Modern Sports, as Rowing, Athletics, Gymnastics, Cycling, Swimming, etc.* (London: Krohne and Sesemann, 1893).

131. F. A. Schmidt and Eustace H. Miles, *The Training of the Body for Games, Athletics, Gymnastics, and Other Forms of Exercise and for Health, Growth, and Development* (New York: E. P. Dutton and Co., 1901), 286–88.

132. See Jacques Thibault *L'Influence du mouvement sportif sur l'évolution de l'éducation physique dans l'enseignement secondaire Français* (Paris: Librairie Philosophique J. Vrin, 1972), 126–37; T. Lauder Brunton, and F. W. Tunnicliffe, "The Effect of Resistance Exercise upon the Circulation in Man, Local and General," *British Medical Journal*, 27 October 1897, 1073–75.

133. Eugene Darling, "The Effects of Training: A Study of the Harvard University Crew," *Boston Medical and Surgical Journal* 141 (1899), 229–33; idem., "The Effects of Training: Second Paper," *Boston Medical and Surgical Journal* 144 (1901), 550–59; R. C. Larrabee, "The Effects of Exercise on the Health and Circulation," *Boston Medical and Surgical Journal* 147 (1902), 318–23.

134. Wilbur O. Atwater and A. P. Bryant, *Dietary Studies of University Boat Crews*. Bulletin No. 75 U.S. Department of Agriculture: Office of Experiment

Stations (Washington, D.C.: Government Printing Office, 1900). The December 1, 1901 *British Medical Journal* reviewed Atwater's work and stated that the American studies had "gone far toward putting the subject of dietetics on a sound physiological basis" (p. 1600). J. B. Blake and R. C. Larrabee, "Observations Upon Long-Distance Runners," *Boston Medical and Surgical Journal* 148 (1903), 195–206; George L. Meylan, "Harvard University Oarsmen," *American Physical Education Review* 9 (1904), 362–76, 543–52.

135. Watson L. Savage, "Physiological and Pathological Effects of Severe Exertion (The Marathon Race)," *American Physical Education Review* 15 (1910), 651–61; idem., "Physiological and Pathological Effects of Severe Exertion (The Marathon Race)," *American Physical Education Review* 16 (1911), 1–11, 144–50.

136. Michael C. Murphy, *Athletic Training* (ed. Edward R. Bushnell) (New York: Charles Scribner's Sons, 1914), vi.

137. Ibid., xiii. Several sources, including Spalding's *Athletic Library* called Murphy "the world's most famous athletic trainer." See, E. J. Giannini, *Rowing* (New York: American Sports Publishing Co., 1909) as one example; also, Herbert Reed, *Football for Public and Player* (New York: Frederick A. Stokes, Co., 1913), 97.

138. Murphy, *Athletic Training*, xxii.

139. Paul Withington (ed.), *The Book of Athletics* (Boston: Lothrop, Lee and Shepard Co., 1914), v; Norman W. Bingham (ed.), *The Book of Athletics and Out-of-Door Sports. . . .* (Boston: Lothrop Publishing Co., 1895).

140. See Hoberman, "Early Development of Sports Medicine in Germany."

141. R. Tait McKenzie, *Exercise in Education and Medicine* (Philadelphia: W. B. Saunders Co., 1910).

142. The Athletic Research Society was founded in the early 1900s, largely to counter a growing tide of professionalism in athletic programs for boys and young men. See especially the address at the 1909 conference by George W. Ehler, secretary of the Public Athletic League of Baltimore, included in "Athletic Research Society," *American Physical Education Review* 15 (1910), 263–67.

143. Fielding H. Yost, *Football for Player and Spectator* (Ann Arbor: University Publishing Co., 1905), 21–22.

144. Walter Camp, *Walter Camp's Book of Sports* (New York: The Century Co., 1910), xiii, 120–23.

145. Ralph Henry Barbour, *For the Honor of the School: A Story of School Life and Interscholastic Sport* (New York: D. Appleton and Co., 1900).

146. R. Tait McKenzie's "Introduction" (and tribute) in Murphy, *Athletic Training*, xxvi.

147. Ibid.

3 *James C. Whorton*

"Athlete's Heart": The Medical Debate over Athleticism, 1870–1920

"What lamentations do we hear?," marvelled two members of the London Athletic Club in 1890. "Rachel weeping for her children: mothers discussing the injuries that have occurred to their athletic progeny; how Ajax is afflicted with valvular disease of the heart, and Priam with most dangerous spasms. They inveigh against sports of all kinds, and wish that athletism had never been an institution."[1]

There was irony as well as error in these anti-athletic lamentations, for the Rachels who were weeping the loudest were physicians. Exercise, after all, had been a cardinal element of the medical profession's code of hygiene since antiquity. Doctors through the centuries had recommended regular and moderate exertion for enjoyment of vitality and resistance to disease. During the nineteenth century particularly, American physicians, worried by the increasing sedentariness of a nation rapidly changing from a rural to an urban life-style, exhorted the public to counteract the staleness of the counting room with the exhilaration of the field and the gymnasium. The people generally refused to comply with the exercise prescription, though, until the post–Civil War boom in games and athletics suddenly roused them to levels of physical activity that often exceeded what had been intended by their physicians. The heart of hygienic philosophy had always been "moderation," and the new enthusiasm of the public for ball games and cycling and other athletic endeavors appeared to many physicians to overleap even the most liberal bounds of moderation. These doctors thus ended up among the staunchest foes of a trend of "athleticism" that had been originally set in motion and pushed ahead with considerable eagerness by the medical profession, and was still being energetically advocated by physicians who saw only good in the expansion of traditional exercise into boat racing and football. The resulting clash of opinions over the medical consequences of athleticism was one of the profession's livelier intramural confrontations around the turn of this century (fought along identical lines in America and in Europe) and was a significant factor both in the crystallization of sports medicine as an area of specialization and in the formation of public attitudes toward strenuous exertion.

While systematic exercise, and even play, had been promoted by physicians before the mid-1800s, there was a heightening of medical interest in the 1850s and 1860s in response to the growth of gymnastics—first the demanding German *Turnen,* and then "the new gymnastics" of Dio Lewis, a gentler system of calisthenics and games employing music and apparatus such as wooden dumbbells and bean bags. Lewis's gymnastics were all the rage in educational circles for a season, but despite its author's assurances that his exercises were "not less fascinating than the most popular games,"[2] the new gymnastics were sometimes perceived as rigidly prescribed drills that lacked spontaneity and unpredictability and heated competition, were more duty than fun, and had, moreover, a touch of the absurd about them. The various posturings required could make a group performance of Lewis gymnastics take on successively the appearance of "a series of windmills—a group of inflated balloons—a flock of geese all asleep on one leg . . . a whole parish of Shaker worshippers—a Japanese embassy performing *Ko-tow.*"[3]

An activity more entertaining to spectators than practitioners was destined for only passing popularity, and as baseball, football, and tennis rose in public esteem, American society passed from the "gymnastic era" to the "athletic era." Edward Hitchcock, Jr., the physician who identified that change of epochs, epitomized the medical profession's initially positive reaction to the advent of athleticism. The first professor of physical education at an American college (Amherst), Hitchcock had originally been a proponent of Lewis gymnastics, but by the 1890s he was certain that although

> a man may get simple muscular development in a gymnasium, and be strong in arms, legs, lungs, and back. . . . he cannot get the real brawn, effective muscle, capacious lungs, a tough skin and the best of digestion, or a really reliable heart, unless he gets more of the natural process of health from mother earth and her surroundings of air, water, temperature, ozone, and the actual touch of soil and grass. . . . Man needs outdoor discipline as well as that of the training master indoors, if he would secure the bodily condition and the physical power that make him the best man to conduct a business, to edit a newspaper, or to make the most effective use of high intellectual attainments in any calling.[4]

Outdoor games, the standard argument for athleticism ran, had greater hygienic value because, being more enjoyable, they attracted more participants; and being conducted in a natural environment, they were more beneficial to the organs of a human animal who was the product of a long process of biological evolution within nature.

The greatest advantage of athletics, however, was not muscular, but moral. It was not just that the strength, energy, and endurance built by sports endowed one, as Hitchcock suggested, with the power to better conduct his business or otherwise use his intellectual attainments. Nor was it sufficient to recognize the worth of open-air games for diverting one from the relentless nervous excitement of the urban bustle. The value of athletics for combatting the great epidemic of civilization—"neurasthenia" or nervous weakness, with accompanying exhaustion of creative energy and spiritual fortitude—was generally and gratefully acknowledged, but doctors were most impressed by the usefulness of sport for building the most prized of Victorian virtues, character. That hope was already being furthered in the public sphere by the penetration of the British ethic of "muscular Christianity" into popular thought during the 1860s. Suggested by the novels of Charles Kingsley and Thomas Hughes, muscular Christianity became a kind of social gospel that affirmed the compatibility of the robust physical life with a life of Christian morality and service, which indeed contended that bodily strength built character and righteousness and usefulness for God's (and the nation's) work.[5]

Even had they been insulated from the popular interpretations of Kingsley and Hughes, physicians could have developed their own version of muscular Christianity from the medical philosophy of sanitary reform. The beginning of modern public health activity, the sanitary reform movement, was a mid- to late-nineteenth century campaign to clean city streets and supply pure water and efficient drainage to city houses, and thereby eradicate the problem of physical disease. Removal of decomposing organic refuse, it was presumed, would prevent the generation of the foul miasmas that polluted the urban atmosphere and were believed to be the source of cholera, yellow fever, and most of the other acute infections that plagued the period. Sanitary reform had a moral face as well. The evangelical equation of ungodliness with uncleanliness encouraged sanitarians to concentrate on the association of immorality and licentiousness with filthy living conditions, too, and to see themselves as crusaders against moral disease as well. The ardent sanitationist was almost as bent on cleansing souls as streets. New York's John Griscom, the first American physician to strongly urge sanitary reform, introduced his 1845 survey of the sanitary condition of his city's laboring population by asking what was the effect of "this degraded and filthy manner of life" upon not only the health and life span of slum residents, but also "their morals, their self-respect, and appreciation of virtue." His summation for the implementation of thorough-going public sanitation had as a critical link the argument that a clean population in a decent environment would not be guilty of nearly so much lawlessness, and therefore be less difficult and expensive to govern.[6] That economic ploy was vital for winning legislative backing of sanitary programs, but Griscom and most other sanitarians were far more deeply concerned about human lives than dollars. As one saw it, "sanitary science" must take as its eventual goal nothing less that the advancement of "human felicity" by every means possible.[7] As late as 1887, as sanitary reform was yielding to "the new public health" founded on the germ theory of disease, the American physician Frances White still felt confident presenting an address entitled "Hygiene as a Basis for Morals," in which she described the ideal city to be built by sanitarians. Her name for the city—Ethica!—underscores the ultimately moral thrust of the sanitationist spirit.[8]

When that professional ethos fused with the pervasive lay excitement over muscular Christianity, there inevitably resulted a medical-moral philosophy of athletics that supposed the personal, internal sanitation of strenuous exercise must perfect the spirit as well as the body. Late Victorian physicians fairly tumbled over themselves searching for character-enhancing elements within the various outdoor games and recreations. Thus the bicycling craze of the 1890s was greeted with ecstatic pronouncements of not only the limitless physical improvement it promised the masses, but also the opportunities for spiritual and social growth it offered. Every societal end from strengthening of the family to the curing of alcoholism and opium addiction was credited to the wonderful exercise of wheeling.[9]

Cycling was still secondary as a character-builder to football, rowing, and other competitive sports. There were a number of professional bicycle racers, but the vast majority of cyclists were interested only in recreation, not competition. And competition was a crucial consideration in determining the character value of a sport. The struggle to win forced a competitor to dig to the bottom of his physical and moral reserves to meet the rival's challenge. "If you abolish contests," an English doctor submitted, "you do away with emulation and stifle the cry of 'Excelsior.'" In truth, he continued, "the more hazardous the game the better for the development of the character of the individual."[10] Such feelings, widely shared among physicians, had special relevance at a time when American football was being attacked as senseless and brutal. The University of Pennsylvania's R. Tait McKenzie, a leader among medical advocates of athletics, rose to the sport's defense with a *moral* argument. "The football is the only field we have, in the absence of actual fighting," he reminded, "for that training in presence of mind, audacity, courage, endurance of pain and fatigue, pluck and 'sand' that must characterize the youth of a nation which must play a leading part in the work of the world."[11] Professional colleagues readily echoed those sentiments, one noting that, "It is your physical wrecks who become perverts,"[12] another announcing that, *"Football has ended a career of debauchery for more than one youth."*[13] At the University of Pennsylvania, it was attested, undergraduate sexual morality became "incredibly higher" after students became involved in athletics,[14] while it was the non-dangerous and relatively non-competitive games like golf and bowling that one found "essentially associated with substantial oaths and Scotch whisky."[15]

All competitions, though football especially, were seen to give the athlete "heart," the self-discipline and drive that "fitted [him] for the stern work of life that assails us all at some time."[16] But his physical, as opposed to metaphoric, heart made the athlete the object of grave disquietude among a second set of physicians. This group was not, it must be explained, blindly anti-athletic. Its members recognized hygienic value in exercise, and usually agreed that physical improvement brought mental and moral improvement in its train. They were nevertheless deeply troubled by the medical implications of competition: that same thirst for victory that put starch in a man's spirit, they realized, might lead him to overextend himself physically and injure his muscles and vital organs. Their aphorism that, "Athletics for health is safe. Athletics for prowess and superiority may be dangerous,"[17] was a logical conclusion from the fear of intemperance ingrained by their medical training (and by Victorian culture generally). Because intemperance is a relative term, applied after subjective evaluation of an activity, it was easy for many physicians (particularly the unathletic) to recoil from competitive sports as debilitating excesses rather than embrace them as muscle and backbone builders. Their distrust of contests was reinforced by the fact that games attracted mostly young men, and while "intemperance in any form is injurious to the body," it must be "especially [so] in its immature condition."[18]

That same youth implied immature judgment, too, the inability of young men to foresee that their "courage and willpower were stronger than their bodies."[19] And though the foolishness of youth had always been a hazard, in many fields other than athletics, the danger had intensified in recent years with the growth of inter-collegiate competition. The injection of do-or-die for *alma mater* spirit into contests had made footballers and rowers seemingly maniacal in their battle for victory. "This was not true in earlier days," a nostalgic doctor complained, "when college men took their sport like gentlemen."[20] Now, though, they were goaded into ungentlemanly, almost superhuman exertions by their own collegiate loyalties, and by fanatical crowds of spectators equally committed to redeeming the school's honor. (The health of those spectators, incidentally, was a subject of some concern also to the critics of competition; those unable to qualify as "the 'beef' of the college," it was charged, were ignored by physical educators and trainers and allowed to degenerate into "a horde of pimply-faced, hollow-chested boys, whose ideal of physical training is to smoke cigarets, drink beer, [and] give the college yell").[21] In giving the yell, furthermore, these "mollycoddles of the bleachers"[22] drove their more muscular classmates to exhaustion: "It is this public admiration which has much to do with the overdoing and therefore the undoing of the student contestant."[23]

The contestant's undoing was supposed to be worked in several ways, beginning with his excessive muscular development. Medical prejudice against extraordinary strength and large muscles dated to the beginnings of the modern physical education movement. In their eagerness to democratize exercise and extend its benefits to the masses, physicians of the 1850s and 1860s had often renounced the apparently difficult and specialized (therefore elitist) accomplishments of *Turners* and weightlifters. This early ridicule of heavy musculature became an article of faith among subsequent generations of physical educators, and many drew no distinction between the physiques of renowned weightlifters like Sandow and the considerably less awesome (but still "abnormal") bodies of college rowers and football players. The big muscles built by concentrated training, according to these analysts, were an evolutionary anachronism. In industrial societies, natural selection favored brain power; heavy muscular work was for "animals or the lower races." Greater than usual bulk was thus a burden in the "race of life;" "piles of parasitic muscles" required "an undue amount of nourishment," lowering bodily efficiency (and thus brain power), and making athletes into "physiological profligates."[24] Clear evidence of that squandering of bodily reserve power was to be had in the incidence of death from infectious disease, which several observers claimed was notably higher for the muscular than for the average population. Tuberculosis particularly was laid to physiological poverty brought on by athletic indulgence.[25]

Lowered resistance to infection was but one, and a relatively minor one at that, of the injuries believed to be the wages of athleticism. Emphysema and other lung ailments were expected to occur as the respiratory rate and pulmonary blood flow surged beyond natural limits. The discovery of protein in the urine of athletes after they had competed (now accepted as a normal condition) was interpreted as evidence of sport-induced kidney damage.[26] Some physicians revived the ancient Greek association of athletic training with decreased libido. At a time when doctors were as worried as the public about the declining birthrate among Anglo-Saxon stock—what Roosevelt sensationalized as "race suicide"—that revival was likely to be accomplished with a vengeance. The life records of America's professional athletes, one commentator reported, demonstrated that "comparatively few athletes marry. Of those that do marry, a small percentage have children. A large percentage are divorced by their wives, and it is doubtless true that not a few completely lose the instinct of the normal man."[27] A fellow physician disclosed that "the best athletes possess poorly developed sexual organs," and rationalized this generalization with the argument that "severe athletic training and muscle building are at the expense of the nervous and glandular systems." The same reasoning accounted for the "fact" that "many athletes are sexual perverts."[28] And though the college sportsman might preserve his normal sexuality, his presumed higher mortality rate meant that he nevertheless participated in race suicide. "If we must have the excitement [of competition]," a medical editor insisted, "we can turn to other fields—the shortening of the life of a race horse, or of a game cock, or even of a professional pugilist need not concern us much." It was racial stupidity to "impair the futures of our best of young men, the college graduates."[29]

Even the relaxation from care and worry enjoyed by the recreational sportsman was denied to the competitor. Not only was the contest itself a nerve-grating struggle to win glory and avoid shame. The between-games anticipation of upcoming battles turned the entire season into a period of nervous turmoil for the athlete: "he can never remain at ease for a minute at a time, and like the caged lion is forever on the move during his waking moments."[30] The final payment exacted by this nervous taxation could actually be mental breakdown. "Our ancestors with fewer gymnasiums were a remarkably sane people," a casual epidemiologist noted, "and we may ask ourselves the question if the great increase in insanity has anything to do with our present system of physical training. Asylums and hospitals are crowded and athleticism increases in proportion."[31]

Such exaggerations of the effects of athleticism dramatize the uncomfortable situation in which doctors found themselves. Faced with an unprecedented mass athletics and armed with only the most rudimentary knowledge of the long-term effects of repeated stressing of the heart, lungs, and nervous system, it was only natural for physicians to err on the side of safety and suspect danger where a later, more experienced and sophisticated generation would see invigoration. That tendency was reinforced by the case of rationalizing pathology by the post hoc assumption that since a condition had no other obvious cause and it had appeared after the patient's involvement in athletics, it must have been caused by the unnatural and peculiar strains of his sport. Doctors made uneasy by heavy or prolonged exercise were also quick to generalize from single incidents. "Pessimists," McKenzie called them, "who argue from the early death of some hero of the gridiron or cinder path, that we are yearly sacrificing the flower of our youth to the molech of athleticism."[32]

Of all the pathological artifacts offered in tribute to this "molech," though, none even approached in frequency and severity the condition of "athlete's heart." The heart was the most obviously vital of organs, and the one whose functioning, in the form of accelerated beat, was most clearly affected by exercise. Heart attack victims were often stricken while engaged in exercise or work, and even though athletes completing a game or race were not experiencing cardiac failure, their appearance of pained breathlessness and exhaustion aroused an uneasy wonder in the spectator. This visceral fear of heart injury from overexertion was being strengthened by the end of the nineteenth century by the medical preoccupation with the rising incidence of heart disease. As infectious diseases were steadily brought under control, chronic degenerative ailments became more prominent. One of America's most eminent cardiac experts, Alfred Stengel, began the new century with a warning that the rate of heart disease had climbed remarkably during the past fifty years.[33] Only ten years later, the editor of the country's most prestigious medical journal despaired that, "Every year the death rate from cardiac disease is increasing, and unless something is done to check this it will become more of a menace than tuberculosis or acute respiratory diseases."[34] Given this alarm over the new epidemic, it is not surprising to find so many physicians urging that, "The relations of violent muscular exertion to such diseases should be thoroughly understood."[35]

The anti-athletic doctor's understanding of those relations was derived from seemingly pertinent observations. The heart of the trained athlete does present different clinical data than that of the "normal" person. The athletic heart is larger, beats less frequently, often exhibits murmurs and a diffuse impulse, and is sometimes subject to arrhythmias. Physicians are still warned not to misinterpret unusual radiographic and electrocardiographic findings in athletes as necessarily pathological. Appreciation that these "abnormalities" are physiological responses to training has developed only very recently, however. To most early twentieth-century physicians, an enlarged and irregular heart with murmurs was a diseased heart, and athletes were thus easily diagnosed as casualities of their sport. To be fair, some probably were victimized by exercise: rheumatic fever was more common, and the fact that heart problems could also result from heavy exertion during other acute infections was not yet known by athletes. Cardiac damage could also occur in competitors with undiagnosed hypertension (a condition that was not commonly detected at the time).[36] Finally, athletes were already notorious for supplementing their competitive labors with less wholesome physical conquests. "No one will dispute," a *proponent* of athleticism acknowledged, that sportsmen often fell into immoral dissipation. If it was true that many athletes emulated John L. Sullivan, a man who made "continuous use of alcohol" and "was no less assiduous in his worship of Venus," then heart disease of syphilitic origin may well have been a common end to the sporting life.[37]

There were numerous other competitors, though, the large majority, whose hearts experienced only a physiological hypertrophy, but who were diagnosed as injured and used as tragic case histories of "athlete's heart." Benjamin Ward Richardson, a leading English sanitary reformer who nevertheless feared athletics required *excessive* exercise, was among the first to warn of the new condition. Already in the early 1870s, he "venture[d] to affirm there is not in England a trained professional athlete of the age of thirty-five, who has been ten years at his calling, who is not disabled." His damning generalization was based on a total of only seven former athletes who might "have lived to a vigorous old age under a system of exercise less lawless against nature and less suicidal." But what he lacked in statistical backing, Richardson more than made up with his compelling pathological rationale. Cardiac hypertrophy was the essence of athletic heart. "Undue muscular development" of the heart, he reasoned, must increase the pressure of the blood on vessel walls and cause steady degeneration of vascular tone and, consequently, lowering of overall vitality. The effects would become particularly noticeable in later years, Richardson believed, as the ex-athlete's body decreased in strength due to aging and cessation of training. The overdeveloped heart, though, he expected to remain strong, too strong for the body, "so that movement is laborious, breathless and even exhaustive."[38]

No doubt had he looked longer he could have found many more than seven middle-aged men who had become laborious and breathless in movement since abandoning the athletic life. Other physicians did find similar cases of post-athletic decay and quickly expanded Richardson's theory into a grand scheme of cardiac pathology. That scheme retained enlargement of the heart as the fundamental type of athletic injury. Heart size was determined (albeit not very reliably) by percussion and auscultation in most instances, and sometimes (after 1900) by X-ray examination of the cardiac shadow. When enlargement was found, it might be explained as either hypertrophy (actual growth of the muscular tissue of the heart) or dilatation (enlargement of the cavities of the heart, due to stretching of the muscular walls). The latter was the more ominous diagnosis, having been long recognized as a common product of heart disease and grounds for a most grave prognosis.[39] Dilatation was also expected to result from an overpowering of the heart by sudden and excessive demands for effort: "a disproportion between the work the heart has to do and its ability to do it." The disproportion might come from "a prolonged debauch," but could result more quickly from such superficially healthful activities as "a hasty run [or] a spurt on a bicycle."[40] All that was required was that the effort be "violent and sustained,"comparable to the regimen of the London distance runner who died during the training season and was found to have ventricles that were "enormously dilated."[41]

The unfortunate runner's dilatation was discovered by autopsy and is not to be disputed. He was undoubtedly not the only case of undiagnosed heart disease who committed unwitting suicide with athletics. The regular implication in the medical reports of such cases, though, that dilatation was *caused* by athletic effort, made doctors unnecessarily jittery about exercise. That readiness to find fault with sport was intensified by the apparent belief of many that murmurs, bradycardia (lowered heart rate), diffuse cardiac impulse, and irregular beat invariably indicated dilatation and/or valvular dysfunction, and by the fact that diagnostic techniques could not always clearly distinguish between dilatation and hypertrophy. Athletic training normally causes a physiologic hypertrophy, which actually represents an improvement in cardiac function, but it is evident doctors often mistook hypertrophy for dilatation and diagnosed their athletic patients as cases of serious heart disease.[42]

It nevertheless appears that the athlete's heart was more often than not correctly recognized as hypertrophied, although that conclusion scarcely improved his outlook, for hypertrophy was also regarded as a necessarily pathological condition. It had been known, for some time, to be associated with such problems as persistent high blood pressure and valvular defects, and was regarded as being almost as threatening a sign as dilatation. The association of pathologic hypertrophy with exertion can be traced to J. M. DaCosta's studies of Union soldiers. As early as 1862 the pioneering cardiologist recognized a functional disorder of "irritable heart" which often affected soldiers with palpitations, tachycardia, and chest pain, as well as breathlessness and dizziness. Attributing the condition to the extreme physical demands of long military campaigns—particularly exhausting forced marches—DaCosta argued that the functional irritation eventually led to an organic injury: hypertrophy.[43] That pathologic progression was not to be substantiated by later investigations; still it was only during the early 1900s that it became clear that "irritable heart" or "soldier's heart" was not a sign of impending structural injury. By that time, the idea that hypertrophy was an abnormality produced by excessive exercise had become securely seated in many physicians' minds. As competitive athletics involved not only unusual physical efforts, but was also a form of war, or at least heroic struggle, it was inevitable that the concept of "soldier's heart" would be enlarged to include "athlete's heart." Already an early reviewer had seen DaCosta's work as timely primarily because of the burgeoning public fascination with athletics. "This excessive devotion to muscular acquirements is fraught with danger to the body," he warned, and ended with the assertion that DaCosta's real service had been to alert the public to the need to "avoid athletic excess."[44]

Even after it became apparent that irritable heart was only a functional syndrome, not an organic disease, and occurred typically in frail and nervous people unable to cope with physical and psychic stress, the new name given the condition—"effort syndrome" (1918)—was hardly calculated to assuage fears of the cardiac effects of athletic effort. By 1940, the experts could agree that many cases of "athlete's heart" had actually been victims of effort syndrome and had not suffered any permanent damage from sports, but that realization had only gradually dawned over the preceding three decades. Through the first third of the century at least, physicians could easily be led to suppose that athletic hypertrophy was pathological.[45] They could also easily formulate a rationale for the pathology. The blood pumped by an enlarged, more powerful heart must apply more pressure to arterial walls, it was reasoned, and that "constant hammering" must certainly shorten the life of the "vital rubber" in those walls. Arteriosclerosis was the consequence, though it might be accompanied or preceded by valvular disease (the enlarged heart's valves were also hammered).[46]

Finally, even when the hypertrophy resulting from competition was recognized as physiological and of no immediate pathological import, it was still commonly supposed to be an eventual threat to health. That the bulging biceps of football players, blacksmiths, and other muscle workers shrank once the individual retired from his activity was a commonplace observation. Either because the muscular shrinkage was more noticeable than for the aging non-athlete, or because too many famous athletes turned to dissipation in their later years and thus dramatized their physical decline, it had become established opinion that muscle fibers built up by athletics suffered serious degeneration once training ceased. "The powerful muscles of the quondam athlete," this conventional wisdom ran, "are turned into flabby, pendulous lumps of tissue."[47] Since the heart was also a muscle, the hypertrophied heart of the athlete would necessarily suffer a similar deterioration once his competitive days ended. "Fatty heart" was the cardiac counterpart to flabby, pendulous biceps. As the hypertrophied heart muscle fibers withered, without compensating growth of intermuscular fibers, the heart wall might be expected to weaken and undergo dilatation.[48]

Middle-age, it was generally agreed, was the critical time period for the manifestation of this postponed damage. An Illinois college president bemoaned the tragic ends of his varsity tennis players by relating that, "Many have died of heart disease between the ages of forty and forty-five, when they should have been at their best physically."[49] Mr. C., a case reported by a New York physician, lived a bit longer, to age fifty-two, but finally the heart he had enlarged through cycling turned on him after sedentary years as a bookkeeper. The weakened organ began demanding beer, then cigars, but in the end even these stimulants proved inadequate. Mr. C. was stricken with shortness of breath and angina while walking up only a moderate incline. "Diagnosis: Myocarditis [inflammation of cardiac muscle], dilated heart, arteriosclerosis."[50] The most shocking demonstration of the inevitability of cardiac degeneration was given by William Blaikie, an exemplar of athleticism. Stroke on the Harvard crew in the mid-1860s, Blaikie turned to weight lifting after college and authored a highly popular volume entitled *How To Get Strong and How To Stay So* (1879). Blaikie remained active until his sixtieth year, but then became so involved in his law practice he gave up physical exercise altogether. At the age of sixty-one, he was dead of a stroke, a cardiovascular complication of his failure to "keep up his heart muscle."[51]

Critics of athleticism were at least willing to allow that keeping up the heart muscle would forestall degeneration and dilatation. They doubted, however, that that theoretical safeguard would have any significant impact on real athletic mortality. Only a small percentage of athletes, they believed, could be expected to continue vigorous exercising for any time beyond their college days, and a smaller percentage still would remain lifelong athletes. Assuming that physical training was drudgery, they could scold that, "The penalty of early athletics is athletics all of one's life;" in that view, the athletic life was a wearisome treadmill, and to step off was to risk early death.[52]

Most would step off anyway, it was believed, and sooner rather than later, for the treadmill was tedious, and the penalty for leaving it so remote in time. The remoteness of the penalty also doomed any efforts to discourage young men from seeking athletic glory and getting onto the treadmill in the first place: "What is invalidism or disability to one who has made a record, and how trivial seems the hypertrophied heart to the winner of the Olympic games."[53] Athletes would be athletes, and doctors could only warn them of the consequences for later life and hope that gradually they would pay heed. In the meantime, it was imperative to stand vigil over young competitors and rescue any showing evidence of immediate injury from athletics by barring them from further participation in sports or any strenuous exercise.

One can only guess at the number of athletic careers ended prematurely, the amount of pleasurable and healthful recreation forbidden to people throughout their lives, the degree of hypochondria and anxiety suffered by athlete's heart "patients." The great Yale economist Irving Fisher, for example, was told in 1896 that he had strained his heart "by hill-climbing on the bicycle." The diagnosis "frightened me. I feared sudden death, and I feared to hear my heart beat on my pillow." Worry caused him to lose sleep for two years, to become run down, and thus contributed, he believed, to his eventual attack of tuberculosis.[54] Even if the patient's fear for his heart did not reduce him to consumption, the misdiagnosis was still an iatrogenic problem of serious proportions. It caused loss of invigorating exercise, worry, depression. How many repetitions were there, one must wonder, of the case of the man who was an athlete in college, but whose father feared he was overstraining himself and insisted he see a physician. The doctor diagnosed cardiac inflammation and demanded he give up athletics. The poor youth was made to squander two decades in fretful inactivity, with accompanying nervous symptoms, until at last finding a physician who was not a believer in athlete's heart. This doctor, in fact, put him on a program of slowly increasing exercise to treat his neurasthenia, until after about six weeks, "he suddenly remarked after quite a bit of lively exercise, 'By jove, for the first time in twenty years I forgot I had a heart while exercising.' " After continued improvement, "He often remarks, 'What would I have given to have been convinced of my condition ten years ago.' "[55]

What might many have given to have been spared the diagnosis of athlete's heart? Fortunately the above physician's skepticism was not an isolated attitude, but one shared by a respectable number of medical supporters of athleticism. Nor did the skeptics confine their denial of sport-induced heart disease to the salvaging of individual misdiagnosed patients. They aired their doubts before the profession, confronted critics with statistical studies indicating the healthfulness of competition, and challenged them to counter with something more solid than anecdote and hypothesis. Indeed, the repudiation of athlete's heart became a major element of the medical campaign to promote the athletic life.

That campaign was waged on several fields, corresponding to the particular sports that at different periods aroused the greatest anxiety among the anti-athletic forces. It actually began as a nautical struggle, for crew racing was the competition that initially forced the issue. Rowing was an especially taxing sport, and the first to generate intense intercollegiate rivalry. The annual University Boat Race between Oxford and Cambridge, especially, was the occasion for extraordinary public excitement, "a kind of Derby day with the Londoners,"[56] a critic disparaged, attendant with drinking, gambling, and wild cheering among the thousands of spectators who lined the Thames. It was obvious to any reflecting person that the roaring of that frenzied crowd, coupled with the collegians' immature notions of the cosmic significance of victory, might drive the young rowers to demand almost impossible, ultimately injurious effort from their still developing bodies. Though statements to that effect had been issued regularly since the inauguration of the race in 1829, they seem to have had no lasting effect until 1867. In the wake of that year's contest followed a warning from the medical Journal *Lancet* that dilatation and aneurysm were the frequent consequences of the race, and then F. C. Skey, a London surgeon, vented his disgust with this "national folly" on the editorial pages of the *Times*. The folly, in Skey's eyes, was *competition*, the "death or victory" obsession that made the rower expend "every inch of power inherent in his muscular system." Perhaps the majority survived that expenditure unscathed, Skey admitted, but a significant minority undoubtedly crawled exhausted from their boats with "a seed sown" in their cardiovascular systems, and with time the seed would become "a formidable tree." For that reason, the English could take little pride in their abolition of animal-baiting and other cruel sports; the cruelest sport of all remained.[57]

Skey's perfervid attack on a cherished institution drew stinging rebukes from retired rowers, but it also elicited a poignant confession from "The Father of a University Oarsman." The correspondent had reluctantly granted his son permission to row in the contest, and the boy had been out of health ever since. Never again, the father vowed, would he give his consent to "the greatest folly and cruelty which has, probably, ever been perpetrated in the annals of athletics."[58] The paper's editor concluded the debate the day following with a summary that perfectly exemplified the ambivalence so many doctors of the next half century would feel about athletic competition. Racing might well have serious physical consequences, he agreed, but if so, they were as desirable as they were unfortunate; they were that element of risk, of adventure, that was vital to the life of a nation. The seeking of complete physical security, the editorial decided, was more deadly than the risk of exertion: "It is not by so niggardly an economy of nerves that noble races acquire or preserve their vigor."[59]

The less impassioned opening paragraph of the editorial had more significance. There it was recognized that the question of the effects of rowing could be answered only by a thorough statistical evaluation of the long-term health of many men who had participated in the sport. John Edward Morgan, a Manchester physician, at once accepted the challenge and produced a study that the champions of athleticism were to regard as the most authoritative analysis of the subject until well into the twentieth century. The favorable conclusions of *University Oars* might have been expected, for Morgan, captain of his crew for three years at Oxford, was hardly a disinterested observer. The whole project, he announced in his introduction, had been "a labour of love" prompted "by a deep-rooted conviction that . . . we should not allow so manly and health-giving an exercise to be unjustly assailed."[60]

Happily, there was no need for Morgan to doctor the statistics to make them support his deep-rooted conviction. Succeeding in locating all but 4 of the 255 survivors of the Cambridge and Oxford oarsmen for the period from 1829 through 1869, Morgan inquired into each man's health and found the overall report to be most reassuring.

True, one forty-one-year-old gentleman lamented he was "quite obsolete from an hypertrophied heart (I believe)," and a few others attributed lesser ailments to their youthful exertions. Most, however, believed improved health to have been the product of their athletic careers. Thirty-nine additional oarsmen had died by 1869, but only three had been diagnosed as heart disease victims; half as many as had died in accidents. Both the heart disease and the pulmonary and total mortality rates were comparable to, or better than, the rates established for the general population. Similarly, calculations projected that surviving oarsmen might expect life spans significantly beyond the average. The University Boat Races, Morgan decided with no little satisfaction, did not destroy, or even weaken, its participants; in fact, the training it demanded actually strengthened the cardiovascular system and made it more efficient for later life. Final gratification was found in the fact that crewmen had gathered relatively more academic honors than their non-athletic classmen.[61]

Morgan's conclusions (as well as most later surveys of athletic longevity) were weakened by being based on a relatively small number of subjects who enjoyed physical, economic, and educational advantages over the general population. One could argue that robust college graduates might be expected to live somewhat longer than ill-nourished and ignorant factory workers even if rowing did damage their hearts. The optimistic slant of *University Oars* nevertheless continued to rule subsequent examinations of the health of American college rowers. Within five years of the publication of Morgan's book, a Dr. E. H. Bradford reported similar statistics regarding the health of men who had rowed for Harvard during the previous twenty-five years.[62] Bradford's figures were derived entirely from correspondence, however; he did not personally examine any of his subjects. A far more thorough survey was conducted in 1903 by George Meylan, medical director of the gymnasium of Columbia University. Meylan secured extensive health data through personal examination, as well as correspondence, from nearly all the men who had rowed for Harvard from 1852 through 1892. His findings were even more favorable to rowing than Morgan's. Comparing his oarsmen to the typical healthy American male as defined in life insurance tables, he found the former to enjoy five years greater life expectancy per man. The rowers were, as a group, freer from disease (including heart affections), more robust and energetic, ruddier in complexion, and more prolific as parents. They even had placed proportionately greater numbers of men in *Who's Who* than had college graduates as a whole, or even members of Phi Beta Kappa. The retired crewman discovered by Meylan bore little resemblance to the dull-witted, flabby, under-sexed, weak-hearted ex-athlete of popular stereotype.[63]

The stereotype persisted nonetheless. As late as 1914 an unusually detailed report of the high frequency of cardiac lesions among athletes at the University of Wisconsin stirred that school's medical faculty to protest. Although the report had suggested damage from football, basketball, and track as well, rowing was the sport singled out for attention by the faculty. The resolution they adopted for transmission to the University Athletic Council warned that "the severe training deemed necessary for preparing crews for intercollegiate contests puts so severe a strain on the heart that an undue proportion of men are seriously injured and that, therefore, a continuation of intercollegiate rowing is indefensible from the health standpoint."[64]

In the meantime, the suspicion of mischief from rowing had been extended to other sports. One of the most unsettling of these was long-distance bicycle racing, a new event that seemed to require unprecedented, nearly unimaginable effort. Medical commentary on the record-seeking exploits of competitive cyclists was filled with awe. Five hundred miles in twenty-four hours, grueling hill-climbing contests, the seemingly insane six-day races: these were "competitions that have never before been dreamed of in the history of the world." This shaking of the head in wonder was a motion immediately transmitted to the physician's finger, which he vigorously wagged at those young men who were "deliberately sacrificing their future health for the sake of winning a few prizes." The sheer enormity of the work accomplished by the racing cyclist's heart—estimated by Richardson to be 200 foot tons in a twenty-four-hour competition—forced amazed doctors to *assume* the organ must be damaged; that it could escape unharmed, Richardson submitted, "is not, as it *seems* to me, within the range of possibility."[65]

The dilatation, hypertrophy, valvular disease, and functional derangement laid to cycling were not reserved for its competitive form exclusively. The bicycle was perceived as a unique sports threat, for it had proved itself so enjoyable as to inspire mass participation at high levels of exertion. The recreational cycling of many, in fact, seemed as strenuous as competitive activity in other sports. Too many wheelmen (and women!) strove to complete "century runs" (non-stop rides of 100 miles), struggled to ride against strong head winds, and pedalled up sharp grades instead of walking. And some cyclists were positively contemptuous of overstrain. The popular magazine *Wheeling*, ignoring the bicycle as a *cause* of heart disease, advocated its use for the diagnosis of *weak* heart: "The cyclist who has doubts as to the strength of his heart may easily put the matter to the test by riding up a steep hill as far as possible, and if there is any heart weakness a sharp pain will strike him in the back, between the shoulders. If the pain does not appear, the cyclist may take it that his heart is practically sound."[66]

There was little cause for wonder, then, at the frequency of reports of sudden death among riders during, or shortly after, cycling outings. The greater concern, however, remained for the chronic effects of the activity, and physicians discovering hypertrophy in devotees of the wheel were quick to diagnose "bicycle heart." Men were actually rejected from military service because they were found to be victims of the complaint![67] That such spurious disabilities were largely the inventions of overprotective physicians personally uncomfortable with athletic endeavor is suggested by the naive limits commonly set on activity. A British heart specialist, for instance, concluded his discussion of cycling as a cause of heart disease with the urgent advice that, "*On no account should the cyclist continue riding after he has commenced to feel short of breath.*"[68] A more sophisticated doctor at once objected that were that rule observed, "no athletic exercise could be practised," but his common sense wisdom was lost on many colleagues.[69]

The epidemic of bicycle heart nevertheless subsided, as the cycling craze itself faded after the late 1890s. It was replaced by the presumption of heart disease from distance running, a sport in which shortness of breath was even more prevalent. Distance running had actually been suspect as long as rowing, but it remained in the latter sport's shadows until the institution of the marathon race. That exceptional test of endurance was adopted as the finale to the Olympic Games when they were revived in 1896. The romantic recreation of the feat of the legendary Pheidippides, the soldier who in 490 B.C. supposedly ran the forty kilometers from Marathon to Athens to herald the Greek defeat of the Persians—then fell dead from exhaustion—immediately captured the fancy of the sports-minded public. The first American running of the race followed within months, the weary winner being greeted by a "crowd . . . howling itself hoarse." "Women . . . waved their handkerchiefs and fairly screamed with excitement. . . . There was a pandemonium of joy."[70]

There was also a pandemonium of medical apprehension, particularly after the Boston Athletic Association (several members of which had competed in the first Olympic marathon) instituted its annual race in 1897. As the *Journal of the American Medical Association* stated so bluntly, that heart damage must be a common result of marathoning was "unquestionable."[71] Still no attempt to actually measure the unquestionable cardiac effects of the Boston Marathon was made until its third running, in 1899. Two Tufts Medical School faculty members examined nearly all of the fourteen men who completed the course, both before and after, to determine their pulse rates, heart sizes, and heart sounds. Most were found to have hypertrophy and, after the race, murmurs, but the physicians were unperturbed. The hypertrophy they recognized as physiological, and the murmurs as temporary manifestations of cardiac fatigue. They doubted any lasting damage had been done and concluded the contest had been "far less injurious than other practices indulged in by exuberant young men." (In fact, they identified only a single casualty—a member of the ambulance corps which accompanied the runners, whose bicycle collided with a dog.)[72]

Quite similar studies were made on marathon contestants over the next three years, and similar findings recorded. A lengthy summary of these observations, published in 1903, concluded all enlargement and murmurs were physiological and that there was no evidence of permanent injury. In this instance, blistered feet comprised the most serious type of injury.[73]

There was nonetheless a definite degree of uncertainty in such interpretations. The authors of both Boston marathon investigations admitted they could not be sure the "abnormalities" they found were only the passing effects of severe exertion. There was room for subjectivity in this still nebulous realm of athletic cardiology, and doctors with less favorable opinions of exercise could draw very different, darker conclusions. Such a reaction became especially likely after 1908. The triumph of Johnnie Hayes, the first American to win the Olympic marathon, fired a national passion for the race akin to (though less intense than) the marathoning enthusiasm that followed Frank Shorter's 1972 victory. The sudden increase in the number of contestants and races, and especially the eagerness of still teenaged boys to join in this epic competition, brought significantly sharper medical attention to bear on the marathon. For many physicians, the sight was most unsettling, the cases of extreme exhaustion, delirium, and collapse triggering an emotional judgment that suffering "is testimony enough that such races menace athletes." "The death of the first marathon runner as he announced a great victory," this Jeremiah went on to decree, "should have been an object lesson for all time."[74]

More sober evaluations of marathoning, however, continued to belie such charges. The most thorough of all marathon medical surveys was conducted during the race's peak period of popularity in 1909. A team of Pittsburgh physicians headed by Watson Savage, physical

director of the Pittsburgh Athletic Association and former president
of the American Association for the Advancement of Physical Education, actually organized the Pittsburgh Marathon that year as an experimental test of the effects of extreme exertion. All fifty-five
entrants were required to submit forms detailing medical history,
physical measurements, training and eating habits, use of alcohol and
tobacco, even the weight of their running clothes. Savage and his co-
workers also performed examinations of heart size and sounds, pulse,
and blood pressure, as well as of temperature and urine, before and
after the race. The contest was run over a very hilly course, in hot
weather punctuated with heavy rain showers, and nearly half of the
entrants failed to finish. But despite the examples of extraordinary
physical depletion, Savage could find no conclusive evidence of permanent injury. He recommended prolonged training prior to attempting the distance, and advised those under twenty and over forty
to abstain from so strenuous an endeavor, but stopped well short of
describing the race as a menace. A colleague in the study published
separate articles that took a slightly dimmer view, suggesting that in
some cases pathological conditions had developed. Even he acknowledged, though, that most returned to normal more or less quickly after the competition, and would venture nothing more than "it may
be" that some would suffer permanent injury.[75]

Comparable inconclusiveness reigned in the discussion of the medical effects of running shorter races; cries of "permanent injury to the
heart" from distances in excess of one mile met retorts that cross-
country and track races were the most beneficial components of a
schoolboy's physical (and moral) education.[76] Exactly the same debate
was waged over all other popular, strenuous sports. Football, for example, was a "wolf in sheep's clothing" to some;[77] to others it was "the
'goat' of all the sports," the one automatically blamed whenever any
mishap befell a participant. "If he dies of heart disease or acute indigestion," a pro-football physician moaned, "If a player is killed in a
railroad wreck; . . . if he dies during the football season, football did
it."[78] In other instances it was basketball that did it, or even baseball![79]

The opponents of athleticism displayed, ironically, impressive endurance and competitive drive, continuing to make a contest of the
athlete's heart issue into the 1910s. Their final shot at victory came
under the leadership of Charles Stokes, surgeon general of the
United States Navy. His 1911 report on the long-term effects of athleticism on midshipmen at the Naval Academy bristled with disdain
for competition. His charge that the training required to allow a
young man to excel in sports caused degenerative physical changes

was backed by his inquiry revealing nearly a third of the Academy athletes of the past two decades to be suffering "disabilities or abnormal conditions." Fully one-quarter of the disabled were afflicted with heart ailments ranging from murmurs to dilatation. The production of "winning teams," he concluded, was not in "the best interests of the Navy."[80]

The anti-athletic forces rallied behind the surgeon general's call, but only, as it turned out, to make their last stand. Their praise of his report, though loud, lacked substance and was easily overcome by the advocates of athleticism. Some critics proposed that it was actually post-Academy ship life, with its lack of opportunity for continued athletics and its boredom that drove men to drink and venery, that was responsible for the distressing statistics. There were others who denied that the statistics were distressing, who calculated that Stokes's ex-athletes still suffered only one-third the mortality rate of all midshipmen during that same recent period, and pronounced the report "entirely devoid" of solid support for his opinions.[81] McKenzie, finally, went beyond the limited question of Naval Academy athletics and seized the Stokes controversy as an opportunity to dismantle the concept of athlete's heart from any source. "The hour has arrived," he proclaimed in 1912, "for a complete reconsideration of the whole question of exercise in relation to the heart."[82] His review of the evidence that cardiac hypertrophy and irregularities of sound and beat were variations within the normal rather than signs of pathology was buttressed by a report of his own examinations of University of Pennsylvania students, and a recitation of others' careful studies of athletic mortality. The latter included not only those analyses of specific sports discussed above, but also surveys of more diverse athletic populations. Such, for instance, was the study of William Anderson, the physician-physical educator who directed the Yale Gymnasium. Anderson determined the mortality rate for Yale participants in crew, football, baseball, and track for the half century from 1855 to 1905 and found that the man who "won the 'Y' . . . does not die young nor is heart disease a leading cause of death."[83] The weight of McKenzie's meticulously organized case was such as to force anti-athletic physicians to yield ground. They did so grudgingly, but over the course of the next quarter century, as maturing cardiology reinforced McKenzie's position, "athlete's heart" gradually became a medical curiosity.

But McKenzie's argument had not stopped at the denial of cardiac injury from sports. He had, in fact, by maintaining that "the heart needs constant and varied movement for its proper development,"[84] identified the athletic heart as the ideal. To a degree, his views were prophetic of the meaning "athletic heart" would acquire during the second half of the twentieth century. Not only would exercise be exonerated of causing heart disease, it would win increasing respect as a means of improving the heart. The "Athletic Heart Syndrome" would be redefined as a desirable condition, the athletic, hypertrophied heart extolled as "a functionally superior pump rather than a liability."[85]

Such a definition holds obvious implications for preventive medicine, and the more sanguine interpreters have envisioned a holistic future in which "society will start thinking of 'mileage' instead of 'medication,' [and] the annual physical will be replaced by a quarterly 42-km. hike." That "hike," of course, is the marathon, the ultimate test of cardiac endurance. The race had seemed unquestionably dangerous in the early 1900s, but seventy years later, as a second wave of marathon mania swept the country, the grueling training regimen required to prepare for that distance was actually presented as the surest method to achieve *immunity* to heart disease. The representatives of the American Medical Joggers Association who offered that guarantee also endorsed participation in the marathon as a program of rehabilitation for men recovering from heart attacks! Such promises and programs have struck more than a few physicians as extreme, and have been subjected to criticism, yet the revival of the controversy over athlete's heart can provide little satisfaction to the shades of the first generation of anti-athletic doctors. The fact that the question now at issue is the superiority, rather than inferiority, of that heart is a rather conclusive indication of the outcome of that first debate.[86]

Notes

1. James Irvine Lupton and James Money Lupton, *The Pedestrian's Record* (London: W. H. Allen, 1890), 56.

2. Dio Lewis, "New Gymnastics," *American Journal of Education* 11 (1862), 535.

3. Thomas Wentworth Higginson, "Gymnastics," *Atlantic Monthly* 7 (1861), 288.

4. Edward Hitchcock, "The Gymnastic Era and the Athletic Era of Our Country," *Outlook* 51 (1895), 817.

5. Bruce Haley, *The Healthy Body and Victorian Culture* (Cambridge, Mass.: Harvard University Press, 1978), 107–19, 149–57; John Lucas, "A Prelude to the Rise of Sport: Ante-bellum America, 1850–1860," *Quest* 11 (1968), 50–57.

6. John Griscom, *The Sanitary Condition of the Laboring Population of New York* (New York: Harper, 1845), 11.

7. Benjamin Ward Richardson, "Felicity as a Sanitary Research," *Asclepiad* 1 (1884), 62–90.

8. Frances White, "Hygiene as a Basis of Morals," *Popular Science Monthly* 31 (1887), 67–79. For a general discussion of sanitary reform in America, see Wilson Smillie, *Public Health. Its Promise for the Future* (New York: Macmillan, 1955), 228–68.

9. James Whorton, "The Hygiene of the Wheel: An Episode in Victorian Sanitary Science," *Bulletin of the History of Medicine* 52 (1978), 61–88.

10. Sir James Barr, "Discussion on the Medical Aspects of Athletism," *British Medical Journal* 2 (1909), 835.

11. R. Tait McKenzie, "Athletes Do Not Die Prematurely from Cardiac Diseases," *Medical Times* 40 (1912), 67.

12. Barr, "Discussion on the Medical Aspects of Athletism," 836.

13. B. W. Mitchell, "A Defense of Football," *Journal of Hygiene and Herald of Health* 45 (1895), 93.

14. Edward Cowles, "Gymnastics in the Treatment of Inebriety," *American Physical Education Review* 3 (1898), 108.

15. Barr, "Discussion on the Medical Aspects of Athletism," 835.

16. Hitchcock, "The Gymnastic Era," 817.

17. G. Frank Lydston, "Remarks on Athletics for Health," *Interstate Medical Journal* 16 (1909), 122. Also see Lydston, "Briefs on Physical Training," *American Medicine* 5 (1903), 300–2, 342–44, 383–85, 418–21, 463–66, for a perfect illustration of medical ambivalence towards exercise—his discussion begins with a call to give physical training an important position in both preventive and curative medicine, but eventually denounces competition as an expression of the "innate savagery of man . . . the instinctive cry of the human animal for a 'kill' of some kind" (p. 385).

18. Clement Dukes, "Discussion on the Medical Aspects of Athletism," *British Medical Journal* 2 (1909), 382. Also see "The Premature Deaths of Athletes," *American Medicine* 13 (1907), 135–36.

19. Robert Coughlin, "The Athletic Life in Its Relation to Degenerative Changes in the Cardiovascular System," *Medical Record* 77 (1910), 576.

20. Woods Hutchinson, *Instinct and Health* (New York: Dodd, Mead, 1909), 91.

21. "The Dangers of Athletic Training," *American Medicine* 13 (1907), 500.

22. Ibid., 500.

23. W. E. McVey, "The Effects of Modern College Athletics on the Heart," *Journal of the Kansas Medical Society* 10 (1910), 179.

24. "The Dangers of Athletic Training," 500–501.

25. Robert Coughlin, "Deaths of Athletes and Fatalities in Athletic Games during the Year," *Medical Record* 69 (1906), 870–73; Hutchinson, *Instinct and Health,* 90–91.

26. Lydston, "Briefs," 384; "The University Boat Races," *Lancet* 2 (1867), 454–55; Eugene Darling, "The Effects of Training," *Boston Medical and Surgical Journal* 141 (1899), 205–9, 229–31; Nathaniel Potter and James Harrington, "Medical Supervision of Athletics among Boys at Boarding School," *Journal of the American Medical Association* 53 (1909), 1957–60; W. Collier, "Functional Albuminuria in Athletes," *British Medical Journal* 1 (1907), 4–6.

27. Edward Beall, quoted by Robert Coughlin, "The Use and Abuse of Athletics," *Medical Record* 60 (1904), 485.

28. Coughlin, ibid., 485.

29. "The Dangers in Competitive College Athletics," *Journal of the American Medical Association* 40 (1903), 993.

30. Coughlin, "Use and Abuse," 485.

31. Robert Coughlin, "The Medical Aspects of Athletics," *Medical Record* 86 (1914), 247.

32. R. Tait McKenzie, "Relation of Athletics to Longevity," *Medical Examiner and Practitioner* 16 (1906), 195.

33. Alfred Stengel, "A Review of the History of Cardiac Pathology, with Especial Reference to Modern Conceptions of Myocardial Disease," *Philadelphia Medical Journal* 6 (1900), 698–706.

34. "Increase in Deaths from Heart Disease," *Boston Medical and Surgical Journal* 163 (1910), 702.

35. Leopold Shumacker and William Middleton, "The Cardiac Effects of Immoderate College Athletics," *Journal of the American Medical Association* 62 (1914), 1142.

36. W. V. R. Viewig, "Left Ventricular Hypertrophy in an Athletic Family; a Variant of the Athletic Heart Syndrome," *Journal of Sports Medicine and Physical Fitness* 15 (1975), 132–37; R. J. Shepard, *The Fit Athlete* (Oxford: Oxford University Press, 1978), 170; Ernst Jokl, *Heart and Sport* (Springfield, Ill.: Thomas, 1964), 104–5; Joseph Wolffe, "The Heart of the Athlete," *Journal of Sports Medicine and Physical Fitness* 2 (1962), 20–22.

37. McKenzie, "Relation of Athletics to Longevity," 199.

38. Benjamin Ward Richardson, *Diseases of Modern Life* (New York: Bermingham, 1882), 105.

39. For descriptions of standard techniques of examination of the heart in use at the time, see Robert Babcock, *Diseases of the Heart and Arterial System* (New York: Appleton, 1903), 1–36; and Arthur Hirschfelder, *Diseases of the Heart and Aorta* (Philadelphia: Lippincott, 1910), 92–96.

40. Babcock, *Diseases of the Heart*, 577.

41. William Broadbent, *Heart Disease and Aneurysm of the Aorta*, 4th ed. (New York: Wood, 1906), 273, 286–87.

42. Thomas Lewis, *The Soldier's Heart and the Effort Syndrome*, 2nd ed. (London: Shaw, 1940), 20–21; Charles Hammett, "Middle and Distance Running," *Popular Science Monthly* 77 (1910), 28–41.

43. J. M. DaCosta, "On Irritable Heart," *American Journal of the Medical Sciences* 61 (1871), 17–52.

44. Review of J. M. DaCosta, *On Strain and Over-action of the Heart,* in *American Journal of the Medical Sciences* 68 (1874), 505.

45. The most thorough treatment of the effort syndrome is Lewis, *The Soldier's Heart;* also see S. Calvin Smith, *Heart Affections. Their Recognition and Treatment* (Philadelphia: Davis, 1922), 352–59, and Paul Dudley White, *Heart Disease* (New York: Macmillan, 1931), 426–43.

46. "The Dangers in Competitive College Athletics," 992; George Herschell, "On Bicycling as a Cause of Heart Disease," *Lancet* 1 1895, 540–42; Lydston, "Briefs," 385.

47. C. H. Melville, "The Physiological Effects of Exercise," *Journal of the Royal Sanitary Institute* 33 (1912–13), 376–77.

48. Coughlin, *Heart Disease,* 577; Broadbent, 283–84.

49. Illinois president quoted by G. Frank Lydston, "The Effects of Athletics on Health," *New York Medical Journal* 82 (1905), 340.

50. Coughlin, "The Athletic Life," 577.

51. Ibid., 578.

52. Ibid., 577; Alfred Stengel, "The Immediate and Remote Effects of Athletics upon the Heart and Circulation," *American Journal of the Medical Sciences* 118 (1899), 544–53.

53. Coughlin, "The Athletic Life," 576.

54. Fisher quoted by Christine Whittaker, "Chasing the Cure: Irving Fisher's Experience as a Tuberculosis Patient," *Bulletin of the History of Medicine* 48 (1974), 400.

55. Watson Savage, "Exercise in the Treatment of Neurasthenia," *Journal of Advanced Therapeutics* 27 (1909), 520. Also see C. O. Carlstrom, "The Treatment of Heart Disease by Therapeutic Gymnastics," *American Physical Education Review* 15 (1910), 508–14.

56. William Wood, "The Hygiene of Athletic Sports," *Lancet* 2 (1867), 517.

57. F. C. Skey, letter to London *Times,* Oct. 10, 1867, p. 9. Also see "The University Boat Races" *Lancet* 2 (1867), 454–55.

58. London *Times,* Oct. 14, 1867, p. 10.

59. Ibid., Oct. 15, 1867, p. 6.

60. John Edward Morgan, *University Oars* (London: Macmillan, 1873), xv–xvi.

61. Ibid., 10–11, 20–29, 44, 61, 63–68.

62. E. H. Bradford, "Health of Rowing Men," *The Sanitarian* 5 (1877), 529–36.

63. George Meylan, "Harvard University Oarsmen," *American Physical Education Review* 9 (1904), 362–76, 543–52.

64. Minutes of University of Wisconsin medical faculty meeting, June 12, 1914 (I am indebted to Professor Ronald Numbers, Department of History of Medicine, University of Wisconsin, for bringing this document to my attention). Also see Shumacker and Middleton, "Cardiac Effects."

65. Benjamin Ward Richardson, "Cycling and Heart Disease," *Medical Society Transactions* 18 (1895), 98–99 (italics mine). Also see Herschell, "On

Bicycling," and E. B. Turner, "A Report on Cycling in Health and Disease," *British Medical Journal* 1 (1896), 98–99.

66. *Wheeling* quoted in "The Cycle as an Instrument of Diagnosis," *Boston Medical and Surgical Journal* 141 (1899), 458.

67. "The Heart, the Bicycle, and the Cigarette," *Medical Record* 54 (1898), 274; "Bicycle Heart," *British Medical Journal* 1 (1898), 908.

68. Herschell, "On Bicycling," 542.

69. W. J. Turrell, "Cycling as a Cause of Heart Disease," *Lancet* 1 (1895), 711.

70. John Lucas, "A History of the Marathon Race—490 B.C. to 1975," *Journal of Sport History* 3 (1976), 131.

71. "The Dangers in Competitive College Athletics," 992.

72. Harold Williams and Horace Arnold, "The Effects of Violent and Prolonged Muscular Exercise upon the Heart," *Philadelphia Medical Journal* 3 (1899), 1233–39.

73. J. B. Blake and R. C. Larrabee (eds.), "Observations upon Long-Distance Runners," *Boston Medical and Surgical Journal* 148 (1903), 195–206.

74. Coughlin, "The Athletic Life," 576, 578. Others condemned the marathon as the single greatest cause of cardiac dilatation (e.g., McVey,"The Effects of Modern College Athletics").

75. Watson Savage et al., "Physiological and Pathological Effects of Severe Exertion (The Marathon Race)," *American Physical Education Review* 15 (1910), 651–61; ibid. 16 (1911), 1–11, 144–50; Joseph Barach et al., "Physiological and Pathological Effects of Severe Exertion (The Marathon Race)," *American Physical Education Review* 16 (1911), 200–5, 262–68, 325–34; ibid., "Physiological and Pathological Effects of Severe Exertion (The Marathon Race) on the Circulatory and Renal Systems," *Archives of Internal Medicine* 5 (1910), 382–405.

76. Lauder Brunton et al., letter to *Lancet* 1 (1909), 441; "Schoolboys and Long Races," *Lancet* 1 (1909), 433; Adolphe Abrahams, "Athletics and the Medical Man," *Practitioner* 86 (1911), 429–46; Hammett 28–41; Potter and Harrington, 1957–60.

77. "Athletic Sports," *Boston Medical and Surgical Journal* 96 (1877), 57.

78. A. H. Sharpe, "Foot Ball Safe for Physically Qualified Men," *Medical Times* 40 (1912), 35.

79. Albert Stern, "Wholesome versus Unwholesome Exercise," *Mind and Body* 17 (1910–11), 243–46; Nathan Allen, "College Sports," *Sanitarian* 3 (1875), 241–47.

80. Stokes's report quoted in "The Effects of Athletics on Young Men," *Medical Times* 40 (1912), 32.

81. For pro-Stokes commentary, see W. L. Estes, "A Radical Change Needed," *Medical Times* 40 (1912), 35–36; George Dearborn, "Athletics and Life," *Boston Medical and Surgical Journal* 168 (1913), 406–7; Charles Young, "The After Effects of Athletic Training," *American Physical Education Review* 19 (1914), 27–30; "Effects of Strenuous Athletics in the Navy," *Journal of the*

American Medical Association 58 (1912), 40–41; "Athletics in the Navy," *Medical Record* 81 (1912), 421–22. The cited criticisms of Stokes are Richard Newton, "After-Effects of Athletics," *Journal of the American Medical Association* 58 (1912), 955; and George Meylan, "The Effects of Athletics in After Life," *Medical Times* 40 (1912), 63–64.

82. R. Tait McKenzie, "The Influence of Exercise on the Heart," *American Journal of the Medical Sciences* 145 (1912), 69–74.

83. William Anderson, "Some Observations on Mortality among Yale Students," *Medical Times* 40 (1912), 32–34. Also idem, "Further Studies in the Longevity of Yale Athletes," *Mind and Body* 23 (1916–17), 374–83.

84. McKenzie, "Influence of Exercise," 74.

85. William Kannel, "Medical Evaluation for Physical Exercise Programs," in Robert Morse, ed., *Exercise and the Heart* (Springfield, Ill.: Thomas, 1972), 82.

86. Thomas Bassler and Frank Cardello, "Jogging and Health," *Journal of the American Medical Association* 231 (1975), 23. Also, Bassler, "Marathon Running and Immunity to Heart Disease," *The Physician and Sportsmedicine* 3 (Apr., 1975), 77–80; Bassler and Jack Scaff, "Marathon Running after Myocardial Infarction," *Journal of the American Medical Association* 229 (1974), 1602–5; editor's note to Bassler, "Physician Deaths," *Journal of the American Medical Association* 223 (1973), 1391; "You Can Run Down Running, But . . . Bikers Are Hit by Cars and Swimmers Drown," *Physician and Sportsmedicine* 3 (Apr., 1975), 81–98.

4 *Roberta J. Park*

Physiologists, Physicians, and Physical Educators: Nineteenth-Century Biology and Exercise, *Hygienic* and *Educative*

In 1893, Francis Amasa Walker (Harvard, LL.D., 1883, and signatory to the call for the 1889 Boston Conference on Physical Training), president of the Massachusetts Institute of Technology, delivered Harvard's Phi Beta Kappa address. The subject was "College Athletics." Three months later the full text of Walker's remarks appeared in the *Harvard Graduates Magazine*.[1] The decision to open the second volume of the new publication with a discussion devoted to athletics—and gymnastics—might have been the idiosyncratic choice of the editor. More likely, however, it was prompted by the intense interest that arose after the Civil War in matters pertaining to health (both personal and public), calisthenics, gymnastics, physical training, out-of-door pursuits, and competitive athletics.

As several sport and social historians have shown, Americans of a wide variety of persuasions expressed a remarkable interest in athletics and "physical education" in the four decades between 1865 and 1906.[2] By 1890, this had found expression in the emergence of "varsity" sports, athletic clubs, country clubs, and the formation of the Amateur Athletic Union. It was also reflected in a spate of books, pamphlets, essays, and articles of a general and a specialized nature on athletics, gymnastics, and physical training. The interest was further expressed in the formation of college and high school physical education programs and various organizations (e.g., American Social Science Association and the Playground Association of America) that devoted at least a portion of their attention to promoting health and development through exercise regimens, gymnastics, play, athletics, and physical education. A professional organization specifically devoted to such matters—the present American Alliance for Health,

Physical Education, Recreation and Dance—held its inaugural meeting on November 27, 1885. The goals of the American Association for the Advancement of Physical Education, as stated in its revised constitution of 1895, were: ". . . to awaken a wider and more intelligent interest in Physical Education; to acquire and disseminate knowledge concerning it; and to labor for the improvement and extension of gymnastics, games, and athletic pastimes in the education of children and youth."[3]

In the minds of many who were associated with the newly emerging field of physical education through their work in schools and colleges, summer courses, Chautauquas, and the like—as well as those who sought to influence and educate their contemporaries by means of the printed word—the goals of physical training, and athletics as well, were: *hygienic* and *educative*.

Speaking in 1894 before the Boston Society for Medical Improvement, W. M. Conant, M.D., instructor in anatomy at the Harvard Medical School and out-patient surgeon at Massachusetts General Hospital, declared: "Exercise . . . has for its aims the promotion of health and the acquisition of correct habits of action. The first is hygienic; the second is educational. . . . The principles of all forms of physical training, however various, are based upon the power of the nervous system to receive impressions and to note them or their effects." Drawing upon the writings of the English physiologist Michael Foster, from Herbert Spencer's *Law of Evolution*, and from Edward M. Hartwell, M.D. (president of the A.A.A.P.E., 1891–91 and 1885–99), Conant upheld the worth of gymnastics, as well as baseball, football, rowing, tennis, track, cricket, and other sports—provided these were not carried to excess.[4]

The first goal—*hygienic*—was especially concerned with bodily health, hygiene, and "fitness" of the muscular, circulatory, digestive, and excretory functions. It was strongly influenced by antebellum health reform movements but drew also from newer discoveries in the biological sciences—especially the physiology of the circulatory, respiratory, and digestive systems. The second—*educative*—emphasized "development,"—a vaguely and variously used term that meant, among other things, the ways in which the organism grew, how "character" was formed, and the way in which the human species had evolved. Here discussions drew heavily upon pre–Civil War millenarian ideologies and older notions of the nature of "the will" as well as selected aspects of nineteenth-century biological science, especially the physiology of the nervous system. Newer concepts of the nervous system and the brain, derived from laboratory experiments of researchers like Helmholtz, DuBois-Reymond, Bain, and Ferrier, were frequently merged with older conceptions of "mind" and "will," resulting in differing, and at times contradictory, notions of man's essential nature. After the 1859 publication of Darwin's *On the Origin of Species*, they also drew increasingly from evolutionary theories—both biological and social.[5]

The belief that exercise can effect mental and moral development, as well as physical health, has a long, if uneven, history. Hippocrates held that, without health, wisdom could not be fully achieved. For the "Socratics, health of the body [was] an aid to, and condition for, the right life of the soul."[6] In the nineteenth century, health of the body in relation to proper moral development of the individual—and, by extension, to the improvement of society—received intense and sustained attention, especially in English-speaking countries. One of the reasons for this was improved technology which made possible a number of advances in medicine, sanitation, and science. Another was the renewed attention given to the body by discoveries in the biological sciences. The prominence of beliefs about man's unique place in Nature, Divine Providence, and "will" in English-speaking cultures, L. S. Jacyna has suggested, fostered a particular interest in the "nervous system."[7] As the century progressed, a belief that muscular action undertaken in physical education or athletics could contribute to strengthening humanity's *moral* qualities received increasing attention in both Britain and the United States.

Shortly after the *Harvard Graduates Magazine* published Walker's commentary on college athletics, it also printed Charles William Eliot's 1892–93 annual Harvard President's Report. By 1893, Eliot had become convinced that American intercollegiate athletics were inimical to both the physical health and the moral development of young men. An inordinate desire to win and the attendant evils of commercialism, "coarse publicity," and "hysterical excitement," he insisted, had turned potentially healthy and beneficial activities into an aberration—a blight on the colleges. The intense excitement drained the "nervous energy" of athletes and the brutality of the contests (football was the chief culprit) blunted the sensibilities of players and spectators alike. For the remainder of his career, Harvard's president would remain an implacable foe of what he considered to be corrupted forms of athletics.[8]

As the twentieth century approached, American views regarding athletics ranged along a continuum from those of Eliot to those of men like Paul Dashiell, former multi-sport athlete at The Johns Hopkins University, football coach at the U.S. Naval Academy, and referee

at the 1905 Harvard-Yale game. It was Dashiell's *alleged* unwillingness—or inability—to prevent repeated slugging and other transgres-
sions that prompted an inquiry from U.S. President Theodore
Roosevelt. A lengthy response from Dashiell, which attempted to explain the action in the 1905 contest, added fuel to an already smol-
dering debate over college athletics. Even further removed from the
views of Eliot were those of men like J. W. Spalding (of A. G. Spalding
and Co.), who wrote to Walter Camp in 1895 urging the Yale coach to
publicly suggest changes in the football rules. Anything that would
stem the current criticisms that threatened football, Spalding stated,
"would be hailed with delight by every lover of the game as well as
those interested in its success financially."[9]

Walker shared the views of Harvard's president regarding commercialism and excess, finding "evil" any form of "athletic competition and contest which injuriously affect[ed] the constitution and
permanently impair[ed] the vital force." However, he rejected Eliot's
extreme position, holding that the benefits of athletics usually
were far greater than the defects. Athletics developed strength,
swiftness, ". . . courage, steadiness of nerve . . . resourcefulness, self-
knowledge, self-reliance . . . the ability to work with others . . . [and]
readiness to subordinate selfish impulses, personal desires, and individual credit to a common end."[10] These and comparable words were
used so frequently in connection with male athletics that they became
a veritable litany. Norman Bingham's *Book of Athletics and Out-of-Door
Sports* (1895), for example, discussed: "sand"—the "steady pegging
away in the face of all discouragements." Significantly, Bingham
placed the effects of athletics on the *disposition* ahead of the "physical
good which comes from regular exercise." The 1893 history of *Dartmouth Athletics* noted "the increased attention given of late to the physical side of man's development," and cited the positive effects of
"stronger physiques" on the nerves of the present and future generations. Readers of Walter Camp and Lorin Deland's *Football* (1896)
were assured: "Great as are the physical benefits to the football player,
there are advantages of a mental or ethical nature which outweigh
them." Football developed physical and moral courage, vigorous
manhood, self-control, discipline, and "power of the will." These were
the qualities needed by both the *soldier* and "the successful man in any
of the affairs of life."[11]

Such ideal attributes appear remarkably similar to those that such
British public school masters as Almond, Welldon, Cotton, and
Warre sought to inculcate in boys who would become both proper
"Christian gentlemen" and future custodians of the Empire.[12] While

Americans did not have an empire to defend and extend, they did have a nation to build. The Western frontier of the continental United States may have closed in 1890, as the Bureau of the Census and Frederick Jackson Turner claimed, but for those of expansionist persuasions there were "new frontiers in the Indies and in the Far Pacific." These impulses would become more evident after "the Splendid Little" Spanish-American War of 1898. For men like Theodore Roosevelt, self-reliance, strength, courage, and "sand" were precisely the qualities needed by those men who were to ensure the fulfillment of the nation's quest for greatness and world leadership. Roosevelt repeatedly upheld the merits of out-of-door pursuits and athletics in the formation of bodily strength and manly virtue, holding that the character of a man and "national greatness" both owed much to vigorous physical activity.[13]

Americans had originally derived both the forms of their games and at least the broad outlines of the values to be associated with them from English sources. By the 1890s, however, few Americans looked back across the Atlantic for their inspiration in sports or in anything else. Proud of their own heritage—and increasingly certain of the power of their young nation—Americans shaped athletics with their own values and to their own purposes. Their ascendancy over British athletes was evident in 1895 when the New York Athletic Club was victorious over the London Athletic Club. The *Quarterly Review* in 1904 expressed alarm that Rhodes scholars were bringing "professionalism" to British university sport; and in 1905, the stewards at Henley decided to instruct American crews to leave their "salaried" coaches at home. Walker's 1893 statement had included a hint of the changes to more "pragmatic" Yankee values when he declared that, among other things, athletic participation developed qualities that were "useful in any profession."[14]

As Anthony Rotundo, Peter Stearns, and others have shown, American middle-class attitudes regarding what defined ideal male qualities and behavior changed during the nineteenth century. By the 1870s, the earlier concept of "inner-strength"—which usually meant self-possession and a balance not "easily disturbed by outward events"—had given way to that of the "self-made" man. *Action* was the watchword of the new ideal.[15] The "self-made" man had shaped himself by acting upon the material world and tested himself in the crucible of competition. Perhaps nowhere were the changes more graphically conveyed than in athletic games where the body in *action* was (and is) spectacularly displayed. (A similar vigorous ideal was also embodied in the icon of the frontiersman, cowboy, and the cavalryman, also popular and powerful expressions of mid- to late-nineteenth century American ideals of maleness.)

Summarizing "The Status of Athletics in American Colleges" for the *Atlantic Monthly* in 1890, Albert Bushnell Hart proclaimed that the sporting element was fast disappearing: "The participants find both practice and match hard, unremitting work."[16] This transformation of "play" into work in the last decades of the century has been noted by Daniel T. Rodgers and others: "There was no missing the gospel of play, reiterated as it was in a thousand sandlot base-ball games and in the frenzied enthusiasms of college football."[17] The gospel of strenuous activity that transformed "colleges into theaters of organized physical combat . . . ," John Higham con-tends, reflected ". . . the dynamism that characterized the whole political and social scene from the turn of the century through World War I."[18]

For those who stressed *hygienic* and *educative* goals, the new gospel of strenuous activity meant something special which partook of, but also differed from, the glorified accounts of athletics that appeared in the popular press and sporting journals. They, too, stressed vigor and activity, but usually within certain well-defined limits and directed to-ward specific goals. A large corps of "experts" would be needed to achieve the desired ends, to plan and direct exercise and athletic pro-grams that placed health and physical and moral development above contest victory. A "new profession" devoted to the study and care of the body—and aimed at perfection of both the individual *and* the race—was to be intrusted with this important goal. That profession, as Luther Halsey Gulick told the A.A.A.P.E. in 1890, was physical education.[19]

The precipitous rise of athletic sports after the Civil War, as Walker asserted, had "carried all before it: Honors in football, in baseball, and in rowing have come to be esteemed of equal value with honors in the classics, in philosophy, or in mathematics." The earlier ideal of the pale, religious, intellectual young man with "towering forehead, from which the hair was carefully brushed backwards and upwards to give the full effect to his remarkable phrenological development" had been replaced by one of vigor and vitality. Now "mass" and "power" in a nation—and in a man—were the things to be admired. The Civil War had provided a new awareness of America's strength and the physical and moral courage of her young men. It was the role of ath-letics to perpetuate in peace what had been forged in battle. Camp and Deland agreed. The "best fighters" in the war had displayed the precise qualities that were needed by a football player, and vice versa.

Yet Walker was slightly anxious about the new cult of strenuous physical prowess, holding that when "the severer forms of athletic competition and contest . . . impair[ed] the vital force," their influence was evil.[20]

Athletics, Physical Culture, and "Modern Biology"

Although much of his Phi Beta Kappa address was substantially a paean to men who had endured the sectional strife, and to those who would become the nation's leaders, Walker included in his remarks another topic: modern *biology* and its relationship to athletics and physical culture. Whereas a "bad physiology, or the absence of anything that could be called physiology" before the Civil War had resulted in devaluation of "physical force, dexterity, and endurance, capacity for action, nerve, and will power," recent developments had cast athletics and physical training in a new light. Modern biology, Walker maintained, had fostered the introduction of gymnastics and physical training into the colleges, with courses in hygiene and human physiology and the appointment of medical doctors to direct gymnasia and organize departments of physical education. It had also helped to legitimize athletics as an appropriate educational investment.[21]

Although it was not usual for late nineteenth-century commentators to make such a direct connection between biology and athletics, this conjunction was frequently made by those who sought to advance the cause of "physical education" and what they considered to be "educational" forms of play and games.[22] What was implied in more general discussions was usually more directly enunciated in pedagogical statements. The *New England Journal of Education,* founded in 1875 by a merger of the *Massachusetts Teacher, Rhode Island Schoolmaster, Connecticut School Journal, College Courant,* and *Maine Journal of Education,* devoted substantial attention to physical education, exercise, athletics, physiology, hygiene, and play. In 1875 G. B. Emerson urged teachers to pay more attention to the training "of all the senses and faculties of the body" and recommended they read Dr. J. C. Dalton's *Physiology and Hygiene.* The author of an accompanying article on exercise urged two hours of activity a day to maintain "the natural force of the muscular system. . . ." The following week readers were told of the moral and physical benefits that the English derived from school sports. In October a lengthy article linked physically active games with the development of "intellectual and moral motives. . . ."[23]

Two decades later, T. M. Balliet, superintendent of the Springfield, Massachusetts schools and member of the A.A.A.P.E., conveyed the sense that a scientific understanding of the ways in which muscular exercise affected moral development could be achieved, even though direct *experimental* evidence for such a statement was lacking:

> Brain cells grow, like other parts of the body, by exercise. The sensory cells . . . can be exercised only by the use of the senses. In like manner the motor cells can be exercised and developed only by making them contract the muscles. Muscular exercise, either in the form of play, gymnastics, or manual training, is therefore absolutely essential for the healthy growth of the brain as a physical organ. Motor education, by developing the motor parts of the brain, develops energy and force of character. It develops pluck and courage. Competitive games are particularly valuable in this respect. It would be difficult to estimate how much cricket has done for the Englishman.[24]

Arguments that linked muscular contractions with functional development of the nervous system, "growth of the brain," strength of mind, "will," and character rested largely upon reasoning by analogy and were embraced by many contemporary social reformers, educators, physicians, theologians, and even physiologists. The power and perseverance of these assumptions need to be seen against the broader background of biology, and especially physiology, in the nineteenth century.

In 1897 a series of articles in *Harper's New Monthly Magazine* outlined recent discoveries that had altered traditional beliefs regarding the human body. Ether and chloroform had made surgery bearable; Pasteur had discovered anaerobic bacteria; the nature of "contagion" had been exposed; Lister's "antiseptic principle" had opened the way to safer surgery. By the 1840s, the improved microscope had given physiologists a powerful instrument for opening new lines of investigation. Schwann, Virchow, and other members of the German scientific community had fixed the nucleated cell as the fundamental organization of organic matter. The function of the red corpuscles in carrying oxygen to the cells had been established, and it had been determined that the muscles burned fuel and transformed energy. The glycogenic (carbohydrate) function of the liver had been experimentally demonstrated by Claude Bernard, and by the end of the century the general role of the glands in metabolic change was known. The third article in the series, "The Century's Progress in Experimental Psychology," gave particular attention to the work of the "nerve physiologists" (e.g., Magendie, Helmholtz, DuBois-Reymond, Wundt).[25]

The Example of "the Blacksmith's Arm"

Historians of science have suggested that the nervous system dominated nineteenth-century thought in much the same way that the heart and circulation had dominated the seventeenth. Early in the century Sir Charles Bell discovered that the anterior roots of the spinal nerves conveyed motor impulses while the posterior roots conveyed sensory impulses. Further investigations found the same divisions in the cranial nerves. Marshall Hall observed the reflex action in 1832. By mid-century the essentials of the nerve tract, with one terminal in a cell of the brain or spinal cord and the other in the muscle or skin, had been determined. Work on the nervous system had an important bearing on questions dealing with the mind—and "will"—and with attitudes toward physical training and athletics.[26]

Arguments based upon a belief that the works of an all-wise God were manifest in the indissoluble joining of form and function had occupied a dominant role in eighteenth-century thought. The power of this belief persisted well into the following century, even in the face of the continuing discoveries of science and medicine. As Karl Figlio has maintained, nineteenth-century physiological investigation initially "focused on the nervous system as the bridge between philosophical/psychological inquiry into the soul and nature of man . . . and the anatomical/physiological study of . . . structure and function. . . ." The requirement that bodily structure and organic action receive equal consideration flowed from the assumption that such harmony was set down by divine design.[27] In *Animal Mechanics: or Proofs of Design in the Animal Frame*, a small work prepared in 1823 for the Society for the Diffusion of Useful Knowledge, Sir Charles Bell had stated that the *structure* of the bones, joints, and muscles confirmed that man was intended to "walk, run, leap, and swim," and that "this apparatus is preserved perfect by exercise." While he spoke approvingly of these types of exercises, Bell had little use for calisthenics and gymnastics as they placed unnatural demands on the body.[28]

In 1834, Andrew Combe, an Edinburgh physician trained in both his native city and at Paris, referred to Bell's recent work (as well as that of Cuvier, Bichat, and Gall) in *The Principles of Physiology Applied to the Preservation of Health, and to the Improvement of Physical and Mental Education*. Written for the benefit of the intelligent layman, this useful little work had gone to a sixteenth American printing by 1854. Combe was too well schooled in anatomy and physiology to contend that brain and "mind" were the same thing; however, because they were closely associated in life, he held that whatever would strengthen one would strengthen the other. Combe made numerous recommendations in support of exercise, and deemed "active sports" superior to "mere measured movements" such as walking or routine calisthenics—the reason being that the more active and social nature of sport brought the "nervous impulse" into fuller and more harmonious operation.[29]

Combe's *Principles of Physiology* was brought to the attention of American readers in the November 1834 issue of the *American Annals of Education*. In introducing his review, editor William Woodbridge declared: "It is more than four years since we began . . . to press the subject of Physical Education upon the community; to urge them to consider the mutual connection and dependence of mind and body. . . ." The subject of "physical education" had been introduced in the first issue in 1826 by the original editor William Russel, who urged schools to institute programs of "healthful exercise and innocent recreation . . . [to meliorate] the condition of our race." The development of the corporeal system and the improvement of health, Russel and his successors repeatedly insisted, were fundamental to achieving mental and moral power.[30] The *Journal of Health*, established in 1829 by a group of Philadelphia physicians, likewise specified that the topics that were to receive attention were: "Air, food, exercise, the reciprocal operation of mind and body . . . [and] the physical education of children."[31]

The "argument from design" had postulated intimate connections and harmony between the body and the "mind" or "will"; however, just what the nature of these was remained obscure. John Jeffries, a Boston physician, wrote for the 1833 *American Quarterly Review:* "The powers of the body should be cultivated, because of its connection with the mind." Although the Creator had not seen fit to reveal to man the mechanisms by which this connection was made, Jeffries held that the "union of the body and the soul . . . [was] clearly seen in the mutual action of mind and matter." The strength of the blacksmith's arm confirmed this fact, as did "the strength and swiftness of the athlete and the prodigious feats of the gymnasium."[32] The example of the "blacksmith's arm" would be repeatedly set forth throughout the century to uphold the assumption that strengthening the muscular system would strengthen the "will." Likewise, a belief that the strength and swiftness of the athlete and the "feats of the gymnasium" were instrumental in developing proper *moral* character underscored the majority of arguments that were advanced in support of *educational* athletics and physical *education* in the second half of the century.

Healthy Bodies, Wholesome Minds, and Prosperous Societies

As Harvey Green and James Whorton have shown in their studies of American health and fitness movements—and Bruce Haley has shown for Victorian Britain—exercise, "physical education," and sports were often advocated as alternatives to the standard ministrations and pharmacopeia of "heroic" physicians.[33] Americans certainly suffered from a host of illnesses and disabilities for which there were few medical cures before the end of the nineteenth century; there was, in fact, often little that could be done about many conditions. Technologies were not advanced and most doctors were poorly prepared in comparison to those standards that would apply after the Flexner Report of 1910. Until the turn of the century, many of the best American physicians had studied abroad at Edinburgh, London, Paris, Berlin, or Vienna. It was this backward and uncontrolled state of medical education that led to the reorganization of the A.M.A. and to the licensing reforms of the early twentieth century.[34]

Physical activity offered one way in which digestive, respiratory, circulatory, and even reproductive complaints might be alleviated—or so many believed. At the very least, calisthenics, games, and outdoor exercises were not likely to induce the same violent results that might ensue from blood-letting or the ingestion of mercury compounds, laudanum (tincture of opium), or other widely used chemical preparations. Calisthenics, simple games, and out-of-door pursuits, therefore, *could* have positive hygienic value. The potential value attributed to such activities was not solely *hygienic*, however; they could also be *educative*. The possibility existed that calisthenics, gymnastics, simple exercise, and even athletic games could strengthen the "will," or so it was believed. In their advocation of bodily exercise for developmental reasons, supporters continued to uphold and extend those assumptions that saw personal hygiene as the necessary foundation for human progress.[35]

According to the physiology of the first six decades of the century, the brain—the "sensorium"—was the organ by which the immaterial mind received sensations and issued the volitions that resulted in bodily movements.[36] In 1839, William B. Carpenter, M.D., F.R.S., and examiner in physiology and comparative anatomy at the University of London, had published *Principles of Physiology, General and Comparative.* The 1854 fourth edition appeared as two massive volumes. In the first, *Principles of Comparative Physiology,* Carpenter addressed the subject of the nervous system and the "will" in members of the animal kingdom, adhering to the notion of the hierarchy of functions. "The successively more complex nervous actions of animals . . . ," he held, "were developments from a primitive functional type." In the case of humans, however, a *discontinuity* in the development of the nervous system had occurred. In humans, the cerebrum was "the instrument of the 'will' and not an organ of reflex action." For Carpenter, the cerebral hemispheres were not only *ganglia*—they were "also agents by which an immaterial principle exerted its Will in the world." The diagram on page 707 of the 1854 edition aptly conveys this conception. Over and controlling the operations of the spinal cord, sensory ganglia, and cerebrum is the "will," which operates "in producing or checking muscular movement, or in controlling or directing the current of thought." Operationally and hierarchically the "will" governed all actions. Carpenter retained this separation of mind and motor-function throughout all the editions of *Principles of Physiology*— the standard English text—and other writings "up to and *including* his review of the experiments of David Ferrier which decisively disproved it."[37]

The living body, however, is a complex mechanism that cannot be fully, or perhaps even adequately, explained by the direct application of the findings of experimental laboratory science. As numerous scholars have shown, conceptions of the body are always grounded in broader social and cultural contexts and often are expressed metaphorically. The anthropologist Mary Douglas maintains that there are deep and persistent pressures to create consonance between the social and physiological levels of experience, and that because consonance can be so satisfying, it is to be found "in layer after layer of experience, and in context after context."[38]

In a study of eighteenth-century conceptions of health, disease, and medical care, W. F. Bynum has stated: "models of physiological function may embody attitudes to children and the aged, to men and women, class and race, refinement and civilization, and to existing and desired social systems." Sally Shuttleworth has shown how Victorian psychological and physiological theory influenced the British author George Eliot's understanding and depiction of contemporary society, and Bruce Haley's excellent study of Victorian health illustrates the pervasiveness of the body metaphor in British thought and institutions. Sharon Cameron has analyzed symbolic representations of the body in the novels of Herman Melville and Nathaniel Hawthorne, concluding that these nineteenth-century American works are preoccupied with identity in corporeal terms.[39] The average person, professionals, physicians, and also scientists use body metaphors in an attempt to understand, explain, and communicate not only physiological functions, but customs, roles, status, fears, aspirations, perceived relationships to nature and to the cosmos, and much more.

Metaphorical thought has influenced the thinking of biologists, in spite of the tendency of scientists to reject analogy and metaphor as "smack[ing] of rhetoric rather than of sober and factual description of things."[40] The noted physiologist Rudolph Virchow, for example, drew upon social theories of the German state in the mid-1800s to explain the nature and function of the "cell." L. S. Jacyna has examined how a "natural" dimension in social and political discourse in Victorian Britain influenced physiological psychology. He finds that as the century progressed the "laws of nature" increasingly supplied the type of social restraints that "the will of God had once provided."[41]

In novels, health guides, and a host of other sources, Americans at mid-century were repeatedly reminded by words and pictures that they had innumerable bodily deficiencies and that they constantly teetered on the brink of physical disaster. Dr. W. W. Hall's *Guide-Board to Health, Peace, and Competence* proclaimed: "It is hard enough to get along in this world when a man is well; but to have to make a living under the depressing influence of sickness, and pain, and suffering, is worse than having to climb a steep clay bank in wet weather." In 1867, what purported to be the Hundredth Edition of *Gunn's New Family Physician or Home Book of Health* (to which an entire section on calisthenics had been added) informed readers: "The faculties with which our Creator has endowed us, both physical and intellectual, are so dependent upon exercise for their proper development, that action and industry must be regarded as among the primary duties of accountable man." Exercise, Gunn proclaimed, was the source of bodily health, vigor, moral evolution, and all happiness. In his opus of some 12,000 pages, the eclectic physician referred to Carpenter's *Physiology*, Wells's *Principles of Chemistry*, the English physician Southward Smith's *Philosophy of Health*, Dio Lewis's *Light Gymnastics*, and other sources to discuss "chylification," animal heat, the sponge bath, early rising, horseback riding, and an enormous number of items that influenced the body, mind, and morals of men and women. Although Gunn's recommendations were more comprehensive than those offered in the health manuals and guidebooks of most of his contemporaries, the coverage was simple, superficial, and often contradictory.[42]

The same year that Gunn's Hundredth Edition appeared, William Jay Youmans, M.D., dedicated the first American edition of *The Elements of Physiology and Hygiene: A Text-Book for Educational Institutions* to "My friend and teacher, professor [Thomas] Huxley." The famous

English biologist had recently published an elementary work on physiology intended for "any person who desires to become acquainted
with the principles of Human Physiology," and had given his former
student permission to modify it for "the circumstances and requirements of American education." Youmans added seven of his own
chapters on Practical Hygiene "in response to a growing demand that
the subject . . . in both its bodily and mental aspects, shall receive increasing attention in general education."[43]

The two goals of applied physiology, Youmans declared, were
hygiene, or "the art of preserving health," and *medicine,* "the art of restoring it." Proper exercise was one way to minimize such physiological hazards of modern society as overcrowding, impure air, bad water,
exhausting labor, and excessive "brain-work." Continued improvement of the race depended on improved "bodily constitution, and especially the qualities of the brain." Invoking the "argument from
design," Youmans continued: "Anatomy and Physiology alike proclaim that the purpose of the human constitution is activity. The pro-
vision for varied and complex movement is seen in the jointed
skeleton, the contractile muscles, the controlling nerves, and the
power supplying apparatus of digestion and circulation." Because
bodily and mental health depended upon the same conditions, both
needed to be "the business of the physiologist." Although he was familiar with the Swedish Movement Cure, which had been introduced
into the United States in the 1850s, Youmans preferred exercise taken
in the open air to that performed in the gymnasium.[44]

A decade later a man considered by many contemporaries to be
America's leading physician published *A Text Book of Human Physiology*
for the use of students and medical practitioners. Austin Flint, Jr.,
(M.D., Harvard 1833) was professor of physiology in the Bellevue
Hospital Medical College, a former president of the New York Academy of Medicine, and soon to become president of the A.M.A. Citing
experiments on the rate of nervous conduction, Flint questioned the
existence of any special "muscular sense" and noted the importance
of "habit and education" to the muscular nerves in making judgments
about weight and resistance. (The importance of "habit" in training
both "motor nerves" and "will" would assume a major role in physical
education theory by the early 1900s.) In a brief section on training,
Flint distinguished between *local* and *general* effects of exercise (i.e.,
increased muscle girth and endurance) and noted that: "training
men . . . have long since demonstrated practically certain facts which
physiologists have been rather slow to appreciate." Trained men, even
pugilists, he held, were healthy specimens. It was *after* their contests

that they lapsed into practices "in which all physiological laws are violated"; this, not training, was what deteriorated their health. In an extended discussion of the nervous system informed by the findings of Helmholtz, DuBois-Reymond, Marey, and other physiologists, he used the example of playing musical instruments to show "to what extent the power of association and disassociation of movements may be acquired by long practice."[45] In eliminating all but the briefest mention of the "will" from his discussions, Flint reflected the more scientific attitude in medicine that was beginning to emerge.

Thomas Wentworth Higginson, who has been called America's preeminent "muscular Christian,"[46] had observed a decade earlier that too few physiologists understood the effects of exercise on the human constitution. Not having been "practical gymnasts," physiologists lacked an understanding and appreciation of vigorous physical activity. Writing for the *Atlantic Monthly* in 1861, he suggested that technical innovations like the Fairbank's scale and stopwatch should be brought to bear on improving physical education and asserted that more attention should be paid to the study of the relation between mental culture and physical power. Although the best physical condition—and the highest standard of civilization—were to be found in the Anglo-Saxon race, in America progress was being purchased by a neglect of the body and "physical decay." To arrest this, the burnt-out man of business needed to frequent the gymnasium for calisthenics, vaulting, and similar exercises and engage in vigorous outdoor activities. Higginson wanted his countrymen to develop a system of physical education that conformed to distinct "American needs"—one that would be scientifically informed and superior to German and Swedish gymnastics and English sport.[47]

Reformers and Professionals: Attempts to Initiate a "Scientific" Physical Education

Higginson anticipated by slightly more than two decades the first *formal* efforts to develop an "American" system of physical education. The Association for the Advancement of Physical Education held its organizational meeting at Adelphi Academy on November 27, 1885. Among those present were ministers, directors of college gymnasia (women as well as men), and representatives from the Y.M.C.A., the U.S. Military Academy, private athletic clubs, and academic and commercial enterprises. Those assembled included eleven men who had earned (in some fashion) the M.D. degree. In calling the meeting together Adelphi's principal Albert C. Perkins "welcomed his guests as co-laborers in a department of service of the highest importance," proclaiming physical education to be the basis for "the intellectual and moral well-being of society." He also commented upon the "progress" that had been made in the last thirty years.[48]

Although those who sought to organize a *profession* of physical education in the last decades of the nineteenth century endorsed "progress"—and often sought to express their goals in modern terms—there was frequently little to separate their aspirations from those who had been a part of the Millenarian health reform endeavors of the 1830s and 1840s. The founding of the A.A.A.P.E. needs to be seen within the broader context of such continuing attitudes toward health, exercise, and physical activity. It also needs to be examined as a part of those tendencies toward professionalization that occurred in several fields in the late nineteenth century.

Between 1880 and 1900, the American Historical Association (1884), the American Physiological Society (1887), the American Association of Anatomists (1888), and the American Psychological Association (1892) were among the many organizations that sought to break with an amateur tradition and establish authority based upon specialized knowledge and intensive preparation.[49] The A.A.A.P.E. had similar aspirations, but its ties to the ideologies of social reform frequently stood in the way of professional as well as scientific advancement.

For most pre–Civil War reformers, individual redemption and regeneration had been seen as fundamental to the reform of society. After the war, reformers increasingly focused their activities through a variety of agencies that aimed at redressing a host of problems that were seen to afflict the nation. The American Social Science Association (A.S.S.A.), often referred to as "the mother of associations," was founded in 1865. Its major goal, Thomas Haskell has asserted, "was not only to understand society, but to improve it as well." Addressing the 1883 A.S.S.A. meetings, Dr. Ezra Hunt, chairman of the Department of Health, equated health with wealth, patriotism, and national strength. Social science, Hunt continued, must begin with the family; but the schools could also contribute by teaching hygiene and physical education, for it was on "physical vigor" that mental and moral culture and "social and civic existence" depended.[50]

Among the founders of A.S.S.A. was Thomas Amasa Walker's father; the younger Walker was an active member in the 1880s and 1890s. Charles William Eliot, Daniel Coit Gilman, president of Johns Hopkins, John Eaton, U.S. Commissioner of Education, William Torry Harris, then superintendent of the St. Louis Public Schools, and Thomas Wentworth Higginson were also early members. Dudley Allen Sargent, M.D., Edward M. Hartwell, M.D., and D. F. Lincoln, M.D., all future members of the still-to-be-formed A.A.A.P.E., presented papers at the A.S.S.A. meetings in the 1870s and 1880s.

As the director of Harvard's Hemenway Gymnasium, Sargent held a position of considerable stature. In his 1883 A.S.S.A. address he stated that American attempts to institute systematic bodily culture had all been adaptations of German, English, and French practices. What America needed was a "combination of these systems, all regulated and adapted to our particular needs and institutions." At Harvard, Sargent had instituted a program of exercises based upon anthropometric measurements, a physical examination, and the use of "developing appliances" (e.g., chest-weights, leg-weights) that he had designed. A program of exercises was devised for each student who worked to shape those parts of the body that had been judged "deficient" on the basis of anthropometric data and functional measurements taken in dynamometer and lung capacity tests. Sargent became the leading proponent of "anthropometry" in the decades between 1880 and 1900. He published charts and directions for taking measurements and actively sought to sell his "developing appliances." The "Sargent System" was one of the three that were extensively discussed at the 1889 Boston Conference on Physical Training.[51]

Modeled upon the British National Association for the Promotion of Social Science, the A.S.S.A. adopted the same four departments: Education; Public Health; Jurisprudence; Economy, Trade, and Finance. As secretary of the Department of Public Health, D. F. Lincoln proposed a plan in 1874 for studying school hygiene, specifying that particular attention should be paid to "School Gymnastics" and "The Effects of Schools on the Nervous System." Lengthy papers on both subjects were given the following year. Neurologist Dr. J. J. Putnam spoke on "Gymnastics for Schools." Introducing his own paper on the nervous system, Lincoln observed: "Muscular functions are in a sense nervous functions . . . nervous force is consumed in the performance of muscular acts, and is reciprocally strengthened by such performance." The blood, by means of the heart and vessels, supplies the "nervous organs" with nutrition. Therefore, "a strong pulse is needed by a strong brain; and if we want a strong pulse we must strengthen the heart. And in no way can this be done except by muscular exercise." It was the responsibility of educators, Lincoln maintained, to provide such exercise by means of singing, dancing, running, gymnastics, and athletic sports.[52]

An infinitely more detailed and precise portrayal of the functional relationships of the body's systems was set forth in Michael Foster's *Text Book of Physiology* (1877), the most authoritative English language treatise on the subject in the last quarter of the century. In his introduction, Foster declared all the various tissues to be but parts of one body bound together by the vascular mechanism and the nervous co-ordinating mechanism. The latter was connected to the muscles, which in higher animal forms were arranged with the greatest precision to achieve the chief end of animal life—*muscular movement.* Foster's influential text included much detailed information about such things as DuBois-Reymond's muscle-nerve and electrode-holder, the theory of the realignment of molecules during a nerve-impulse, the pendulum myograph, the muscle curve, and tetanus produced by means of the magnetic interrupter. Even the noted British physiologist, however, found it necessary to resort to making "will" the stimulus that puts the machinery of the cerebral hemispheres into action.[53]

In 1862, Emil DuBois-Reymond, whose theory of muscle and nerve current (derived from analog models expressed in terms of Faraday's theories of electricity and magnetism) had been cited by Foster, had written a short and acerbic article in which he linked muscular activity and development of the nervous system to gymnastics and physical activities. The renowned German physiologist's stature as an experimental scientist provided additional legitimacy for those who argued that strengthening muscles would strengthen nerves and "mind."

Swedish gymnastics had been introduced at Berlin's Royal Central Gymnasium by Major Hugo Rothstein, who had studied Ling's work at Stockholm. The installation of a foreign system at the Prussian national school for training gymnastic teachers for schools and the military infuriated many Germans. Issues embedded in a discussion of "physiology" soon aroused an acrimonious debate that focused on: (1) whether exercises on the parallel bars were dangerous, and (2) whether it was possible to exercise "single muscles."[54] The Prussian Minister of Education appointed several members of the Royal Medical Department of the University of Berlin (including Virchow and DuBois-Reymond) to look into the matter. In "Swedish Gymnastics and German Gymnastics From a Physiological Point of View," DuBois-Reymond attacked the so-called physiological theories upon which the Swedish system was based. Even the simplest body movements, he pointed out, were not "performed by the action of a single muscle, but by several muscles which are similar in their actions."

This, he claimed, was confirmed by his research experiments and his experience in the Gymnasium of Eiselin. Invoking Helmholtz's work on the production of heat, and his own on the velocity of nerve impulse and sequence of action, DuBois-Reymond declared: "All forms of bodily skill, such as dancing, skiing, riding, swimming, fencing, etc., depend in the end on a complicated activity and on the suitable interaction of impressions obtained through the senses of which we are only partially conscious. All these accomplishments, therefore, pertain equally as much to the nervous system as to the muscles."[55]

This statement, which was subsequently cited by numerous commentators, was brought to the attention of members of the newly created A.A.A.P.E. in 1886 by Edward M. Hartwell, associate in physical training at The Johns Hopkins University. A recent recipient of the Ph.D. in biology from Hopkins and the M.D. from Cincinnati's Miami Medical College, Hartwell was one of the most scientifically prepared of the early leaders of American physical education. In an address entitled "On the Physiology of Exercise" (subsequently published in the *Boston Medical and Surgical Journal*) Hartwell declared DuBois-Reymond's definition of exercise to be the most comprehensive he had encountered, stating "such bodily exercises as gymnastics, fencing, swimming, riding, dancing, and skating are much more exercises of the central nervous system, of the brain and spinal marrow." He also invoked the example of the "blacksmith's arm," observing that the analogy had been repeatedly used as the standard proof that "muscles grow larger, harder and stronger when duly exercised." Moreover, Hartwell continued, exercise produced similar effects on sensory and motor cells, even if this was less easily observed.[56]

Hartwell brought his training in both medicine and biological science to bear on many of the issues regarding exercise and physical education that were being debated at the end of the nineteenth century. One was the problem of the many, mixed, and imprecise meanings that were attached to the term "exercise." While he readily acknowledged that in actual life they were intimately related, Hartwell distinguished between: (1) exercise that was aimed at perfecting the "more familiar systems of organs" (commenting here on smooth and striated muscle, the circulatory system, production of "carbonic acid," etc.); and (2) exercise that "exerts a potent influence upon the important growth of the body" (commenting here upon the effects of exercise on nerves and the brain, and emerging theories of evolution).[57]

In "On the Physiology of Exercise," "The Nature of Physical Training and the Best Means of Securing Its Ends" (which he presented at

Figure 4.1 Edward M. Hartwell, from Fred E. Leonard, *Pioneers of Modern Physical Training* (New York: Association Press, 1915).

the 1889 Boston Conference on Physical Training), and in other writings, Hartwell's familiarity with contemporary scientific and medical work was evident: e.g., Ferrier's research on the brain; the medical writings of J. Crichton-Brown and S. Weir Mitchell; studies of height, weight, and growth conducted by Henry Pickering Bowditch, M.D., professor of physiology in the Harvard Medical School; the anthropometric studies of Charles Roberts, M.D., F.R.S. The importance of physical education, he maintained, was increasingly confirmed by discoveries in the biological sciences, notably work on the central nervous system. Although the nature of the mechanisms was still not well understood, "there is a settled conviction among those who know most about healthy and diseased nerves, that the frequent or habitual passage of stimuli from a given group of cells through definite fibres to the muscles concerned in a given movement, leads to some kind of rearrangement of the molecules composing the irritable protoplasm of fibres and cells so that less and less resistance is required to the passage of subsequent impulses from the same source."[58]

This depiction of the effects of muscular movement on nervous tissue, drawn from the work of DuBois-Reymond, provided the basis for Hartwell's claim that "the centres of motor ideation" need to be exercised so that proper development will occur. It was also used to substantiate the role that "muscular training" must perform "in our educational systems of the future." It was these important ends, and not the mere outward form of gymnastics and athletics, that legitimized physical education.[59]

Hartwell repeatedly upheld the distinction between gymnastics and athletics that was shared by most of his contemporaries—the essential difference being the goals: "The aim of athletics, unless of the illegitimate professional sort, is pleasurable activity for the sake of recreation; that of gymnastics is discipline or training for pleasure, health, and skill. . . . Gymnastics . . . are most comprehensive in their aims, more formal, elaborate, and systematic in their methods, and are productive of more solid and considerable results." This did not mean that Hartwell deprecated athletics. Indeed, as the head of Hopkins's Department of Physical Training, he had already spent considerable time providing athletic opportunities for students. While he had "no disposition to disparage athletic sports," he wished they could be better regulated and accessible to more students. Because athletics called for "self-subordination, public spirit, and co-operative effort" they were of particular value for their *moral* effects, but this could only be achieved when they were directed to *educational* ends.[60]

In his 1889 address Hartwell had also touched upon a subject that would receive increased attention from physical educators, social reformers, psychologists, and professional educators: the *healthful play instinct.* Indeed, the athletics of young men—properly conceived and responsibly directed—offered the "highest and fullest expression of the play instinct."[61] That same year Harvard's N. S. Shaler authored an article for the *Atlantic Monthly* entitled "The Athletic Problem in Education" in which he observed that the child's natural disposition to play served important biological purposes. By actively reliving the experiences of the race, the child learned "habits of command, of cooperation, and of laboring under defeat, qualities of the utmost value in maturer life, on which the very success of the race may depend." While calisthenics and gymnastics could benefit the body, Shaler held, because they lacked "the cooperative element" they could not provide for *moral* education to the same extent as games and sports.[62]

Shaler's article sketched arguments that were presented in much greater detail by G. Stanley Hall, professor of psychology and pedagogy and president of Clark University, especially in his influential *Adolescence, Its Psychology and Its Relations to Physiology, Anthropology, Sociology, Sex, Crime, Religion, and Education* (1904). America's leading proponent of the *recapitulation* theory of development, Hall was extremely interested in physical education, play, and athletic games. In his epochal work on adolescence (and in scores of other writings) he declared play to be of inestimable value to the child: "I regard play as the motor habits and spirit of the past of the race, persisting in the present, as rudimentary functions sometimes of and always akin to rudimentary organs." To act vigorously gave the "organism a sense of superiority, dignity, endurance, courage, confidence, enterprise, power, personal vitality, and virtue [manliness] in the entomological sense of that noble word." Hall, too, considered play superior to gymnastics because it called forth the social instincts of the child. Using terms that gave his statement a scientific patina, Hall declared that in vigorous activity "the products of decomposition are washed out by oxygenation and elimination, the best of the ganglionic and sympathetic activities is aroused. . . ." Athletics, the more mature form of play, provided a defense against weakening of the will, loss of honor, and degeneration of both the individual and the race.[63]

The Boston Conference of 1889 and the Establishment of College Programs

The full incorporation of play—and the recapitulation theory—into physical education was, however, still in the future when U.S.

Commissioner of Education William T. Harris opened the 1889 Boston Conference on Physical Training. Although Harris acknowledged the hygienic (e.g., dietary, digestive, circulatory, respiratory) benefits of physical training, it was "the exercise of the muscles by voluntary effort [that] calls into action the higher nervous motor-centers of the body and brain," that the Commissioner stressed: "physical training such as is advocated by us relates especially to the will." In closing his introduction, the Commissioner optimistically proclaimed the emergence of a *new physical education.*[64]

Harris, Hartwell, and participants at the Boston Conference were not alone among those who spoke enthusiastically of a "new physical education." It was not always clear, however, what "new" meant. In a lengthy article in 1887 for *Lippincott's Magazine,* "A Physician's View of Exercise and Athletics," J. William White, M.D., cited Hartwell's 1885 report "Physical Training in American Colleges and Universities" and DuBois-Reymond's statement about the influence of exercise on the nervous system. In rambling praise of both gymnastics and athletics, White touched upon sources as diverse as Homeric Greece, Martin Luther, Dudley Allen Sargent, Archibald Maclaren (director of the Oxford Gymnasium), Dr. John Morgan's study of Oxford and Cambridge crew members between 1849 and 1869, the Harvard-Yale boat race, Wilkie Collin's *Man and Wife,* Eugene L. Richard's comments on "body brain-work," and recent meetings at which problems of college sport had been discussed. White concluded that competitive athletics were "far less dangerous and much more beneficial than is generally supposed." The manly games of the Anglo-Saxon race—expunged of all excess—needed to be extended to all schools and colleges, and to the dyspeptic, the nervous, the overworked professional, and the businessman. Exercise was, White concluded, "the most important therapeutic and hygienic agency at the command of the physician of to-day."[65]

In 1884, *Popular Science Monthly* had published two articles on college athletics by Eugene L. Richards, professor of mathematics and director of the gymnasium at Yale. Although "disadvantages" existed, Richards was convinced that the "advantages" of college athletics far outweighed them. Referring to Dr. Edward Clarke's book *Building of a Brain* (1874), Richards pointed out that the development of the brain and the development of the muscles were intimately related. Young men, he asserted, were in particular need of maintaining the right "reciprocal action between body and brain" if they were to withstand the intellectual and emotional strains of college life. By providing a goal to strive for, "an ideal of strength or skill," athletics encouraged men to engage in "*body* brain-work": that is, the type of physical activity that benefited the mind, not the type that drained away "vital energy." Invoking an argument that would be repeated ad nauseam for the next hundred years, Richards insisted that the men on university crews, "nines," and "elevens" served as models that encouraged others to emulate their efforts; hence, varsity athletics served a good that was far greater than only that of those who were on the teams.[66]

Not everyone, however, was convinced that varsity teams provided any such stimulus. A series of editorials in the *Medical News* in late 1892 (published separately as a small pamphlet entitled "Some of the Moral and Physical Effects of the Game of Foot-Ball") decried the current state of affairs: "Wise educators are today frightened at the influence of the foot-ball problem. . . . Ninety-nine let one do their exercising . . . for them, and we have the noteworthy result—vicarious athletics, or gymnastics by proxy." The growing number of injuries and deaths incurred in the game was noted apprehensively, as was the game's "pernicious influence upon the morals of the players and of the community."[67]

While college presidents and others grappled with the problem of what to do with the burgeoning and immensely popular sports of the student extracurriculum, departments of physical training were being organized at colleges and universities. Influenced by local circumstances, type of the institution, and the training and predilections of those who served as directors and faculty, these took several forms. Some included athletics as well as physical training; others did not. Many were headed by men who possessed a medical degree. The nature of this training might have been anything from a short course at a proprietary institution, where whatever physiology had been learned was gained from textbooks and lectures (and perhaps a few demonstrations), to the type of scientifically based medical education that Henry Pickering Bowditch had begun to institute at Harvard in the 1870s. Few American-trained physicians before 1910, however, had much experience with experimental science.[68] The consequences of this soon became apparent in the types of programs that were developed and the debates that appeared in the professional physical education literature.

Collegiate departments of physical training that were organized in the 1890s and early 1900s for the most part endeavored to devote attention to the goals that Harris, Hartwell, and others had set forth at the Boston Conference. In 1892, for example, the Division of Physical Culture and Athletics at the University of Chicago was opened, with Amos Alonzo Stagg as its director. This arrangement placed athletics under university rather than student control, while physical training was made a requirement for graduation. The aims of the Division, as set forth in the 1892–93 *Register,* were specified as *hygienic* and *educative.* Under *hygienic* were included: activities to aid circulation, respiration, and digestion; exercises to develop posture and the symmetry of the body; and "recreational" activities that would draw blood from the nerve centers, congested by mental work, out to the skeletal muscles. The *educative* goals included perfection of the nervous system; production of mental and moral self-control (e.g., action, courage, the ability to subordinate personal will for the good of the whole) and the development of muscular strength.[69]

A "New" Physical Education

Although there was considerable agreement that a "modern ideal" must define and inform the *new* physical education, the achievement of this goal was not easily accomplished. It is a tall order to attribute to any field *all* of the potential that so many commentators have assigned to physical education. By setting goals that came close to embracing total human perfection—a kind of professionalized Millenarianism—physical education extended its boundaries so broadly that almost anything might be—and often was—included. Even the more scientifically inclined often found it easy to slip into this mode of thought. Addressing fellow members of the A.A.A.P.E. in 1890 on the topic "Physical Education: A New Profession," Luther Halsey Gulick declared:

> There are a few scientific fields to-day which offer opportunities for the study of the problems of greater value to the human race. . . . [It] is in line with the most thorough modern physiological psychology . . . [and] with our modern conception of evolution, as it works to develop a superior race. This profession offers to its students a large and broad field for intellectual activity, involving for its fullest appreciation a profound knowledge of man through physiology, anatomy, psychology, history and philosophy.[70]

In a speech before the International Congress of Education at the 1893 Chicago World's Fair, Thomas Dennison Wood, M.D., director of physical training at Stanford University, declared that although "there is today, in an embryonic and crude form, a science of physical education," greater dedication to a *scientific attitude* was needed among its practitioners.[71] George Fitz, M.D., instructor in physiology and hygiene at Harvard University, was more emphatic!

Figure 4.2 Luther Halsey Gulick, from *Official Handbook of the Academic Athletic League of California, 1910* (San Francisco: A. G. Spalding and Bros., 1910).

The same issue of the *Harvard Graduates Magazine* that opened with Walker's "College Athletics" also contained Fitz's brief article "Problems of Physical Education." Fitz had graduated from Harvard Medical School in 1891 where the influence of Bowditch's new experimental approach had made a considerable impact on the curriculum. As Walter Kroll has suggested, it was surely Fitz who was a guiding force in establishing a laboratory in the Lawrence Scientific School "for the experimental study of the physiology of exercise." Here attention was given to "the hygiene of muscles, conditions under which they act . . . and the effects of various exercises upon muscular growth and general health."[72]

Fitz's insistence that physical education could become a respectable field only if it was grounded in a systematic, scientific study of the effects of physical activity on the body was evident early in his career. At the 1891 A.A.A.P.E. meetings, he had criticized the uninformed debate regarding which "system" of gymnastics was best, saying: "Physical training today is an art, not a science. . . . What we need is scientific work, not the assumption that certain laws require certain exercises." In "Problems of Physical Education," he set forth numerous questions regarding gymnastics and athletics for which no adequate information existed, even though practitioners continued to advance extravagant claims for a bewildering assortment of "theories" of exercise. The entire "question of the relative value of games *versus* arbitrary systems of gymnastics" could only be intelligently discussed, he held, when the appropriate research studies had been completed.[73]

In an attempt to place physical education and athletics on a secure scientific foundation, Fitz set about establishing a four-year B.S. degree program in "Anatomy, Physiology, and Physical Training" for "those who expect to take charge of gymnasiums as well as for those who wish to obtain a general education preparatory to the study of medicine." The only contributions that physical educators could claim, he held, were in anthropometry, the production of "tables of measurements," and the design of various pieces of exercise equipment. This was not the type of work, however, that was likely to do much to further the *scientific* study of physical training. In making such a statement, Fitz was indicting (even if this was not his intention) the work of his Harvard contemporary, Sargent. Anthropometry had become a preoccupation of many physical educators in the late nineteenth century; however, the compiling of endless height, weight, girth, and strength tables could do little to explain the *functional* effects of exercise. *Experimental* research in physiology and psychology was indispensable. As a condition of their work, therefore, every advanced student in the Harvard B.S. program was required to undertake original research and report the results in a thesis.[74]

The curriculum of Harvard's four-year degree program (which terminated in 1899) was far more scientific and rigorous than that offered by any other contemporary institution that trained physical educators. Fitz taught the first year physiology and hygiene course, the senior course in the physiology of exercise (which included experimental work), and the course in remedial gymnastics. With Sargent he also taught the senior course in the history of physical education. General physiology was taught by Bowditch and William T. Porter, also a professor in the Harvard Medical School. William James taught the psychology course. The curriculum included: experimental physics, zoology, morphology (animal and human), chemistry, medical chemistry, general anatomy, comparative anatomy, English, and foreign languages. Sargent taught the anthropometry course and the course in applied anatomy and animal mechanics. With James Lathrop he also instructed the students each year in a course entitled "Gymnastics and Athletics."[75]

At the nearby Boston Normal School of Gymnastics, young women received instruction in anthropometry from Bowditch; Josiah Royce lectured on psychology and pedagogy; Dr. W. M. Conant, Harvard's assistant demonstrator of anatomy, taught "Emergencies"; M.I.T.'s Thomas Drown, M.D., taught chemistry; and William T. Sedgwick, Ph.D., and Theodore Hough, Ph.D. (both of M.I.T.) were in charge of general biology, comparative anatomy, histology, physiology, and sanitary science. Applied anatomy, physiology, and Swedish pedagogical and medical gymnastics were taught by Claes Enebuske, Ph.D., a graduate of the Royal University at Lund, Sweden. Students at the B.N.S.G. were required to undertake laboratory work—dissecting frogs and various mammals. Although examination questions suggest that a high standard of performance was expected, it does not appear that they had much experience with original research other than, perhaps, in anthropometry.[76]

The type of curriculum offered at the B.N.S.G., impressive by contemporary standards, was much more reflective of the better college physical education baccalaureate programs that would begin to emerge in the twentieth century. While comparable endeavors were undertaken at several other institutions (e.g., the program that Wood initiated at Stanford in 1891), many of the teachers who were needed to fill posts in the rapidly growing public school physical education programs—and even at institutions of higher learning—were trained in two-year, or shorter, courses. It was the limited and unscientific nature of these that presented a serious threat, Fitz told the Physical Education Section of the National Education Association in 1899. This was also a concern of Dr. C. E. Ehinger of the State Normal School at West Chester, who declared at the Seventh Annual Meeting of the A.A.A.P.E. that, in spite of the recent interest in physical education, there was "a lamentable neglect and dense ignorance of this subject." Although educators, physicians, and parents were coming to appreciate the hygienic and educational value of exercise, Fitz maintained, a persistent failure to apply "scientific investigation" to the field impeded its growth while competing and uninformed claims of various groups "threaten[ed] the unity of purpose and heartiness of cooperation upon which our future progress rests." Accurate physiological and psychological knowledge, he remonstrated, must be sought by physical educators, who must become "students of the problems of physical education, not merely exponents of fixed systems."[77]

Most of the men and women who headed the newly emerging teacher-training programs—either by choice or by necessity—were oriented more toward the practical concerns of curriculum, facilities, and teaching methods than they were toward experimental science. Gerald Geison has observed in "Divided We Stand: Physiologists and Clinicians in the American Context" that medical doctors and research physiologists have persistently held substantially different views of the body.[78] In general, although there were important exceptions, those medical doctors who were directors of college programs had been trained more in accordance with a "clinical" than an experimental model. This influenced the types of programs that emerged under their direction.

In an effort to foster scientific work, Fitz, Sargent, Springfield College's James H. McCurdy, M.D., Hough, and others formed an American Society for Research in Physical Education. Thirteen of the group's initial twenty-two members spoke at the first annual meeting in April 1904; of these, nine held medical degrees and an additional two held the Ph.D. in biological science.[79]

Science or Service: Which Shall Prevail?

The nature of the assumptions upon which most Americans based their ideas of physical education, however, militated against the type of scientifically based profession that Fitz and others aspired to attain. Health reform, after all, had been anyone's prerogative—and often business—throughout the century; and "physical education" was closely, even if often ambiguously, involved with a very substantial number of these health reform activities. The close association of many antebellum reform efforts with notions of total human perfection also continued to influence the way in which many individuals perceived the field of physical education. (Indeed, it is not difficult to discern a vacillation between objective, scientific goals and subjective, Millenarian aspirations through the hundred years since the profession was founded.) It was difficult for the emerging A.A.A.P.E. and its members to counter this legacy. There were, moreover, continuing opportunities to make money by writing books, giving lectures, and opening proprietary training schools, especially as there were no licensing laws or other mechanisms to control unqualified practitioners.[80]

The inclusion of physical education in the curriculum of public high schools in the 1890s and the enthusiasm for "child study," which had begun in the 1880s, exacerbated the problem. The *1891–92 Report of the U.S. Commissioner of Education* concluded a 100-page article on the history and present status of physical education with tables showing the rapid increase in the number of cities that had instituted public school programs: eighty-four employed "specialists" and an additional eighty-one required regular instruction in some form of gymnastics. The need to provide teachers fostered the expansion of "normal," Chautauqua, and private-venture courses. Some, like the Sargent Normal School of Physical Training (established in 1881 as a two-year program and expanded to a three-year course in 1902) brought in medically trained faculty to instruct students; others offered much thinner fare. Athletic clubs, the Y.M.C.A., Turner societies, and private individuals like health seeker Bernarr Macfadden and strongman Eugen Sandow also vied for a portion of the current enthusiasm for exercise. The American Physical Education Association was sufficiently concerned about the "manifold and confusing systems" that it held a symposium on the problem in 1903. A.P.E.A. member James A. Babbitt, M.D., of Haverford College, one of the discussants, urgently called for more scientific men and women to "add strength and dignity to our profession."[81]

The same volume of the *American Physical Education Review* that published Babbitt's remarks included Dr. Delphine Hanna's survey of colleges preparing students in public school gymnastics. Of the sixteen institutions listed, only three (University of California, University of Nebraska, and Oberlin College) offered four-year courses. Two years later, James McCurdy reported the results of a survey that found that 128 American cities employed a total of 291 teachers of physical training, the overwhelming majority of whom had been trained at normal or proprietary schools; the largest numbers had studied at the Boston Normal School of Gymnastics and the Turnlehrer Seminar of the North American Turnerbund.[82] Only the best of these schools could provide the time and resources to give students any experience with laboratory work, and it is doubtful that any were able to offer extended experience in experimental science. As a consequence, large numbers of those individuals who trained for the field were left with learning the outward "forms" of exercise and games, gross anatomy, hygiene (personal and school), anthropometry, kinesiology and postural work, and some basic physiology. McCurdy also expressed anxiety over the fact that a man was hurried "into active work before he ha[d] fully prepared himself," noting that the additional demands of conducting competitive athletics programs further complicated the situation.[83]

As McCurdy had observed, the burgeoning interscholastic and intercollegiate athletic programs created a dilemma for the embryonic field of physical education. At numerous institutions physical educators—both male and female—were asked or chose to devote much of their attention and energy to competitive sports. The persistence of values that postulated a "separate sphere" for members of the female sex made it relatively easy to hold to what was claimed to be an "educational" model for girls and women. Highly visible competitive sports for males, however, had attained such prominence by the 1890s—as Walker pointed out in his Phi Beta Kappa Address—that attempts to organize athletics solely for "educational" ends were constantly overshadowed by the presence of the more spectacular "intercollegiate" model.[84] Although various efforts had been made since the 1880s to place the control of athletics in the hands of the faculty, little success was achieved until the founding of the Intercollegiate Athletic Association of the United States (now the N.C.A.A.) in 1906 and the organization of high school athletic leagues in the early 1900s.

Since at least the 1890s, some members of the A.A.A.P.E. had acknowledged that athletics (subject to certain constraints) might be an appropriate—even important—form of physical training. By 1906, as Guy Lewis has shown, the emphasis in curricular physical education was rapidly moving from gymnastics to sport.[85] The assumed "developmental" potential of athletics, long associated with what were believed to be desirable male qualities, was given added luster by Victorian ideologies that attributed to them such values as

"manliness," "character," and "sand." Those who maintained that athletics as well as formal gymnastics might serve both *hygienic,* and more
importantly, *educational* ends drew upon this tradition. The transition
from a gymnastics-centered to a sports-centered curriculum was facilitated by developments in evolutionary biology, physiological psychology, and work on the association of ideas, instinct, interest,
recapitulation, and play during the late 1800s and early 1900s. These
combined, within the broader context of Progressive Era concerns
about society and social issues, to move the professional field of physical education toward an emphasis on questions dominated by social
science and psychology rather than physiology. The new interest in
play and games also drew heavily upon the Child Study Movement,
educational reforms that G. Stanley Hall had initiated in the 1880s,
and assumptions about the nature and role of "habit."

In 1887, William James had written in *Popular Science Monthly:* "every state of ideational Consciousness which is either very strong or
habitually repeated leaves an organic impression on the cerebrum."
James's conception of "habit" was expanded in his influential text *Psychology* (1891): "An acquired habit, from the physiological point of
view, is nothing but a new pathway of discharge formed in the brain."
Drawing upon Henry Maudsley's *Physiology and Pathology of the Mind*
(1867), he used the examples of proficiency in swimming, skating,
fencing, writing, and singing to support the physical basis of habit
and the plasticity of the nervous system in the formation of ethical
behavior.[86]

Addressing the Boston Medical Improvement Society in 1896,
Hartwell referred to various contemporary views of "habit" and evolutionary theory. The two ends of exercise, the A.A.A.P.E. president
reminded his audience, were "the promotion of health . . . and the
formation of proper habits." The former was a *hygienic* end; the latter,
distinctively *educational.* Citing Mercier's *Nervous System and the Mind*
(1888), he distinguished between muscular *action* (predominantly a
physiological function) and muscular *movements* (identified as a psychological function). The first, Hartwell continued, concerned processes that occurred *within* the organism; the latter involved the
adjustment of "the *processes that occur within the organism to the conditions
that exist outside of it.*" The study of the psychological functions of the
nervous system, then, was "the study of conduct";[87] and "conduct"
implied action in accordance with the standards of a social group.

Drawing from Drummond's Lowell Lecture on the Ascent of Man
(1894) and Kidd's *Social Evolution* (1894), he urged his listeners to devote attention to recent work on evolution and criticized earlier the-

ories that saw education as an unfolding rather than a series of developmental stages, each with its need for particular forms of physical activity. While both were always needed, *hygienic* forms were most appropriate from birth through age thirteen; *educative* forms should increasingly predominate from age fourteen to twenty-four. Although he continued to reject "rampant athleticism," Hartwell acknowledged that "the predilection of collegiate youth for athletic sports and contests may be justified as natural and fitting by the teachings of neurology and psychology, if once it can be admitted that the development of mind and character, as well as brain and muscles, is subject to the laws of evolution." Finding the problems of education to be fundamentally problems of evolution, he concluded that "the new education will be . . . the quintessential of the biological sciences." The basis of all education, of course, was clearly physical training.[88]

Given his training in physiology and medicine, it is not surprising that Hartwell would proclaim education to be a biological science. Yet, like most of his contemporaries, he recognized that humans were social as well as biological creatures. Other proponents of physical education, also drawing upon evolution, recapitulation theory, work on heredity and environment, and the growing volume of "play" literature, intentionally and unintentionally moved the field closer to the social sciences. In 1898, Luther Gulick discussed "Some Psychical Aspects of Physical Exercise" in *Popular Science Monthly,* dividing the play life of the child into five stages. Whereas the play of early childhood was "individualistic" and "non-competitive," that of later childhood and adolescence was "competitive" and "socialistic." Gulick followed with an article for the *Pedagogical Seminary* in March 1899 in which he equated group games and "team work" with "qualities indigenous to the Anglo-Saxon youth." It was now recognized, he asserted, that it was necessary to attend to the types of social issues that sociologists had recently begun to raise. Six months later T. R. Croswell published his survey of the *variety* and *character* of the games and amusements of 2,000 Worcester, Massachusetts, schoolchildren, a lengthy article that also summarized the main points of the major recent studies of play.[89]

Even the irascible George Fitz was caught up in the new enthusiasm for "play" and the importance of the social environment. Speaking to the Primary Section of the Massachusetts Teachers Association in 1897, the director of the Harvard B.S. program in anatomy, physiology, and physical training drew heavily upon Karl Groos's *Die Spiele der Thier* (1895) to argue the importance of "play as an educational factor." Pointing to "instinct" and the association of pleasure with the satisfaction of instinct, Fitz concluded by informing his audience: "Play thus relates itself to the truest conception of evolution, the development of power, the power of the individual to act as a self-directed unit in civilization."[90]

Although Fitz was predominantly interested in psycho-physiological questions, others focused far more on psycho-social concerns. The 1898 volume of the *American Physical Education Review* reflects the diversity of approaches. Boston's mayor Josiah Quincy emphasized the social influences of the gymnasium in winter and the playground in summer, while Dr. Henry Ling Taylor discussed the value of gymnastics over games in training "the nerve centres, the intelligence, and the character, as well as the muscles." George E. Johnson, one of Hall's students at Clark University, drew upon Maudsley, James, Groos, recapitulation theory, and "instinct" to argue that because play was driven by "inner necessity and impulse," it was a more valuable educational tool than was routine gymnastics. Games—the more formal and *social* form of play—were of most value when they retained play's basic elements.[91]

The Incorporation of the Social and Psychological Sciences

The ascendance of a psycho-social over a physiological perspective—and an *educational* over a *hygienic* emphasis—was fully evident in the "Tentative Report of the Committee on a Normal Course in Play" published by the Playground Association of America three years after its founding in 1906.[92] The P.A.A. and the A.P.E.A. shared a number of similar goals with regard to physical exercise and the welfare of children, and many of the same men and women were active with both groups. Gulick, for example, was president of both the P.A.A. and the A.P.E.A. and, in 1903, the founder of New York's Public School Athletic League. Clark Hetherington was deeply involved with the P.A.A., A.P.E.A., and N.C.A.A.

In 1906, Hetherington composed a lengthy article, "Analysis of Problems in College Athletics," in which he went to great pains to distinguish between "sporting" and "educational" athletics: "From the educational view point, [athletics] are encouraged or promoted, sometimes sought, for the values which they contain as an educational discipline. Consciousness of social values is prominent. Nature made the play instinct the guardian of an organic need. The educational interest interprets and idealizes nature's aims and advocates athletics for the good of race and society."[93] The aims of physical education, therefore, were: organic development; psycho-motor development; health; mental, moral, and social discipline. In 1907, Hetherington was instrumental in founding the Athletic Research Society in order to "study athletic problems" and "widen the public consciousness of the moral and social values of play and athletics."[94] By 1908, the *American Physical Education Review,* the official organ of the A.P.E.A., was regularly publishing annual reports of the P.A.A. and the N.C.A.A.

Paul Phillips, M.D., professor of hygiene and physical education and director of Pratt Gymnasium at Amherst College, summarized the new impulses in the field of physical education when he declared in 1912: "Thanks to the work of Groos, Gulick, Fitz, Hetherington, and others it has been shown that normal play is not only important but also absolutely necessary to the normal development of boys and girls physically and mentally, and morally as well. Play and the play spirit constitute perhaps the most important single element in growth and education."[95] While physiological and other laboratory research was by no means abandoned by the field of physical education, it was relegated to a proportionally much smaller sphere of influence for the next half century. So, too, were physicians, who occupied a diminishing role in the leadership of the profession as the twentieth century progressed.

Notes

1. Francis A. Walker, "College Athletics," *Harvard Graduates Magazine* 2 (1893), 1–18. Walker's speech was published in abstract form, and with high endorsements, in the "Clippings" section of *Physical Education* 3 (1894), 14–16. "Addendum," *Report of the Commissioner of Education for the Year 1889–90,* vol. 2 (Washington, D.C.: U.S. Government Printing Office, 1893), 1103. Also Edward M. Hartwell, *Report of the Director of Physical Training,* School Document No. 22—1891 (Boston: Rockwell and Churchill, 1891), 65–66.

2. The literature on this subject is now quite extensive. One useful source is the Special Issue of the *Journal of Sport History* 10 (1983). Athletics, and sport, have been the subjects of by far the largest percentage of historical studies, although several of these have also touched upon "physical culture," "physical training," and "physical education." The terms are not quite synonymous, but were often used somewhat indiscriminately. In general, but with many exceptions, "physical culture" was the broader term and the term used more by non-professionals. "Physical training" tended to be the preferred term among those who were interested in its educational dimensions and by members of the American Association for the Advancement of Physical

Education (A.A.A.P.E.). "Physical education," a term that has a long history, increasingly replaced "physical training" in the late 1890s and early 1900s.

3. A.A.A.P.E. General Constitution, Article II. In *Report of the Tenth Annual Meeting of the American Association for the Advancement of Physical Education, April 25, 26, and 27, 1895* (Concord, N.H.: Republican Press Assoc., 1896), appendix, 7.

4. W. M. Conant, "The Educational Aspects of College Athletics," *Boston Medical and Surgical Journal* 18 Oct. 1894. Published and distributed as part of a separate pamphlet by Damrell and Upham, Boston, 1894.

5. In *The Descent of Man and Selection in Relation to Sex,* Darwin had included a chapter in which he discussed "the moral sense" at some length. It was "the moral sense" that distinguished man from the lower animals, and it was the social instincts that were "the prime principle of man's moral constitution." "[T]he state of the body by affecting the brain . . . ," Darwin held, "ha[d] a great influence on moral tendencies." Right actions could be reinforced by "habit," and it was expected that "virtuous habits will grow stronger, becoming perhaps fixed by inheritance" (rev. ed. [Chicago: Rand, McNally and Co., n.d.], 94–123, especially 120–21).

6. Ludwig Edelstein, "The Dietetics of Antiquity," in Owsei Temkin and C. Lilian Temkin, eds., *Ancient Medicine: Selected Papers of Ludwig Edelstein* (Baltimore: The Johns Hopkins University Press, 1967), 315. See also Michel Foucault, *The History of Sexuality,* part 2 (New York: Random House, 1985).

7. L. S. Jacyna, "Principles of General Physiology: The Comparative Dimension to British Neuroscience in the 1830s and 1840s," In William Coleman and Camille Limoges, eds., *Studies in the History of Biology* (Baltimore: The Johns Hopkins University Press, 1984), 47–92; idem, "The Physiology of Mind, the Unity of Nature, and Moral Order in Victorian Thought," *British Journal for the History of Science* 14 (1981), 109–32.

8. [Charles William Eliot], "President Eliot's Report of 1892–'93," *Harvard Graduates Magazine* 2 (1893), 374–83. In 1906 Eliot responded to a letter from the president of the University of California, Benjamin Ide Wheeler, stating irascibly that Americans were "morally inferior" to the English in competitive sports. Harvard students, he held, "in any keen competition would make it a rough and cheating game in fifteen minutes." Eliot, letters to Wheeler, 8 Feb. 1906 and 19 Sept. 1906 (Bancroft Library, University of California; by permission).

9. Paul Dashiell, letter to President [Theodore Roosevelt], 7 Dec. 1905 (Harvard University Archives; by permission); J. W. Spalding, letter to Walter Camp, 20 Nov. 1895 (Yale University Archives; by permission).

10. Walker, "College Athletics," 11–13.

11. Norman Bingham, ed., *The Book of Athletics and Out-of-Door Sports* (Boston: Lothrop Publishing Co., 1895), 9–14; Walter Camp and Lorin F. Deland, *Football* (Boston: Houghton, Mifflin and Co., 1896), 42–52. Other authors repeatedly set forth the same slogans. Fielding H. Yost, *Football for Player and Spectator* (Ann Arbor: University Publishing Co., 1905), talked

about "self-reliance, moral courage, energy, discipline, and 'sand' " (10–11). See also John Henry Bartlett and John Pearl Gifford, *Dartmouth Athletics: A Complete History of All Kinds of Sports at the College* (Concord, N.H.: Republican Press Association, 1893).

12. See, for example, James A. Mangan, *The Games Ethic and Imperialism* (Harmondsworth: Penguin Books, 1985); idem, *Athleticism in the Victorian and Edwardian Public School: The Emergence and Consolidation of an Educational Ideology* (Cambridge: Cambridge University Press, 1981).

13. Quoted in Walter La Feber, *The New Empire: An Interpretation of American Expansion, 1860–1898* (Ithaca: Cornell University Press, 1963), 71. See for example, Theodore Roosevelt, *The Strenuous Life: Essays and Addresses* (Philadelphia: Gebbie and Co., 1903), especially chap. 1, 5, 6, 10, 15, and 17.

14. See Roberta J. Park, "Sport, Gender and Society in a Transatlantic Victorian Perspective," *British Journal of Sports History* 2 (1985), 1–28. Ralph D. Paine, "The Spirit of School and College Sport: American and English Rowing," *The Century* 70 (1905), 483–503; idem, "The Spirit of School and College Sport: English and American Football," *The Century* 71 (1905), 99–116; "The Cricket Mania," *Nation* 9 (2 Sept. 1859), 658; "Some Tendencies in Modern Sport," *Quarterly Review* 199 (1904), 127–52; Walker, "College Athletics," 13.

15. Anthony Rotundo, "Body and Soul: Changing Ideals of American Middle-Class Manhood, 1770–1920," *Journal of Social History* 16 (1983), 23–38; Peter Stearns, *Be a Man!: Males in Modern Society* (New York: Holms and Meier, 1979); Elizabeth H. Pleck and Joseph H. Pleck, eds., *The American Man* (Englewood Cliffs, N.J.: Prentice-Hall, 1980); John G. Cawelti, *Apostles of the Self-Made Man: Changing Concepts of Success in America* (Chicago: University of Chicago Press, 1965). The whole notion of *action*, with regard to the body and to the rise of athletics and new "scientific" attempts to understand and control both, needs further attention. I attempted to grapple with this in my 1979 Seward Staley Address before the North American Society for Sport History—"Action as Moral Necessity: Reflections on Healthful Exercise and 'Wholesome' Sport, 1815–1915." Donald J. Mrozek, *Sport and American Mentality, 1880–1910* (Knoxville: University of Tennessee Press, 1983) adds important new dimensions to this fascinating and still too little analyzed concept.

16. Albert Bushnell Hart, "The Status of Athletics in American Colleges," *Atlantic Monthly* 66 (1890), 63–71.

17. Daniel T. Rodgers, *The Work Ethic in Industrial America, 1850–1920* (Chicago: University of Chicago Press, 1974), 108.

18. John Higham, "The Reorientation of American Culture in the 1890s," in John Higham, ed., *Writing American History: Essays on Modern Scholarship* (Bloomington: Indiana University Press, 1970), 79.

19. Luther Halsey Gulick, "Physical Education: A New Profession," in *Proceedings of the American Association for the Advancement of Physical Education,*

Cambridge and Boston, 1890 (Ithaca, N.Y.: Andrus and Church, 1890), 65; Walker, "College Athletics," 1–2; Camp and Deland, *Football,* 48. See also George M. Frederickson, *The Inner Civil War: Northern Intellectuals and the Crisis of the Union* (New York: Harper Brothers, 1965), chap. 9.

20. Walker, "College Athletics," 11. Anxieties over the loss of "vital force" or energy, though they took somewhat different forms before and after the Civil War, existed throughout the nineteenth century. See Harvey Green, *Fit for America: Health, Fitness, Sport, and American Society* (New York: Pantheon Books, 1986), 68–76, 167–79, passim.

21. Walker, "College Athletics," 3–5, 9–10.

22. To the extent that just about every commentator contended that the participant "learned" something from engaging in athletics, one could say that they were all educational. The majority of those who had some official capacity in an educational institution, or in an organization that took seriously its responsibilities for the body, mind, and spirit of a young man, *educational* athletics meant something special. In the *Young Men's Christian Association Handbook,* rev. ed (1891), chap. 25, Luther Halsey Gulick wrote that outdoor work and athletics added to the value of work done in the gymnasium, and that athletics could have greater *educational* value provided they were carefully supervised and controlled (32–38). A society for the study of athletics (Athletic Research Society) was organized on December 30, 1907 to seek a "solution of the problems and difficulties in competitive athletics and . . . study the educational, moral, and social forces involved" ("News Notes," *American Physical Education Review* 8 [1908], 65).

23. G. B. Emerson, "Physical Education," *New England Journal of Education* 1 (Feb. 13, 1875), 76; "Exercise", ibid, 76–77; "Physical Culture among English Students: Competitive Tests," *New England Journal of Education* 1 (Feb. 20, 1875), 91; "The Nature of Play, and Its Importance as a Means of Education," *New England Journal of Education* 2 (Oct. 2, 1875), 147–48.

24. T. M. Balliet, "Value of Motor Education," *New England Journal of Education* 48 (Nov. 17, 1898), 317.

25. Henry Smith Williams, "The Century's Progress in Anatomy and Physiology," *Harper's New Monthly Magazine* 96 (1898), 621–32; idem, "The Century's Progress in Scientific Medicine," *Harper's New Century Magazine* 99 (1899), 38–52; idem, "The Century's Progress in Experimental Psychology," ibid., 513–27.

26. Smith, "Experimental Psychology," 515–17; Karl E. Rothschuh, *History of Physiology* (Huntington, N.Y.: Robert E. Kreiger Co., 1973), 181–87.

27. Karl Figlio, "Theories of Perception and Physiology of Mind in the Late Eighteenth Century," *History of Science* 12 (1975), 177. See also Thomas L. Hankins, *Science and the Enlightenment* (Cambridge: Cambridge University Press, 1985), chap. 5.

28. Charles Bell, *Animal Mechanics or the Proofs of Design in the Bones of the Head, Spine and Chest, Shown by Comparison with Architectural and Mechanical Contrivances* (Cambridge: Riverside Press, 1902), 1–2, 87–89.

29. Andrew Combe, *The Principles of Physiology Applied to the Preservation of Health, and to the Improvement of Physical and Mental Education* (New York: Harper and Brothers, 1836), 1, 109–20, 208–9, passim.

30. "Review of Combe's Physiology," *American Annals of Education* 1 (1834), 485–91; "Physical Education," *American Journal of Education* 1 (1826), 19–23.

31. *Journal of Health, Conducted by an Association of Physicians* 1 (1830), announcement inside book cover.

32. John Jeffries, "Physical Culture, the Result of Moral Obligation," *American Quarterly Review* 1 (1833), 253, 259–60.

33. Green, *Fit for America;* James C. Whorton, *Crusaders for Fitness: The History of American Health Reformers* (Princeton, N.J.: Princeton University Press, 1982); Bruce Haley, *The Healthy Body and Victorian Culture* (Cambridge: Cambridge University Press, 1978).

34. See, for example, William G. Rothstein, *American Physicians in the 19th Century: From Sects to Science* (Baltimore: The Johns Hopkins University Press, 1972); Martin Kaufman, "American Medical Education," in Ronald L. Numbers, ed., *The Education of American Physicians: Historical Essays* (Berkeley: University of California Press, 1980), 7–28; Richard H. Shryock, *Medical Licensing in America, 1650–1965* (Baltimore: The Johns Hopkins University Press, 1967).

35. See William Coleman, *Biology in the Nineteenth Century: Problems of Form, Function, and Transformation* (Cambridge: Cambridge University Press, 1977).

36. Jacyna, "Principles of General Physiology"; idem, "Physiology of Mind."

37. William B. Carpenter, *Principles of Comparative Physiology,* 4th ed. (London: John Churchill, 1854), 690–709. See also, Jacyna, "Principles of General Physiology"; Roger Smith, "The Background of Physiological Psychology in Natural Philosophy," *History of Science* 11 (1973), 75–123; Robert M. Young, "The Functions of the Brain: Gall to Ferrier (1808–1886)," *Isis* 59 (1968), 251–68.

38. Mary Douglas, *Natural Symbols: Explorations in Cosmology* (New York: Pantheon Books, 1982), 65–71.

39. W. R. Bynum, "Health, Disease and Medical Care," in G. S. Rousseau and R. Porter, eds., *The Ferment of Knowledge: Studies in the Historiography of Eighteenth-Century Science* (Cambridge: Cambridge University Press, 1984), 224; Sally Shuttleworth, *George Eliot and Nineteenth-Century Science: The Make-Believe of a Beginning* (Cambridge: Cambridge University Press, 1984); Haley, *Healthy Body;* Sharon Cameron, *The Corporeal Self: Allegories of the Body in Melville and Hawthorne* (Baltimore: The Johns Hopkins University Press, 1981). See also Roberta J. Park, "Hermeneutics, Semiotics, and the 19th-Century Quest for a Corporeal Self," *Quest* 38 (1986), 33–49.

40. Owsei Temkin, "Metaphors in Human Biology," in Owsei Temkin, ed., *The Double Face of Janus and Other Essays in the History of Medicine* (Baltimore: The Johns Hopkins University Press, 1977), 271. See also Karl M. Figlio,

"The Metaphor of Organization: An Historiographical Perspective on the Bio-Medical Sciences in the Early Nineteenth Century," *History of Sciences* 14 (1976), 17–53.

41. Paul Weindling, "Theories of the Cell State in Imperial Germany," in Charles Webster, ed., *Biology, Medicine, Society: 1840–1940* (Cambridge: Cambridge University Press, 1981), 99–155; Jacyna, "Physiology of Mind"; Smith, "Physiological Psychology," 105.

42. W. W. Hall, *Guide-Board to Health, Peace and Competence, or the Road to Happy Old Age* (Springfield, Mass.: D. E. Fisk and Co., 1867), preface; John C. Gunn, *Gunn's New Family Physician: or, Home Book of Health; Forming a Household Guide . . . With Supplementary Treatises on Domestic and Sanitary Economy, and on Physical Culture and Development* (New York: Moore, Wilstach and Baldwin, 1867).

43. Thomas H. Huxley and William Jay Youmans, *The Elements of Physiology and Hygiene: A Text-Book for Educational Institutions* (New York: D. Appleton and Co., 1881), preface to the revised edition (1872).

44. Ibid., 344–45, 420–32.

45. Austin Flint, Jr., *A Text-Book of Human Physiology; Designed for the Use of Practitioners and Students of Medicine* (New York: D. Appleton and Co., 1876), 54, 78–79, 150–51, 498–99, 513–14, 586–99, 750–51.

46. John A. Lucas, "Thomas Wentworth Higginson: Early Apostle of Health and Fitness," *Journal of Health, Physical Education, and Recreation* 42 (1971), 30–33.

47. Thomas Wentworth Higginson, "Barbarism and Civilization," *Atlantic Monthly* 7 (1861), 51–61; idem, "Gymnastics," ibid., 283–302.

48. *Proceedings of the Association for the Advancement of Physical Education, at its Organizational Meeting at Brooklyn, N.Y., November 27, 1885* (Brooklyn, N.Y.: Rome Brothers, 1885), 3. For a discussion of the first twenty years of the A.A.A.P.E., see Roberta J. Park, "Science, Service, and the Professionalization of Physical Education: 1885–1905," *Research Quarterly for Exercise and Sport,* Special Centennial issue (Apr. 1985), 7–20.

49. See Thomas Haskell, *The Emergence of Professional Social Science: The American Social Science Association and the Nineteenth-Century Crisis of Authority* (Urbana: University of Illinois Press, 1977); Sally G. Kohlstedt, *The Formation of the American Scientific Community: The Association for the Advancement of Science* (Urbana: University of Illinois Press, 1976).

50. Haskell, *Professional Social Science,* 100; Ezra M. Hunt, "Health and Social Science," *Journal of Social Science* 18 (1883), 28–43.

51. Haskell, *Professional Social Science,* 91–110; Dudley A. Sargent, "Physical Training in Homes and Training Schools," *Journal of Social Science* 18 (1883), 44–52; Edward M. Hartwell, "The Study of Anatomy, Historically and Legally Considered," *Journal of Social Science* 9 (1880), 54–88; D. F. Lincoln, "The Nervous System as Affected by School-Life," *Journal of Social Science* 7 (1876), 87–110.

52. J. J. Putnam, "Gymnastics for Schools," *Journal of Social Science* 7 (1876), 110–24; Lincoln, "Nervous System," 89–92.

53. Michael Foster, *A Text-Book of Physiology* (London: Macmillan and Co., 1878), 1–8, 490. For a discussion of DuBois-Reymond's work on the electro-magnetic theory of the action of nerves and muscles see Timothy Lenoir, "Models and Instruments in the Development of Electrophysiology, 1845–1912," *Historical Studies in the Physical and Biological Sciences* 17 (1986), 1–54.

54. Emil DuBois-Reymond, "Swedish Gymnastics and German Gymnas-tics from a Physiological Point of View," Biewind, trans., in *Essays Concerning the German System of Gymnastics* (Milwaukee: Freuekner Publishing Co., n.d.); Lehnert et al., "Exercises on the Parallel Bars from a Medical Point of View," ibid. Virchow was a signatory to the latter report. These were published as a small pamphlet by the executive committee of the North American Turnerbund.

55. DuBois-Reymond, "German Gymnastics," 5–10.

56. Edward M. Hartwell, "On the Physiology of Exercise," *Boston Medical and Surgical Journal*, 31 Mar. 1887, 297–302; ibid., 7 Apr. 1887, 321–24. Pub-lished separately as *On the Physiology of Exercise* (Boston: Cupples, Upham and Co., 1887).

57. See Roberta J. Park, "Edward M. Hartwell and Physical Training at The Johns Hopkins University, 1879–1890," *Journal of Sport History* 14 (Spring 1987), 108–19; Edward M. Hartwell, "The Nature of Physical Train-ing, and the Best Means of Securing Its Ends," in Isabel C. Barrows, ed., *Phys-ical Training: A Full Report of the Papers and Discussions of the Conference Held in Boston in November 1889* (Boston: George H. Ellis, 1899), 5–20.

58. Hartwell, "Physiology of Exercise," 26–29.

59. Hartwell, "Nature of Physical Training," 15.

60. Ibid., 20.

61. Ibid., 19.

62. N. S. Shaler, "The Athletic Problem in Education," *Atlantic Monthly* 63 (1889), 79–88.

63. G. Stanley Hall, *Adolescence, Its Psychology and Its Relations to Physiology, Anthropology, Sociology, Sex, Crime, Religion, and Education* (New York: D. Ap-pleton and Co., 1904), vol. 1, 202–5, 217–30.

64. William T. Harris, "Physical Training," in Barrows, *Physical Training, 1889*, 1–4.

65. Ibid.; J. William White, "A Physician's View of Exercise and Athletics," *Lippincott's Magazine* (1887), 1008–33. See Edward M. Hartwell, *Physical Train-ing in American Colleges and Universities*, Circulars of Information of the Bu-reau of Education, No. 5, 1885 (Washington, D.C.: U.S. Government Printing Office, 1886).

66. Eugene L. Richards, "College Athletics: Advantages," *Popular Science Monthly* 24 (1884), 446–53; idem, "College Athletics: Evils and Their Reme-dies," *Popular Science Monthly* 24 (1884), 587–97. In an encomium to football

the following year, Richards compared the sport to the feelings a lover has for his *mistress* and the *patriot* for his country! Idem, "Foot-Ball in America," *Outing* 6 (1885), 62–66.

67. "Some of the Moral and Physical Effects of the Game of Football, Selections from Editorials in the *Medical News* of November 18, November 25, December 2 and December 9, 1893" (published as separate pamphlet). Compare, for example, Joseph Hamblen Sears, "Foot-ball: Sport and Training," *North American Review* 153 (1891), 750–53.

68. John Harley Warner, "Physiology," in Numbers, *Education of American Physicians*, 48–71.

69. "The Division of Physical Culture and Athletics," *University of Chicago Register, July 1, 1893,* 169–70; "Physical Culture and Athletics," *The University of Chicago President's Report, July 1892–July 1902* (Chicago: University of Chicago Press, 1903), 336–39; Hal A. Lawson and Alan G. Ingham, "Conflicting Ideologies Concerning the University and Intercollegiate Athletics: Harper and Hutchins at Chicago, 1892–1940," *Journal of Sport History* 7 (1980), 37–67.

70. Gulick, "Physical Education: A New Profession," 65. See also H. P. Bowditch, "Reform in Medical Education," *Science* 8 (1898), 921–27.

71. Thomas D. Wood, "Some Unsolved Problems in Physical Education," *Addresses and Proceedings of the International Congress of Education, Chicago, 1893* 3 (1893), 621–23, as cited by Walter P. Kroll, *Graduate Study and Research in Physical Education* (Champaign, Ill.: Human Kinetics Publishers, 1982), 43. To date, Kroll's is the only attempt to analyze efforts to establish "academic/scientific" degree programs in physical education in the 1890s.

72. George W. Fitz, "Problems of Physical Education," *Harvard Graduates Magazine* 2 (1893), 26–31; Kroll, *Graduate Study,* 27–60; *Harvard University Catalogue, 1893–94,* 246–47; *Harvard University Catalogue, 1895–96,* 297–99.

73. George W. Fitz, "Discussion," in *Proceedings of the American Association for the Advancement of Physical Education, Philadelphia, 1892* (Springfield, Mass.: Springfield Printing and Binding Co., 1893), 203.

74. Fitz, "Problems of Physical Education," 30; *Harvard University Catalogue, 1895–96,* 297.

75. *Harvard University Catalogue, 1895–96,* 297–99. The Department of Physical Training and Hygiene at Stanford University opened with the 1891–92 academic year. Professor Thomas Denison Wood, M.D. was its director. The course for teachers included sanitary science, personal and general hygiene, bodily mechanics, physiology of exercise, anthropometry, history of gymnastics, and medical gymnastics—all taught by Wood. Miss Lowell and Mr. Black (with Wood) taught a variety of practical courses in Swedish and German gymnastics, health gymnastics and athletics. *Stanford University Register, 1891–92,* 72–73.

76. *Boston Normal School of Gymnastics, Second Annual Catalogue of the Instructors, Students, and Graduates, with a Statement of the Course of Instruction and Examinations, 1892–1893; Boston Normal School of Gymnastics; Fourth Annual*

Catalogue of the Instructors, Students, and Graduates, with a Statement of the Courses of Instruction, 1894–95.

77. George W. Fitz, "Conditions and Needs of Physical Education," *American Physical Education Review* 4 (1899), 337–39. Hartwell had criticized colleges and universities for a failure to show any great insight or scientific interest in physical training as early as 1891. He and other discussants objected to a paper delivered at the 1891 A.A.A.P.E. meetings entitled "Is the Teaching of Physical Education a Trade or a Profession?" in which Dudley A. Sargent had complained that manufacturers and entrepreneurs were appropriating the gymnasium equipment that had been invented by "experts"—by which Harvard's Gymnasium Director almost certainly meant his "developing appliances." Gulick and J. Gardner Smith, director of the Harlem, New York, Y.M.C.A., both medical doctors—as was Sargent—retorted that in medicine it was considered unprofessional for a man to use his name in connection with a patent. See *Proceedings of the American Association for the Advancement of Physical Education, Boston, 1891* (Ithaca, N.Y.: Andrus and Church, 1891), especially 22–24; C. E. Ehinger, "Physical Culture in Normal Schools," in *Proceedings of the American Association for the Advancement of Physical Education, Philadelphia, 1892* (Springfield, Mass.: Springfield Printing and Binding Co., 1893), 184–204.

78. Gerald Geison, "Divided We Stand: Physiologists and Clinicians in the American Context," in Morris J. Vogel and Charles E. Rosenberg, eds., *The Therapeutic Revolution: Essays in the Social History of American Medicine* (Philadelphia: University of Pennsylvania Press, 1979), 67–90.

79. James A. Babbitt, "Present Condition of Gymnastics and Athletics in American Colleges," *American Physical Education Review* 8 (1903), 280–83; "American Society for Research in Physical Education," *American Physical Education Review* 9 (1904), 60–61.

80. Ronald G. Walters, *American Health Reformers, 1815–1860* (New York: Hill and Wang, 1978), especially chap. 7. See Green, *Fit for America;* Whorton, *Crusaders for Fitness;* and items such as *A Synopsis of the Course of Instruction in the Department of Gymnastics of the Northwestern Normal Institute for Physical Education* (Chicago: H. A. Newcome and Co., 1864).

81. "Physical Training in America," *Report of the Commissioner of Education for the Year 1891–92,* vol. 1 (Washington, D.C.: Government Printing Office, 1894), 494–594; Delphine Hanna, "Present Status of Physical Training in Normal Schools," *American Physical Education Review* 8 (1903), 293–97; James E. Sullivan, "Present Status of Athletic Gymnastics and Gymnasiums," ibid., 268–72; Henry Hartung, "The Present Condition of Gymnastics and Athletics in the North American Gymnastic Union," ibid., 273–79; George T. Hepbron, "The Present Status of Physical Training in the Young Men's Christian Associations," ibid., 284–92; Babbitt, "Present Condition of Gymnastics and Athletics in American Colleges." See also Donald J. Mrozek, *Sport and American Mentality, 1880–1910* (Knoxville: University of Tennessee Press, 1983), especially chap. 7. Although Macfadden had been publishing books

and journals for years, his several volume *Macfadden's Encyclopedia of Physical Culture*, first issued in 1911, may have been the most extensive. The A.A.A.P.E. was renamed the American Physical Education Association in 1903.

82. Hanna, "Physical Training in Normal Schools"; reprinted in Kroll, *Graduate Study in Physical Education*, chap. 2. James H. McCurdy, "A Study of the Characteristics of Physical Training in the Public Schools of the United States," *American Physical Education Review* 10 (1905), 202–13.

83. McCurdy, "Characteristics of Physical Training."

84. Walker, "College Athletics."

85. Guy M. Lewis, "Adoption of the Sports Program, 1906–1939: The Role of Accommodation in the Transformation of Physical Education," *Quest* 12 (1969), 34–46.

86. William James, *Psychology* (New York: Henry Holt and Co., 1913), 65–66, 134–50; Henry Maudsley, *The Physiology of Mind* (New York: D. Appleton and Co., 1883), especially chap. 7; see also Anita C. Fellman and Michael Fellman, *Making Sense of Self: Medical Advice Literature in Late Nineteenth-Century America* (Philadelphia: University of Pennsylvania Press, 1981), chap. 7.

87. Edward M. Hartwell, "Physical Training, Its Function and Place in Education," *American Physical Education Review* 2 (1897), 148. The quote is attributed to Mercier. Italics in the source.

88. Ibid., 133–51.

89. Luther Gulick, "Some Psychical Aspects of Physical Exercise," *Popular Science Monthly* 52 (1898), 793–808; idem, "Psychological, Pedagogical, and Religious Aspects of Group Games," *Pedagogical Seminary* 6 (1899), 135–51; T. R. Croswell, "Amusements of Worcester School Children," ibid., 314–71.

90. George Fitz, "Play as a Factor in Development," *American Physical Education Review* 2 (1897), 209–15.

91. Josiah Quincy, "Playgrounds, Baths and Gymnasia," *American Physical Education Review* 3 (1898), 235–41; Henry Ling Taylor, "Exercise and Vigor," ibid., 249–57; George E. Johnson, "Play in Physical Education" ibid., 179–87. See also idem, "Education by Plays and Games, *Pedagogical Seminary* 3 (1894), 97–133.

92. "Tentative Report of the Committee on a Normal Course in Play of the Playground Association of America," *Proceedings of the Third Annual Playground Congress and Yearbook, 1909.*

93. Clark W. Hetherington, "Analysis of Problems in College Athletics," *American Physical Education Review* 12 (1907), 154–81.

94. J. Thomas Jable, "The Public Schools Athletic League of New York City: Organized Athletics for City School Children, 1903–1914," in Wayne M. Ladd and Angela Lumpkin, eds., *Sport in American Education: History and Perspective. A.A.H.P.E.R.D. History of Sport and Physical Education Academy Symposia, March 24, 1977 and April 6, 1978*, ix-18; Arnold W. Flath, *A History of Relations between the National Collegiate Athletic Association and the Amateur Athletic Union of the United States: 1905–1963* (Champaign, Ill.: Stipes Publishing

Co., 1964), chap. 3. Although physical educators by no means ever formed a major part of the governance of the N.C.A.A., Hetherington (Missouri), Stagg, Phillips, and C. W. Savage (Oberlin) had all served on the executive committee by 1910, and Savage and R. Tait McKenzie, M.D. (Pennsylvania) had been vice presidents.

95. Paul C. Phillips, "The Extension of Athletic Sports to the Whole Student Body at Amherst," *American Physical Education Review* 17 (1912), 339–42.

5 *Patricia Vertinsky*

Exercise, Physical Capability, and the Eternally Wounded Woman in Late Nineteenth-Century North America

During the latter part of the nineteenth century, arguments about women's limited physical and mental capacity and the centrality of reproduction for understanding women's bodies defined medical views of women's health and the productive boundaries of their lives. Ostensibly basing their views upon new scientific evidence, influential medical practitioners, many of whom were men, utilized pseudo-scientific theories about the effects of the reproductive life cycle upon women's physical capabilities to control the life choices of middle-class women and set limits upon their activities.

Though women were held to be victims of their reproductive apparatus in general, the onset of menstruation and its recurring cycle were believed to be the cause of particular handicap. Women's limited physical achievements as compared to men were increasingly ascribed to the burden placed upon them by their reproductive apparatus, especially menstruation. The onset of menses at puberty was considered an illness to be weathered only with particular care. For the next thirty years of life's pilgrimage, women were advised to treat themselves as invalids once a month, curtailing both physical and mental activity during the "catamenial week" lest they succumb to accidents, disease, and loss of fertility.

The widespread notion that women were chronically weak, and that they had only a finite amount of mental and physical energy due to the recurring fact of menstruation had a strong effect upon the medical profession's attitude and consequently the public's attitude toward female exercise and participation in sport. Furthermore, these attitudes have continued to persist throughout the twentieth century despite accumulating scientific and medical evidence that menstruation need not affect physical performance.

Wells, in a recent summary of the scientific literature related to exercise and menstruation, notes that misinformation and traditional views concerning the menstrual function are still major blocks to the active participation of girls and women in competitive sports. Until quite recently, for example, the International Olympic Committee believed that sports training and competition were detrimental to proper reproductive functioning in women and used these beliefs to delimit female participation in certain sports.[1] Female athletes and feminists have worked hard to dispel such myths.[2]

This paper explores how long-standing propositions about women's capacity for sport and strenuous exercise developed in response to late nineteenth-century physicians' interpretations of biological theories about menstruation. In issuing popular medical advice to middle-class women in the last three decades of the nineteenth century, establishment physicians on both sides of the Atlantic promoted a theory of menstrual disability that contributed substantially to a deepening stereotyping of women as both the weaker and a periodically weakened sex. In their professional and popular writings, and in their medical practice, these physicians disseminated widely their understandings of the menstrual function and offered their notions of the therapies and life-style behaviors that were required to help women cope with the "illness of menstruation" and its baneful and limiting effects upon female physical capabilities.

Looked upon as an "eternal wound," an illness, and as a shortcoming, menstruation came to be seen as a process that required certain kinds of moderate physical activity, suitable exercises in the open air, and the kind of sport that would be appropriate for physical renewal. Perceived as a pathological condition, however, it necessitated the exclusion of women from vigorous and competitive sports and from any physical exertion that the medical experts considered overtaxing. Thus, though certain requirements for exercise were among the most frequent prescriptions for the recurring drain of menstruation, constraints were imposed with increasing regularity upon the extent and nature of female participation in exercise and sporting activities. Medical advice concerning exercise and physical activity came to reflect and perpetuate understandings about woman's "abiding sense of physical weakness" and the unchangeable nature of her physical inferiority.

Increasingly, medico-biological arguments concerning menstruation were generalized to buttress the special position of establishment physicians as arbiters of female physical behavior, hence legitimizing their claim that women had special needs for constant medical guardianship. With this mandate, doctors could render judgments as to who was physically fit and who was not (these judgments carrying with them implications of being fit or unfit for particular tasks, physical activities, and certain types of sports).

A study of how medical reasonings about the menstrual function developed to define and delimit the parameters of female physical activity is instructive in understanding the shaping of scientific and popular thought by a dominant group of physicians operating within the technical and ideological framework of their era. For many perceived disorders, the labeling of disease or disability, the delimiting of disease characteristics, and the choices made among possible therapies depend heavily upon social and professional convention (and/or convenience). Furthermore, "there are complex ambiguities in the application of medical models and practices to chronic disorders and especially to normal processes.[3] In their attempt to root views of womenkind in biology, late nineteenth century regular medical practitioners played the role of human engineers, conditioning middle-class females to view their normal menstrual function as pathological, thus distorting their perception of their own vigor and physical abilities.

Theories of Menstruation: Myth, Magic, and Science

The widespread notion that women were rendered imperfect, less whole, and physically disabled due to the recurring fact of menstruation was not a fiction of the nineteenth century but had deep roots in magical, religious, and medical mythologies. Menstrual taboos are among the most inviolate in many societies. Indeed, few taboos "evoke as forceful and as universal a response as those surrounding menstruation."[4]

The cyclical character of menstruation has generated a particular set of long-standing beliefs. Primitive society connected the rhythm of menstruation with the cycles of the moon, the seasons, and the rhythm of tides. Many ancient legends developed explanations to relate the cyclic occurrence of the moon with the recurring menses. Fluhman, in his treatise on menstrual disorders, noted the persistence of the saying in ancient treatises, "luna vetus vetulas, juvenes nova luna repurgat" (The old moon repurifies old women, the new moon [repurifies] young women).[5] Aristotle considered the moon to be female since "the menstrual flux and the waning of the moon both take place towards the end of the month, and after the wane and the discharge, both become whole again."[6] Centuries later, one of King George II's physicians explained that "the ancients observed, and everyone knows, how great a share the moon has in forwarding those evacuations of the weaker sex. . . . in countries nearest the equator where we have proved lunar action to be strongest, these monthly secretions are in much greater quantity than in those near the poles where the force is weakest."[7]

Many traditional beliefs reflected a fear of the powers of menstrual blood, where the menstruating woman, albeit weakened, was also seen as a contaminating agent.[8] Thus, many taboos developed around female contact with food and with people (especially men). Sometimes seen as a healing agent, menstrual blood was more often believed to have destructive powers or bring bad luck. Contact with it, said Pliny the Roman, "turns new wine sour—hives of bees die—to taste it drives dogs mad and infects their bite with an incurable poison."[9] Many primitive societies thus excluded menstruating females from public life, especially from food gathering and preparation, so that they would not contaminate members of the tribe.

Taboos also extended to intercourse during menstruation. In the Judeo-Christian scriptures, the rule was underscored in Leviticus, "And if a woman have issue, and her issue in her flesh be blood, she shall be put apart seven days: and whoever toucheth her shall be unclean until the even."[10] Christianity clung to the Old Testament belief in the imperfect nature of woman that was believed to be, in part, a consequence of the menstrual flow.[11]

Thomas Aquinas described woman as "defective and misbegotten," a result of a defect in the active power (of the male seed) or some external influence such as a moist south wind.[12] To the early monks, woman was impure as a result of the pollution of menstruation and was forbidden to take communion in the early Christian churches. Orthodox Jews insisted upon Niddah, a minimum of twelve days separation of wife and husband during and after the menses with strict prohibitions about food handling and other intimate practices.[13]

Ideas about the contaminating possibilities of menstruating women increased their currency during the nineteenth century. John Elliotson wrote in 1840 that it was very useful to regard menstruating women as unclean, for they could not cure meat at such a time.[14] Thirty-eight years later, the *British Medical Journal* published an extensive correspondence concerning whether a menstruating woman could contaminate the food she touched. One contributor extended the argument to oppose medical education for women: "If such bad results accrue from a woman curing dead meat whilst she is menstruating, what would result, under similar conditions, from her attempt to cure living flesh in her midwifery or surgical practice?"[15]

Scientific and medical theories of menstruation were strongly colored by these traditional beliefs. Two general propositions tended to dominate medical thought about menstruation. On the one hand, the condition was seen as a regular release of accumulated excess blood and body impurities—a form of purification. The second proposition related to the reproductive process. During pregnancy, the accumulated blood was believed to be used as a nutritive source for the fetus—this being the contribution of the woman to reproduction. Aristotle observed that menstruation was the outward sign of female inferiority, a result of the passive part played by women in reproduction. The active male was believed to be able to transform matter with heat to produce semen; the colder female could not transform matter, hence had to discharge the residue of useless nourishment from her blood vessels each month unless she was pregnant. Thus, noted Aristotle, the menses must be a substance intended to nourish the fetus, and this was the only contribution of the female to reproduction.[16] Hippocrates and Pliny shared the same belief, one that persisted for centuries. Pliny wrote that "women who do not menstruate are incapable of bearing children because it is of this substance that the infant is formed. The seed of the male, acting as a sort of leaven, causes it to unite and assume a form, and in due time it acquires life and assumes a bodily shape."[17]

Other theorists agreed with the unique need of women to periodically shed extra blood, though for different reasons. In the second century A.D., Galen believed that menstruation consisted of fluids accumulated from leading an idle life, which were thus regularly evacuated for the body's relief.[18] Soranus felt that both men and women generated surplus matter; women eliminated it as menses, men through athletics.[19] Smellie, in 1766, concurred that "the catamenia is no more than a periodic discharge of that superfluous blood which is collected through the month."[20]

Medical theorists later focused upon the mode of evacuation. Avicenna, an eleventh-century Arab physician, suggested that menstrual blood was eliminated through the womb because that organ had been the last formed and was, therefore, the weakest.[21] His idea was further developed in the seventeenth century by Regnier de Graaf, who likened the escape of blood from the weakened uterus to fermented wine or beer seeping out of a defective barrel.[22]

The demonstration of the graafian follicle by Dr. Graaf and others was predicated upon the notion that ovulation occurred at the time of conception. Subsequently, a number of physicians began to suspect that ovulation might be a spontaneous process and that menstruation was intimately connected with the ovarian function. In 1793, Dr. John Beale Davidge, a prominent Maryland surgeon, wrote a dissertation citing evidence to support his belief that the menstrual flow was a secretion of the uterus under the control of the ovaries. In 1812, John Power of London further enunciated the relationship between menstruation and specific changes in the ovaries, and studies of the ovulation process appeared increasingly in print in the first half of the nineteenth century.[23]

By 1865, Pfluger was arguing that the development of the graafian follicle produced an irritation of the ovarian nerve leading to a reflex stimulation that resulted in simultaneous ovulation and menstruation.[24] Pfluger's theory that nervous stimulation triggered menstruation was widely accepted by American physicians in the last three decades of the nineteenth century, despite a number of studies that suggested that such a view might be mistaken.[25] Graaf's theory of ferment, or "vehement effervescence," laid the basis for the Stephenson wave theory which was expounded in 1882. Stephenson, a physician, understood menstruation to be related to cyclical waves of vital energy, shown in the body temperature, daily urine, and pulse rate. In his view, menstruation coincided with changes in the average body temperature and sought the weakest exit (the womb) when excessive nutritive material and vital energy were not required for reproduction.[26] Stephenson's theory also explained vicarious menstruation, for he believed that if there was an obstruction anywhere in the body, the resulting wave would be thrown to the weakest part of the system. G. Stanley Hall later used Stephenson's theory to explain why every trouble in a woman demanded special attention to the pelvis.[27]

Stephenson based his wave principle on the experimental findings of Mary Putnam Jacobi and John Goodman, a Louisville physician, which were essentially a reformulation of Galen's plethoric theory.[28] Goodman claimed that menstruation was presided over by a law of monthly periodicity, a menstrual wave that affected the entire female and rendered her periodically unstable and liable to serious derangement.

Mary Putnam Jacobi explained that women experienced a rhythmic wave of nutrition, such nutritive material being expelled in menstruation when not used for reproduction. This caused a perturbation of the economy periodically and could lead to hysteria.[29] Though she criticized those who considered menstruation to be a morbid circumstance, she did report evidence that because of it women might be unfit to bear the physical fatigues and mental anxieties of such activities as obstetrical practice.[30] Dr. King went further than Goodman to view menstruation as a totally abnormal process, associated with civilization and logically, therefore, an interference with nature.[31] Dr. King maintained that menstruation must be unnatural since, though conception occurred at that time, the intercourse necessary to cause conception might cause gonorrhea in the male. Dr. Gardner, author of *Conjugal Sins,* similarly warned that menstrual blood was corrupt and virulent, threatening an unwitting penis with "disease, excoriations and blenorrhagias."[32] John Cowan predicted that the fetus might be damaged should intercourse take place at menstruation. "Do not, I pray you, . . . do this unclean thing . . . while a new body is being developed."[33] King's cure for the menstrual disease was to repress it altogether through continual pregnancies, since in her primitive state woman was constantly conceiving and menstruation was therefore rare.

Such views, taken together, helped cement the picture of the female as somehow "driven by the tidal currents of her cyclical reproductive system, a cycle . . . reinforced each month by her recurrent menstrual flow."[34] Each month, for a woman's thirty-year pilgrimage, menstruation was seen to present itself as a trauma—a morbid and unnatural activity, a disease requiring specific therapies.[35] It was a circumstance over which woman had little control, yet it shaped her personality and physical ability to respond to life's demands. As Dr. Van de Worker explained, women's limited physical achievements as compared with men were due to the fact that the menstrual cycle handicapped her, rendering her periodically susceptible to accidents and hysteria.[36] Menstruation, some physicians warned, could drive a woman temporarily insane.[37]

Not until 1896 was the reflex nerve irritation theory refuted by Westphalen who began to describe the cyclical changes in the uterine lining and the continual process of building up and breaking down of that lining. Important discoveries about the endocrine function in menstrual physiology came only after 1900, when the cycle of changes in the endometrium and the role of ovarian hormones in triggering the cycle became more clearly understood.[38]

Explaining Menstrual Disability

Though clearly hampered by a lack of knowledge about the precise functioning of the menstrual system, late nineteenth-century physicians developed a remarkably elaborate set of explanations and accompanying prescriptions to offset what they insisted were the deleterious effects of recurring menstruation. Neglect of the ramifications of the periodical function was considered by Dr. Edward Clarke to be the principal source of disease among the women of the land—its repression or overproduction to be equally fatal to health.[39] Michelet referred to the menstrual function as "the cause of the whole drama."[40] Hayes called it "an internal wound, the real cause of all this tragedy."[41]

Underlying the perceived need to regulate girls' and women's behavior during menstruation was an overriding concern of the age with order and with scarcity. The anxieties of physicians (and other health advisers) were demonstrated through constant reference to the need to obey the laws of nature lest loss of control, disorder, and disease follow. Perceived as a discrete energy field, the body was believed to contain a certain amount of vital energy. If energy was used in one direction, then less would be available for another. Consequently, scarce energy had to be husbanded for the particular needs of mind and body. Furthermore, one's quota of energy for the life span had to be spent carefully. Since what you spent in one period of life was bound to be missed at another, energy had to be carefully apportioned. Any overuse could well be billed to future generations who would have to pay for it out of their own limited supply. The belief in a limited energy pool was a kind of "mercantilism of self" for, "in the great economy of nature, force answers to force and everything must be paid."[42] "Nature," warned Herbert Spencer, "is a strict accountant . . . and if you demand of her in one direction more than she is prepared to lay out, she balances the account by making a deduction elsewhere."[43]

The writings of Herbert Spencer were enormously influential in explaining the particular physical disabilities of women. Spencer was perhaps the supreme ideologue of the Victorian period, reflecting the dominant ideas and values of the middle class.[44] His prolific writings were widely disseminated and his influence extensive. In North America, his main forum was the *Popular Science Monthly,* a serious and widely read journal that was initially founded as a spokespiece for his ideas.[45] In his numerous books and articles, Spencer carefully delineated the relationship of women to evolutionary theory and the social and physical energy scheme. His argument went as follows. Men were always physically stronger than women. Though primitive women had more nearly approached the physical status of civilized men, the progress of evolution had freed them from the necessity of hard physical work. In the process, they had lost their physical strength, for the Lamarckian mechanism decreed that disease developed when organs were not used.[46] Though males and females both needed physical strength for growth and development, girls developed more rapidly than boys and used up their available strength quota faster.[47] Thus, not only did they start with less strength and lose it more quickly, women were subsequently "taxed" with the special energy demand necessitated by menstruation and reproduction. This tax was a biological one and a social one for women were obliged to pay the price for the preservation of society. It was a "reproductive sacrifice" that was bound to limit individual development, but that could only be seen as a requirement for the fitness of the race.

Thus, Spencer set up the central argument against female emancipation by elucidating the conflict between self-development and reproduction. To social theorists of his ilk, self-development for females could only mean self-sacrifice and this meant spending their cachet of physical and mental energy at the motherhood bank. There simply was not enough vital force left over from the demands of the reproductive system for women to develop their intellects.[48]

Though such arguments explained why women were particularly subject to energy limitations, boys and men, too, were often warned of the dangers of excessive or imbalanced use of physical and mental activity. In their case, intellectual activity was not considered a drain upon the physical energy of the male. What could debilitate was excessive sexual vigor and the deliberate loss of sperm, which led to mental disability and disease.[49] Women, however, were believed to have constitutions that demanded a reverse kind of caution in balancing the energy supply, for they were at the mercy of the physical demands of their reproductive physiology. Parsons has argued that late nineteenth-century physicians also considered males as extensions and victims of their reproductive systems, equating at times the prostate with the uterus.[50] Certainly, the loss of seminal fluid was considered to be as detrimental to body and brain as was the loss of blood.[51] Also, certain energetic exercises were thought to be provocative of masturbation, and hence loss of vital fluid; "those in which the whole weight of the body [is] sustained by the hands" would be better excluded from the gymnasium, said Dr. Howe.[52] However, males could use force of will to prevent loss of fluids, while females could not. A life-style of self-denial could turn away weakness and disease from the male whereas women's loss of blood was spontaneous and ungovernable and was required for the sake of the race.

The constant emphasis upon the need for race betterment at this time tended to focus the physician's spotlight upon the menstrual disability theory. A woman who consumed her vital force in brain work depleted the amount of energy required by the reproductive system, especially during menstruation or pregnancy. Male physicians felt there could be no competition between the pursuit of culture and the demands of nature. Women could not do two things well at the same time. "We would rather err on the safe side and keep the mental part of the human machine back a little, while we would encourage bulk, and fat and bone and muscular strength . . . this applies to the female sex . . . more than to the male (since) women's chief work (is) to the future of the world."[53]

Since a woman's chief function was motherhood, the laws of nature demanded that not only must a bountiful supply of energy be reserved for the demands of the reproductive system, but that more energy still must be earmarked to compensate for the monthly drain of energy imposed by menstruation. As Dr. A. Hughes Bennett explained it, even under the best of circumstances, the frequently recurring processes of menstruation rendered a woman "specially liable to derangements of her general health—under adverse conditions she is almost certain to fall a victim."[54] Dr. Taylor concurred in *A Physician's Counsels to Women in Health and Disease:* "We cannot too emphatically urge the importance of regarding these monthly returns as periods of ill health, as days when the ordinary occupations are to be suspended or modified. . . . every woman should look upon herself as an invalid once a month since the monthly flow exaggerates any existing affection of the womb and readily rekindles the expiring flames of disease."[55]

Notions of menstrual disability became widespread in both Europe and North America. Dr. Tilt was an eminent and widely read authority in England. "For thirty years," he wrote in *The Lancet*, woman is "thrown into a state of haemorrhagic and other orgasm every month."[56] At such time, explained a supporting authority, they are "unfit for any great mental or physical labor. . . . They suffer under a languor and depression which disqualify them for thought or action."[57] Michelet, in *L'Amour*, explained that for a period of fifteen or twenty days out of twenty-eight, the woman was "not only an invalid, but a wounded one. It was woman's plight to ceaselessly suffer love's eternal wound."[58] From Germany, Dr. Runge insisted that "since a woman needs protection during menstruation all demands on her strength must be remitted. Every month for several days she is enfeebled, if not downright ill."[59] G. Stanley Hall summed up many of the arguments in his monumental treatise *Adolescence*. At this time, he said, "they can do less work with mind and body (and) make less accurate and energetic movements."[60]

Though women had to expect to be disabled by menstruation for thirty of their best years, the onset of menarche was believed to be a time of particular physical stress and crisis. At this time, the entire developing female organism was thrown into turmoil. Adolescence was the period of maximum growth when all energies were to be conserved rather than dissipated. Puberty for boys marked the onset of strength and enhanced vigor; for girls it marked the onset of the prolonged and periodic weaknesses of womanhood. George Austin warned girls that at the time of the appearance of menstruation, special dangers awaited, all of them due to their sexual functions.[61] J. H. Kellogg wrote repeatedly that the first occurrence of menstruation was a very critical period in the life of a female, each recurrence rendering her "specially susceptible to morbid influences and liable to serious derangements."[62] Nineteenth-century physicians recalled Hippocrates' analysis that "nubile virgins, particularly about the menstrual periods, are affected with paroxysms, apoplexies."[63] Many were sure that the onset of menarche made a girl ripe for disease, and that special precautions were absolutely necessary.

"To Be" Is Greater Than "To Do": Life-style Prescriptions for Coping with Menstrual Disability

The protection of pubertal girls from excessive mental and physical activity at the time of menarche became a veritable campaign among the proponents of menstrual disability. Girls of the better classes, said Thomas Emmett in a widely quoted medical textbook, should spend the year before and two years after puberty at rest. "Each menstrual period should be passed in the recumbent position until her system becomes accustomed to the new order of life."[64]

John Thorburn feared "disproportion between development of muscle and of nerve in women." Agreeing with Emmett, he insisted that girls should do hardly any steady work for the three years surrounding puberty. Furthermore, they should "plan to lie fallow about a quarter of the time." "Girls," he continued, "should develop the dignity and efficiency of going slow."[65] The best of medical specialists, said G. Stanley Hall, agreed that a girl should be "turned out to grass" and allowed to withdraw from other activities to "let nature do its beautiful work of inflorescence." "Periodicity, perhaps the deepest law of the cosmos, celebrates its highest triumphs in woman's life." Once regular menstruation was established, he added, "the paradise of stated rest should be revisited in the monthly sabbath." Idleness should be actively cultivated, and woman, realizing that " 'to be' is greater than 'to do' should step reverently aside from her daily routine and let Lord Nature work."[66]

Hall's volumes on adolescence underscored widespread medical concerns about the appropriate life-style behavior of girls and young women. In a variety of public arenas he carried on the campaign that "every girl should be educated," not to become self-supporting but, "primarily to become a wife and mother."[67] Education for the adolescent girl should consist of courses in "heroalogy"—the teaching of the noble lesson of service to the collective soul of the people wherein women, as bearers of the race, would become the conduit through which "mansoul" might some day become a "supermansoul."[68] Since the efficient functioning of the reproductive system was the raison d'être of woman's existence, efforts to explain and prescribe appropriate adolescent female activities were considered critically important. Hall used the fact that American girls had their first menses, on average, at fourteen years of age, rather than fifteen and a half in Europe, to support medical claims that American girls must be too precocious. This precocity he blamed upon "mentality and nerve stimulation" resulting especially from inappropriate female education.[69] He thus strongly buttressed the popular medical feeling that "there are, in the physiological life of women, disqualifications for continuous labor of the mind."[70]

The precise physiological disqualifications of young women were elaborated most clearly by Dr. Edward Clarke in 1873. His treatise on *Sex and Education* (which ran through seventeen editions in thirteen years) mounted a major attack upon the educational and professional aspirations of late nineteenth-century middle-class women, and his chief weapon was the theory of menstrual disability. "Let the fact be accepted," he declared, "that there is nothing to be ashamed of in a woman's organization, and let her whole education and life be guided by the divine requirements of her system." Clarke, a professor of medicine at Harvard, was convinced that girls between twelve and twenty should concentrate solely upon the physiological development of their reproductive system. Energy expended upon mental activity (i.e., female education) at this time could only lead to a depletion of the energy required for full physical development. Mental activity during the catamenial week destroyed feminine capabilities and might well interfere with ovulation and arrest reproductive development. Studying forced the brain to use up the blood and energy needed to get the menstrual process functioning efficiently. Indeed, Clarke warned, if a girl "puts as much force into her brain education as a boy. . . . the special apparatus will suffer."[71]

Clouston went further, attributing stunted growth, nervousness, headaches, hysteria, and insanity to overstimulation of the female brain.[72] Maudsley drew upon Clarke's portraits of the ill-effects of education upon young women to describe the girl who "enters upon the hard work of school or college at the age of 15 or thereabouts, when the function of her sex has perhaps been fairly established; ambitious to stand high in class she . . . (allows) herself no days of relaxation or rest. . . . paying no attention to the periodical tides of her organization, unheeding a drain that would make the stroke oar of the University crew falter. . . . in the long run nature asserts its powers. . . . (she) leaves college a good scholar but a delicate and ailing woman, whose future is one of more or less suffering."[73] Dr. Kellogg agreed. "There is no doubt," he said, "that many young women have permanently injured their constitutions while at school by excessive mental taxation during the catamenial period."[74]

Though there were a number of immediate objections to its implications, the menstrual disability theory of Clarke and his physician contemporaries in Europe and North America became widely accepted. Julia Ward Howe was a leading critic of Dr. Clarke's thesis. "Despite Dr. Clarke's prominent position in this community," she wrote in a collection of essays by leading public figures, "we do not feel compelled to regard him as the supreme authority on the subjects of which he treats." In her effort to disprove his thesis that you cannot feed a woman's brain without starving her body, she pointed instead to the powerful influence of climate upon the health of American women, as well as a young female's particular need for special guardianship. "Many young women," she insisted, "are periodically kept from all violent exercise and fatigue so far as the vigilance of elders can accomplish this . . . [but] . . . a single ride on horseback, a single wetting of the feet . . . may entail lifelong misery. . . . I have known of repeated instances of incurable disease and even of death arising from rides on horseback taken at the critical period."[75] Thus educators, she explained, should not shoulder all the blame for exacerbating female weakness, yet she and many other critics of Clarke did not take issue with the notion that the periodic function should be regarded as a potentially debilitating condition requiring specific lifestyle prescriptions.

Instead, in light of a number of studies pointing out the excellent health of many college women, they attributed the problems of menstrual disability more to a school or household regimen that did not provide sufficient rest and careful exercise during menstruation, than to the actual physical drain of studying.[76] W. LeC. Stevens collected

data from the presidents of Cornell, Michigan, and Wesleyan that suggested that education need not be unfavorable to the health of women
if proper care was taken.[77] The resident physician from Vassar, for
example, claimed that all possible precautions were taken not to over-
tax Vassar girls during the critical period. All students

> are carefully instructed regarding precautions which are periodically nec-
> essary for them. . . . they are positively forbidden to take gymnastics at all
> during the first two days of their period . . . they are also forbidden to ride
> horseback then; and . . . strongly advised not to dance, nor run up and
> down stairs, nor do anything else that gives sudden and successive. . . .
> shocks to the trunk. They are encouraged to go out of doors for quiet
> walks or drives, or boating and to do whatever they can to steady the ner-
> vous irritation.[78]

Arguments about the ramifications of menstrual disability theory
upon adolescent education took a similar tack in England. Though
rebuking Henry Maudsley for his exaggerated conclusion that
women could not compete with men since "for one quarter of each
month during the best years of life (they were) . . . more or less sick
and unfit for hard work," Dr. Elizabeth Garrett Anderson did encourage teachers to protect adolescent girls from mental and physical fatigue and from violent activities such as long walks, riding, dancing,
or lifting heavy weights. Instead, she advocated gymnastics, active
games, daily baths, and other hygienic reforms for girls in schools in
order that their physical condition might be improved.[79]

Thus, the onset of menarche brought the adolescent girl and her
guardians face to face with the need to concentrate upon the regulation of her menses and the honing of her reproductive capacity.
Indeed, said Dr. Wilson, "such is the tendency of most American
girls . . . towards functional disorders, that to inaugurate a proper hygiene that should lead to healthy and vigorous womanhood in most
cases needs nothing less than medical supervision."[80] While vigorous
activity was frowned upon, and periods of rest strongly encouraged, a
certain amount of healthy exercise was definitely indicated. Physicians
elaborated a detailed regimen for young women consisting of an appropriate blend of rest and restorative exercise. As Dr. Henry Ling
Taylor explained, the problem presented to the physician lay in de-
ciding "not merely the prescription of exercise but rather such pro-
portioning and contrasting of the muscular activity to periods of rest
that the total result [would] be beneficial."[81]

Clearly, the argument for physical activity had to be carefully con-
strued. On the one hand, definitions of femininity and the menstrual

disability theory implied a lack of physical vigor and robustness, and a recurring energy drain that prevented participation in education and hard labor. On the other hand, the development of physical strength and health was a necessary attribute of a robust and potentially productive mother.[82] There was a difficulty, then, says Rosenberg, of providing the appropriate regimen to smooth the path taken by the dependent, fragile child en route to the demanding responsibilities of motherhood.[83] Some experts, such as Dr. Kellogg, advocated a more active vigorous childhood including outdoor play and exercise for young girls. An active tomboy would surely develop the physical health for future motherhood through boyish sports, he reasoned, yet the carefree romping and vigorous activity had to cease at puberty. Appropriate activity could then be obtained in the kitchen, the washroom, and the garden which was "nature's gymnasia" for adolescent girls.[84] Rest and carefully regulated exercise were to be the norm in the abrupt transition from activity to relative passivity. The sportive competitiveness which could be encouraged in childhood was to give way to selfless femininity. Indeed, after puberty, women were never to compete, for to do so would challenge the whole notion of complementary spheres of influence and competence. Nor were they to be encouraged to assert mastery "in such masculine areas as physical skill, strength and courage."[85] "Certain games, like football and boxing, girls cannot play," said Hall.[86] Rather, girls were to be primed to understand that from puberty on, all bodily strength was to be dedicated to the ceaseless routine of maternity and caring for others—most notably, husband and children. From this time until they were forty years old, said Miss Hardaker, 20 percent of their energy had to be diverted for the maintenance of maternity and its attendant functions.[87] Indeed, every time menstruation occurred, a period of comparative repose, mental and bodily, was to be sought.[88]

Menarche, then, abruptly ushered girls toward their natural vocation, at which stage they "were exempted from the necessity of engaging in violent exercises."[89] Bodily changes associated with the time of menarche also dictated an alteration in exercise prescription. At puberty, said Dr. Roberts, the "pelvis alters its shape . . . and the effect . . . is to bring the knees closer together, and to produce a weak-kneed condition and awkward running gait peculiar to women. Much walking or standing should be avoided and short but vigorous gymnastics exercises substituted, and when possible the recumbent position assumed."[90]

Clouston summed up the general attitudes of the establishment medical profession toward physical education for adolescent girls. The right kind, he explained, is "that which hardens the muscles, adds to the fat, softens the skin, enriches the blood, promotes but does not overstimulate the bodily functions."[91] To exercise the muscles, romping and play, especially out of doors, were the perfect answer.[92] Gymnastic exercises, if well selected and proportioned, would promote muscular development, grace and vigor, but were easily carried to extremes where they could break down the constitution.[93]

Dr. Madison Taylor proposed that the "enfeeblement, so common among pubescent girls, should be combated by romping, ball, beanbags, battledore, hoops, running, golf, tennis, bicycling, self-bathing in cold water, deep breathing exercises once or twice a day rather than by systematic physical culture."[94] Especially appropriate, reminded Alice Tweedy, were "homely gymnastics," or in other words, housework.[95]

To develop fat, "that most essential concomitant of female adolescence," the blood needed enrichment by good nutrition. "Fat is to the body what fun is to the mind" explained Clouston. It is "an indication of spare power for future use."[96] Though physicians did not understand the exact relationship between the onset of menarche and a critical level of body fat, they did worry about "anorexia scolastica," a debilitating thinness and weakness that they believed to result from too much mental stimulus, especially during menstruation.[97] They were also acutely aware of the linkage between the body changes of puberty and chlorosis, a common form of anemia named for the greenish tinge that marked the skin of young women.[98] Chlorosis was linked variously to poor diet, lack of exercise, lack of fresh air, impoverished blood, and mental effort.[99] The menstrual function was almost always implicated. Its derangement resulted in anemic and chlorotic girls, some of whom manifested amenorrhea, while others appeared to show increased blood volume which was interpreted as a promise of fecundity.[100] Loss of strength and appetite were the most frequently reported symptoms of the condition and medical guides noted that common characteristics of chlorotic girls included menstrual problems, a distaste for meat in any form, and a low tolerance for physical activity.[101] Physicians prescribed a combination of rest, moderate exercise in the fresh air, blood and nerve remedies, iron pills, and the eating of red meat to combat what they perceived to be the crisis evoked by the establishment of periodicity.[102]

Life-style prescriptions for the adolescent girl thus took the form of a set of signposts, erected to assist her in coping with the passage from girlhood to womanhood that had been initiated by menarche. "Puberty for a girl," said G. Stanley Hall, "is like floating down a broadening river into an open sea . . . [where] . . . the currents are more complex and the phenomena of tides make new conditions and new dangers."[103]

The metaphorical use of tides and currents in relation to the periodic crises of menstruation was indicative of the generalized fear, at the end of the nineteenth century, that the order and well-being of society was being threatened by waves of uncontrollable elements— among them, demands by the "new woman" to break out of the "separate sphere" that had been defined for her. Establishment physicians saw themselves as being in a special position to stem the tide of female demands for higher education, entrance to the professions, and new bodily freedoms such as birth control and competitive sporting activities, by invoking the authority of science to assert a broader form of control over women's bodies and their regular functions. "We must not abet woman as a sex in rebelling against maternity, quarreling with the moon, or sacrifice wifehood to maidenhood."[104] We must protect them from being "dashed to pieces on the rock of childbirth, . . . ground on the ever-recurring shallows of menstruation."[105] We must warn them of "the effeminacy of wealth, the new woman movement and foeticide."[106] We must not countenance these women who "strive to theoretically ignore and practically escape the monthly function."[107]

Summarizing the scientific findings that had contributed to "our modern knowledge of women," Hall repeatedly underscored established medical opinion that women's periods must be more respected and reiterated the role that physicians must assume as medical guardians, almost moral directors of the intimate, personal behavior of females.[108] Thus, the same mechanistic, closed model of a finite store of nervous energy used by physicians to explain physical and mental health and disease served equally to account for incidences of fragility and disorderliness in social and moral affairs.[109] To many late nineteenth-century American doctors, increasingly anxious about the tensions of American life, the golden key to the desired state of equilibrium was moderation. Excess was morally and physiologically foolhardy. Energy-discharging activities must always be compensated for by energy-conserving ones. Activity must be countered with rest and relaxation; indoor work must be balanced with activity in the open air, and so on. "With a peculiar appropriateness," says Rosenberg, "science provided a vocabulary and a sense of imagery to express and support these beliefs, and from among them, physicians selected those scientific plausibilities which fitted most conveniently into their professional paradigm."[110]

Thus, those who supported most staunchly the theory of menstrual disability were the most uneasy about the dangers of feminine excess, whether it be in study, professional work, or in sports and exercise. Not necessarily considering themselves conservative in their attitudes toward women, they nevertheless were quite convinced that medical evidence demonstrated the physiological undesirability of strenuous and prolonged exertion in mental and physical activities. "When we thus look the matter honestly in the face," said Maudsley,

> it would seem plain that women are marked out by Nature for very different offices in life from those of men, and that the healthy performance of her . . . special functions renders it improbable she will succeed, and unwise for her to persevere, in running over the same course at the same pace with him. For such a race she is certainly weighted unfairly . . . women cannot rebel successfully against the tyranny of their organization. This is not the expression of prejudice nor of false statement, it is the plain statement of a physiological fact.[111]

Sporting activities, just as educational pursuits, had to be compatible with female physiology and always focused upon health and balance rather than the recklessness of unregulated competition. The demands of periodicity were monthly reminders that nineteenth-century women could not, and should not, play the game like men.[112] The burgeoning demands of the "new woman" at the end of the century, however, suggested that, in athletics as well as in other endeavors of the male sphere, women were not wholly committed to the notion that they were eternally wounded.[113]

Epilogue

Paradoxically, one hundred years after the heyday of the menstrual disability theory, current research studies are adding new grist to traditional anxieties that vigorous exercise might indeed be harmful to the female's reproductive function under certain circumstances. Evidence associating endurance-type exercise with changes in the menstrual cycle and ovulation disruption is accumulating.[114] Studies explain that the teenager who begins an intensive physical exercise program prior to normal menarche may experience a delay in the onset of her first period of several years. Furthermore, amenorrhea and infertility appear not to be unusual among female ballet dancers, gymnasts, cross-country skiers, swimmers, and distance runners. Physicians and exercise physiologists demonstrate that to achieve optimum performance, many female athletes go to extraordinary lengths to reduce their body fat stores with severe consequences to their general and reproductive health.[115] Indeed, the relationships between exercise, body fat, and the onset and persistence of menstruation are being explored from a variety of disciplinary viewpoints, due, in part, to an alarming increase in the incidence of pathogenic weight-control behaviors among girls and women.[116]

There is a growing fear that young females, especially athletes, in pushing back the frontiers of corporeal existence in a quest for self-identity and distinctiveness, may close off options available to normally functioning females and damage their reproductive health for the safe of fitness.[117] Within this anxiety do we hear perhaps the echo of Dr. Clouston's warning rebounding? "Women," he wrote in 1884, "have a peculiar power of taking out of themselves more than they can bear. All should carry a reserve to meet emergencies and not use up all their power and thus rob future generations."[118]

Notes

1. Christine L. Wells, *Women, Sport and Performance: A Physiological Perspective* (Champaign, Ill.: Human Kinetics, 1985).

2. See, for example, M. Ann Hall and Dorothy A. Richardson, *Fair Ball: Towards Sex Equality in Canadian Sport* (Ottawa: The Canadian Advisory Council on the Status of Women, 1982); Carole A. Oglesby (ed.), *Women and Sport, From Myth to Reality* (Philadelphia: Lea and Febiger, 1978). Mary C. Boutilier and Lucinda Sangiovanni, *The Sporting Woman* (Champaign, Ill.: Human Kinetics, 1983). G. Pfister has described how, in Germany, female doctors and athletes have had to battle against prejudice and discrimination generated by the scientific assertions of male physicians that the female body is naturally inferior. "The Influence of Women Doctors on the Origins of Women's Sports in Germany," *Medicine and Sport* 14 (1981), 58–65.

3. Eric Holtzman, "Science, Philosophy and Society," *International Journal of Health Services* 11, no. 1 (1981), 125.

4. Menstrual taboos are discussed by Elaine and English Showalter in "Victorian Women and Menstruation," *Victorian Studies* 14, no. 1 (1970), 83–89; Vern Bullough and Martha Voght, "Women, Menstruation, and Nineteenth-Century Medicine," *Bulletin of the History of Medicine* 47, no. 1 (Jan.–Feb. 1973), 66–82; Janice Delaney, Mary Jane Lupton, and Emily Toth, *The Curse: A Cultural History of Menstruation* (New York: E. P. Dutton, 1976); E. Novak, "The Superstition and Folklore of Menstruation," *Johns Hopkins Hospital Bulletin* 27 (1916), 270–74. A major national study on menstruation, *The Tampax Report,* published in 1981 notes that menstruation still remains a taboo subject for most Americans. Of the 1,034 men and women interviewed by a research consortium, most of them thought that menstruation affected women

physically and emotionally, and one third believed that women should restrict their physical activities. *The Tampax Report* (New York: Tambrands, 1981).

5. C. Frederic Fluhman, *Menstrual Disorders, Pathology, Diagnosis and Treatment* (Philadelphia: W. B. Saunders, 1939), 18.

6. Aristotle, quoted in R. Crawford, *The Lancet* 2 (1915), 1331.

7. Richard Mead, *The Medical Works* (Edinburgh: A. Donaldson and J. Reid, 1765). Some nineteenth-century physicians remained convinced that climate affected menstruation, especially the age of menarche. According to the research of Dr. Pye Henry Chavasse, girls in warm climates menstruated at ten or eleven but those in Russia might wait till they were twenty to thirty years old, and even then only menstruate a few times a year. Pye Henry Chavasse, *Woman as a Wife and Mother* (Philadelphia, 1871), 90–91.

8. Freud, for example, saw in men's fear of blood an ambivalence toward women as both sacred and cursed, both pure and unclean. Devereux discusses examples of the central theme of the psychoanalytic approach to menstruation, which is the menstruating woman as "witch," possessing special dangers and powers. He concludes that taboos on menstruation reflect women's real power as propagators of men (G. Devereux, "The Psychology of Feminine Genital Bleeding," *The International Journal of Psycho-Analysis* 31 (1950), 252–53). Bruno Bettelheim, in *Symbolic Wounds* (Glencoe, Ill.: The Free Press, 1954) discusses psychoanalytic interpretations of male envy and fear of female menstruation and the taboos and ceremonies that developed around these beliefs. Psychoanalysts have contributed to notions that menstruation is a monthly neurosis fraught with numerous psychic fears. According to Karen Horney, man devalues woman's functions in order to keep her out of his domain, creating an ideology that will keep him powerful and her inferior. By viewing the menarche and menstruation as problematic, the male can see the female as biologically incapable of assuming positions of power (Karen Horney, "The Problems of Feminine Masochism," *Feminine Psychology* [N.Y.: Norton, 1967]).

9. Pliny the Younger, *Natural History*, trans. H. Rackham (Cambridge, Mass.: Harvard University Press, 1961), book 7, 549.

10. Leviticus 15:19 (New Revised Standard Translation).

11. Mary Douglas explains that much of Leviticus is taken up with outlining the physical perfection (completeness) required in being holy and, therefore, blessed. The idea of holiness was given an external, physical expression in the wholeness of the body, seen as a perfect container. Natural functions producing bodily waste, especially menstruation, degraded this notion of completeness and rendered women somehow less able to conform to the holiness essential for gaining God's blessing. Thus, a polluting person was always seen as marginal and a source of weakness to the social unit (*Purity and Danger: An Analysis of the Concepts of Pollution and Taboo* [Boston: Routledge and Kegan Paul, 1966]).

12. *Basic Writings of St. Thomas Aquinas*, ed. Anton C. Pegis (New York: Random House, 1948), 880.

13. Though Orthodox Jews believe these laws to have originated from the time of Adam and Eve, when Eve was punished by God with menstruation and pain in labor for bringing mortality to Adam (Genesis Rabbah 17:13), and to be underscored in the writings of Leviticus, a book, *Baraita de Niddah,* published by a heretical Jewish sect in 1890, reinforced a number of traditional taboos concerning menstruation. See Cora Goldberg Marks, "In Purity and Love. An Introduction to the Jewish Attitudes towards Marriage." *Lifestyles* 13 (1986), 98–106.

14. John Elliotson, *Human Physiology,* 5th ed. (London: Green and Longmans, 1840), 770–71.

15. W. Storey, *British Medical Journal* 1 (1878), 324. The correspondence columns of the *Journal* debating menstruation and contamination are discussed in detail in Ronald Pearson, *The Worm in the Bud. The World of Victorian Sexuality* (London: Penguin Books, 1969).

16. Aristotle, *On the Generation of Animals,* trans. A. L. Peck (London: Heinemann, 1943), 2.4.185.

17. Pliny the Younger, *Natural History,* book 7, 13.

18. Fluhman, *Menstrual Disorders,* 19. Galen, quoted by John Freind, *Emmenologia,* trans. Thomas Dale (London: 1729), 19, 67.

19. Soranus, *Gynecology,* trans. Oswei Temkin (Baltimore: Johns Hopkins University Press, 1956), 23.

20. W. Smellie, *A Treatise on the Theory and Practice of Midwifery,* 5th ed. (London: Wilson, 1766).

21. Fritz Vosselmann, *La menstruation, légendes, coutumes, et superstitions* (Lyon: University of Lyon, 1935), 16–17.

22. Regnier de Graaf, *Histoire anatomique des parties génitales de l'homme et de la femme* (Paris: Baritel, 1699).

23. John Power, *Essays on the Female Economy* (London: Burgess & Hill, 1831); C. Negrier, *Recherches sur les ovaries* (Paris: Deehet & Labe, 1840).

24. E. P. F. Pfluger, *Ueber die Bedeutung und Ursache der Menstruation* (Berlin, 1865).

25. J. Williams, *Obstetrical Journal of Britain and Ireland* 3 (1875–76), 496.

26. W. Stephenson, *American Journal of Obstetrics* 15 (1882), 287–94.

27. G. Stanley Hall, *Adolescence* (New York: D. Appleton & Co., 1904), 1, 487.

28. J. Goodman, "The Cyclical Theory of Menstruation," *American Journal of Obstetrics* 11 (1878), 3–44; Mary Putnam Jacobi, *The Question of Rest for Women during Menstruation,* Boylston Prize Essay of Harvard University for 1876 (New York: G. P. Putnam's Sons, 1877).

29. Mary Putnam Jacobi, "Hysterical Fever," *Journal of Nervous and Mental Disease* 15 (1890), 373–88.

30. Quoted by Mary Jacobi from an address to the Obstetrical Society of London in 1874, reported in the *British Medical Journal* 16 (January, 1875).

31. A. F. A. King, "A New Basis for Uterine Pathology," *American Journal of Obstetrics* 8 (1875), 242–43.

32. Augustus Kinsley Gardner, *Conjugal Sins: Against the Laws of Life and Health and Their Efforts upon the Father, Mother and Child* (New York: J. S. Redfield, 1870), 17, 145–46.

33. John Cowan, *The Science of a New Life* (New York: Cowan and Co., 1871).

34. Carroll Smith-Rosenberg, "Puberty to Menopause: The Cycle of Femininity in Nineteenth-Century America," in *Disorderly Conduct: Visions of Gender in Victorian America* (New York: Alfred A. Knopf, 1985), 183.

35. W. W. Bliss, *Woman and Her Thirty Year Pilgrimage* (New York: William M. Littell, 1869).

36. Ely Van De Worker, "New Basis for Uterine Pathology," *American Journal of Obstetrics* 8 (1875), 242–43.

37. Edward Tilt, *The Change of Life in Health and Disease*, 4th ed. (New York: Bermingham and Co., 1882) 16, 39, 94–95; and, Tilt, *On the Preservation of the Health of Women at the Critical Periods of Life* (London, 1851); P. J. Moebius, *Über den Physiologischen Schwachsinn des Weibes* (Berlin: Halle, 1908); P. S. Icard, in *La femme pendant la periode menstruelle* (Paris: F. Alcan, 1890), was widely quoted as stating, "The menstrual function may . . . induce sympathetically a mental state varying from a slight psychosis to absolute irresponsibility."

38. R. Leonardo, *History of Gynecology* (New York: Froben, 1944); see also E. Novak, *Menstruation and Its Disorders* (New York: D. Appleton & Co., 1921). New theories did not mean, however, that medical opinions were quick to cast off traditional ideas. The *New York Times,* on March 28, 1912, commented, "No doctor can ever lose sight of the fact that the mind of a woman is always threatened with danger from the reverberations of her physiological emergencies."

39. Edward H. Clarke, *Sex in Education; or A Fair Chance for Girls* (Boston: James R. Osgood and Co., 1873), 37–38.

40. Jules Michelet, *L'Amour* (Paris: I. Hachette, 1859). He stated, "Woman is forever suffering from cicatrisation of an interior wound which is the cause of a whole drama" (p. 48).

41. Albert Hayes, *Physiology of Women* (Boston: Peabody Medical Institute, 1869), 84–85.

42. J. S. Jewell, "Influence of Our Present Civilization in the Production of Nervous and Mental Energy," *Journal of Nervous and Mental Disease* 1 (Jan. 1874), 70–73, quoted by Anita Clair Fellman and Michael Fellman, *Making Sense of Self: Medical Advice Literature in Late Nineteenth-Century America* (Philadelphia: University of Philadelphia Press, 1981), 70–71.

43. Herbert Spencer, *Education: Intellectual, Moral and Physical* (London: Williams and Norgate, 1861), 179.

44. For a discussion of Spencer's views on women and biological determinism, see Louise Michele Newman (ed.), *Men's Ideas/Women's Realities; Popular Science, 1870–1915* (New York: Pergamon Press, 1985), 1–11; Sara Delamont and Lorna Duffin (eds.), *The Nineteenth-Century Woman: Her Cultural and Physi-*

cal World (London: Croom Helm, 1978); John S. Haller and Robin M. Haller, *The Physician and Sexuality in Victorian America* (Urbana: University of Illinois Press, 1974).

45. E. L. Youmans started *Popular Science Monthly* in part to bring Spencer's ideas to America. See Robert C. Banister, *Social Darwinism: Science and Myth in Anglo-American Thought* (Philadelphia, 1979); and Susan Sleeth Mosedale, "Science Corrupted: Victorian Biologists Consider the Woman Question," *Journal of the History of Biology* 11 (Spring 1978), 9.

46. The Lamarckian mechanism explained that the use of an organ resulted in its development, and disuse resulted in its degeneration over time. Due to prolonged disuse, women lacked a number of abilities that men had developed, especially abstract thought and reason. Female brains were thus marred by disuse and Darwin considered "catch up" to be impossible for the female since the male was advancing so rapidly. Woman, in short, was less completely evolved than the male and was likely to remain so, for male traits were strengthened by use somewhat differently than were those of the female. Charles Darwin, *The Descent of Man and Selection in Relation to Sex*, 2d ed. (Akron: Werner, 1874), 576–77. This kind of reasoning, David Ritche noted in 1890, was tantamount to shutting up a bird in a narrow cage and then pointing out that it was incapable of flying (David Ritchie, *Darwinism and Politics*, 2d ed. (London: Mosdale, 1890; reprinted, New York: Charles Scribner's Sons, 1909), 68–69.

47. A note in *Popular Science Monthly* 17 (July 1880), 431, suggested that M. G. Delaunay had advanced the opinion that precocity was a sign of biological inferiority and that in all domestic animals the female was formed sooner than the male. Furthermore, the precocity of organs and organisms was in an inverse ration to the extent of their evolution. See also G. Delaunay, "Equality and Inequality in Sex," *Popular Science Monthly* 20 (Dec. 1881), 184–92.

48. Susan Sleeth Mosedale, in "Science Corrupted," analyzes Spencer's and other's arguments about the mental and physical capacity of women.

49. Ben Barker-Benfield, "The Spermatic Economy: A Nineteenth-Century View of Sexuality," *Feminist Studies* 1 (Summer, 1972), 45–74.

50. Robert Ultzman, *The Neuroses of the Genito-Urinary System in the Male, with Sterility and Impotence* (Philadelphia, 1890), 11. See Gail Pat Parsons, "Equal Treatment for All: American Medical Remedies for Male Sexual Problems, 1850–1900," *Journal of the History of Medicine* 32 (Jan. 1977), 55–71.

51. G. B. H. Swayze, "Spermatorrhea," *Medical Surgery Report* 33 (1875), 61.

52. Joseph W. Howe, *Excessive Venery, Masturbation and Continence* (New York, 1883), 63–66.

53. T. S. Clouston, "Female Education," (12), 1884.

54. A. Hughes Bennett, "Hygiene in the Education of Women," *Popular Science Monthly* 16 (Feb. 1880), 521.

55. W. C. Taylor, *A Physician's Counsels to Woman in Health and Disease* (Springfield: W. J. Holland and Co., 1871), quoted in Barbara Ehrenreich

and Deidre English, *Complaints and Disorders: The Sexual Politics of Sickness* (New York: The Feminist Press, 1973), 21.

56. Dr. Tilt, *The Lancet* 11 (1862), 480, quoted by Lorna Duffin, "The Conspicious Consumptive: Woman as an Invalid," in Delamont and Duffin, *The Nineteenth-Century Woman*, 32.

57. J. McGrigor Allan, "On the Real Differences in the Minds of Men and Women," *Anthropological Review* 7 (1869), cxcviii.

58. Jules Michelet, *L'Amour*, 48.

59. Max Runge, *Das Weib in seiner geschlechtliche Eigenart*, 5th ed. (Berlin: J. Springer, 1900), 3.

60. G. Stanley Hall, *Adolescence* (New York: D. Appleton and Co., 1904), vol. 1, 472.

61. George L. Austin, *Perils of American Womanhood, or a Doctor's Talk with Maiden, Wife and Mother* (Boston: Lee & Shepard, 1883), 150.

62. J. H. Kellogg, *Plain Facts for Old and Young* (Burlington, Iowa: I. F. Segner, 1889), 183.

63. Robert Barnes, "Lumleian Lectures: The Convulsive Diseases of Women," *The Lancet* 1 (1873), 514.

64. Thomas E. Addis Emmett, *The Principles and Practice of Gynecology* (Philadelphia: Henry C. Lea, 1879), 21.

65. John Thorburn, *Female Education from a Medical Point of View* (Manchester: J. E. Cornish, 1884).

66. G. Stanley Hall, *Adolescence*, vol. 1, 618, 639.

67. G. Stanley Hall, "The Ideal School Based on Child Study," *The Forum* 32 (Feb. 1902), 35.

68. Clarence J. Karier, "G. Stanley Hall: A Priestly Prophet of a New Dispensation," *Journal of Libertarian Studies* 7 (Spring, 1983), 54.

69. G. Stanley Hall, *Adolescence*, vol. 1, 478.

70. Silas Weir Mitchell, *Lectures on Diseases of the Nervous System Especially in Women* (Philadelphia: Lea Bros. and Co., 1885), 15. Dr. Mitchell was famous for his rest cures for women who had become, he claimed, nervous and hysterical due to improper life-styles. For an excellent analysis, see Ellen L. Bassuk, "The Rest Cure: Repetition or Resolution of Victorian Women's Conflicts?" *Poetics Today* 6 (1985), 245–57.

71. Edward H. Clarke, *Sex in Education or a Fair Chance for the Girls* (Boston: J. R. Osgood, 1873).

72. T. S. Clouston, "Female Education from a Medical Point of View," *Popular Science Monthly* 24 (December 1883), 322–33.

73. Henry Maudsley, "Sex in Mind and Education," *Fortnightly Review* 15 (1874), 475.

74. J. H. Kellogg, *Plain Facts for Old and Young* (Burlington, Iowa: I. F. Segner, 1882), 83.

75. Julia Ward Howe, ed., *Sex and Education: A Reply to Dr. Clarke's Sex in Education* (Boston: Roberts Brothers, 1874), 8, 15, 18–19.

76. The Association of Collegiate Alumnae, Health Statistics of Women College Graduates (1885). See also Leta Stetter Hollingworth, *Functional Periodicity: An Experimental Study of the Mental and Motor Abilities of Women During Menstruation* (New York: Columbia University, 1914) and John Dewey, "Health and Sex in Higher Education," *Popular Science Monthly,* 29 (March 1886), 606–15.

77. W. LeC. Stevens, *The Admission of Women to Universities* (Boston: S. W. Green's Sons, 1883).

78. Alida C. Avery, "Testimony from Colleges (Vassar, 1873)," in Julia Ward Howe, *Sex and Education,* 193.

79. Elizabeth Garrett Anderson, "Sex in Mind and Education. A Reply," *Fortnightly Review* 15 (1874), 503. She and other female physicians such as Mary Jacobi did attempt to counter the belief that rest was necessary or even desirable for women who menstruated normally. Mary Putnam Jacobi, *The Question of Rest for Women during Menstruation* (New York: G. P. Putnam, 1877). Clelia Mosher pointed out that "the tradition that women must be incapacitated at periods strongly tends to increase the idea that efficiency is impaired" ("Normal Menstruation and Some of the Factors Modifying It," *Johns Hopkins Hospital Bulletin,* April-May, June 1901).

80. J. T. Wilson, "Menstrual Disorder in School Girls," *The Texas Sanitarium* (June 1885), 18.

81. Henry Ling Taylor, "Exercise as Remedy," *Popular Science Monthly* 48 (March 1896), 626.

82. The female role in reproduction, note Ehrenreich and English, required stamina, and if you counted in the activities of child raising and running a household, it required full-blown energetic health. Barbara Ehrenreich and Deidre English, *For Her Own Good. 150 Years of the Experts' Advice to Women* (New York: Doubleday, 1979), 134. Such stamina appeared to many physicians in the latter part of the nineteenth century to be palpably lacking among white, Anglo-Saxon, middle-class American women. They pointed to an alarming drop in the birthrate among the "native stock" and challenged women to do their duty and improve their health or accept a "new rape of the Sabines" to save the race. See, for example, G. Stanley Hall, *Adolescence,* vol. 2, 561–647.

83. Carroll Smith-Rosenberg, "The Hysterical Woman: Sex Roles and Role Conflict in Nineteenth-Century America," in *Disorderly Conduct,* 658.

84. J. H. Kellogg, *Ladies' Guide in Health and Disease* (Battle Creek, Mich.: Modern Medical Publishing, 1883), 188. For a discussion concerning the integration of tomboyism with a traditional view of women's domestic role, see Sharon O'Brien, "Tomboyism and Adolescent Conflict: Three Nineteenth-Century Case Studies," in Mary Kelley (ed.), *Woman's Being, Woman's Place: Female Identity and Vocation in American History* (Boston: G. K. Hall & Co., 1979), 351–72.

85. Smith-Rosenberg, "The Hysterical Woman," 212.

86. G. Stanley Hall, *Adolescence*, vol. 1, 615.

87. M. A. Hardaker, "Science and the Woman Question," *Popular Science Monthly* 20 (March 1882), 581.

88. John Thorburn, *Female Education from a Physiological Point of View* (Manchester: J. E. Cornish, 1884).

89. Felix L. Oswald, "Physical Education," *Popular Science Monthly* 19 (May 1881), 23.

90. C. Roberts, "Bodily Deformities in Girlhood," *Popular Science Monthly* 22 (January 1883), 324.

91. T. S. Clouston, "Female Education from a Medical Point of View, (1)," *Popular Science Monthly* 24 (Dec. 1883), 227. Clouston echoed Clarke that physical education for girls was to be stressed only as it connected with the duties of maternity.

92. T. S. Clouston, "Female Education from a Medical Point of View (2)," *Popular Science Monthly* 24 (January 1884), 320.

93. Henry Ling Taylor, "Exercise as a Remedy," *Popular Science Monthly* 18 (March 1896), 630. As Nathan Allen put it, "stated, and out of door and not excessive physical culture had a normative influence upon the monthly function" ("The Education of Girls as Connected with Their Growth and Physical Development," *Sanitarian* [1879]).

94. J. Madison Taylor, "Puberty in Girls and Certain of Its Disturbances." *Pediatrics* (July 15, 1896), 15.

95. Alice B. Tweedy, "Homely Gymnastics," *Popular Science Monthly* 40 (Feb. 1892), 527.

96. Clouston, "Female Education (2)," 323.

97. M. G. Van Rensselaer, "The Waste of Woman's Intellectual Force," *Forum* (1892), 616. Although S. Weir Mitchell admitted he did not understand the relationship between fat and health, gaining weight, he felt, improved the blood and made the skin ruddy, which was a certain sign of physical health (*Wear and Tear, or Hints for the Overworked*, 4th ed. [Philadelphia: J. B. Lippincott & Co., 1885]).

98. R. P. Hudson, "The Biography of Disease: Lessons from Chlorosis," *Bulletin of the History of Medicine* 51 (1977), 440–63; A. C. Siddall, "Chlorosis: Etiology Reconsidered," *Bulletin of the History of Medicine* 56 (1982), 254–60; T. Clifford Allbutt, "Chlorosis," in *A System of Medicine*, T. C. Allbutt, ed. (New York: Macmillan, 1905); R. L. Tait, *Disorders of Women* (Philadelphia: Lea, 1889).

99. Joan Jacobs Brumberg, "Chlorotic Girls 1870–1920: A Historical Perspective on Female Adolescence," in Judith Walzer Leavitt, ed., *Women and Health in America* (Madison: University of Wisconsin Press, 1984), 188.

100. L. Warner, *A Treatise on the Functions and Diseases of Women* (New York: Manhattan, 1875); Taylor, "Puberty in Girls and Certain of Its Disturbances," 10–15.

101. E. L. Jones, *Chlorosis: The Special Anemia of Young Women* (London: Balliere, Tindall & Cox, 1897); Allbutt, "Chlorosis."

102. As many commentators on nineteenth-century nutritional practices have noted, it was not surprising that Victorian adolescents eschewed, or were not offered, red meat for the link between animal flesh and rampant sexuality had been well established by numerous physicians and health reformers. See, for example, John S. Haller and Robin M. Haller, *The Physician and Sexuality in Victorian America* (Urbana: University of Illinois Press, 1974); James C. Whorton, *Crusaders for Fitness: The History of American Health Reformers* (Princeton, N.J.: Princeton University Press, 1982); Bullough and Voght, "Women, Menstruation and Nineteenth-Century Medicine."

103. G. Stanley Hall, *Adolescence,* vol. 1, 507–8.

104. Grant Allen, "Plain Words about the Woman Question," *Popular Science Monthly* 36 (Dec. 1889), 181.

105. George J. Engelman, "The American Girl of Today. The Influence of Modern Education on Functional Development," President's Address, *American Gynecological Society* 25 (1900), 8–45.

106. Havelock Ellis, *Determinants of Puritan Stock and Its Causes* (New York: Charles Scribner's Sons, 1894).

107. G. Stanley Hall, *Adolescence,* vol. 1, 609.

108. John Chynoweth Burnham, in "Psychiatry, Psychology and the Progressive Movement," *American Quarterly* 12 (Sept. 1960), 457–65, discusses how the role of many doctors had expanded by the end of the nineteenth century to become "moral directors of their patients." See also the Hallers, *Physician and Sexuality* for a broader discussion of male medical guardianship.

109. In their analysis of the medical advice literature of the late nineteenth century, the Fellmans note that "a general sense that the world outside is coming undone is frequently related to the haunting fear that the body and the mind are fragile structures. The imperiled body is both metaphor and ideological focus" (Fellmans, *Making Sense of Self,* 138).

110. Charles E. Rosenberg, "Science and American Social Thought," in David D. Van Tassel and Michael G. Hall (eds.), *Science and Society in the United States* (Illinois: The Dorsey Press, 1966), 139.

111. Henry Maudsley, "Sex in Mind and in Education," *Fortnightly Review* 15 (1874), 468.

112. James Whorton has described the debate about the medical consequences of athletics for men and the effect it had upon the formation of public attitudes toward strenuous exertion and competitiveness in sport. Those physicians fearful about the squandering of bodily reserve power by young men in their battle for victory pointed to cardiac hypertrophy, emphysema and kidney damage, and insanity (see chap. 3).

The debate over athlete's heart, however, was well over by the time of World War I. The debate about the medical implications of female sport, especially during menstruation, has been more enduring.

113. See, for example, Carroll Smith-Rosenberg, "The New Woman as Androgyne: Social Disorder and Gender Crisis, 1870–1936," in *Disorderly Conduct: Visions of Gender in Victorian America;* and Donald J. Mrozek, *Sport*

and American Mentality, 1880–1910 (Knoxville: University of Tennessee Press, 1983).

114. American College of Sports Medicine, "Opinion Statement on the Participation of the Female Athlete in Long-Distance Running," *Medicine and Science in Sports and Exercise* 4 (1979), ix–xi; Jerilyn Prior and Yvette Vigna, "Reproductive Responses to Endurance Exercises in Women: From Corsets to Shin Splints," *Canadian Women's Studies* 4 (Spring, 1983), 35–39; R. Bloomberg, "Coach Says Running Affects Menstruation," *The Physician and Sportsmedicine* 5 (1977), 15; E. Dale, D. H. Gerlach, and A. L. Wilhite. "Menstrual Dysfunction in Distance Runners," *Obstetrics and Gynecology* 54 (1979), 47–53; B. Schwartz, D. C. Cumming, E. Riordan, H. Selye, S. S. C. Yen, and R. W. Rebar, "Exercise-Associated Amenorrhea: A Distant Entity?" *American Journal of Obstetrics and Gynecology* 141 (1981), 662–70.

115. Recent studies show that menarche occurs at a significantly later age in the American female athlete than in her non-athletic counterpart. R. M. Malina, W. W. Spirduso, C. Tate, A. M. Baylor, "Age at Menarche and Selected Menstrual Characteristics in Athletes at Different Competitive Levels and in Different Sports, *Medicine and Science in Sports* 10 (1978), 218–22; Robert M. Malina, Albert B. Harper, Henrietta H. Avent, and Donald E. Campbell, "Age at Menarche in Athletes and Non-Athletes, *Medicine and Science in Sports* 5 (1973), 11–13; M. P. Warren, "The Effects of Exercise on Pubertal Progression and Reproductive Function in Girls," *Journal of Clinical Endocrinology and Metabolism* 51 (1980), 1150–57; J. H. Wilmore, C. H. Brown, and J. A. Davis, "Body Physique and Composition of the Female Distance Runner," *Annals of the New York Academy of Sciences* 32 (1977), 764–76. J. L. Cohen, P. B. May, C. S. Kim, and N. J. Ertel, "Exercise and Amenorrhea in Professional Ballet Dancers," *Clinical Research* 28 (1980), 23.

116. Lionel W. Rosen, Douglas B. McKeag, David O. Hough, Victoria Curley, "Pathogenic Weight-Control Behavior in Female Athletes," *The Physician and Sportsmedicine* 14 (January, 1986), 79–86; N. J. Smith, "Excessive Weight Loss and Food Aversion in Athletes Simulating Anorexia Nervosa," *Pediatrics* 66 (July 1980), 139–42. The suppression of menstruation is a distinguishing feature of anorexia nervosa which is a phobic fear of fat. It is known that the initiation of menses depends upon the attainment of critical body weight and composition, and that a lack of food and/or the large energy drain of habitual physical activity delays menarche. Rose E. Frisch and Janet W. McArthur, "Menstrual Cycles: Fatness as a Determinant of Minimum Weight for Height Necessary for Their Maintenance or Onset," *Science* 185 (Sept. 1974), 942–49. Thus, fat and the female reproductive system cannot be separated physiologically, for the art of starvation not only promises control of the shape that distinguishes the female body, but leads to a cessation of menstruation as well. See, for example, Noelle Caskey, "Interpreting Anorexia Nervosa," *Poetics Today* 1–2 (1985), 259–73; and Kim Chernin, *The Obsession: Reflections on the Tyranny of Slenderness* (New York: Harper and Row, 1981).

117. Frans de Wachter, "The Symbolism of the Healthy Body: A Philosophical Analysis of the Sportive Imagery of Health," *Journal of the Philosophy of Sport* 11 (1985), 56–62.

118. T. S. Clouston, "Female Education from a Medical Point of View," *Popular Science Monthly* 24 (1884), 319–34.

6 *Jan Todd*

Bernarr Macfadden: Reformer of Feminine Form

On October 5, 1905, Anthony Comstock of the Society for the Suppression of Vice accompanied the officers of the New York Police Department as they raided the offices of the Physical Culture Publishing Company and arrested its founder and owner, Bernarr Macfadden. The charge was the spreading of pornography and at issue were the posters for a "Mammoth Physical Culture Exhibition" to be held at Madison Square Garden—posters that showed the winners of the physique competitions held as part of the previous year's extravaganza. There were apparently two posters that Comstock found objectionable; the first, as the *New York Times* reported, showed "the women prize winners, ten or twelve young women in white union suits with sashes around their waists . . ." while the second featured Al Treloar, the men's winner, "wearing a pair of sandals and a leopard's skin as a breechcloth."[1] Once inside the offices, Comstock found even more to offend his delicate sensibilities: various classical renderings, a number of physique photographs, and a painting of the Venus de Milo which, according to Macfadden biographer Clement Wood, Comstock called "obscene."[2]

Though a large number of posters were confiscated from the Macfadden offices, most of them had already been distributed throughout the city. The ensuing furor raised by the New York press surrounding Macfadden's litigation in the days between his arrest and the opening of the show whetted the public's curiosity to such an extent that special police units had to be called out on opening night to handle the 20,000 spectators, 5,000 of whom had to be turned away.[3] As the *Times* pointed out on the morning after the show's opening, Comstock's efforts to preserve the morals of the citizenry of New York failed because they generated an enormous amount of free publicity for Macfadden, and because those who were able to get in and see the show saw only a "tame programme of athletic sports, backed up by a dozen women who stood on pedestals behind a muslin curtain."[4]

What had aroused Comstock to action was his belief that nudity (or women whose bodily forms were revealed by union suits) was obscene when it was able to be viewed by others. Comstock claimed to find nothing intrinsically ugly or obscene about the naked human form, but argued that the display of such in any truly public way was immoral. As he so delicately put it, "Let the nude be kept in its proper place and out of the reach of the rabble."[5] Thus it was almost inevitable that he and Macfadden, who more than any other publisher of the era made extensive use of the nude and semi-nude form, should clash.

But as Fulton Oursler, one of Macfadden's hand-picked biographers, observed, the main issue in the Comstock case was not the bare torso of Al Treloar, but the fact that Macfadden was exhibiting "athletic girls" in the Garden.[6] It was, of course, these "ideal women" that the large crowds turned out to see, though not necessarily to worship. In fact, as the *Times* reported, the introductions to the audience of the "most superbly developed lady from Long Island" and the "Venus from Hoboken" were not received without a bit of "guying." And in a tone of dismay, the *Times* noted that the costumes worn by the women were no more revealing than those seen nightly in burlesque houses throughout the city.[7]

The most revealing thing about the entire episode may well have been its symbolic value. We should keep this in mind as we look back to those heady times and attempt to understand Macfadden's leading role in establishing the physicality of women in our culture, a role that has received too little serious consideration. Apparently, Macfadden's forceful personality, Barnum-like love of publicity, and unbridled zeal on the subject of physical culture projected the image of a "crack" reformer and thus put off many of his contemporaries. Consequently, most historians have simply considered Macfadden "not worth writing about,"[8] as if the persona of the man somehow outweighed his achievements. But the simple fact is that this strongman-publisher not only established one of the most successful physical fitness ventures of all time—*Physical Culture* magazine—but also created, in 1919, with *True Story,* the "confessional" magazine genre, and helped to redefine the tabloid with his New York *Graphic,* often called the "Pornographic."[9] It is significant that of the few scholarly efforts produced in the thirty years since Macfadden's death in 1955,[10] none has

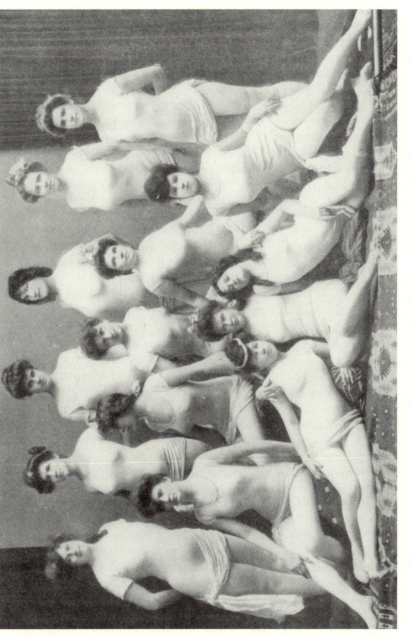

Figure 6.1 The revealing costumes worn by the women finalists in Bernarr Macfadden's "perfect woman" contest scandalized Anthony Comstock, who charged Macfadden with spreading obscenity. This photograph, showing the finalists of the 1904 competition, is included in a souvenir program entitled *The Human Form Divine*, later marketed through the pages of *Physical Culture*. (*The Human Form Divine*, Physical Culture Publishing Company, 1904, p. 3.)

made any specific attempt to address his views on women and bodily beauty, despite the fact that his magazines were brimful of scathing attacks on restrictive women's fashions and prudery and contained articles on the public's conception of beauty and the role of exercise in producing an ideal female form.

In many ways, Macfadden's early views on these subjects seem to echo those of Catharine Beecher, to whom he refers in *The Power and Beauty of Superb Womanhood,* published in 1901. Though known primarily for her efforts on behalf of women's education, Beecher was also a staunch health reformer who introduced calisthenic exercises in her schools as early as 1827.[11] She also published two books advocating calisthenics and light dumbbell drills for women: *Letters to the People on Health and Happiness* (1855) and *Physiology and Calisthenics* (1856).[12] The most striking similarity in the thought of Beecher and Macfadden is that both valued improved health and strength of women primarily as a boon to motherhood.

Since Beecher's writings on health reform influenced most of the writers who came after her, it is difficult to know how much Macfadden gleaned directly from her works, how much came to him second-hand, and how much was original. But he was clearly influenced by her in regard to corsets and the "natural" beauty of the ancient Greeks. In fact, from the 1850s onward, the literature of "physical culture" and "gymnastics" was filled with references to "the Greek ideal" and classical statuary. The idea of the healthy, "natural" body of the ancient Greeks, unfettered by the confining form of Victorian costumes, was exploited by the dress reformers who used it as an argument against the corset and other uncomfortable and unhealthy fashions. In the United States, Greek revivalism enjoyed its greatest popularity during the World's Columbian Exposition in 1893, an event that played a pivotal role in Macfadden's life.

Prior to that time, Macfadden had given ample evidence of the peripateticism that characterized his entire career. But in the summer of 1893, like thousands of other Americans, Macfadden made his way to Chicago to view the Columbian Exposition and his life was never the same again. Nor was America, as this World's Fair marked a turning point in American cultural history. It was a "celebration of America's coming of age—a grand rite of passage."[13] It was also America's chance to show the world that she was ready to take a place among the "civilized" nations.

According to Macfadden's autobiography, he arrived at the Fair by boat, landing at the "peristyle," a row of huge columns supporting massive, classical statues of athletic figures. As he later wrote, "I shall never forget it."[14] Performing at the Fair on the midway was a man who was also to have a lasting impact on young Macfadden—Eugen Sandow, the professional strongman. From Sandow, Macfadden learned the showman's tricks of muscular display. But although this same showmanship was later used by the smaller Macfadden in his own posing exhibitions, Sandow was not mentioned in any of the three "authorized" biographies, no doubt because Macfadden and Sandow became rivals for the physical culture dollar.[15] In any case, after an enormously successful American tour (It is reported that Sandow, who became a household name in the U.S., was paid $1500-$2500 a week for his performances),[16] Sandow returned to England. There he gave lectures and demonstrations, wrote books on physical culture advocating exercise for men *and* women, opened several physical culture studios, and, in 1904, began *Sandow's Magazine,* which continued through thirteen volumes, thus helping to create the proper climate for Macfadden's later efforts.[17]

Following the Chicago exposition, Macfadden manufactured a home-use exercise machine composed of cables and pulleys and, in 1895, published *McFadden's System of Physical Training.* Though largely a how-to supplement for the "McFadden exerciser," the book contained three chapters on training for women, and a fourth entitled, "Restrictive Dress—Corsets, Belts, etc." Buoyed by his success, he decided to expand his market into England, and it was there that he finally found the combination of marketing, bombast, common sense, hard work, and chutzpah that was to form the pattern of his life.

As he had hoped, Great Britain turned out to be remarkably receptive to his ideas on health and exercise.[18] Modeling himself after Sandow, he traveled from city to city, lecturing and posing, selling his exerciser, and handing out a four-page brochure that described how to use his machine.[19] Soon the advertising brochure began to carry a few factual articles, and so it evolved into *Macfadden's Magazine,*[20] under which name it operated for approximately a year before he returned to the United States. Upon his return, having finally realized that the only forum that would carry his ideas was one of his own creation, he almost immediately founded *Physical Culture,* which was to remain his first love throughout his publishing career.[21] With it, Macfadden finally had a megaphone for his campaign to reform America—and American women.

The first issue of *Physical Culture* was released in March of 1899 and sold for only five cents;[22] the only reference to women it contained was in an installment of his novel, *The Athlete's Conquest.* But in the

Figure 6.2 Professional strongman Eugen Sandow as he
appeared in 1893 at the World's Columbian Exhibition.
Sandow was then twenty-five years of age and at the
height of his physical development. (Photo by Roland
White of England, in the Todd-McLean Collection at the
University of Texas at Austin.)

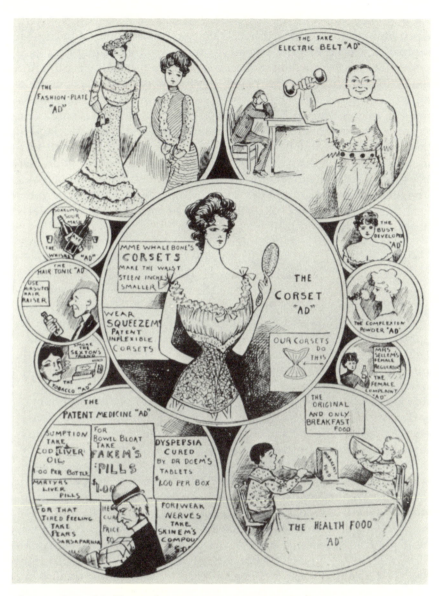

Figure 6.3 As this illustration from *Women's Physical Development* shows, Macfadden's campaign against the corset was in the forefront of his concerns for American women. The pages of *Physical Development* were filled with cartoons such as this, in which the corset, and other unnatural aids to beauty and/or health, are satirized. (*Women's Physical Development* 2 [Aug. 1901] 198.)

April number he began shaping one of the cornerstones of his health campaign: that a healthy sex life is necessary for ultimate physical perfection. Here, Macfadden discussed women's sexuality for the first time and laid out his earlier belief that the married state is the natural lot of women: "The highest degree of attainable physical perfection can certainly never be acquired unless this condition is entered at the proper period of life."[23] Throughout his early writings, Macfadden held up the image of healthy, vigorous wild animals, living in harmony with nature, as an example for men and women to emulate. He saw human sexuality in Darwinian terms: that mating is part of a natural life-style and that each person's eugenic responsibility is to find a healthy, vigorous counterpart with whom he or she can have similarly healthy, perhaps even healthier, offspring.

Macfadden's interest in human sexuality was, of course, not uncommon in his time. The progressive era was filled with reform movements, and as historian John C. Burnham says, "the so-called revolution in morals became one of the lasting legacies of progressivism to American life."[24] One of the chief thrusts of the progressive campaign was to break the conspiracy of silence that kept people in ignorance about the most basic facts of human life. For his part, Macfadden used the pages of *Physical Culture* to wage a constant battle with public censors, saying that they stood "for mystery, secrecy, ignorance, superstition and for the most depraved conception of all that should be divine and holy."[25] But his advocacy and prominence had a price, and he received much criticism through the years as a result of his writings on sexual topics and his illustrations of the semi-nude human form. But sex was hardly the only thing Macfadden covered in the second and succeeding issues of *Physical Culture*. In fact, it is in the same second issue that the first "women's" articles appear, including Macfadden's first magazine exercise prescription for women—a series of "gymnastic movements" for developing the muscles of the neck. And by June 1899 a special section of *Physical Culture* was established for women, the "Department for Information Relative To THE CULTIVATION OF PHYSICAL BEAUTY." In this section, two of Macfadden's major themes regarding women and beauty are expressed: that all beauty has its roots in a physical, active life[26] and that "there can be no beauty without fine muscles."[27] His words are surprisingly modern, reminiscent of many recent articles on women's weight training and bodybuilding: "women have the idea that 'being muscular' means the possession of 'big knots' of muscle. . . . To illustrate the absurdity of such a fear, one has merely to call attention to the rounded, smooth and symmetrical development of most professional women athletes, though under this beauty of contour there are muscles of steel."[28]

Unlike Beecher, Dio Lewis,[29] and other earlier advocates of exercise for women, Macfadden firmly believed that exercise should do more than simply make women "fit." And in this opinion he was a legitimate pioneer. In *The Power and Beauty of Superb Womanhood,* he again employed his animal metaphors, arguing that the small variation in the strength of male and female animals is proof that women can be nearly as strong as men, and pointing out that "those very women who marvel at the strength of these athletes [female acrobats] could, in numerous instances, have been as strong, and even stronger, had they gone through the same course of training. . . ."[30] Again, Macfadden harkened back to the Greeks by reminding his readers that the greatest beauty is seen in those bodies where the muscles are fully developed, as in the statues of Venus, Juno, Diana, and Minerva.

Though Macfadden's notions of feminine strength and muscular beauty seem at first glance amazingly modern, his thinking was not altogether ahead of his time. Though the stereotype of the delicate, weak, even ailing, Victorian woman described by Catharine Beecher[31] was probably accurate for the first part of the nineteenth century, the increase in college education for women in the second half of the century meant that more women were exposed to sports and methods of physical training in the United States than had been the case in most countries since the days of Sparta.[32] And, since many of these same women were to become involved with the various reform movements that dominated American life in the late nineteenth century, they were especially amenable to discussions of dress reform. As historian Valerie Steele put it, "The increasing popularity of sports for women probably gradually influenced the ideal of feminine beauty and this may have had a delayed and indirect effect on fashion."[33]

What these late Victorian sportswomen (and Macfadden) had to fight was the culturally ingrained notion that, unlike animals, each of the human sexes has a definite and particular beauty that "would be ugliness with the other, and vice-versa."[34] To the men and women in the first half of the nineteenth century, any sort of muscular development on women was seen as useless and unattractive: strength was beautiful in men and ugly in women. According to Steele, many early Victorians believed that feminine beauty was a compensation for feminine weakness.[35] But by the 1870s ethereal frailty was on its way out and the "combination of points recognized as a good figure" consisted of a well-developed bust, a tapering (corseted) waist, and large hips.[36] By the 1890s, however, the plump, hourglass figure had further

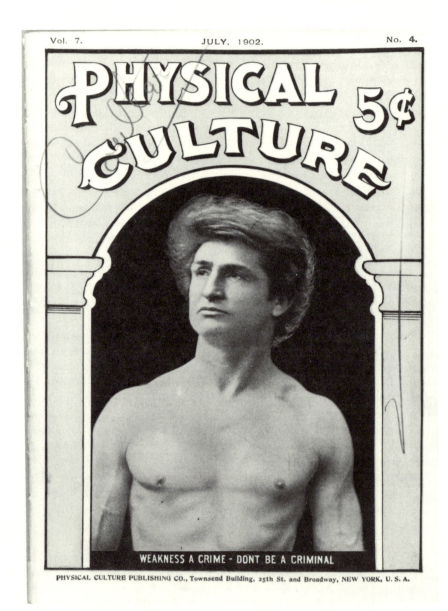

Vol. 7. JULY, 1902. No. 4.

PHYSICAL CULTURE 5¢

WEAKNESS A CRIME - DONT BE A CRIMINAL

PHYSICAL CULTURE PUBLISHING CO., Townsend Building, 25th St. and Broadway, NEW YORK, U. S. A.

Figure 6.4 Bernarr Macfadden never hesitated to use himself as a living illustration of the effectiveness of his methods. He frequently appeared on the cover of *Physical Culture* magazine. (*Physical Culture* 7 [July 1902] cover.)

COMSTOCK, KING OF THE PRUDES

EXCESS

THE COMSTOCK THEORY OF TEACHING BOYS AND GIRLS

Figure 6.5 Following the vice squad's raid on Physical Culture Publishing, Macfadden launched a full-front attack against Anthony Comstock and the narrow-minded world-view he represented. This cartoon is only one of several that appeared in *Physical Culture* in the following months as the "evils of prudery" became a dominant theme in the magazine. (*Physical Culture* 15 [Feb. 1906] 162.)

evolved into an "S" shape (with the bust thrust more forward and in greater prominence and the hips thrust further back), and "prettiness" had given way to height, grandeur, and sturdiness.[37]

Historian Thomas Beers coined the term "Titaness" for this "new woman"[38] who rose like a phoenix from the ashes of the "White City" of 1893 Chicago. As Ernest P. Earnest wrote in *The American Eve in Fact and Fiction*, "Whether or not the American government had discovered women [following the Chicago World's Fair] the American public did so . . . the papers and magazines were full of accounts of titanesses."[39]

The other feminine image that dominated the American consciousness during these years was that of the Gibson Girl, who also came into prominence as a result of the Chicago World's Fair.[40] As drawn by illustrator Charles Dana Gibson, the Gibson Girl was tall, relatively slim, though well formed, and often engaged in sports and exercise, creating a fashionable, fresh image. It has even been said that the appeal of the Gibson Girl was in the knowledge that she would mature into the Titaness[41] and find, as Macfadden might have put it, the "power and beauty of superb womanhood."

One thing that must be said about Macfadden is that, although he lacked formal education, he was never ignorant of the *zeitgeist,* and this insight led him to launch the first women's fitness magazine, *Women's Physical Development,* in October 1900. *Physical Culture* had by then been in operation little more than a year, but it had grown so rapidly—there were more than 100,000 subscribers by 1900[42]—that Macfadden was convinced the market could support separate publications for men and women. Another example of his firm belief involving the relationship of women and exercise is his placing on the cover of the August 1900 issue a buxom young woman with dumbbells in hand—the first *Physical Culture* cover girl. As for *Women's Physical Development,* the magazine did well enough, although according to Oursler the "cumbersome" title hampered public acceptance.[43] But in March 1903 the title was changed to *Beauty and Health: Woman's Physical Development* and circulation soon exceeded 80,000.[44]

The success of the magazine, however, owed less to a name change than it did to Macfadden's instinct for the mood of fin de siècle America. For example, in a stroke of editorial and public relations genius, he announced in the December 1902 issue of *Women's Physical Development* that, "knowing as I do the vast importance of strength and beauty and health in women, I have determined to offer for the year 1903, a prize of $1,000.00 to be presented to the best and most perfectly formed woman."[45]

In the months that followed, Macfadden's editorial column carried a reference to the contest every month. The brilliance of the idea was that besides generating an enormous amount of publicity throughout the country, it provided his new magazine with hundreds of photographs and stories of "physical culture women," all of which helped to humanize *Beauty and Health.* By the May issue the contest had grown and the plan now called for regional competitions to be held in thirteen cities across the country: New York, Boston, Buffalo, Philadelphia, Washington, Pittsburgh, New Orleans, Cincinnati, Chicago, St. Louis, Minneapolis, Denver, and San Francisco. These preliminary competitions were to be conducted under the auspices of local physical culture clubs and the winners would be sent to the semi-finals at Madison Square Garden in New York. The winners of this competition would then be furnished round-trip passage plus expenses for a two-week stay in London where they would meet the European semi-final winners for the world title. As it turned out, however, the European winners traveled to New York[46] where the finals were held between December 28, 1903, and January 2, 1904, as the climax of a "Monumental Physical Culture Entertainment." Besides the two physique contests, races for men and women, fencing championships, wrestling bouts, and several fasting competitions were held during the exposition.[47]

Emma Newkirk of Santa Monica, California, won the 1904 competition; she stood $5'4\frac{1}{2}''$, weighed 136 pounds, and had a 35-inch bust, 25-inch waist, 36-inch hips, and $23\frac{1}{2}$-inch thighs.[48] It is especially interesting to note that the panel of judges who chose Miss Newkirk was composed not only of athletes but of "prominent sculptors, physicians, and physical culturists."[49] As for Newkirk, Macfadden also featured the fact that, despite the many offers she received after the contest to pose for artists and appear in theatrical reviews, she, "like a true woman," returned to Santa Monica and married her sweetheart.[50] Though Macfadden lost money on the show,[51] the publicity generated by it was beyond price, and so plans were soon underway for a second competition, set for October 1905. This time, thanks to Anthony Comstock, Macfadden did not have to hype the gate and the women's contest went off on schedule, although the rules had changed considerably from the previous year. At the 1905 show, the competitors had to be more than simply aesthetically pleasing to the panel. In addition to the posing contest, all the competitors had to participate in a series of eight athletic events: 50-yard run, 220-yard run, 440-yard run, running high jump, two-hands lift, half-mile run, one-mile run, and three-mile "go as you please." This altered format meant that though Marie Spitzer of New Haven, Connecticut, placed only fourth in the posing part of the competition, she was chosen as the "perfectly developed woman" by virtue of the fact that she finished first in six of the eight athletic events.[52]

As the years passed and more such contests were held, *Physical Culture* continued to grow, reaching a high of more than 340,000 subscribers early in the Depression.[53] By that time, Macfadden was reportedly worth more than $30 million and his publishing empire had spread so widely that the combined circulation of his magazines was over 7,355,000, more than those of either William Randolph Hearst or Henry Luce.[54]

Macfadden's bold campaign to change the way American culture viewed womanly beauty, rooted as it was in the late nineteenth-century ideals of neo-classicism and naturalism, was essentially a campaign for functional beauty. To Macfadden the body should not only have proportion and symmetry but should also be servicable—strong, capable, enduring, and therefore healthy. Though Macfadden's zeal for the family unit and the role of the woman-wife within it grates a bit in these more modern times, it is not surprising considering his early childhood and the loss of his mother, after which he seems to have always yearned for supportive feminine influences. Furthermore, the Industrial Revolution had made dramatic changes in the social structure of America, so that in 1900, for instance, when *Women's Physical Development* was first launched, more than 6 million American women worked outside the home. And it must be remembered that America had just passed through a decade in which the number of women who entered the work force increased at a rate faster than the birth rate. A further telling statistic is that in the decade following 1900, an unprecedented 954,000 divorces were granted,[55] which gave Macfadden and hundreds of other Americans another substantial reason to be concerned about the future of the American family.

But his concern was real and it helped to fuel his reformist engine. Historically, Macfadden is difficult to define because his interests and impacts on American culture were so diverse. But if he did nothing else, he took the verse from Corinthians seriously, "Whatsoever cometh to thy hand, do it with all thy might." And, as Hofstadter points out in *The Progressive Movement: 1900–1915*, a distinguishing characteristic of the era was not simply a belief in "progress" but activism. The progressives argued that "social evils will not remedy themselves, and that it is wrong to sit by passively and wait for time to take care of them . . . they did not believe that the future would take care of itself."[56]

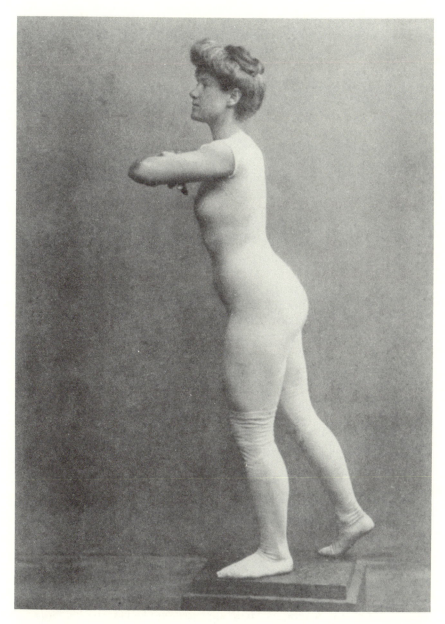

Figure 6.6 In 1904, Santa Monican Emma Newkirk was judged to have the most perfect figure in Macfadden's first physique contest for women. This publicity shot was taken at the time of the show. (*The Human Form Divine*, Physical Culture Publishing Company, 1904, p. 4.)

Macfadden's activism found a focus in the Victorian belief, expressed best by Herbert Spencer, "that the preservation of health is a *duty* . . . all breaches of the laws of health are *physical sins.*"[57] Working within this concept, Macfadden adopted his famous motto, "Weakness Is a Crime, Don't Be a Criminal." And with typical turn of the century eclecticism, he took those aspects of popular culture that met his needs—neo-classicism, Darwinism, dress reform, and concern for the family—and synthesized them into a "new woman" who satisfied his philosophical, aesthetic, and sexual tastes and filled the role of surrogate maternal figure. That he was so successful in his efforts is partly a result of technological printing advances such as the Hoe rotary art press that made it possible for magazines to print photos and pictures at less expense than ever before,[58] thereby enabling him to use the very sorts of images that had so profoundly stirred him and many other Americans at the Chicago World's Fair. That he would be roundly criticized for his efforts was, of course, all in the best tradition of the reformer.

But was Macfadden really successful in his campaign to change the American image of feminine beauty? Did he make a significant contribution to the aesthetic shift that caused Dorothy Dix, in 1915, to describe the type of girl that was attractive to men of her era as a "husky young woman who can play golf all day and dance all night?"[59] The evidence suggests that clearly he did. Though Macfadden was only one voice in the campaign against such things as the corset, his voice was the loudest and it reached hundreds of thousands of men and women in the early part of this century. And, in particular, his boldness in putting the bodies of stronger, fitter and more vigorous womanhood on proud display in his magazines and in Madison Square Garden, dressed in their union suits and sashes, meant that women who longed to live more vigorous and active lives, and be athletic as well as attractive, now had role models, even if it was only a "Venus from Hoboken."

Notes

Since the original version of this article was published in the *Journal of Sport History* in 1987, two biographies have appeared on Macfadden's life. William R. Hunt's *Body Love: The Amazing Career of Bernarr Macfadden* (1989) was published by Bowling Green State University Popular Press, Bowling Green, Ohio. Robert Ernst's *Weakness Is a Crime: The Life of Bernarr Macfadden* was released in December 1990 by Syracuse University Press.

1. *New York Times,* 6 Oct. 1905, p. 9.

2. Clement Wood, *What It Takes* (New York: Liberty Publishing Corporation, 1934), 105.

3. Bernarr Macfadden, "The Physical Culture Exhibition," *Physical Culture* 14, no. 6 (Dec. 1905): 575.

4. *New York Times,* 10 Oct. 1905, p. 9.

5. Heywood Broun and Margaret Leech, *Anthony Comstock: Roundsman of the Lord* (New York: Literary Guild of America, 1927), 225.

6. Foulton Oursler, "Bernarr Macfadden: His Life and Work," *Physical Culture* 60, no. 3 (Sept. 1928): 41.

7. *New York Times,* 10 Oct. 1905, p. 9.

8. William H. Taft, "Bernarr Macfadden: One of a Kind," *Journalism Quarterly* 45, no. 4 (Winter 1968): 627.

9. Ibid., 627–33.

10. William H. Taft, now retired from the School of Journalism at the University of Missouri, is our foremost Macfadden scholar with three published critical articles and a book in process. His interest has, not surprisingly, been centered on Macfadden's career as a publisher and on his early days in Missouri. In a telephone interview with the author on December 5, 1985, Taft corroborated the fact that no scholarly attention has been paid to Macfadden's views on women. Other scholarly treatments include one dissertation, Clifford Waugh's "Bernarr Macfadden: The Muscular Prophet" (State University of New York at Buffalo, 1979), and a single article by Ben Yagoda, which appeared in *American Heritage* 33, no. 1 (Dec. 1981): 22–28. The best discussion of Macfadden's early life is found in Taft's "Bernarr Macfadden," *Missouri Historical Review* 63, no. 1, (Oct. 1968): 71–89. None of these sources examine Macfadden's impact on women's exercise.

11. Catharine Beecher, *Educational Reminiscences* (New York: J. B. Ford and Co., 1874), 43.

12. Catharine Beecher, *Letters to the People on Health and Happiness* (New York: Harper and Brothers, 1855) and *Physiology and Calisthenics* (New York: Harper and Brothers, 1856).

13. David F. Burg, *Chicago's White City of 1893* (Lexington: University Press of Kentucky, 1976), xiii.

14. Bernarr Macfadden, "My Fifty Years of Physical Culture," *Physical Culture* 69, no. 10 (Oct. 1933): 99.

15. In 1929, three biographies appeared, written by Macfadden associates: Fulton Oursler, *The True Story of Bernarr Macfadden;* Grace Perkins (Oursler), *Chats with the Macfadden Family;* and Clement Wood, *Bernarr Macfadden: A Study in Success.* All three were published by the Lewis Copeland Company in New York. A shortened version of Wood's work, retitled *What It Takes: A Study in Success,* was published in 1934 by Liberty Publishing in New York. Oursler's biography was serialized in *Physical Culture* under the title "Bernarr Macfadden—His Life and Work," running from September 1928 through May 1929. Through the years, Macfadden included much biographical information in *Physical Culture Magazine,* of which the most important sources are

the twenty-three articles that comprised "My Fifty Years of Physical Culture," from April 1933 to February 1935. Macfadden's third wife, Mary, tells the story of her years with Macfadden in *Dumbbells and Carrot Strips*, coauthored by Emile Gauvreau, in 1951 (New York: Henry Holt and Company); while Johnny Lee Macfadden, the last wife, published *Barefoot in Eden* (Englewood Cliffs, N.J.: Prentice Hall) in 1962.

16. David P. Webster, *Barbells and Beefcake: An Illustrated History of Bodybuilding* (Irvine, Scotland: privately printed, 1979), 33.

17. Charles T. Trevor, *Sandow the Magnificent* (London: Mitre Press, n.d.), 40.

18. For an excellent discussion of Great Britain's attitudes regarding health and exercise in the nineteenth century, see Bruce Haley's *The Healthy Body and Victorian Culture* (Cambridge: Harvard University Press, 1978). Haley's belief is that "no topic more occupied the Victorian mind than Health— not religion, or politics, or improvement, or Darwinism" (p. 3) and that the mind-body (*mens sana in corpore sano*) relationship involved fundamental questions "about the relation of natural law to human growth or culture" (p. 22).

19. Bernarr Macfadden, "My Fifty Years of Physical Culture," *Physical Culture* 70, no. 5 (Nov. 1933): 99.

20. Bernarr Macfadden, "My Fifty Years of Physical Culture," *Physical Culture* 70, no. 6 (Dec. 1933): 23.

21. David P. Webster, "Bernarr Macfadden," *Muscle Mag International* (Summer 1975): 20–21. The Coulter Papers, File "Macfadden," The Todd-McLean Sports History Collection, University of Texas, Austin. When Macfadden returned to America, the magazine was purchased by his business partner, Hopton Hadley, who changed the name to *Health and Strength*. It continued to specialize in weight-lifting and bodybuilding news while Macfadden's new *Physical Culture* turned more to health. *Health and Strength* ceased publication in 1984, making it the longest running physical culture magazine ever.

22. William H. Taft, "Bernarr Macfadden," *Missouri Historical Review* 63, no. 1 (October 1968): 82.

23. [Bernarr Macfadden], "Can the Highest Degree of Attainable Physical Perfection Be Acquired If Absolute Continence Be Observed?" *Physical Culture* 1, no. 2 (Apr. 1899): 28.

24. John C. Burnham, "The Progressive Era Revolution in American Attitudes toward Sex," *Journal of American History* 54, no. 4 (Mar. 1973): 885.

25. William H. Taft, "Bernarr Macfadden," *American Newspaper Journalists: 1901–1925.* Perry J. Ashley, ed., vol. 25 of *Dictionary of Literary Biography* (Detroit: Gale Research Company, 1984).

26. [Bernarr Macfadden] "The Exhilaration of a Superb Physique Necessary to Beauty," *Physical Culture* 1, no. 4 (June 1899): 81.

27. [Bernarr Macfadden], "Erroneous Ideas of Muscle," *Physical Culture* 1, no. 4 (June 1899): 82.

28. Ibid.

29. During the middle years of the nineteenth century Dr. Dio Lewis, following in Catharine Beecher's footsteps, advocated physical training for women, publishing his classic work, *The New Gymnastics for Men, Women and Children* in 1864 (Boston: Ticknor and Fields). He is also credited with establishing the first normal college for physical education instructors in 1861, in Boston. For further biographical information on Lewis see Fred Eugene Leonard's *A Guide to the History of Physical Education,* 2d ed. (Philadelphia: Lea and Febiger, 1927), 225–67.

30. MacFadden, *The Power and Beauty of Superb Womanhood* (Spotswood, N.J.: Physical Culture Publishing Company, 1901), 22.

31. In *Letters to the People on Health and Happiness,* Beecher reported on an informal survey she conducted during her travels throughout the United States. It convinced her "that there was a terrible decay of female health all over the land" (p. 121) and that "the standard of health among American women is so low that few have a correct idea of what a healthy women is" (p. 122).

32. Ernest P. Earnest, *The American Eve in Fact and Fiction* (Urbana: University of Illinois Press, 1974), 229.

33. Valerie Steele, *Fashion and Eroticism: Ideals of Feminine Beauty from the Victorian Era to the Jazz Age* (New York: Oxford University Press, 1985), 96. See also Lois W. Banner, *American Beauty* (New York: Oxford University Press, 1983) for further discussions of the links between exercise, sport, and the ideal feminine form in America.

34. Gabriel Prevost, quoted by Valerie Steel in *Fashion and Eroticism,* 102.

35. Steele, *Fashion and Eroticism,* 103.

36. Ibid., 108.

37. Ibid., 218.

38. Earnest, *The American Eve in Fact and Fiction,* 208.

39. Ibid., 228.

40. Ibid., 208.

41. Ibid., 231.

42. Printed on the cover of *Physical Culture* 4, no. 2 (Nov. 1900) are the words "Paid Circulation for October, 102,000."

43. Oursler, "Bernarr Macfadden: His Life and Work," *Physical Culture* 60, no. 6 (Dec. 1928), 111.

44. Ibid.

45. [Bernarr Macfadden], "$1,000 for the Most Perfect Woman," *Women's Physical Development* 5, no. 3 (Dec. 1902): 126.

46. Webster, "Bernarr Macfadden," 22.

47. "5,000 in Prizes," *Physical Culture* 6, no. 7 (Oct. 1903): 332.

48. L. E. Eubanks, "The Female Form—Ideal and Real," *Physical Culture,* magazine clipping in the "Women's Physical Culture" file, Todd-McClean Sport History Collection, University of Texas, Austin.

49. "The Great Physical Culture Exhibition," *Physical Culture* 11, no. 2 (Feb. 1904): 113.

50. Marion Walford, "A Rival of Miss Newkirk," magazine clipping in the "Women's Physical Culture" file, Todd-McLean Sport History Collection, University of Texas, Austin (article appears to be from *Physical Culture*).

51. Macfadden, "My Fifty Years of Physical Culture," *Physical Culture* 71, no. 3 (Mar. 1934): 70.

52. "The Athletic World," *Physical Culture*, 14, no. 6 (Dec. 1905): 494. The "two-hands lift" was done using a "lifting machine" of the type popularized by George Barker Windship in the mid-nineteenth century. The athlete stood on a platform above the weight and pulled upward, using a handle attached by chains or pipe to the weights below. In modern terminology it is called a hand-and-thigh lift and as the weights are moved only a few inches, exceptionally large poundages can be raised. One of the women competitors in this contest lifted 550 pounds.

53. Taft, "Bernarr Macfadden: One of a Kind," 624.

54. Yagoda, "The True Story of Bernarr Macfadden," *American Heritage* 33, no. 1 (Dec. 1981): 26.

55. 1900 Census statistics reported in Rheta Childe Dorr's, "The Role of American Women" (1910), in Richard Hofstadter, ed., *The Progressive Movement: 1900–1915* (Englewood Cliffs, N.J.: Prentice Hall, 1965), 84.

56. Hofstadter, *The Progressive Movement*, 84.

57. Haley, *The Healthy Body in Victorian Culture*, 17.

58. Richard L. Watson, *The Development of National Power* (Boston: Houghton Mifflin Company, 1976), 63.

59. Quotation from Dorothy Dix cited in James R. McGovern, "The American Woman," *Journal of American History* 55:2 (Sept. 1968): 317.

7 *John M. Hoberman*

The Early Development of Sports Medicine in Germany

The development of sports medicine[1] in Germany is of historical interest for several reasons. First, the emergence of a scientifically based sports medicine at the end of the nineteenth century occurred earlier and more intensively in Germany than in any other country, at a time when Germany had produced the most advanced research in the fields of animal and human physiology.[2] In a similar fashion, French physiologists of the late nineteenth century pursued many of the same topics, such as the nature of fatigue, sensory reaction times, physiologically traumatic states, and pharmacological effects, which anticipated the concerns of high-performance sports medicine at a time when interest in performance-enhancing techniques hardly existed. Section 1 of this essay looks first at the nineteenth-century origins of modern ambitions to investigate and enhance human athletic potential and then at the emergence of the German medical thinking that attempted to convert physiological research findings into improved athletic performance.

German sports medicine is also of interest to the cultural historian because, like any substantial subculture, it absorbed prevailing social and ideological trends, which can be studied in this context. Many German sports physicians, as we shall see, were exponents of culturally conservative (*völkisch*) and, in some cases, Nazi values, and it is interesting to see how these values could be combined with an interest in high-performance sport. Section 2 examines how early German sports medicine expressed, even as it occasionally challenged, a profoundly conservative value system.

The dramatic growth of German sports medicine during the 1920s coincided with the popularization of a theory of human "constitution"

(*Konstitution*) made internationally famous by the German psychiatrist Ernst Kretschmer. The publication of *Köperbau und Charakter* (*Physique and Character*, 1921) produced an intense scientific controversy that, although it has long been out of fashion, has never been fully resolved.[3] Section 3 shows how German sports physicians attempted to apply Kretschmer's "doctrine of types" (*Konstitutionslehre*) to the problem of correlating body types with specific athletic aptitudes. In addition, Kretschmer's human typology was situated within the contemporary trend in Weimar Germany to promote an interest in the human body in the form of idealized images of health, racial vigor, and sportive dynamism.

Turn-of-the-century European physiologists were well aware of the psychological dimension of physical performance. In his study of the relationship between nutrition and athletic achievement published in 1905, the German physiologist W. Caspari referred to "the enormous influence of willpower on maximal physical performances,"[4] and this connection, though even more mysterious then than it is today, was widely recognized.[5] Section 4 examines how and where German sports physicians looked for psychological factors affecting athletic performance.

Pharmacological research was a major branch of nineteenth-century physiology. German research on muscle physiology included studies of how a variety of substances—including alcohol, caffeine, cocaine, curare, digitalis, strychnine and glucose—affected muscle functioning. Section 5 examines the attitudes of early German sports physicians toward the use of allegedly performance-enhancing substances and the evolution of the concept of "doping."

Finally, German sports medicine can add to our understanding of modernity itself. If sport as we know it is a kind of modernism, then the sports medicine that attends it must be a part of that modernism. One could even argue that performance-enhancing sports medicine has turned out to be the crucial modernizing force within the subculture of modern sport. Section 6 examines the "premodern" attitude of German physiologists and physicians toward human athletic potential, their striking indifference to athletic performance per se,[6] and the transition to a distinctively "modern" fascination with record performances in sport.

1. The Prehistory of Sports Physiology and the Birth of German Sports Medicine

Scientific speculation about the physiological foundations of human abilities is evident in both the physical anthropology and the experimental physiology of the nineteenth century. It must be emphasized, however, that the investigation of human *athletic* potential was never a primary goal of the ethnographers and biological scientists who studied the human organism during this period. Quantified sports performances—excluding those of seventeenth- and eighteenth-century racehorses[7]—became a familiar part of the cultural landscape only during the last few decades of the century;[8] and it was only at the end of the century that the application of physiological thinking to athletic performance appeared as a wholly peripheral theme in the scientific literature of Germany, France, and England. From the perspective of a "postindustrial" civilization seemingly obsessed with extreme muscularity and record athletic performances, this lack of scientific ambition has a quaintly "premodern" quality that ought to stimulate our curiosity rather than our condescension.

Anthropological and physiological assessments of the human organism during this period were early expressions of a scientific Age of Calibration that continues unabated to this day. As Jacques Guillerme has pointed out, scientific interest in objective assessments of muscular energy—a requirement for any future sport science—developed along with a general trend toward quantification in the medical realm.[9] The dynamometer (for measuring gross muscular strength), the sphygmograph (for recording the movements of the pulse), the pneumatometer (for measuring exhaled air), the ergograph (for measuring the work accomplished by a single muscle or set of muscles) are examples of calibrating devices that, having served mainstream experimental physiology, were eventually applied to sports physiology, as well.

But the nineteenth-century obsession with measuring every conceivable organic phenomenon, whether physiological or psychological, was not confined to the now familiar assessments of bodily functions carried out by physicians and physiologists. "Physical anthropology," one cultural historian has noted, "inaugurated the sustained effort to measure and record the differences among human beings in the middle and late nineteenth century." As a result of this demand for "a rigorously precise physical anthropology," a "preoccupation with bodies, with things tangible and measurable, narrowed the vision and cramped the understanding of many" scientists and physicians who sought to make sense of humanity in its almost limitless variety.[10]

This trend toward the quantification of human physiological and psychological variables took its place within what Stephen Jay Gould has called "a strong Western tradition for ordering related items into a progressive chain of being." This virtual mandate to interpret human differences in a hierarchical fashion coincided with the revolutionary impact of Darwin's theory of evolution. "Evolution and quantification," Gould writes, "formed an unholy alliance; in a sense, their union forged the first powerful theory of 'scientific' racism—if we define 'science' as many do who misunderstand it most profoundly: as any claim apparently backed by copious numbers."[11] This is the dynamic that converted early physical anthropology into a racial anthropology whose vestiges linger even today in the form of apparently inextinguishable folkloric ideas about racial difference. Modern theories of black athletic superiority, however empirically based they may appear to be, are variations on a highly differentiated racialistic physiology that blossomed during the nineteenth century.

The European anthropology of this period offered a theory of racial differentiation that perceived a series of differences more profound than the merely external features—skin color, hair texture, and bodily dimensions—that had been so evident to early European visitors to Africa, Australia, and other remote places. The more "scientific" racial physiology distinguished between races—and primarily between Negroes and Caucasians—in terms of reactions to various drugs, sensitivity to pain, reaction time, glandular chemistry, acuteness of the senses, muscle strength and composition, brain size and structure, perceived body odor, physical dexterity, and even the structure and functioning of the nervous system. Several of these criteria are clearly related to human athletic potential.

Nineteenth-century Germany was fertile ground for biological and characterological theories about racial differences,[12] including "premodern" thinking about the physiology of human performance. Writing at a time when physical anthropologists were primarily interested in cranial measurements—and in the mental capacities they mistakenly derived from this scrupulously quantified physical evidence—the anthropologist Theodor Waitz asserted: "That the convolutions in the Negro brain are less numerous and more massive than in the European (in whom they vary) appears certain." But while the principal aim of anthropologists like Waitz was to deny blacks a fully human brain and nervous system, racial differentiation encompassed a wider variety of physical differences. Waitz's version of this sort of comparative anatomy and physiology included the size and weight of bones, the sense of smell, the strength of the legs (Waitz argues for Negro inferiority in this respect), the size of the genitals, body odor, and even the capacity for blushing.[13]

This comparative anthropology, to which Waitz made his own contribution, also included a proto-sportive agenda that called for frequent judgments about the physical strength, agility, and endurance of the different races. Although Waitz shared the contemporary romantic tendency to exaggerate the physical and sensory (if not the intellectual) capacities of "savage" peoples, he actually concluded that "greater muscular strength is found among civilized nations, owing to their protecting themselves from injurious influences of all kinds, in combination with superior nutrition and regular exercise."[14] This early racial anthropology of sportive aptitudes eventually reappeared in Germany during the 1920s and 1930s (see section 3).[15]

The physiology of proto-athletic performance that developed during the nineteenth century did not focus on probing the capacities of the Caucasian males who happened to be directing this project. The examination of European aptitudes occurred when amateur or professional ethnographers attempted to situate primitive peoples on a developmental scale by comparing the quantified aptitudes of Europeans and the "savage" types who served as their experimental subjects. The dynamometer, for example, was supposed to measure the hand strength of any given individual. But Waitz, for one, realized that such comparative measurements were of questionable value. Such experiments, he wrote, "can only be decisive when performed on individuals of the same nature and the same practice in physical efforts."[16] There was, after all, no reason to assume that people of different cultures approached any given physical performance in the same frame of mind. Decades later the physiologist Adolf Basler added a racist logic to this sort of cultural relativism by claiming that "colored" peoples were unable to develop the mental concentration required to achieve a high score on a muscular strength test.[17]

The animal world provided another group of experimental subjects for physiologists investigating the inherent biological limits of living organisms. Late nineteenth-century German physiologists studied canine metabolism during physical exertion, the locomotion of sharks, epilepsy in frogs, the psychic qualities of ants and bees, and they used animals to develop a simple artificial respirator. Animal athleticism was best exemplified by horses[18] and birds, whose flying abilities were studied as early as 1846.[19] At the dawn of the age of aviation, physiologists acknowledged, perhaps a bit grudgingly, that the avian machine was much more efficient than its man-made equivalent.[20]

During the second half of the nineteenth century, the German scientific establishment produced what may be called a latent sports physiology, a science of humanity quite unaware of its future role in exploring the biological foundations of specifically athletic achievements. The scientific marginality of sport during this period, its status as just one more potential application for physiological knowledge, cannot be sufficiently stressed. A pioneering scientist like Nathan Zuntz (b. 1847) did not do basic work on metabolism and muscle physiology, or put horses on his laboratory treadmill, to promote the fortunes of German athletes. Zuntz's research on the energy efficiency of the mammalian organism stimulated his interest in the physiology of the marching soldier, the alpinist, the high-altitude balloonist, and the (sportive) cyclist,[21] about whom his son Leo did significant research.[22]

We must keep in mind that, a century ago, the high-performance athlete was still a curiosity, not a charismatic figure at the center of huge commercial enterprises. In summary, sport occupied a very humble position within that much broader range of performances required by modern civilization. The very insignificance of sport at this time reminds us that sports medicine must be seen as only one part of the much larger investigation of human potential—physical and psychological—that was accelerating dramatically at the end of the nineteenth century.

The "latent" sports science of this period may be divided into five categories. *Muscle physiology* investigated the biochemistry and thermodynamics of muscular contractions, measured muscular strength with the ergograph developed by the Italian physiologist Angelo Mosso, studied the effects of alcohol and other drugs on muscle functioning, and looked at the effect of muscular exertion on blood pressure, glycogen consumption, and so forth.

Respiratory physiology studied the relationship between metabolism and the oxygen content of inhaled air, the effects of drugs like alcohol and morphine derivatives on breathing, the effects of rapid air pressure changes on organisms, and the physiological effects of breathing at high altitudes, including the critical red blood cell count. The development by Nathan and Leo Zuntz of an apparatus for collecting and analyzing exhaled gases greatly facilitated the study of extreme physical exertion, including that of athletes.[23]

Endocrine physiology, or the study of glandular functioning, was in an undeveloped state during the last decades of the nineteenth century, although a rough theory of "internal secretions" developed during the 1890s. The idea of the hormone was not clarified until 1905.[24] German physiologists, along with important French colleagues like C.-E. Brown-Séquard, were left to grope their way toward an understanding of the relationship between the sex glands and secondary sexual characteristics, or to speculate on the fate of unejaculated spermatozoa.[25] The development of reproductive endocrinology between the World Wars led to an explosion of research on the steroid hormones in Germany during the late 1930s and, eventually, to the widespread use of anabolic steroids in high-performance sport.

The *neuromotor physiology* of this time looked at such issues as the anatomical structure of the nervous system, the relationships between nerves, muscle tissue, and organs such as the glands, lungs, and heart, the effects of drugs and other chemical compounds on nervous functioning, the effects of electrical stimulation, and the speed of nerve impulses. The preoccupation with fatigue during this period raised the intriguing question of whether nerves, like muscles, experience an analogous exhaustion.

Finally, the *cardiac physiology* of this era probed the neural regulation of cardiac functioning, rhythmic and arrhythmic heartbeats, pharmacological effects of drugs and toxic substances, including the boosting of cardiac functioning with aspirin, artificial stimulation (chemical, electrical, mechanical) of the heart, the heart-lung relationship, the calibrating of cardiac performance, reviving the heart after cardiac arrest, and the detection of audible cardiac anomalies. Contemporary sports physicians were particularly concerned about the effects of athletic exertion on the size of the heart. Mallwitz (1908), for example, spoke with much concern about "the hypertrophy of the heart muscle"[26] as a result of physical overexertion.

The physicians who shaped German sports medicine during the first three decades of this century naturally tended to address physiological issues relevant to the study of athletes, but they did not do so in a spirit of narrow-minded practicality. Overspecialization was hardly possible in so underdeveloped a field, and the early sports physicians recognized that progress in sports medicine depended on their acquiring an understanding of the basic physiological processes involved in athletic performance. Even as late an "early" text as Herbert Herxheimer's *Grundriß der Sportmedizin* (1933) offers very little practical advice to the trainer, one example being a warning against the "virilizing" of female athletes.[27]

German sports medicine originated after the turn of the century as a specialty within mainstream medicine among physicians with a personal interest in sport. For example, Arthur Mallwitz, a prominent sports physician for decades (and, eventually, a Nazi sympathizer), defended his dissertation on the effects of high-performance sport on the human organism in 1908. Two years earlier, as a pentathlete at the Athens Olympic Games, he had contributed a urine specimen to a German scientific team conducting research similar to his own.[28]

The early history of German sports medicine includes a series of pathbreaking events. The term "sports physician" (*Sportarzt*) was first used in 1904 by Mallwitz, who three decades later played an important role in organizing the International Sports Physicians Congress held in conjunction with the Berlin Olympiad in 1936.[29] The International Hygiene Exposition held in Dresden in 1911 provoked considerable interest in sports medical issues. The first official sports physicians' congress ever held took place in September 1912 in Oberhof/Thüringen. The first university lecture course on sports medicine was given in Berlin by Arthur Mallwitz and August Bier during the summer semester of 1919 under the title "The Hygiene of Sports and Performance." The world's first sports college, which included a sports medical curriculum, was founded in Berlin in 1920. The world's first sports medical journal was founded in 1924 by the German Association of Physicians for the Promotion of Physical Culture, which was formed the same year after the second German Sports Physicians' Congress held in July 1924. "The aim of the Association," its founding document stated, "is the promotion of physical culture (*Leibesübungen*) through the exchange of ideas regarding scientific and practical issues; addressing these issues by means of special committees, the advising of associations and responsible officials; and the addressing of issues pertaining to hygiene and the organization of sports medical research."[30] Research carried out on athletes participating in the second Winter Olympic Games at St. Moritz in 1928 was led by the Swiss physician Wilhelm Knoll. Finally, the establishment of FIMS (Fédération Internationale Médico-Sportive) in 1928 was initiated by the president of the German sports physicians, Dr. Walter Schnell.[31]

German sports physicians tended to agree that they should be active or former athletes, and several arguments were advanced to support this view. Physicians could teach good health by example.[32] A related point was that an intimate familiarity with the lived experience of the athlete was a prerequisite for treating the athletic client. In the opinion of the Berlin physiologist René du Bois-Reymond: "Without wishing to offend the medical establishment, it should be acknowledged that the judgment of an untrained layman regarding sport and its excesses is worth more than that of an inexperienced physician."[33] It is possible this judgment was aimed at the opposition to sport among many physicians encountered by the pioneering sports physicians.

The physician-athlete could also observe his own body's reactions to the stress of competition. Mallwitz, for example, noted in his dissertation (though his reasoning is not always clear) that his success as a pentathlete in Athens, and that of a German teammate, had confirmed another scientist's prognostications in that their relatively small hearts had not precluded successful performances.[34]

There was also widespread agreement among these men that sports medicine should not become a separate medical discipline. (Today many West German sports physicians feel otherwise.) On the purely practical level, Dr. Walter Schnell pointed out in 1927 that physicians specializing in sports medicine, and especially those serving "proletarian" sports clubs, would quite simply have trouble making a living.[35] A more profound point was that the physiology of sportive functioning could not be divorced from human physiology as a whole. "The specific nature of the sports medical examination," Schnell wrote in 1925, "does not involve the development of a specialized method, but rather the application of established medical science of a specific area." Sport physiology was a part of, and would inevitably enrich, general physiology.[36] In his 1913 essay on the "pathological physiology of sport," A. Albu had noted that the study of sportive overexertion could lead to "useful conclusions regarding the pathogenesis of kidney disorders."[37]

It is senseless, said Schnell, to separate sport-induced bodily changes from the same kinds of changes resulting from occupational stress.[38] This is only one aspect of the sport-labor synthesis that emerged along with a unified conception of performance (*Leistung*) embracing various types of physiological exertion. These observers saw no reason to distinguish between job-related exertion and the exertions of athletes. In either case, the human organism was put under stress, and its responses to stress could be studied by physicians and "psychotechnicians" (see section 4).

The most important—and truly modern—theme for this modern sports medicine was the stress on objectively verifiable performance and its measurement. But sportive performance is best understood as only one type of performance favored by an industrial civilization that demands a wide range of performances—from prime ministers to coal miners—in addition to sportive ones. The interest in sport so evident in the "psychotechnics" (industrial psychology) movement of the 1920s and 1930s shows again how many observers did not differentiate between sportive effort (the phrase *sportliche Arbeit*—"sportive labor"—was commonly used) and the physical performances required by factory production lines.

Like the European physiology from which it derived, early German sports medical literature offers a highly variegated idea of physical performance, even as it neglects to mention that physical performances were part and parcel of factory life.[39] The preferred analogues to sportive performance were roles associated with male adventure. In his article on "Sport and Stimulants" (1913), Dr. Ferdinand Hueppe discussed the role of alcohol on polar expeditions (such as those of the Norwegian explorer Fritjof Nansen) and in the tropics, where meat extract could be useful.[40] Professor A. Albu described (in 1913) the research opportunities offered by military marches (with heavy packs) which, having been introduced in 1905, had by 1907 become a kind of competitive sport. "During these pack marches I have made a series of observations which seem to me of interest for both the physiology and psychology of modern sport."[41] Dr. August Bier's 1926 article on the psychological foundations of extraordinary physical performances described how the fatigue built up during a long trek through the forest was overwhelmed by "the passion of the hunter," the strength of which "can only be appreciated by someone who has had it in his blood since he was a boy."[42]

This elastic concept of performance extended as well into the animal realm, which had been providing experimental subjects for medical research throughout the nineteenth century and would perform the same service for sports medical research well into the twentieth. German scientists, for example, would train dogs like athletes, then kill them in order to study the changes that had occurred in their internal organs.[43] Ferdinand Hueppe argued that breeding the racehorse for performance had produced a more beautiful as well as a fitter body.[44] Bier wrote of the "amazing flying performances" of migratory birds, although he refuted what he called the widespread idea that these birds actually embarked upon "training exercises" prior to making the great migrations.[45]

Performances rooted in natural instincts could not, of course, be "new" in an historical sense. The novel elements are the highly elastic nature of the performance concept in the first decades of the twentieth century and the self-consciousness about observing, quantifying, and even creating new types of quantifiable and implicitly competitive performances within an emerging industrial civilization based upon an ideal of high performance ("productivity"). Intelligence testing, for example, developed simultaneously with the new culture of "sport." More than ever before, human beings were seen as physical and psychological specimens whose performances could be measured, and possibly improved, within limits that were still unknown.

The practical challenge to sports physicians in Germany and elsewhere was to convert physiological science into scientifically valid training regimens. Over the past century the relationship between theory and practice has changed dramatically. Early sports medicine was essentially observational, restorative, and therefore limited in its ambitions to enhance performance. As high-performance sports medicine has evolved, and as its powers of observation have greatly increased, it has become much more prescriptive and ambitious both with respect to restoring the injured body and to increasing its level of performance. This trend is evident in F. Heiss's three stages in the history of German sports medicine: (1) the application of general medical knowledge to the athlete (1912–c.1925); (2) the acquiring of a systematic understanding of the effects of sport on the human body (c.1925–1955); and (3) the development of sports medicine into a component of most medical disciplines (c.1965–   ).[46]

To appreciate the significance of this third stage of development we may turn to Ernst Jokl's retrospective survey (1985) of some of German sports medicine's contributions to general medicine: (1) the concept of the "sports heart" as distinguished from the pathologically hypertrophic cor bovinum; (2) the elucidation of sudden death in sport; (3) the decreased immune capacity of the athlete; (4) the adaptational limits of the autonomic nervous system; (5) revising the concept of the "aging heart"; and (6) establishing that athletic training does not reverse pathological-anatomical processes.[47]

Klaus Carl's study of training methods in Germany during the first decades of this century enables us to observe the emergence of sports medical thinking in relation to training and to construct an overall idea of what separates "premodern" from "modern" thinking in the combined area of training and sports medicine. It should be emphasized that the ideas enumerated below do not always appear in a straightforward chronological sequence; in a few cases, "modern" ideas can appear even before the turn of the century, and "premodern" thinking can appear in Germany as late as the 1930s. Here we encounter German sports medicine's affinity for certain culturally conservative attitudes, including during the Nazi period (see section 2).

The "premodern" attitude toward sports medicine emphasizes the limitations both of sports medical practice and of the human body itself. In 1906 one author expressed concern about the consequences of the sport-induced "hypertrophic heart"—a topic that generated much discussion in the medical literature in and outside of Germany.[48] In 1909 Arthur Mallwitz defined the role of the sports physician as essentially limited to providing "the necessary clinical assistance" and "observing the athlete's mode of life." In 1910 another author feared the effects of "overtraining," which became a standard term. Such anxieties recall one cultural conservative's use in 1908 of the pejorative term *Hypersport*.[49]

"Premodern" attitudes also include: training norms derived from generalizations based on individual cases rather than systematic research, and a failure to treat athletic performance as the complex result of independent variables such as data about the heart, metabolism, and the blood. In 1895 Ferdinand Hueppe had talked about developing the heart, blood vessels, and lungs; but his goal was a "harmonious development of the body" rather than the improvement of athletic performance.[50]

The "modern" period, which began around 1912 for German track and field, was characterized by training regimens that were more frequent, more strenuous, and more closely studied and supervised by medical personnel. The use of weight-training increased. Training became less casual and more of a problem to be thought about. First photography and later cinematic techniques were used to study athletic movements. A bureaucratic structure that included sports physicians aimed at improving athletic performance began to take shape, and the average age at which athletes achieved their peak performances began to decrease.[51] In short, the stage was set for modern sport as we know it.

2. Cultural Conservatism and the Origins of German Sports Medicine

The alliance between medical science and high-performance sport has become a unique, and at times controversial, adventure in the history of the human species. Over the past century, the quantifiable elite sports (such as weightlifting and track and field) have developed into nothing less than an enormous biomedical experiment on the human organism itself.[52] The birth of modern sports medicine allows us to examine the emergence of specifically modern physiological and psychological doctrines of human functioning within a fundamentally conservative culture which, at the same time, was being transformed into the quantified and functional world of both industrial and sportive technologies. How did traditional medical men adapt to a modern role—that of the high-performance sports physician—that required a new, and widely resented, functional approach to the treatment of the human organism in its entirety?

It is a curious fact that the early and intensive development of German sports medicine occurred within a fundamentally conservative society, and within a nationalistic, even chauvinistic, medical subculture,[53] which had first resisted the advent of sport. The allegiance of many physicians to traditional German gymnastics and its system of values created a tension between this culturally based antimodernism and the scientific modernism inherent in their own medical research and practice (see the discussion of August Bier below).

During the century preceding the appearance of sports medicine, the predominant form of physical culture had been the German gymnastics (*Turnen*) founded at the time of the Napoleonic Wars by the racial nationalist Friedrich Ludwig ("Father") Jahn.[54] The gymnasts opposed sport, and its modernized forms of traditional physical culture, as a foreign (primarily British) import, making the argument for its inferiority on nationalistic, racial, and aesthetic grounds.

This resentment of sport among German right-wingers lasted well into the 1930s. In his essay "Prussianism and Socialism" (1920), Oswald Spengler denounced "the English mentality" as follows: "Even in sports and recreation the Englishman sees a test of personal, and especially physical superiority. He engages in sports for the sake of national and world records; he enjoys prizefighting, a sport that is closely related to his economic habits and is quite alien to the minds of gymnasts in Germany."[55] It is worth noting that Spengler's conservatism in this regard was not shared by Adolf Hitler, whose favorite sport happened to be prizefighting. What is more, Hitler's sponsorship of the 1936 Berlin Olympiad required significant concessions to the modern sport culture Spengler clearly resented.

As I have argued elsewhere,[56] the conservative (*völkisch*) critique of sport in Germany is deeply embedded in a comprehensive critique of modernity that appeared in Germany even before the turn of the century and constituted the cultural soil in which Nazi doctrine grew. "What differentiated the Germany of this period from other nations," George Mosse has written, "was a profound mood, a peculiar view of man and society which seems alien and even demonic to the Western intellect."[57] German cultural conservatism at this time was racially chauvinistic and anti-international; resentful of industrialism and the city; hostile to rationality, technology, and science even as many German scientists and engineers were making basic contributions to their fields; and deeply attached to an aesthetic of the human body that implied both a racial doctrine and the presumed superiority of a well-proportioned, muscular male type whose authority derived from the aesthetic norms of ancient Greece and assumptions about the physical and emotional ferocity of ancient Germanic warriors. The glorification of this physically superior male type, and his taste for violent and predatory action, has been an important aspect of

German culture over the past two centuries. All of these themes appear in the sports medical literature of this period.

But the early sports physicians could not adopt a purely *völkisch* outlook. As we have just seen, many sports physicians could and did embrace *völkisch* themes—nationalist chauvinism, the cult of virility, the racial aesthetics of the body, a resentment of modernity itself. But resistance to performance-enhancing sports medicine was inherent in the *völkisch* critique of sport as a whole. First, sport was criticized as unhealthy: it was an overspecialized form of physical culture that promoted "one-sided and repetitive movements" (*Einseitigkeit und Einförmigkeit der Bewegungen*).[58] And there were other objections to sport that were incompatible with any sports medical project whose ambitions extended beyond mere hygienism. There was, for example, a critique of stress. One author pointed out in 1884—two years after Germany's first (British-style) track and field meet—that sport encouraged people to train like racehorses.[59] An early sports medical study published in 1908 would later compare the enlarged hearts of athletes to those of racehorses.[60] And another critic claimed that people were "training—to the point of madness."[61]

But this sort of concern was incompatible with the goals of early sports medicine, which began in large part as the study of the human organism under stress. Objections that sport caused the body to be treated as a machine, or that sportsmen were employing electrical devices to measure performance as precisely as possible,[62] could not be welcomed by physicians who were trying to acquire a scientific understanding of what we call exercise physiology. Nevertheless, we must keep in mind the capacity of German sports medicine to accommodate conservative, and even anti-scientific, attitudes. The noted surgeon August Bier was one of the founders in 1920 of the German College for Physical Culture in Berlin; but that did not prevent his commenting ten years later that the three greatest threats to physical culture were "the record epidemic," "medicalization," and "pedagogification."[63]

A third conservative objection to sport focused on the psychological state of the athlete. One commentator referred in 1914 to the "hypnotic state" of the competitor.[64] But what the cultural conservative regarded as an unhealthy mental state the sports physician saw as a challenge to his healing or counseling skills. The early German sports medical texts make it clear that a rudimentary sports psychology had to develop along with sports medicine as an ancillary field of study; for this reason, the first sports psychology laboratory was set up at the German College for Physical Culture.[65]

The cultural conservatism of the German medical establishment during the first decades of the twentieth century is well illustrated in the case of the prominent surgeon and sports physician August Bier (1861–1949), who served as the first rector of the German College for Physical Culture. Bier is a useful representative figure in that his conservative orientation was in tune with that of the German medical community in general and surgeons in particular.[66]

Bier described his personal outlook on ancient and modern medicine, and his views on the political condition of Germany, in a series of essays ("A Physician's Thoughts on Medicine") that appeared in the right-wing *Münchener medizinische Wochenschrift* (*Munich Medical Weekly*) in 1926.[67] Like many other Germans of the Weimar period, Bier was profoundly disturbed by the ineffectiveness of parliamentary government and by the "political poisoning" of the body politic.[68] He looked back nostalgically to the Prussian state of Frederick the Great and Bismarck's *Reich* and called for the "towering statesman" who might redeem modern Germany.[69] Such attitudes made Bier a typical German conservative of his era, inside or outside of the medical profession. His anti-modernism was primarily concerned with what one might call the nature of modern experience. His description of "Americanism" as "repulsive" and "fundamentally alien to the soul of the German" referred to the "specialized" and "mechanized" nature of modern work, to the illusory progress of technology and "all the triumphs of cold intellect."[70]

It should be emphasized, however, that Bier was a selective anti-modernist whose primary interest was not to promulgate blind reaction, but rather to assert the healing authority of a classical past over a confused and superficial modern age. As a physician, he could not reject modern science out of hand, since to do so would have meant joining "the army of fakes and quacks" who had attempted to exploit his prestige for their own ends.[71] Instead, Bier's conservativism took the form of a venerated medical canon rooted in a philosophy of "healing" (*Heilkunde*) and based on "teleological concepts"[72] that had been forgotten by modern physicians in favor of mere "medicine." Heraclitus, the creator of a doctrine of the world's ultimate "harmony," had anticipated the basic principle of homeopathy—the curative power of minute doses of poisons[73]—to which Bier subscribed. Hippocrates, "the greatest physician who ever lived," had made "observations and discoveries which are still valid and superior to what the most refined technical instruments have taught us."[74] Bier made much of the fact that Hippocrates had called the physician both a philosopher and an artist and emphasized the invidious comparison between the pre-technological, "godlike" physician and a modern medical establishment, imprisoned within a "mechanical" materialism, which is content to believe that it can live and prosper without a grounding in philosophy, or without—in Bier's words—"our sober, practical teleology."[75]

Bier's pantheon of legendary medical figures includes Paracelsus von Hohenheim (1493–1541), the travelling physician and pharmacological pioneer[76] (once known as "the medical Luther") who became a right-wing cult figure in Germany before and during the Nazi period. For a modern German scientist like Bier, Paracelsus served to reconcile science with a transcendental spirituality whose purpose was to hold in check the technical hubris of science itself.

It was easy for Bier to identify with Paracelsus's heretical position outside the medical establishment of his time. Bier's open advocacy of homeopathy—an aberrant pharmacology without scientific credibility[77]—identified him with the natural healing movement (*Naturheilkunde*) of which many German physicians disapproved on both scientific and self-interested economic grounds. As a scientific outsider, Bier lamented that the young surgeons of the 1920s had embraced the newly fashionable colloidal chemistry and had dismissed him as a mystic.[78]

The Paracelsus legend was easily incorporated into Nazi doctrine.[79] "Paracelsus appeared in Nazi books and magazines as the personification of German medical science. Paracelsean medicine was said to embody the natural, earthbound, experimental character of German medicine—medicine that was 'close to the people' and not based on 'a lot of complicated theories.'" And Bier, like Paracelsus, was eventually honored by the Nazis. In 1937, along with his fellow surgeon Ferdinand Sauerbruch, Bier became one of the first five recipients of the German National Prize.[80]

Bier's anti-scientific instincts were part of a larger ambivalence toward the modern world as a whole. His cultural conservatism had several dimensions: the need to romanticize and spiritualize science, which resulted in his sympathy for homeopathy; the cult of the ancient Greeks, which merged effortlessly with an analogous reverence for Germanic heroes like Paracelsus and Goethe; the hostility toward specialization and "materialism"; the homophobia,[81] which both antedated and was part of what Robert N. Proctor has called the "masculine self-image of Nazi medical science,"[82] and the nationalism that yearned for a *Führer* to heal Germany.

At the same time, Bier was a modern physician who was fully capable of embracing real scientific developments and who did not endorse the racial biology of the 1920s. His belief in "the autonomy and uniqueness of living things" had its limits. "For the physician who thinks biologically," he wrote, "it goes without saying that he may not disregard the physical-chemical dimension of life"; nor does his attachment to a "teleological conception of the organism" exclude a scientific theory of causality.[83]

Bier did not object to scientifically based training in sport, stating that "for the physicians almost everything remains to be done." But it is important to recognize that Bier's endorsement did not refer to scientific performance-enhancement in the modern sense. Bier's primary point was that physical culture could serve medicine, not the other way around. His endorsement of physical culture, especially gymnastics, did not mean, however, that such exercise is a panacea, and he made a point of listing many substances of pharmacological value to the sick person.[84]

It is important to note that Bier objected vigorously to the "one-sided" genetic doctrine promulgated by the racial hygienists and eugenicists of the time, which made the biological "constitution" of the human being subject to an "iron and immutable" law of heredity. "I am well aware," he writes, "that one will never make a Negro out of a white man, an athlete out of a constitutional weakling, or a genius out of a dunce. But within the framework of inherited constitution a great deal can be accomplished if one knows how to deal with the other side of the organism, its mutability, in the correct fashion."[85] Here, says Bier, is where physical culture has an important role to play in modern medicine.

3. Ernst Kretschmer's Constitutional Theory and the "Athletic" Type

The publication of Ernst Kretschmer's *Physique and Character* in 1921 had a profound influence on European psychiatry. Kretschmer's theory of constitutional types was actually a refurbished, if ostensibly more scientific, version of a nineteenth-century French somatology that can be traced back to Hippocrates' theory of temperaments.[86] Kretschmer's novel achievement was to demonstrate an apparent correlation between three body types and two forms of mental illness.[87] He had observed that a disproportionate number of manic-depressive (cyclothymic) patients showed the heavy, compact, fatty body structure he called the *pyknic* type; whereas a disproportionate number of schizophrenic (schizothymic) patients showed the *athletic* or *asthenic* body types, the former characterized by a well-developed skeleton and musculature, and the latter by thinness and above-average length.[88] Nor was Kretschmer content to limit these conclusions to the mentally ill patients he had studied. As one of his critics wrote in 1930: "He generalizes beyond the limited confines of psychopathology by developing a theory of physique and character which embraces the normal personalities found in everyday life. He seizes upon the now generally accepted conclusion that there is no hard and fast dividing line between the normal and the abnormal, the latter merely exhibiting normal mental mechanisms to an exaggerated degree."[89]

Kretschmer's influence on medical thinking during the 1920s and 1930s can be explained as the result of two factors. First, his theory of physique and character was only the latest of many such theories which for centuries had responded to a deeply rooted curiosity about the deeper meaning of physical appearance. Kretschmer himself was well aware that this sort of speculation amounted to a kind of popular folklore about body and temperament. "In mind of the man-in-the-street," he wrote, "the devil is usually lean and has a thin beard growing on a narrow chin, while the fat devil has a strain of good-natured stupidity. The intriguer has a hunch-back and a light cough. The old witch shows us a withered hawk-like face." "It may be," he continued, "that phenomena, which the phantasy of the people has crystallized into the tradition of centuries, are objective documents of folk-psychology—jottings from the observation of mankind, worthy, perhaps, of a glance even from the eyes of the experimenter."[90] This little masterpiece of understatement appears on the first page of a book intended to turn "folk-psychology" into a branch of biological science. Its emphasis on the interpretation of the physical organism further stimulated a racial aesthetics of the body—including an idealized athletic type—which had flourished in Germany throughout the nineteenth century.[91]

Kretschmer's impact can also be related to certain intellectual trends of this period. By the time his book appeared, the biologizing of psychology had been underway for more than a century,[92] promoting the idea that the human organism was a psychosomatic entity that could be analyzed with the latest theories of biological science.

German sports physicians wanted to know whether constitutional theory could correlate specific body types with specific athletic aptitudes. In 1923 the physician Wilhelm Kohlrausch published the results of an anthropometric survey of athletes he had carried out at the "Deutsche Kampfspiele" competitions the previous year. Kohlrausch's sport typology described the following types according to body structure and temperament: sprinter, middle-distance runner, long-distance runner, long-distance skier, ski jumper, high jumper, multi-event athlete (*Mehrkämpfer*), swimmer, throwing athlete, weight-throwing athlete, wrestler, boxer, soccer player, gymnast.

Kohlrausch's observations demonstrated the similarities that link any constitutional sport typology to sports psychology. He claimed, for example, that sprinters and high jumpers were generally "sanguine" types, while long-distance runners and weight throwers were predominantly "phlegmatic." Although Kohlrausch published this work only a year after the second edition of *Physique and Character* appeared, he did not mention Kretschmer. It has been pointed out, however, that Kohlrausch's constitutional types correspond to those of Kretschmer to a striking degree. It is also worth noting that Kohlrausch, like others, presented the multi-event athlete (pentathlete, decathlete) as a physical and characterological ideal type: "He is the most symmetrical, best proportioned and seems to be so temperamentally, as well. His gait, like his facial expression, is energetic and calm. . . ."[93] In summary, the sport typology of Kohlrausch is an applied constitutional psychology that looks for the foundations of performance within the organism as it is already constituted. It is prescriptive only to the extent that it proposes to match constitutional types with appropriate athletic challenges; its function is to identify talent rather than develop it further. As one author put it: "No one ever became an athlete on the basis of a scientific examination."[94] It is this conservatism of approach that makes it an early sport psychology as opposed to the more interventionist techniques (hypnosis, mental imaging, etc.) that have become a familiar, if scientifically unproven, part of high-performance sport.

The application of constitutional theory to sport was one example of what became known as "aptitude testing" (*Eignungslehre*). Carl Krümmel's essay (1930) on this topic illustrates the limited role of body typing within the sportive aptitude testing of this period. Krümmel's point of departure, like that of Kretschmer, is the total impression made by a human being on the trained observer, for which Krümmel used the term "Habitus." But this impression is based on more than body structure; it comprises both the "external impression" and the "internal state" of the human body. The components of "Habitus" are age, growth pattern, biological reactivity, inheritance, and life-style, and Krümmel noted the importance of the biological dimension. "The constitutional science of our era," he wrote, "no longer sees the human being as the plaything of his environment, but rather emphasizes the interplay between these external influences and the individual's own innate and developed resiliency (*Widerstands-kraft*) and adaptability."[95]

While Krümmel was interested in the anthropometrical side of the constitutional theory, he recognized its limitations. He offered a series of arithmetic formulas to establish the body measurements of "healthy men between the ages of twenty and thirty," and he even proposed a formula for middle- and long-distance runners: if the body weight in kilograms divided by 8/10 of the length of the leg in centimeters is greater than 1, then the runner is too heavy. Krümmel also introduced his readers to Kretschmer's three body types: the athletic, pyknic, and leptosome (asthenic). At the same time, he pointed out that "the widest range of racial characteristics, head shapes, skin-, hair- and eye-colors, eyelids and nose shapes" could be found within either the "athletic" or "asthenic" types. As for constructing a sport typology, Krümmel noted: "It is, however, too early to apply the interplay between physique and temperament (or character) to the area of sport, since the fundamental research is still ahead of us, and because no responsible advice about aptitudes can be built on mere hypotheses. What do remain, however, are the trait clusters particular to the individual types." Krümmel concluded: "The value of pursuing typological questions in sport depends on training the observer to spot those natural abilities which are expressed in the body structure." In the last analysis, Krümmel's assessment of sportive aptitude had more to say about the mind than about the body. The most effective kind of "doping," he said, is the carefully trained athlete's will to win. Yet winning is not the point of this activity. The point of sport psychology, said Krümmel, is "to train a human being to transcend himself (*über sich hinaus wachsen*) at a given moment."[96]

Kretschmer was not interested in sport; indeed, *Physique and Character* refers to sport only as an eccentric interest of certain subjects described in the book. The athletic type (*Athletiker*) is a constitutional type rather than a sportive one. Its male and female representatives are also subject to aesthetic (and, therefore, value-laden) judgments: "The bodily constitution of the athletic woman gives us on an average more the impression of abnormality, of extreme over-development, of unpleasant stolidity and massiveness than does that of the athletic male, and for this reason: these men at times come quite near our aesthetic ideal, while our ideal of female beauty is far overstepped by the athletic female." This viewpoint, which Kretschmer presented here in a spirit of neutrality, was promulgated in a more polemical fashion by other prominent contemporary writers on sport and the body. "Here is the point," Kretschmer said, "where we must warn our readers that we do not bring the subjective valuation of the laity into our diagnostic of bodily constitution."[97] Needless to say, it is easier to proclaim this value-free attitude than it is to enforce it. Still, it is clear that Kretschmer proposed the athletic type as an empirically valid scientific construction and not as a modern version of the Germanic heroic ideal.

Kretschmer's unromantic intentions are evident in his monograph on *The Personality of the Athletic Type* (*Die Persönlichkeit der Athletiker*, 1936), in which he argued that the athletic type is not simply an intermediate form between the pyknic and leptosome (asthenic) types. Franz Weidenreich—whom Kretschmer does not cite—had argued in 1927 that Kretschmer had erred in basing the athletic type on as superficial (and malleable) a trait as muscular development. "It seems questionable," Weidenreich wrote, "that the degree to which the musculature can be developed is linked to the presence of a special constitutional factor."[98]

Weidenreich did concede that extraordinary physical performances might be connected to a special constitutional factor,[99] but Kretschmer again was not interested in looking at constitution from this point of view. For example, the brief chapter on "Constitution and Performance" which appeared in the 1948 edition of *Physique and Character* did not appear in the original edition; what is more, this later addition dealt only with mental performance[100]—an apparent concession to the widespread interest in performance boosting he did not share. In the 1936 monograph Kretschmer associated the (physical) performances of "athletic" soldiers and athletes with their phlegmatic dispositions and diminished responsiveness to external stimuli.[101] But he showed no interest in devising ways to improve physical performance.

Nor did Kretschmer show any interest in promoting the athletic type as an ideal type. At a time when some sports physicians and scientists were invoking German athletic successes at the 1936 Berlin Olympiad as evidence of Germany's new greatness, Kretschmer offered his colleagues a portrait of the athletic type that was downright unflattering. According to Kretschmer, the "athletic" temperament has a bipolar structure that includes both a "viscous placidity" and an "explosive tendency." These people are presented as physically clumsier than others and, in particular, as intellectual and emotional dullards. Relative to other human types, they lack imagination, humor, and the capacity to be critical; even their gait and speech habits have a distinctive quality.[102]

Kretschmer even made a point of debunking the current image of the athletic life-style. At the present time, he wrote, "there is a widespread notion that the athletic individual is above all the active and energetic person, where the musculature is regarded as standing for the will pure and simple. This idea does not stand up to scrutiny, but rather contradicts the conclusions we have reached. . . . The energy of the athletic type is far more and predominantly passive, oriented toward calmness and tenacity."[103]

Kretschmer's lack of interest in sportive applications has not been emulated by all who have read him. For example, an Austrian psychologist writing in 1954 does not hesitate to correlate the schizothymic and cyclothymic types with athletic styles. "The schizothyme [soccer player] becomes the fine technician who, in the course of indefatigable training, strives for the utmost precision and achieves an artistic level of ball-handling. . . . The cyclothyme is versatile and adaptable, making up for his deficient technique with his passionate effort and astonishing tricks."[104]

The transition from a constitutional to a sportive typology was a gradual one. Despite Kretschmer's lack of interest in sport, his constitutional psychology could not avoid alluding to physical performance. Early German sports psychology, in turn, leaned heavily on constitutional theory to develop a "doctrine of types" that could be applied to athletes. Over time these sport typologies became less concerned with body types and more focused on the psychological foundations of performance.

4. Physiology and the Origins of German Sport Psychology

In Germany, as elsewhere in the Euro-American world throughout most of the nineteenth century, physical training was associated with a healthy harmonizing of the various human faculties; by the late nineteenth century, sport was assigned the additional function of providing therapeutic relief from the "one-sided" and deforming effects of industrial labor and other strains of modern life. But this kind of mental hygiene was still not a "sports psychology" in the modern, performance-oriented sense of the term.

The application of psychological thinking to the area of high-performance sport appeared shortly after the turn of the century. In 1913 A. Albu pointed out that scientific observations of participants in military marches should be of interest to "the psychology of modern sport," even if his own approach was entirely physiological.[105] Ferdinand Hueppe's article on "Sport and Stimulants" (1913) demonstrated that a kind of proto-sport psychology is inherent in any discussion of sport and pharmacological substances that are believed to improve athletic performance. Hueppe went so far as to claim that modern men and women cannot live without stimulants, and that more harmful stimulants should be replaced by lesser harmful ones.[106] This openly functional approach to the use of drugs appears to be one of the reasons why Hueppe, like others during this period, did not editorialize against doping as providing an unfair physiological or psychological advantage to the athlete who used them.

Early German sport psychology is best understood as a psychophysical anthropology that was more interested in finding the sources of human capacities than in improving these capacities in a programmatic fashion, and one frequently discussed source of energy was psychopathology. In an unusually interesting article titled "High Performances as a Result of Mental Factors and the Exigencies of Life" (1926), the surgeon August Bier argued that the amazing physical feats of certain epileptics and the mentally disturbed offered clues to the psychophysiological origins of high-performance sport. "Our bodies," he wrote, "are constructed in such a way that under normal circumstances they never exert all of their strength, in these cases muscular strength. This sort of exertion is a very rare event made possible by powerful mental stimuli and the simultaneous elimination of inhibitions." Bier's observations led him to conclude that the human organism possessed "reserves of strength" that even experienced scientists had ignored; more specifically, he speculated that individual groups of muscle fibers almost never experience simultaneous maximal stimulation, accounting for the limited range of "normal" performances. He also cited the observation of the psychiatrist Richard Krafft-Ebing that there are mentally ill people who are virtually immune to feelings of fear, exhaustion, and pain.[107]

The nature of fatigue was an important preoccupation of biological science during the last decades of the nineteenth century,[108] and Bier applied his observations concerning mentally disturbed subjects to the current theory of this mysterious phenomenon. Bier cited findings that involuntary ("automatically performed") effort had been found to be less fatiguing than voluntary effort, suggesting that the contemporary theory of "fatigue substances" and their accumulation in the body was mistaken. Krafft-Ebing, comparing genuine lunatics with imposters, had concluded that the physical movements of the former operated independent of volition and were "the product of spontaneous excitation."[109]

Bier rejected Krafft-Ebing's theory as superficial on the grounds that it was not sufficiently materialistic. "No one is going to claim," he wrote, "that the effects of stimulants (*Reizkörper*) are dependent on the will or that they do not act quite automatically. The fatigue substances are produced and affect the organism independent of the will and of mental and spiritual activity in general." Bier believed, however, that the "mental and spiritual" life of the individual can suppress the effects of the fatigue substances in certain situations. What is more, the source of extraordinary energy within the human organism did not have to be of pathological origin. The exhausted hunter who is suddenly energized by the prospect of an imminent kill is "not crazy, but rather completely healthy." The "passion of the hunt" has its origins, not in insanity, but in "an inherited, idealized version of the predatory instinct."[110]

The anthropological dimension of Bier's thinking was evident in his assumption that the hunter's physical performance—the mobilizing of his "reserves of strength"—is a literally atavistic trait, and he amplified this point elsewhere: "Even before I became aware of Polland's observation that epileptics in a state of semiconsciousness climb with their feet like apes and the most primitive peoples, I had come to the conclusion that in these people the thin veneer of civilization so-called has been stripped away, and that primeval drives and capacities concealed in their genomes are brought back to life again."[111] Among German sports-physicians and others writing in the field, this sort of speculative anthropology about "primitives" commonly took the form of observations on the distinct athletic aptitudes of different races, and particularly black Africans.[112] Such speculations actually continued a tradition within German racial anthropology. As early as the late eighteenth century, the theologian and historian Johann-Gotfried Herder had written of the Negro who "runs and climbs as if each were his sport."[113]

Bier's meditations on the uninvestigated sources of high performance accentuated the importance of sheer emotion. In conformity with a general tendency within German sports medical thinking to conflate different types of performance into a single category, Bier proposed that a variety of performances were rooted in a specific temperament: "The geniuses of the body (the so-called 'big guns' of sport), especially the one-sided ones, like the geniuses of the intellect, are very often nervous types," he wrote. Expanding the performance concept even further, Bier claimed that the seemingly inexplicable failures of sports stars were comparable to sexual impotence, in that both were of "psychic" origin. "And here is the old cliché to which science has paid far too little attention: joy, interest, passion to the point of fanaticism and even madness—it is a gradual transition from one to the other—boost performance to an extraordinary degree."[114] It is worth noting that, even today, sports psychology has not made much progress beyond this fundamental insight.

Constitutional psychology, as we have seen, included an implicit typology of sportive aptitudes. A constitutional sport psychology is based on the idea that sportive aptitudes can be rooted in specific temperaments of constitutional origin. In "Sport Type and Performance" (1932), Dr. Walter Schulz showed how the psychologizing of sportive aptitude could be carried out within the constitutional model made famous by Ernst Kretschmer.

Schulz began his article by demonstrating the inadequacy of the body-typing approach to sportive talent. He had no trouble showing that a variety of body types is represented in groups of elite sprinters, and so forth, and he bolstered his argument by pointing to the case of the great Finnish middle- and long-distance running star Paavo Nurmi, whose feats, he said, had astonished medical science. According to a Finnish sports expert, Nurmi had once been "a heavy-limbed youth with a barrel chest" who had gone on to transform his body through training. Nurmi's high-performance body could not, therefore, be identified with a specific constitutional type.[115]

Schulz emphasized environmental factors over genetic ones. The formative influences, he said, are ethnological and climatic. The hard winter of Northern Europe promotes toughness and endurance (e.g., the long-distance skier); the lively and impulsive Rhinelander differs from the more taciturn and self-willed Westfalian type, and so on. But Schulz stayed within the constitutional model by claiming that these "essential inner differences" are manifested in outer (physical) traits such as language, gesture, and movement. "The style of movement in particular is a distinctive expression of inner essence: differences in physical movement, seen from a psychological standpoint, are nothing other than a reflection of inner differences." These differences become evident in the contrasting physical styles of "mechanical, almost machine-like" distance runners like Nurmi and the "more temperamental, more elastic, more rhythmic" sprinters.[116]

The theoretical basis of Schulz's system was the "structural psychology" of Professor Erich Jaensch, whom Schulz described as "one of the most distinguished minds in the world of German scholarship." (Jaensch eventually became a pillar of Nazi psychology.[117]) Jaensch's bipolar model contrasts the "disintegrated type" (D-type) with the "integrated" type (J-type). Whereas the D-type is characterized by his

willpower and insensibility toward those around him, the J-type allows feeling a greater role in his life and consequently forms ties to
the world beyond himself. Within gymnastics, Schulz distinguished
between a "performance motor style" (*Leistungsmotorik*) and an "ex-
pressional motor style" (*Ausdrucksmotorik*). In the world of sport, too,
there are "two completely different structures." The first is characterized by an iron will to win, the second by a self-consciousness and sensitivity to external stimuli that is absent in the former type.[118] It is not
surprising that Walther Jaensch, a medical doctor and brother of the
more famous Erich, took the latter's typology even farther than
Schulz by equating the D-type and J-type with masculine and feminine types, respectively. Writing in the same periodical several issues
after Schulz's essay had appeared, Walther Jaensch contrasted the
characterological style of the "sportive man of willpower" with that of
artists, women, and children.[119] Such developments within constitutional theory show how easily it could be adapted to the ideological
program of the German cultural conservatives.

Just as the early sports physicians found themselves engaged in
psychology, psychologists who analyzed the athletic potential of the
human organism had to integrate a biomedical viewpoint into their
work. Perhaps the most active of these investigators was Dr. Robert
Werner Schulte, described by the Berlin correspondent of *Scientific
American* as "[o]ne of the pioneers in the field of practical psychology"
at a time when Berlin "boasts two colleges of sport where everything
pertaining to gymnastic exercises and outdoors games, as well as the
behavior of the human body under the most varied conditions of
physical activity, is investigated, practiced and taught in the same scientific spirit that is so characteristic of higher education at the university." One of Schulte's more striking approaches to this subject was
"the experimental arrangement for testing will power in connection
with sporting activities, individual courage being the particular quality studied. The candidate is asked to hold in his hand a metal ball
into which the experimentor is able unawares to pour hot water. Persons easily frightened and devoid of energy and courage let go most
rapidly, with all the symptoms of extreme fright."[120]

Like certain contemporaries, including his fellow psychotechnician
Fritz Giese and the surgeon August Bier, Schulte's analysis of sport
was an eclectic combination of psychology, biology, and the sort of
musings one might charitably call anthropological and philosophical
speculation. Like Bier, Schulte could not resist the opportunity to interpret physical culture (*Leibesübungen*) in virtually metaphysical
terms. *The Psychology of Physical Culture* (*Die Psychologie der Leibesübun-*

gen, 1928) begins with a discussion of the *telos* (purpose) of this activity within "contemporary cultural life." But this purpose can be understood only by following it back to "the primeval origins of the Bios," an argument that reaches the notable conclusion that the purpose of exercise (*Übung*) in this context is not high performance but rather an organismic " 'exercise' in the true sense, that is, a facilitating and perfecting of performance" whose justification requires no quantitative measurement.[121]

It is worth noting that in 1881, almost half a century before Schulte wrote these lines, the great German physiologist Emil Heinrich du Bois-Reymond (1818–96) had offered a less metaphysical, and more scientifically phrased, argument to the effect that "whether we understand it or not, man is capable of perfecting himself by exercising."[122] The important point here is that du Bois-Reymond, even more than Schulte, had been referring to "exercises" of the entire nervous system, including the sense of distance, visual impressions, the musical sense, the sense of smell, the sense of time, and even memory. This totalistic approach to the human organism, symptomatic of the exciting developments in phsyiology at this time, is the extremely interesting context in which early sports psychology emerged as one more way to investigate human potential.

Schulte's lack of interest here in quantification is curious coming from an author whose *Aptitude and Performance Testing in Sport* (*Eignungs-und Leistungsprüfung im Sport*, 1925) is filled with photographs of ingenious devices for measuring a variety of psychophysiological phenomena with the greatest possible precision. But Schulte's writings, like those of Giese and Bier, present a melange of cultural conservatism and technological ambition. Five years after being photographed for *Scientific American* as a perfect specimen of the laboratory-coated technician, Schulte was writing ecstatic passages about "the Teutonic type of the early Christian period . . . the sheer force of whose bodily energy reserves made possible the unstoppable drive to Spain and North Africa." This heroic figure, he said, is a "profoundly physical" type, and his inheritor is the German gymnast (*Turner*) of Friedrich Ludwig Jahn. At the same time, however, Schulte understood that "the age of scientific, and especially natural-scientific and technical, development" had put an end to the idyllic world of Prussian discipline. The progress of civilization can be understood as the rise of a new Nietzschean man who subdues nature. It is all the more interesting, then, that Schulte did not identify the high-performance athlete as a Nietzschean hero. The pursuit of sportive high performance, he said, is the victory of quantity—measurability and the exceeding of previous performances—over "quality, that is, beauty, elegance, or grace of line."[123]

Schulte had earlier discussed the pursuit of sportive high performance as a purely scientific subject, noting that his battery of aptitude tests was quite useful in this regard. His description of "the fully healthy record-setter who represents the maximum performance capacity within the bounds of normal physiology" reminds us that this era (1925) was sport physiology's age of innocence, a time when record-setters were still healthy and the boundaries of normal physiology were still widely respected. For Schulte treated the high-performance athlete as only one variation, and not the most important variation, on a more significant type. "The hero," he said, "puts himself in the service of moral ideas and concepts and becomes thereby both the prophet of values and the one who fulfills them." The marathon runner, the mountaineer who risks his life, the lifeguard who saves the lives of others are "shining examples" of this character type.[124] But the cult of sheer performance is not acceptable within this communitarian ethos and its neo-Hellenic ideal of moderation.

Schulte made biology the foundation of his "psychotechnical" approach. "No serious scientific psychology of physical culture can neglect the somatic foundations and parallels [with psychic life]," he wrote. Physical culture embodies values because it reinacts the logic of the "primitive biological" *telos* that condemns living organisms to struggle for survival. The whole concept of the "exercise" (*Übung*) is rooted in the organic life process and is applicable to organisms ranging in size and complexity from cells to human beings.[125] This is the larger biological context in which Schulte situated human potential and performance.

Schulte's sports medical approach included the use of X-rays, research on the circulatory system, blood analyses, spirometric analyses of respiration, the electrocardiograph, and the ergograph and dynamometer (to measure muscular force). He was also interested in physiological problems such as fatigue and pre-competition anxiety (*Startfieber*). On a scientifically more exotic level Schulte speculated about a hypothetical "motility hormone," analogous to the sexual hormone, that actually caused human movement.[126]

Schulte's interest in these medical issues and technologies illustrates the natural interpenetration of sports medicine and sports psychology. Just as a conscientious psychologist like Schulte had no choice but to deal with physiological problems, so the conscientious sports physician had to confront psychological problems that were even less tractable than the mysteries of human physiology. Herbert Herxheimer's well-known textbook *Fundamentals of Sportsmedicine* (*Grundriß der Sportmedizin,* 1933) shows that by the time of its publication a number of psychological topics had become standard themes within German sports medicine. These included hypnosis, pre-competition anxiety, willpower (like that of the much discussed Nurmi), "overtraining," and the so-called "dead point" of apparently terminal exhaustion[127] which appeared in the medical literature as early as 1891 and was still being discussed seventy years later.[128]

5. Early German Sports Medicine and the "Doping" Issue

Pharmacological attempts to improve athletic performance were widely discussed in German sports medical circles prior to the First World War and especially during the 1920s, as competitive sport became a mass culture in Europe and the United States. Robert Werner Schulte, who wrote enthusiastically about a "psychochemistry" that would banish "psychic deformities," both confirmed and endorsed the use of "minor remedies" like coffee, tea, and chocolate to reduce pre-competition anxiety and thereby produce improvements in athletic performances.[129] As we shall see, Schulte's nonjudgmental approach (in 1925) to these and other substances thought to boost performance (such as theobromine and sodium phosphate) may have represented a minority position regarding what was already known as "doping." It is important to recognize that Schulte felt the purpose of these substances to was restore emotionally impaired athletes to a non-anxious (and, therefore, normal state) rather than to transform healthy athletes into superhuman ones.

The use of alcohol and various other drugs to improve athletic performance appeared in Europe during the last decades of the nineteenth century.[130] In Germany, where the doping issue was being publicly discussed just after the turn of the century, it was sometimes associated with Americans. In an account (1910) of his experimental attempts to cancel out the effects of fatigue in dogs, the prominent exercise physiologist A. Loewy wrote: "Stimulants which supposedly produce increases in strength and endurance—so-called 'doping'— played a major role in the six-day bicycle races held here recently [in Berlin]. The Americans, in particular, used these substances. It is not clear which substances are involved, since the various drugs are secret ones whose composition is not revealed. How these compounds work is also unknown; to the best of my knowledge, no accurate investigations in this area have been done."[131]

At the meeting of the German sports physicians held in Berlin in 1924, a Dr. Willner made a similar point: "At the first American six-day [bicycle] race it was said that after the competition some of the participants went completely crazy and climbed in the trees like apes, behavior that was attributed to the extreme physical overexertion of the riders. I can report with the greatest certainty, however, that this behavior was the result of serious cocaine poisoning, a drug that was commonly used for doping." Dr. Willner indicated that he had encountered doping practices throughout his twenty-year medical practice. Prior to the First World War, for example, he had examined a professional bicycle racer who had taken digitalis in the mistaken belief it would strengthen his heart; in fact, it had ruined him. At the first German sports physicians' meeting in 1912, he had found athletes so interested in hearing about doping practices that he had resolved not to publish in this area.[132]

Addressing his German colleagues in 1924, during the European sports boom of the interwar period, Dr. Willner condemned doping as an absolute evil, a "poisonous plant" threatening the sports movement, which he and many other German sports physicians saw as nothing less than a form of social and racial hygiene. "At competitions we want to measure physical performances, not test the effects of drugs. . . . In my view, there is nothing more reprehensible than using pharmacological substances in an attempt to improve one's performances in competition with others who bring to the sporting encounter only that fitness they have achieved through training. It is no longer an honorable struggle when one competes with the assistance of pharmacological substances rather than with what one has acquired through training." It is also important to note Dr. Willner's improbable claim that on this issue "there is absolutely no difference of opinion among the physicians." The whole problem, he said, is "a sad sign of the times" bearing with it both moral and medical consequences.[133]

While Dr. Willner claimed that sports physicians were unanimous in their opposition to doping after the War, earlier commentaries on doping by German sports physicians and interested scientists tended not to address doping as a moral issue. Albu's (1913) treatise on "the pathological physiology of sport" did not mention doping, even when he discussed long-distance marches (where experimentation with drugs had been underway for years) and the notorious six-day bicycle races. He referred to allegedly performance-enhancing substances only in that he devoted considerable space to discrediting the claims of vegetarians that their way of life had produced a number of competitive long-distance march champions.[134]

The prevailing attitude toward performance enhancement prior to the War seems to have been one of scientific curiosity. Loewy, for example, drew no judgmental conclusions about the secret substances employed by the six-day bicycle racers; his point was that experimentation might elucidate the chemical mechanisms that made these drugs effective. What was more, Loewy had some news of his own regarding enhanced performance in his trained dogs: "I have now carried out an extended series of experiments on the effects of prolonged muscular exertion which show that it is actually possible to increase the performance capacity of muscles with medications, and which provide a basis for conceptualizing how these substances work. These were experiments on gas-exchange mechanisms in dogs which had to run on an upwardly inclined, electrically driven treadmill for a long period of time, until signs of fatigue became clearly apparent and also showed up in the gas-exchange process." As Loewy pointed out, earlier experiments of this kind had studied soldiers on a twenty-five-kilometer march, bicycle riders, and horses.[135]

Loewy's experiment actually combined two important theories in a scientifically incorrect fashion. "I now wanted to see," he wrote, "whether harmless pharmacological agents could defer the increase in the oxygen requirement which is characteristic of fatigue. I proceeded on the assumption that fatigue involved an accumulation of acidically reactive metabolic products, and I wanted to try to neutralize them with sperminum," a testicular extract derived from animals whose therapeutic—if scientifically unfounded—use had been pioneered by the French physiologist C.-E. Brown-Séquard in 1889. At a meeting of the Paris Biological Society in 1889, Brown-Séquard announced that, having injected himself with an animal-derived "liquide testiculaire," he had experienced a kind of physiological rejuvenation, including a dramatic increase in muscular strength.[136] Although scientifically invalid, this early example of hormonal organ therapy is considered a pathbreaking experiment.

Loewy concluded that the sperminum reduced fatigue by increasing the alkalinity of the blood, thereby neutralizing the acidity produced by exertion.[137] Loewy was correct, of course, in theorizing that fatigue produced an acidic compound; in fact, lactic acid had been associated with muscle fatigue since the mid-nineteenth century, and a classic paper on lactic acid in amphibian muscle had appeared in 1907.[138] The problem was that he had chosen as his alkalizing agent a biological compound whose real significance lay elsewhere, namely, in the contemporary theory of "internal secretions" which eventually became modern endocrinology.

Ferdinand Hueppe's essay "Sport and Stimulants" (1913), presented the previous year as a lecture to the Association for Scientific Research into Sport and Physical Culture, did not editorialize against performance-enhancing substances. Hueppe used the German word *Doping* to denote the use of arsenic, prussic acid, strychnine, cocaine, cola nuts, caffeine, and alcohol in what we may assume to be a sportive context; apparently, the association between "doping" and sport was so clear by this time that Hueppe felt no need to point it out.

Hueppe's basic approach to stimulants was functional, and most of his lecture dealt with alcohol, which he described as a stimulant rather than a nutrient—a distinction of fundamental importance to the debate over doping which continues today, since stimulants are easily conceived of as artificial while nutrients are generally regarded as natural substances. Hueppe discussed alcohol and physical performance within a conceptual framework that encompassed sport, the physical rigors of military life, and the demands—both physical and emotional—of polar expeditions. "In general," he said, "alcoholic beverages have more disadvantages for sportive exercise, and the stimulant effect of small amounts of alcohol which is useful in some circumstances becomes wholly superfluous if the body has been taught to function more economically and with better technique through planned exercises and the right sort of training." In this passage and elsewhere, Hueppe recommended alcohol as a stimulant of very limited value. Fifteen years later, the sports physician Johannes Müller would draw an interesting distinction that Hueppe disregarded. Alcohol, he argued, is for two reasons a justifiable stimulant of last resort in military emergencies, but not in sport. First, in a military emergency the advantages of alcohol as a stimulant outweigh its disadvantages (such as impaired coordination); second, the athlete has not reached the soldier's state of extreme physiological distress.[136] Here we encounter the idea that athletic exertion does not warrant extraordinary measures like doping, and that it should be kept within certain healthy limits.

Hueppe's attitude toward alcohol, while generally negative, stopped well short of prohibition. "Given our climatic and military situations," he said, "it is in general not necessary to require complete abstinence from alcohol." For one thing, abstinence itself can become a kind of mania that Hueppe associated with hysteria and neurasthenia; the teetotaler who substitutes a caffeine addiction (*Coffeïnismus*)—with its heart spasms, hallucinations, anxiety attacks, and vertigo—for an alcohol problem is simply jumping out of the frying pan into the fire. In addition, Hueppe saw modern society as a whole in a state of addiction to certain stimulants, "since it is impossible for civilized man to live entirely without stimulants and intoxicants." But he did not see this as a desirable state of affairs; it was rather a result of modern civilization's failure to inculcate in its citizens the ancient Greek *sophrosyne*, which Hueppe defined as "self-control with respect to intoxicants."[140]

"Doping" became an elastic concept during the 1920s and 1930s, including stimuli as heterogeneous as chemical substances, artificial ultraviolet radiation, and emotional encouragement during competition ("psychisches Doping")—a clear sign of the "premodern" sensitivity about the limits of intervention into the human organism that coexisted with the more value-free scientific curiosity described above. Dr. Willner's (1924) list of pharmacological substances includes substances affecting blood pressure, circulation, the heart; stimulants like alcohol, coca leaves (cocaine), coffee and tea (caffeine), tobacco (nicotine), hashish, morphium, heroin, strychnine, ether, camphor, ammonium hydroxide; and diuretics including digitalis.[141] The use of ultraviolet radiation provoked a debate wholly analogous to that surrounding drugs of various kinds.[142] The sheer variety of the "doping" practices considered dubious or worse testifies to the "premodern" strength of the taboo regarding performance enhancement which has survived to this day.

In 1924 the German Association of Physicians for the Promotion of Physical Culture issued a resolution condemning "the use of artificial stimulants" (*künstliche Reizmittel*)—synonymous with doping—on both ethical and medical grounds. While the elastic interpretation of doping seems to be implicit in this statement, the sports physician who cited it in 1926 offered an interesting and more detailed commentary: "Even if it must be conceded that it is difficult to draw a sharp line between what is and what is not permitted in the area of artificial methods for enhancing physical performance (I need mention only baths and massage), technical and mechanical devices, no matter how good they are at producing a temporary and objectively demonstrable improvement in physical performance, must be firmly rejected as both culturally unacceptable and contrary to the comradeship of sport."[143] The interesting feature of this passage is the specific reference to mechanical technology rather than drugs of various kinds. Unfortunately, this author did not further describe the devices he had in mind, which arguably might have included the numerous diagnostic instruments in the psychotechnical laboratory of Robert Werner Schulte.

Doping also took on a kind of exotic aura among some athletes. Modern science has always been a medium for wish fulfillment, as the paradoxical term "scientific miracle" amply demonstrates, and over the past century the sports medical enterprise has contributed its own quota of misleading reports and spurious "advances." The ambition to boost human physical performance contains a romantic Promethean impulse which easily imagines what science has not achieved. Dr. Willner pointed out in 1924 that athletes had circulated some "highly exaggerated and sometimes wild (*fabelhafte*) notions" about the powers of the cola nut.[144] While enthusiasm about "wonder drugs" is one kind of scientific romanticism in this sense, the romantic temptation can infiltrate science in subtler ways. Within the field of pharmacology the concept of the "stimulant" provided a case in point during the 1920s.

Doping is synonymous with stimulation. But it is easier to assume than to demonstrate the efficacy—let alone the mechanism—of any given "stimulant." The concept of the stimulus (*Reiz*) was, in fact, one of the classic problems of physiology during the seventeenth, eighteenth, and nineteenth centuries,[145] and it was still a controversial topic in the 1920s. One scientist—making an invidious distinction between sophisticated physiologists and naive physicians—claimed in 1926 that "medical 'public opinion,' as it is expressed in the general tone of the best known medical journals, is far more inclined to piously accept all kinds of hypotheses than are biological theorists, who, for understandable professional reasons, tend to keep more clearly in mind the limited value of hypotheses in general." One result of this credulity, he said, is a general acceptance of the "stimulus" concept by the medical profession.[146]

W. Heubner argued that two prevailing generalizations about the stimulus (*Reiz*) concept were actually invalid. The first holds that different types of external stimuli—physical pressure, electrical potential, a rapid increase in temperature, an osmotic pressure differential—"stimulate" living organisms in different ways. The second assumes that an "effective stimulus" (*Reizerfolg*) is the same as an increased rate of metabolism. Huebner's basic point was that the entire subject is poorly understood, and that there is no proof that "stimulants" have any demonstrable role in the metabolic functioning of normal cells. The problem is that this uncertainty had not prevented the spread of currently fashionable terms like "stimulant cells" (*Reizkörper*) and "cell stimulation" (*Zellreizung*).[147] It is worth noting that this terminology recalls the discredited theories of Wolfgang Weichardt, the controversial immunologist and fatigue researcher whom Heubner did not mention but of whom he may well have been aware. Weichardt's ideas about "protoplasm activation," "protein cell therapy" involving a "stimulus effect" (*Reizwirkung*), and his sensational "antikenotoxin" theory of fatigue reduction suggest the eager scientific romanticism for which Heubner had no patience.[148]

The central importance of stimulus theory resides in the fact that any science of physiology must describe the various movements of the living organism, including muscular contractions, and attempt to determine what actually causes them. During the nineteenth century, stimulus theory also played an important role in discrediting the vitalistic notion of a "life-force" (*Lebenskraft*)[149] in favor of the more scientific model of the "human engine" that forms the basis of exercise and sports physiology. During the eighteenth century, the early physiologist Albrecht von Haller (1708–1777) conducted pioneering experiments on the effects of various stimuli on muscle tissue, including heat, cold, scalpel pricks, electric jolts, alcohol, and other chemical substances.[150] Over the course of the next century many more experiments of this kind were carried out employing a wide variety of chemical compounds, including alcohol, ammonia salts, vomiting agents, meat broth, bile acids, and glucose, as well as the more familiar coffee, curare, and strychnine.[151] These experiments constitute the prehistory of doping in sport.

German medical and scientific opinion in the 1920s and 1930s about the feasibility of doping was divided. A most significant contribution to this debate appeared in 1930 in the physical culture journal *Die Leibesübungen*. In "Is Pharmacological Intervention in Sport Possible?" the scientist and physician Otto Riesser, director of the Institute of Pharmacology and Experimental Therapy at the University of Breslau, approached this topic with the scientific caution Heubner had prescribed for all biological theorizing several years earlier. Riesser's first paragraph directly addressed the role of fantasy in the area of doping: "The athlete should not expect me to be able to write him a prescription for some new substance which will permit him to achieve an astonishing level of fitness. He should realize instead what a difficult area this is, and that the extolling of performance-enhancing substances should be received with both criticism and profound scepticism." Riesser noted that there are two basic approaches to doping. The first assumes the efficacy of pharmacological intervention and discusses the effects of the relevant substances. Riesser preferred the more scientific attitude which inquires into the possibilities for influencing muscle functioning in the first place. Yet another problem is assessing the effects of a given medication: "Determining whether in a given case an improvement in performance, in one sense or another, has actually occurred is one of the most difficult and thankless tasks, even when, as is the case with sport, we can measure performance objectively. These performances are already so subject to variation due to countless internal and external factors that it is very difficult to make reliable judgments about the performance-enhancing properties of a medication. In no other field are there so many possibilities for subjective illusions on the part of both the observer and the observed."[152]

Riesser argued that performance-enhancing medications are conceivable but currently impractical. As for the conditions affecting a muscle's reaction to stimuli, he stated: "Artificial, and particularly chemical [*medikamentös*] modification of these factors, which is possible in one way or another, can undoubtedly influence the performance of the muscle, even if the nature and extent of the influence remain unclear and if *the systematic application of such methods is still in the distant future*" (emphasis added). Riesser pointed out that one important obstacle to performance boosting is a kind of negative feedback provoked by pharmacological intervention. For example, it "is to be expected that an increased buffering capacity of the blood and an increase in its alkali reserves would affect endurance favorably." But buffering against lactic acid buildup in muscle tissue is not a simple, or necessarily successful, procedure: "It is possible to increase the alkali reserves of the blood by administering heavy doses of alkaloid salts. Lacking the appropriate tests, we cannot say whether this is practically feasible. Nor should we forget that increasing the alkalinity of the blood, thereby producing a genuine alkalosis, means a depletion of calcium which may well impair performance. To test the idea of boosting performance through alkalosis would require direct experimentation on human beings." And Riesser made a similar point about the putative value of using adrenalin as a stimulant: "As for the question of to what extent these findings might be of practical significance, we do not want to forget that [the experiments] were all carried out on frogs, and that we were always stimulating [the muscle] with single jolts of artificial electricity applied to the nerves (*vom Nerven aus*), so that this did not involve the natural tetanic excitation (*Erregung*) of the muscle. It is therefore difficult to say without more specific experiments whether adrenalin can produce a temporary enhancing of muscle performance in a human being. The strong impact on the sympathetic nervous system, and especially the rise in blood pressure due to adrenalin, will rule out its practical usefulness."[153]

Riesser's 1930 article refers only once to the ethics of doping, and it is worth noting that when he did raise this issue it was in conjunction with his general scepticism about performance-enhancing interventions. "It is well known," he wrote, "that cardiac stimulants like digitalis apparently do nothing for the healthy heart simply because it is already functioning in an optimal manner. Still, one could imagine that for heavy sportive exertions of long duration, like cross-country skiing, a moderate digitalis treatment administered in advance might prevent general fatigue (*Ermüdung*) and overexertion (*Übermüdung*) of the heart. *I do not know whether this sort of thing has been tried.* In and of themselves such experiments stand opposed to *the healthy inner resistance all of us feel* toward the artificial boosting (*unterstützen*) of athletic performance and, perhaps, in addition the not wholly unjustified fear that any pharmacological intervention, no matter how small, may provoke a disturbance in the healthy organism" (emphasis added).

It should be noted that the ethical and the medical objections are linked in two ways. First, as Riesser implied, it may be unethical to incur medical risks on behalf of boosting athletic performance. And second, "the pharmacological influencing of athletic performance will always mean impairing the capacity to perform."[154] Riesser's second argument points to the fact that doping that does not work is less threatening to the ethos of sport than doping that does work, and this may account for his relative lack of interest here in the ethical issue. He was much more interested in exposing the unscientific premises of doping lore than in denouncing doping as an offense to sportsmanship.

Not long after the Nazi seizure of power in January 1933, Riesser presented a lecture to the German Swimming Federation titled "On Doping and Drugs." For whatever reason, this account of the doping issue emphasizes the dishonesty, rather than the impracticality, of performance-enhancing drugs. "From a sporting standpoint," Riesser stated, "the use of artificial techniques (*Mittel*) has been regarded as wholly incompatible with the sportsman's way of thinking and has been forbidden for that reason. Nevertheless, we all know that this rule is constantly being violated, and that athletic competition is often more dependent on doping substances than training. It is a highly regrettable fact that the supervisory bodies of sport seem to invest little energy in combatting this evil, and a fateful laxness is spreading. Nor are physicians innocent parties in this situation, partly out of ignorance about these matters, and partly because they have been writing prescriptions for powerful doping substances athletes cannot get by themselves."[155]

It would be interesting to know why Riesser's 1933 speech repeatedly stressed the immorality of doping. Perhaps he felt this emphasis better suited an audience of non-scientists; the longer and more technical 1930 text had been presented during a continuing education course sponsored by the German Association of Physicians for the Promotion of Physical Culture. But it is also possible that the new moralistic emphasis was a response to the new political climate of Nazi Germany. Riesser's critical comments about physicians, sports officials, and the "fateful laxness of attitude" about doping in German sports circles appeared rather suddenly. They could hardly have been a reaction to current events; as we have seen, concern about doping among German sports physicians had appeared long before 1933.

What we may presume to be official Nazi disapproval of doping in sport appeared in an address by Hanns Baur to the sports medical congress held in conjunction with the 1936 Berlin Olympic Games.[156] But research on the physiology of human performance, including the effects of stimulants, was carried out and published throughout the Nazi period, not least as a contribution to the war effort.[157] Scientists even refer to the Berlin Olympiad as a showplace for human potential.[158] It is likely that public anti-doping sentiment after 1933 was related to Nazi strictures against the self-serving, individualistic, record-breaking athlete and the abstract ideal of performance.[159] It is also consistent with Nazi rhetoric about sportsmanship, for example, the importance of the "noble contest" and the "chivalric" attitude of the German athlete.[160]

Riesser's disapproval of doping in the 1933 speech was only one side of his fundamental ambivalence about this sort of experimentation. Here, for example, as in his 1930 address, Riesser took up the use of digitalis. "Digitalis," he stated, "has some promise in this area because it does not have an effect until several hours after it is administered. One might arrange its use in such a way that it would first begin to act on the heart when it began to relax after a long period of exertion. Experimentation in this area suggests that it is probable such an effect could be achieved. From a theoretical standpoint all of this is very interesting. As a physician, however, I would not take the responsibility for giving digitalis to a long-distance runner several hours before his race." Discussing the administering of oxygen to the athlete, Riesser again ruled out an interesting theoretical application on ethical grounds and affords us another glimpse of what athletes were actually doing at this time: "If we want to pursue the goal of dilating blood vessels to provide as much oxygen as possible to the working muscles, we can also try something similar by increasing the oxygen concentration in the air which is ingested. One can, in fact, reduce the need for air for some period of time, and this technique has been used recently in swimming competitions. But there should be no doubt that, although oxygen is not a powerful drug, in a sporting sense this is doping plain and simple and must therefore be prohibited."[161]

Riesser's texts show that the doping problem has changed very little over the past half-century. New substances and techniques that allegedly enhance athletic performance continue to appear, but their potential use is debated within a conceptual framework that has remained essentially intact for most of a century. The most fundamental problem remains the definition of doping itself. But the role of moral intuition here makes it unlikely that a truly systematic "solution" to this problem will be found. In Riesser's view, for example, "a procedure which does not involve a single abrupt effect cannot be counted as doping. It is also instructive that, as surely as the injection of 0.1 gram of caffeine must be regarded as doping, drinking a cup of coffee with the same caffeine content, although it is by no means medically advisable, does not fall under the heading of doping. In such borderline cases, common sense and the dictates of conscience must decide."[162]

6. German Sports Medicine and the Transition to Modernity

Distinguishing between "premodern" and "modern" phases in the history of German sports medicine is not always a straightforward procedure. On the one hand, there are certain unambiguously premodern characteristics: early resistance to making sports medicine a separate and specialized discipline; physicians' exaggerated fears about the dire physiological consequences of strenuous athletic effort, resuling in widespread criticism of or ambivalence about the pursuit of the record performance and suggested lower[163] and upper[164] age limits for high-performance training; a general disinterest in challenging the apparent limits of human physiology; and a "negative" emphasis on the limitations imposed by fatigue, which eventually became a "positive" emphasis on the potential residing within the human organism.[165]

Yet even this classification is not immune to challenge. While it is true, for example, that the early German sports physicians tended to emphasize the limits of the human organism and the risks associated with high-performance sport, it is equally true that a modern version of this viewpoint exists today. The prominent West German sports physician Wildor Hollmann, president of the World Association of Sports Physicians, has been particularly outspoken about the physiological stress that is endured by many world-class athletes. "We have reached the maximum," Dr. Hollmann said in 1984, "the athletes have entered the biological border zone."[166] In 1985 the president of the Federal Republic of Germany, Richard von Weizsäcker, addressed a meeting of the West German National Olympic Committee on the dangers confronting modern high-performance sport. "That we should not exceed the specific limits which have been set by nature itself," he stated, "is beyond all doubt. What remains in question is precisely how these limits are to be defined. . . . The danger that specific body-types will be developed for specific sport disciplines is no longer a matter for science fiction; we can already see on the horizon the danger that specific athletic types will be bred by quasi-concealed chemical or even genetic manipulations."[167]

The crucial difference between the early period and our own is that modern sports physicians are haunted—and sometimes tempted—by scientific developments that could not affect the thinking of their "premodern" colleagues. The following episode from the prehistory of doping serves to illustrate how differently early and modern scientists have viewed the application of pharmacological agents to the problem of physical performance.

Nearly a century ago Dr. Oskar Zoth, himself a cyclist and swimmer, was a junior scientist at the Physiological Institute at the University of Graz (Austria). In 1894 he and a colleague, following in the footsteps of Brown-Séquard, performed an experiment in which they injected themselves with a liquid extract of bulls' testicles and then tested their strength with the ergograph designed by the famous Italian fatigue researcher Angelo Mosso. Zoth regarded the results as "a new probable indication (*Wahrscheinlichkeitsbeweis*) of the unusual effects of testicular extract." And he added: "The training of athletes offers an opportunity for further research in this area and for a practical assessment of our experimental results."[168]

Today the equivalent of Zoth's experiment would be properly controlled and officially sanctioned research on the athletic value of anabolic steriods. However, this hypothetical research is currently impossible on ethical grounds: these compounds are regarded as too dangerous to administer to human subjects, and they have been banned by the International Olympic Committee and other organizations that regulate high-level sports competitions. But to a late nineteenth-century scientist like Oskar Zoth, the introduction of such "orchitic" treatments into the athletic life of his era was nothing more than a natural extension of his research into new territory at a time when the campaign against physical and mental "fatigue" was being carried on in many European laboratories. He did not know for a fact that these injections were safe. But the two thousand experiments and therapeutic interventions which had been carried out since Brown-Séquard's first trials in 1889 had apparently convinced Zoth that his own experiment presented no medical hazard to him or his colleague.

From an historical standpoint, the most important point is that the proscription of scientific performance-enhancement on ethical grounds did not yet exist. For one thing, Zoth understood neither the physiological basis of his own research nor that the injections were ineffective. Thus he was in no position to feel sportsmanlike qualms about a proven "unfair" advantage. The scientific immaturity of contemporary sports physiology made it unlikely that the nascent sport culture of this era would see a need to evolve a code of sportsmanship incorporating scientific performance-enhancement into its conceptual apparatus.

A century before Zoth reported his findings the gymnastics theorist J. Chr. Fr. GutsMuths had confessed his own scientific shortcomings. "I am well aware," he wrote, "that an authentic theory of gymnastics should be built on physiological foundations. But this sort of perfection will not be found in my work. . . ."[169] A century later the European physiology that had made such dramatic progress since the era of GutsMuths was essentially uninterested in developing high-performance athletes. In his 1881 essay on exercise, Emil du Bois-Reymond wrote that, "if the supreme goal were the creation of accomplished runners" and other athletic types, then one might as well proceed directly to programming the nervous system with the correct movement sequences. But the great physiologist states his preference for German gymnastics and its lack of "any practical application."[170] The application of "dynamogenic" biological principles to athletic performance still lay in the future.

Notes

The author wishes to thank Charles Bearden and Arnd Krüger for their assistance in collecting materials for this study and the University Research Institute of the University of Texas at Austin for its support of this work.

1. Sports medicine is a comprehensive term that includes the treatment of sports-related injuries, the prescription (and proscription) of certain sportive activities for individual athletes, and physiological research intended to maximize athletic performance. This essay concerns what will be referred to in the text as high-performance sports medicine.

2. K. E. Rothschuh, "Emil Heinrich du Bois-Reymond," in *Dictionary of Scientific Biography,* ed. C. C. Gillispie (New York: Charles Scribner's Sons, 1971), 4.201. For observations on the different "national styles" of English, German, and French physiology, see Gerald L. Geison, "Social and Institutional Factors in the Stagnancy of English Physiology, 1840–1870," *Bulletin of the History of Medicine* 46 (Jan./Feb. 1972): 32–35.

3. See, for example, James Q. Wilson and Richard J. Herrnstein, "Constitutional Factors in Criminal Behavior," in *Crime and Human Nature,* ed. James Q. Wilson and Richard J. Herrnstein (New York: Touchstone Books, 1985), 73–103.

4. W. Caspari, "Physiologische Studien über Vegetarismus" (Physiological studies on vegetarianism), *Pflüger's Arkiv* (1905): 568.

5. See, for example, N. Vaschide, "Neuro-Muscular Force: A Psychical Element in Muscular Force" [1904], *British Journal of Psychology* (1905): 317.

6. See Hans Langenfeld, "Auf dem Wege zur Sportwissenschaft: Mediziner und Leibesübungen im 19. Jahrhundert" (On the way to sport science: Physicians and physical culture in the 19th century), *Stadion* 14 (1988): 130, 133, 135, 136–37, 139, 140–44.

7. Henning Eichberg, *Leistung Spannung Geschwindigkeit* (*Performance tension speed*) (Stuttgart: Klett-Cotta, 1978), 41–42.

8. For a useful schematic chart of these developments, see Jacques Guillerme, "Le sens de la mesure: Notes sur la protohistoire de l'évaluation athlétique" (The meaning of measurement: Notes on the early history of athletic assessment), in Christian Pociello, ed., *Sports et société: Approche socio-culturelle des pratiques* (Sport and society: a socio-cultural approach) (Paris: Editions Vigot, 1987), 64–65.

9. Ibid., 62.

10. Cynthia Eagle Russett, *Sexual Science: The Victorian Construction of Womanhood* (Cambridge, Mass.: Harvard University Press, 1989), 16, 7, 48.

11. Stephen Jay Gould, *The Mismeasure of Man* (New York: W. W. Norton & Co., 1981), 23, 74.

12. See, for example, Léon Poliakov, *The Aryan Myth: A History of Racist and Nationalist Ideas in Europe* (New York: New American Library, 1974); George L. Mosse, *Toward the Final Solution: A History of European Racism* (New York: Harper Colophon Books, 1978); idem, *The Crisis of German Ideology: Intellectual Origins of the Third Reich* (New York: Schocken Books, 1981).

13. Theodor Waitz, *Introduction to Anthropology* (London: Longman, Green, Longman, and Roberts, 1863), 93, 95, 97, 98, 100, 135.

14. Ibid., 109.

15. See Ferdinand Hueppe, *Hygiene der Körperübungen* (Hygiene of physical exercise) (Leipzig: Verlag von S. Hirzel, 1922), 70, 76, 89, 93, 99, 100–106; Adolf Basler, *Einführung in die Rassen- und Gesellschafts-Physiologie* (Introduction to racial and social physiology) (Stuttgart: Frankh'sche Verlagshandlung, 1924), 66, 75, 106; Carl Krümmel, "Eignungslehre" (Doctrine of aptitudes), in Carl Krümmel, ed., *Athletik: Ein Handbuch der lebenswichtigen Leibesübungen*

(Athletics: A handbook of essential physical exercises) (Munich: J. F. Lehmanns Verlag, 1930), 103, 106, 107; Wilhelm Knoll, "Konstitutionstypen und ihre Leistungen" (Constitutional types and their performances), in *Leistung und Beanspruchung* (Performance and stress), ed. Wilhelm Knoll (St. Gallen: Verlag Zollikofer & Co., 1948), 43, 46, 53.

16. Waitz, *Introduction to Anthropology,* 117–18.

17. Basler, *Einführung in die Rassen- und Gesellschafts-Physiologie,* 76.

18. On the physiology of the horse see René du Bois-Reymond's review of N. Zuntz and O. Hagemann, *Untersuchungen über den Stoffwechsel des Pferdes bei Ruhe und Arbeit* (Investigations of the metabolism of the resting and working horse) (Berlin, 1898), in *Centralblatt für Physiologie* (1899): 810–16. The movements of the horse were also studied by the important French physiologist Etienne-Jules Marey (1830–1904), who developed graphical recording and chronophotographic techniques for the analysis of human and animal locomotion including that of horses and birds.

19. Prechtl, *Untersuchungen über den Flug der Vögel* (Investigations of avian flight) (Vienna, 1846).

20. See, for example, A. Pütter, "Vogel und Flugzeug" (Birds and flight), *Die Naturwissenschaften* (1914): 861, 865.

21. W. Caspari, "Nathan Zuntz zu seinem 70. Geburtstage" (Nathan Zuntz on his seventieth birthday), *Die Naturwissenschaften* (1917): 619–20.

22. See Leo Zuntz, "Ueber den Gaswechsel und Energieumsatz des Radfahrers" (On the respiration and energy metabolism of the cyclist), *Pflüger's Arkiv* (1898): 346–48. On Nathan and Leo Zuntz, see Langenfeld, "Auf dem Wege zur Sportwissenschaft," 135.

23. See Caspari, "Nathan Zuntz zu seinem 70. Geburtstage," 619.

24. See Merriley Borell, "Organotherapy and the Emergence of Reproductive Endocrinology," *Journal of the History of Biology* 18 (Spring 1985): 1–30.

25. Hans Königstein, "Über das Schicksal der nicht-ejakulierten Spermatozoen" (On the fate of unejaculated spermatozoa), *Pflüger's Arkiv* 114 (1906): 199–215.

26. Arthur Mallwitz, *Körperliche Höchstleistungen mit besonderer Berücksichtigung des olympischen Sportes* (Top performances in athletics with special reference to olympic sport) (Berlin: Aus dem hygien. Institut der Kgl. Universität Berlin, 1908), 34.

27. Herbert Herxheimer, *Grundriß der Sportmedizin* (An outline of sports medicine) (Leipzig: Georg Thieme Verlag, 1933), 150.

28. A. Albu, "Beitrage zur pathologischen Physiologie des Sports" (Contributions to the pathological physiology of sport), *Zeitschrift für klinische Medizin* 78 (1913): 168.

29. See *Sportmedizin und Olympische Spiele 1936: Festschrift der Sportärzteschaft* (Sports medicine and the 1936 olympic games: A sports medical festschrift) (Leipzig: Verlag Georg Thieme, 1936). Mallwitz's speech is on pp. 8–9.

30. W. Hollmann and E. J. Klaus, "Die Sportmedizin in der Bundesrepublik Deutschland" (Sports medicine in the federal republic of germany), *Sportarzt und Sportmedizin* (1966): 246, 248.

31. F. Heiss, "Sportmedizin im Wandel der Zeiten—50 Jahre internationaler Sportärzteverband (FIMS)" (Sports medicine over the years—50 years of the international federation for sports medicine), *Deutsche Zeitschrift für Sportmedizin* 7 (1978): 180.

32. "Die Leibesübungen und der Arzt" (Physical Exercises and the Physician). Gesellschaft für Natur- und Heilkunde zu Dresden: Sitzung von 2. Oktober 1922 (Dresden Society of Science and Natural Healing, meeting of October 2, 1922), *Münchener medizinische Wochenschrift [M.M.W.]* (1922): 1676.

33. Quoted on Mallwitz, "Körperliche Höchstleistungen," 48. See also Walter Schnell, "Herr Strube und die Sportarzte" [Mr. Strube and the sports physicians], *Die Leibesübungen* (1927): 10.

34. Ibid., 28–29.

35. Schnell, "Herr Strube und die Sportarzte," 11.

36. "Die Leibesübungen und der Arzt," 1676; Walter Schnell, "Der Sportarzt" (The sports physician), *Die Leibesübungen* (1925): 135.

37. Albu, "Beitrage zur pathologischen Physiologie des Sports," 166.

38. Schnell, "Herr Strube und die Sportarzte," 11.

39. But see also Friedrich Hueppe, *Hygiene der Körperübungen* (Hygiene of physical exercise) (Leipzig: Verlag von S. Hirzel, 1922), 86.

40. Ferdinand Hueppe, "Sport und Reizmittel" (Sport and stimulants), *Berliner klinische Wochenschrift* (1913): 550, 551.

41. Albu, "Beitrage zur pathologischen Physiologie des Sports," 168.

42. August Bier, "Höchstleistungen durch seelische Einflüsse und durch Daseinsnotwendigkeiten" (Top performances due to psychological and circumstantial factors), *Die Leibesübungen* (1926): 37.

43. Walter Thörner, "Sportsphysiologische Untersuchungen an trainierenden Hunden" (Sports physiological investigations of trained dogs), *Forschungen und Fortschritte* 13, no. 1 (Jan. 1, 1937): 12–13.

44. Hueppe, *Hygiene der Körperübungen*, 88.

45. Bier, "Höchstleistungen," 39.

46. F. Heiss, "Sportmedizin im Wandel der Zeiten," 191–92.

47. E. Jokl, "Aus der Frühzeit der Deutschen Sportmedizin" (From the early period of german sports medicine), in *Training und Sport zur Prävention und Rehabilitation in der technisierten Umwelt* (Training and sport for prophylaxis and rehabilitation in the technological environment), ed. I.-W. Franz, H. Mellerowicz, and W. Noack (Berlin: Springer Verlag, 1985), 8.

48. See James C. Whorton, " 'Athlete's Heart': The Medical Debate over Athleticism, 1870–1920," *Journal of Sport History* 9 (Spring, 1982): 30–52.

49. Klaus Carl, *Training und Trainingslehre in Deutschland* (Training and training doctrine in germany) (Schorndorf: Verlag Karl Hofmann, 1983), 155, 130, 128; Edmund Neuendorff, *Geschichte der neueren deutschen Leibesübung vom Beginn des 18. Jahrhunderts bis zur Gegenwart* (History of modern

german physical culture from the beginning of the 18th century to the present) (Dresden: Wilhelm Limpert-Verlag, n.d.), 4.499.

50. Carl, *Training und Trainingslehre in Deutschland* 128, 158.

51. Ibid., 140; 126, 132, 133, 134; 126; 119, 154, 155, 162; 146, 152, 159; 142; 138.

52. See especially W. Hollmann, "Risikofaktoren in der Entwicklung des Hochleistungssports" (Risk factors in the development of high-performance sport), in *Sportmedizin-Kursbestimmung*, ed. H. Rieckert. Deutscher Sportarzte-kongreß Kiel, 16.-19. Oktober 1986 (Congress of German Sports Physicians) (Berlin: Springer-Verlag, 1987), 14–22.

53. For a relatively mild reaction to doubts from abroad about nationalism in German medicine, see Hans Kohn, "Pan-germanism in Medicine—To What Will It Lead?" *Berliner klinische Wochenschrift* (1914): 1715.

54. On Jahn see Horst Ueberhorst, *Zurück zu Jahn? Gab es ein besseres vorwärts?* (Back to Jahn: Was there a better path forward?) (Bochum: Universitätsverlag, 1969); Gerhard Stöcker, *Volkserziehung und Turnen: Untersuchung der Grundlagen des Turnens von Fr. L. Jahn* (Popular education and gymnastics: An examination of the foundations of gymnastics from Fr. L. Jahn) (Schorndorf bei Stuttgart: Verlag Karl Hofmann, 1971); Léon Poliakov, *The History of Anti-Semitism: From Voltaire to Wagner* (New York: Vanguard Press, 1975), 383–91.

55. Oswald Spengler, "Prussianism and Socialism," in *Selected Essays* (Chicago: Henry Regnery Company, 1967), 63.

56. See John Hoberman, *The Olympic Crisis: Sport, Politics, and the Moral Order* (New Rochelle, N.Y.: Aristide D. Caratzas, 1986), 100–106.

57. Mosse, *The Crisis of German Ideology*, 1.

58. Neuendorff, *Geschichte der neueren deutschen Leibesübung*, 482, 483.

59. Ibid., 481.

60. Mallwitz, "Körperliche Höchstleistungen," 35.

61. Neuendorff, *Geschichte der neueren deutschen Leibesübung*, 482.

62. Ibid., 485.

63. Ibid., 689.

64. Ibid., 499.

65. Carl, *Training und Trainingslehre in Deutschland*, 157.

66. Robert Proctor, *Racial Hygiene: Medicine under the Nazis* (Cambridge, Mass.: Harvard University Press, 1988), 255; 170, 258.

67. On the political orientation of the *Münchener medizinische Wochenschrift*, see ibid., 26, 75, 92, 97, 157, 160, 169.

68. August Bier, "Gedanken eines Arztes über die Medizin" (A physician's thoughts about medicine), *M.M.W.* (Apr. 2, 1926): 555; Bier, "Gedanken eines Arztes über die Medizin," *M.M.W.* (Aug. 13, 1926): 1362.

69. Bier, *M.M.W.* (Aug. 13, 1926): 1363, 1362.

70. Ibid., 1362.

71. Bier, *M.M.W.* (Apr. 2, 1926): 555.

72. Bier, *M.M.W.* (July 9, 1926): 1161.

73. Bier, *M.M.W.* (Aug. 13, 1926): 1360, 1362.

74. Bier, *M.M.W.* (Apr. 2, 1926): 557, 558.

75. Bier, *M.M.W.* (July 2, 1926): 1102; (July 16, 1926): 1194; (July 2, 1926): 1103, 1102; (July 9, 1926): 1162.

76. Béla Issekutz, *Die Geschichte der Arzneimittelforschung* (The history of pharmacological research) (Budapest: Akadémiai Kiadó, 1971), 15–16.

77. "Magier der Verdünnung" (Magicians of Dilution), *Der Spiegel* 42, no. 51 (Dec. 19, 1988): 58–59.

78. Bier, *M.M.W.* (July 2, 1926): 1103.

79. In 1937 the Nazi sport philosopher Alfred Baeumler called Friedrich Ludwig Jahn "a Paracelsian man," "the political Paracelsus" who "experiences nature; always wandering, always in immediate touch with man and beast, plants and rocks; this is how Jahn experiences his Volk and his epoch." See Winfried Joch, *Politische Leibeserziehung und ihre Theorie im nationalsozialistischen Deutschland* (The politics and theory of physical education in Nazi Germany) (Bern: Herbert Lang, 1976), 192.

80. Proctor, *Racial Hygiene*, 233, 94.

81. Bier, *M.M.W.* (Aug. 20, 1926): 1404.

82. Proctor, *Racial Hygiene*, 119.

83. Bier, *M.M.W.* (July 2, 1926): 1103; (July 9, 1926): 1162, 1163.

84. Bier, *M.M.W.* (Aug. 20, 1926): 1405; 1405, 1406.

85. Ibid., 1404.

86. See Antonio Ciocco, "The Historical Background of the Modern Study of Constitution," *Bulletin of the History of Medicine* 4 (1936): 23–38; W. H. Sheldon, *The Varieties of Human Physique* (New York: Harper & Brothers, 1940), 10–28.

87. For a recent, if brief, assessment of Kretschmer's work see Brian W. P. Wells, *Body and Personality* (London and New York: Longman, 1983), 2–5; for an earlier and more detailed critical commentary see Donald G. Paterson, *Physique and Intellect* (New York and London: The Century Co., 1930), 232–46. See also Hans W. Jürgens and Christian Vogel, "Der Typus in der morphologischen Biologie und Anthropologie," in *Beitrage zur menshlichen Typenkunde* (Contributions to the study of human typology), ed. Hans W. Jürgens and Christian Vogel (Stuttgart: Ferdinand Enke Verlag, 1965), 45–72.

88. Kretschmer's brief summary of these theories is found in his *Physique and Character* (New York: Harcourt, Brace & Company, 1925), 34–36.

89. Paterson, *Physique and Intellect*, 237.

90. Kretschmer, *Physique and Character*, 3.

91. See Hermann Glaser, *The Cultural Roots of National Socialism* (Austin: University of Texas Press, 1978), 44–50; George L. Mosse, *Nationalism and Sexuality: Respectability and Abnormal Sexuality in Modern Europe* (New York: Howard Fertig, 1985).

92. See, for example, Robert M. Young, *Mind, Brain and Adaptation in the Nineteenth Century* (Oxford: Clarendon Press, 1970).

93. Rolf Albonico, *Mensch Menschentypen: Entwicklung und Stand der Typenforschung* (Man and his types: The development and current state of typological research) (Basel: Birkhäuser Verlag, 1970), 77–89.

94. Carl Krümmel, "Eignungslehre" (Doctrine of aptitudes), in *Athletik: Ein Handbuch*, 85.

95. Ibid., 85, 86, 98.

96. Ibid., 90–92, 107, 109, 101.

97. Kretschmer, *Physique and Character*, 105, 160, 195; 27.

98. Franz Weidenreich, *Rasse und Körperbau* (Race and body-structure) (Berlin: Verlag von Julius Springer, 1927), 131.

99. Ibid., 132.

100. Ernst Kretschmer, *Körperbau und Charakter* (Body structure and character) (Berlin-Göttingen-Heidelberg: Springer-Verlag, 1948), 251–56.

101. Ernst Kretschmer and Willi Enke, *Die Persönlichkeit der Athletiker* (The personality of the athletic type) (Leipzig: Georg Thieme Verlag, 1936), 64.

102. Ibid., 67; 22; 42, 46, 58, 41, 44; 60.

103. Ibid., 64.

104. Heinz Seist, "Die psychische Eigenart der Spitzensportler" (The psyche of the high-performance athlete), *Wiener Arkiv für Psychologie* 4 (1954): 195–96.

105. Albu, "Beitrage zur pathologischen Physiologie des Sports," 159.

106. Hueppe, "Sport und Reizmittel," 551.

107. Bier, "Höchstleistungen," 34, 34, 35, 35–36.

108. See, especially, Anson Rabinbach, "The Body without Fatigue: A Nineteenth-Century Utopia," in *Politicial Symbolism in Modern Europe: Essays in Honor of George L. Mosse,* ed. Seymour Drescher, David Sabean, and Allan Sharlin (New Brunswick, N.J.: Transaction Books, 1982), 42–62.

109. Bier "Höchstleistungen," 37.

110. Ibid.

111. Ibid., 35.

112. See note 15.

113. Cited in Poliakov, *The Aryan Myth*, 174.

114. Bier, "Höchstleistungen," 38.

115. Walther Schulz, "Sporttypus und Leistung" (Sport-type and performance), *Die Leibesübungen* (1932): 338.

116. Ibid., 339.

117. Geoffrey Cocks, *Psychotherapy in the Third Reich: The Göring Institute* (New York: Oxford University Press, 1985), 56.

118. Schulz, "Sporttypus und Leistung," 339, 340, 341.

119. Walther Jaensch, "Körper-seelische Entwicklung und Leibesübungen" (Mental-physical development and physical culture), *Die Leibesübungen* (1932): 438.

120. Alfred Gradenwitz, "Making Sport a Science," *Scientific American* 129 (Dec. 1923): 398, 445.

121. Rob. Werner Schulte, *Die Psychologie der Leibesübungen* (The psychology of physical culture) (Berlin: Weidmannsche Verlag, 1928), 3, 6.

122. E. du Bois-Reymond, "L'exercice" (On exercise) ["Über die Übung," 1881] *Revue Scientifique* (Jan. 28, 1882): 104, 103.

123. Schulte, *Die Psychologie der Leibesübungen*, 72, 73, 90.

124. Rob. Werner Schulte, *Eignungs- und Leistungsprüfung im Sport* (Testing for aptitude and performance in sport) (Berlin: Verlag Guido Hackebeil A.-G., 1925), 30, 53, 65; Schulte, *Die Psychologie der Leibesübungen*, 81.

125. Schulte, *Die Psychologie der Leibesübungen*, 23, 4, 7.

126. Schulte, *Eignungs- und Leistungsprüfung im Sport*, 69, 71, 72, 79, 108, 253ff.; Schulte, *Die Psychologie der Leibesübungen*, 29.

127. Herxheimer, *Grundriß der Sportmedizin*, 12, 24; 23, 97; 24, 40, 115; 115, 116; 38.

128. See, for example, A. Z. Puni, *Abriß der Sportpsychologie* (Berlin: Sportverlag, 1961), 171–78.

129. Schulte, *Eignungs- und Leistungsprüfung im Sport*, 80; 112, 266.

130. Ludwig Prokop, "Zur Geschichte des Dopings," in *Rekorde aus der Retorte* (Records from the test tube), ed. Helmut Acker (Stuttgart: Deutsche Varlags-Anstalt, 1972), 22–23; Tom Donohoe and Neil Johnson, *Foul Play: Drug Abuse in Sports* (Oxford: Basil Blackwell, 1986), 3–4.

131. A. Loewy, "Versuche über die Rückgängigmachung der Ermüdungserscheinungen bei Muskelarbeit" (Experiments on the reversal of fatigue symptoms due to muscular exercise), *Berliner klinische Wochenschrift* (1910): 882.

132. Willner, "Sport und Doping," in *Die Sportärztetagung Berlin 1924*, ed. A. Mallwitz (Munich: J. F. Lehmanns Verlag, 1925), 132, 134.

133. Ibid., 131, 133, 149, 150, 150.

143. Albu, "Beitrage zur pathologischen Physiologie des Sports," 159ff., 173; 160–62.

135. Loewy, "Versuche über die Rückgängigmachung," 882.

136. See, for example, [C.-E.] Brown-Séquard, "Expérience démontrant la puissance dynamogénique chez l'homme d'un liquide extrait de testicules d'animaux" (An experiment demonstrating the dynamogenic influence on man of a testicular extract derived from animals), *Archives de Physiologie normale et pathologique* (1889): 651–58.

137. Loewy, "Versuche über die Rückgängigmachung," 882, 883, 884.

138. Dorothy M. Needham, *Machina Carnis: The Biochemistry of Muscular Contraction in Its Historical Development* (Cambridge: Cambridge University Press, 1971), 41, 45.

139. Hueppe, "Sport und Reizmittel," 549, 550, 549; Johannes Müller, *Die Leibesübungen* (Leipzig and Berlin: Verlag von B. G. Teubner, 1928), 314.

140. Hueppe, "Sport und Reizmittel," 551.

141. Willner, "Sport und Doping," 136–37.

142. See. for example, Dr. med. Hering, "Ultraviolette Strahlen für Sportzwecke" (Ultraviolet Radiation in the Service of Sport), *Die Leibesübungen* (1926): 331.

143. Ibid.

144. Willner, "Sport und Doping," 138.

145. See Hans-Jürgen Möller, *Die Begriffe "Reizbarkeit" und "Reiz": Konstanz und Wandel ihres Bedeutungsgehaltes sowie die Problematik ihrer exakten Definition* (The concepts "sensitivity" and "stimulus": The development of their meaning and definition) (Stuttgart: Gustav Fischer Verlag, 1975).

146. W. Heubner, "Über den Begriff 'Reizstoff' " (On the concept of the "stimulant"), *Klinische Wochenschrift* 5 (Jan. 1, 1926): 1.

147. Ibid., 3.

148. See, for example, Wolfgang Weichardt, "Ueber unspezifische Leistungssteigerung (Protoplasmaaktivierung)" (On Unspecific Performance-Enhancement [Protoplasma Activation]) *M.M.W.* (Jan. 23, 1920): 91–93; "Über Proteinkörpertherapie" (On Protein Cell Therapy) *M.M.W.* (Jan. 22, 1922): 107–108.

149. Brigitte Lohff, "Die Entwicklung des Experimentes im Bereich der Nervenphysiologie: Gedanken und Arbeiten zum Begriff der Irritabilität und der Lebenskraft" (Experimental development in Neural physiology: Reflections on the concept of irritability and vital force), *Sudhoffs Arkiv* 64 (1980): 121–22.

150. Möller, *Die Begriffe "Reizbarkeit" und "Reiz,"* 150.

151. For lists of substances used in such experiments during the period 1865–1885, see *Pflüger's Arkiv,* index vols. 1–30 (1885): 127, 129.

152. Otto Riesser, "Ist Medikamentöse Beeinflussung im Sport möglich?" (Is pharmacological intervention in sport possible?), *Die Leibesübungen* 18 (1930): 537, 538.

153. Ibid., 538, 538, 539.

154. Ibid., 541, 542.

155. Otto Reisser, "Über Doping und Dopingmittel" (On doping and doping substances), *Leibesübungen und körperliche Erziehung* 17 (1933): 393–94.

156. Hanns Baur, "Angewandte Sportmedizin" (Applied sports medicine), in *Sportmedizin und Olympische Spiele 1936: Festschrift der Sportärzteschaft,* ed. A. Mallwitz (Leipzig: Georg Thieme Verlag, n.d.), 13.

157. See, for example, Helmut Dennig, "Über Steigerung der körperlichen Leistungen durch künstliche Veränderungen der Säurebasenhaushaltes" (On the boosting of physical performances by means of artificial changes in the acid-base balance), *Forschungen und Fortschritte* 13 (Apr. 20, 1937): 153; Gunther Lehmann, "Menschliche Leistung und Leistungsfähigkeit" (Human performance and performance capacity), *Forschungen und Fortschritte* 18 (Mar. 1 and 10, 1942): 80–82.

158. Thörner, "Sportphysiologische Untersuchungen an trainierenden Hunden," 12; Adolf Bickel, "Die Art der Eiweißernährung als Grundlage körperlicher Leistungssteigerung" (Protein nutrition as a basis for the boosting of physical performance), *Forschungen und Fortschritte* 18 (Apr. 10 and 20, 1942): 121–22.

159. See, for example, Joch, *Politische Leibeserziehung,* 117, 114.

160. Franz Ochsenkühn, "Von der menschlichen zur sportlichen Höchstleistung" (From human to sportive performance), *Leibesübungen und körperliche Erziehung* (1937): 567, 568.

161. Riesser, "Über Doping und Dopingmittel," 395.

162. Ibid.

163. Review of H. Buchgeister, "Wie trainiere ich Leichtathletik?" (How do I train track and field athletes?), in *Die Leibesübungen* (1928): 292.

164. Albu, "Beitrage zur pathologischen Physiologie des Sports," 170.

165. This German author identifies the "negative" emphasis on fatigue with the period prior to about 1930. See G. Lehmann, "Der Einfluß von Nahrungs- und Genußmitteln auf die Leistung" (The influence of nutritional and stimulant substances on performance) *Die Naturwissenschaften* (1941): 553.

166. "Typen wie aus dem Panoptikum" (Types out of the wax museum), *Der Spiegel* (July 23, 1984): 71.

167. Richard von Weizsäcker, "Der Sport befindet sich in einer Grenzsituation" (Sport on the edge), *Süddeutsche Zeitung,* Nov. 18, 1985.

168. Oskar Zoth, "Zwei ergographische Versuchsreihen über die Wirkung orchitischen Extracts" (Two series of ergographic experiments on the effects of orchitic extract), *Pflüger's Arkiv* (1896): 377.

169. Quoted in Langenfeld, "Auf dem Wege zur Sportwissenschaft," 130.

170. du Bois-Reymond, "L'exercice," 108.

8 *Donald J. Mrozek*

The Scientific Quest for Physical Culture and the Persistent Appeal of Quackery

Now, reader, tell me . . . just where the line of scientific practice ends, and the line of quackery practice begins.

—*James C. Jackson*

It was with completely unintended irony that James C. Jackson, the noted health reformer who believed that diet "cured" masturbation, scorned men who prescribed drugs for illnesses as "quacks."[1] Genuine physicians, Jackson asserted in *The Sexual Organism and Its Healthful Management* (1861), were the ardent and enduring enemies of patent medicines. Indeed, Jackson emerged rather as a categorical enemy of drugs themselves, seeing them as a block to natural processes and as a destroyer of natural self-healing. Although he accepted surgery as a means of restoring the proper structure of the body so that natural healing could take place, he doubted that introducing chemical substances could ever be beneficial—the very notion that one might "heal" a "disease" struck him as self-contradictory.[2]

"Genuine" medicine and faddish quackery are often remarkably close and disturbingly similar. Moreover, neither institutional sanction, scientific method, nor the validity of medical claims and procedures seems sufficient to establish a substantive difference between accepted medicine and dubious fad. As an arbitrary matter of definition, one might argue that true medicine is whatever the organized medical professionals say it is at any specific time. Yet authoritative endorsements do not automatically sway the public mind; and, amid the extraordinary medical advancements of the twentieth century, unproven schemes promising health, strength, and renewal still abound.

In a way, the prospects for quackery may have increased because of the great scope of scientific advancement rather than lessened.

The persistence of sweeping health schemes has depended greatly on the asymmetry between the nature of scientific medicine and the psychological inclinations of modern American culture. However broad the reach of medicine, its ultimate grasp depends on testing and verification, often in small and tedious degrees. But the reach of quackery is complete, much like the sweep of the American vision of perfectibility. Rather like a Puritan conversion experience, commitment to a health regimen popular in the past implied sudden virtue, producing instant rectitude and uncomplicated zeal for burning away the traces of earlier sin. Whether for soul or body, the miracle of faith was that the cure was total. Obedience to the regimen allowed one to fulfill the nineteenth-century quest for "character," even as the promise of perfect health fed the twentieth-century hunger for "personality."[3] As genuine medical achievements such as those in anesthesia made pain seem abnormal, the expectation of total comfort was bolstered.[4] And as medicine attended to the details of proof, fads and cure-alls catered to the warped notion that Americans had not only a right to pursue happiness but a right to possess it—all at once, all complete.

Ultimately, such ways of thinking affected physical culture and sport—how one trained for it and through it, what one expected from it, what one claimed it had achieved, and how much it seemed to promise for a better future. To some degree, the interest in sport was explicitly linked to concern for personal and public health.[5] Physical culture thus had clear potential for impact on society. But it also meant that society had enormous impact on sport and physical culture—as in the transference of medical and scientific information from one field to another.

The scientific impulse held sway in sport in certain periods, promising predictable social "payoffs" for executing carefully prescribed regimens. The last decades of the nineteenth century especially bore the marks of this view. Yet, as the goals of sport altered and increasingly centered on the individual's own satisfaction as the object of one's efforts, the scientific impulse was to falter. If the goal of sport became the service of the individual and if the individual was by definition unique, then one could not truly test and verify results nor predictively reproduce them. To this degree, science became impossible. And to this extent, quackery was merely a state of mind.

Examples abound showing the American preference for total solutions to health risks and degeneration. These same examples necessarily testify to the elusiveness of the border between science and quackery. Some devotees of remedies that were offered for serious ailments showed great personal eccentricity and even clear madness, and they risked associating enthusiasm for physical culture with sheer derangement. While the eminent "muscular Christian" Thomas Wentworth Higginson was merely a bit odd and remained socially engaged and productive, there were far different and less reputable devotees of physical culture, too.[6] A chilling example was Charles J. Guiteau, who assassinated President James A. Garfield in 1881 and was convicted of murder the next year.[7] For Guiteau, bodily development appears to have been but one of many truly strange enthusiasms—vehicles of personal transformation, testimonies of his belief in salvation, and signs of his impulse toward perfectionism, which was highly developed despite a life of compounded failures. His experience with the Oneida Community from 1860 to 1865 added to his belief that perfection on earth was possible, even though he finally rejected the Community's leadership. The philosophical and medical views of his age bolstered the understanding of mind and body as inseparably fused—indeed, as an indivisible entity. Hence, such moral accomplishments as Guiteau imagined to be within his grasp required physical training to maintain the requisite moral force. And so, in 1859, at the age of 28, he took up gymnastics and weight lifting. As Charles Rosenberg has noted, after three months of his new regimen, Guiteau had become "a convert" to "the utopian health enthusiasms of the day," temporarily confirmed in his faith by the rapid increase of his chest from 29 to 33 inches.[8] Meanwhile, he became an "avid reader" of W. W. Hall's *Journal of Health* and closely followed the phrenological writings of Orson and Lorenzo Fowler.[9] He raided across the range of schemes for health and physical improvement with little discrimination, lusting after a single and simple solution to his complex of difficulties. When he finally set upon the murder of Garfield, Guiteau thought himself in direct personal communication with God, whose orders he was merely carrying out. Thus, Guiteau was outraged when lawyers sought to defend him by a plea of insanity—a plea that violated his own immense sense of self-esteem and that impeached his claim to divine guidance. For Guiteau, then, physical development, physical education, and health reform were hardly the full or final answer to his own problem or the world's. Instead of bringing Guiteau to a new day of stability and respect, they formed just one in a wretched series of false dawns.

Despite Guiteau's sorry example, nineteenth-century notions of what medicine might encompass were broad enough to include much in physical education and physical culture. Physical culturists and health reformers outside the established medical societies made claims for their efforts which were often as sweeping as those of arrant quacks. The claims of some physical educators were not always much better. So the endorsement that later generations have given to such respected physical educators as Dudley Sargent obscures the kinship that many of his ideas had with more eccentric views.[10] Born in 1849 in Belfast, Maine, Sargent had a brief flirtation with cigars and card playing when he was 14, but he later dismissed these as "fads."[11] He was ever more attracted to sports and organized exercise, which he later described as having "moral" force.[12] In 1866, he became interested in gymnastics, influenced by an article on the subject written by Charles Caldwell and also under the spell of Thomas Wentworth Higginson. For all the later talk of science in Sargent's study of the body, his views were founded in the intertwining of physical and moral dimensions.

In September 1879, Sargent went to Harvard as director of the gymnasium and assistant professor of physical training. His emphasis on "corrective gymnastics" in order to achieve a "symmetrical" body was hailed as a triumphant step for scientific method in physical education, in which tasks were clearly tailored to well-defined goals and in which each such task was seen as part of a comprehensive whole. Yet the insistence on symmetry itself paralleled the view of neurologists and many psychiatrists that physical asymmetry was a sign of insanity, an opinion that clearly put a high premium on balance and order. It also recalled the theories of phrenology, which were widely discredited by Sargent's time. Still more, the concern for symmetry pointed down the same path that led toward chiropractic and overblown posture reform. Even the emphasis on physical development—so often assumed to be a virtue by observers in the latter decades of the twentieth century—was often seen as an eccentricity during the middle and even later decades of the nineteenth.

Health reformers concerned with diet faced a similar confusion of identity. For example, although the reputation of a health reformer such as Sylvester Graham has retrospectively prospered due to his emphasis on raw natural foods, it must be remembered that the source of his inspiration lay more in faith than in science. Even a scientist such as Horace Fletcher, who won some governmental support in the early twentieth century, frequently erred, although he was taken seriously due to his insistence on careful method in studying the chemistry of foods.[13] One example was his advocacy of the "all potato" diet. Other diets advocated by WASP Americans would surely have contributed to a serious surge in such ailments as rickets and scurvy had they been followed.

A notorious example of the dangers posed by an error-prone science came in the diet peddled by the New England Kitchen in the 1880s, a reform enterprise run largely under the inspiration of Edward Atkinson. Thinking that immigrants' heavy use of spices in cooking caused them to be sexually hyperactive, Atkinson and his colleagues sought to reduce the non-WASP population by putting immigrants on a bland diet. Although the promotion of Atkinson's own Aladdin stove as the slow cooker of choice provides an amusing sidelight to this dietary escapade, the more important fact is that the recommended diet would surely have produced massive deficiencies and spawned disease including rickets and scurvy if it had been followed.[14] Such were the limits even of well-intentioned science, let alone scientific notions infected with self-interest such as Atkinson's personal business prospects. For example, the chemist W. O. Atwater, who worked for the U.S. Department of Agriculture and pioneered in analyzing the energy-value of food, knew nothing of vitamins. Here, too, the food intake deemed ideal was vitamin deficient; and "science" would have fostered disease.[15]

The career of physical culturist Bernarr MacFadden extended the tradition of Atwater, Atkinson, and Horace Fletcher—whose work MacFadden admired. Even more than many others, MacFadden's life confuses personal eccentricity with professional quackery, even if he was at least manifestly less lethal than Charles Guiteau.[16] MacFadden's advocacy of dietary reform had some measure of popular appeal and substantial medical support. Yet some specific measures were couched in such extreme terms as to threaten their acceptance. MacFadden's rejection of inherited customs in food preparation reflected an insistence on scientific method in determining the nutritional properties of foods and the means of maximizing them in preparation. But his claims for "chewing your way to health" seemed extreme; and one can only speculate on reaction to his defense of the "nut and fruit diet" as the way of eating most suited to "our nearest animal relatives, the anthropoid apes. . . ."[17] In an age when Darwinian ideas remained the subject of lively controversy, the merit in showing family ties with the ape remained moot. So, too, he opened a string of "physical culture restaurants" in New York City, extending his gospel of health—yet opening himself to charges of mere huckstering.

Even more, though, MacFadden's career ranged broadly from the serious through the frivolous—from the mainstream to the outer fringes. He worked briefly as a circus acrobat, competed as a wrestler, and claimed to be a "kinesitherapist"—that is, a "healer of disease, by use of movements."[18] He published *Physical Culture,* beginning in 1898, and *True Story Magazine,* founded in 1919. He boosted sales of the *Graphic,* established in 1924, with vivid pictures that led critics to nickname it the *Pornographic.* His prescription for health, too, was couched in extremes—all ailments were really variations on the one and only disease besetting humankind, impurity of the blood. Specific ailments which doctors called diseases were Nature's way of removing the impurities. Thus, MacFadden railed against the "medical trust" and opposed the use of drugs.[19] Even the term he gave to his method of cure—"physcultopathy," or healing by use of physical culture— hinted at his distance from conventional medicine. In addition, he was unabashedly in love with his own body, let alone the body as an abstraction. "I freely admit I love my body," he said. "I respect and reverence it."[20] As his "court biographer" indicated, few of MacFadden's conventional contemporaries could quite make sense of his stance on major issues. He opposed the use of alcohol but also opposed the Volstead Act. He attacked prudery and public governance of morals but demanded that sexual contact be strictly limited. By his own lights, MacFadden was a miracle of consistency. But where those lights faded into society's glare, he seemed an arbitrary eccentric.[21]

MacFadden's thoughts on dress suitable for athletic competition made for conflict when he first revealed them—such as his advocacy of swimming suits for playing tennis. He denounced hats, explaining that hair was the natural and sufficient insulation provided by Nature. He insisted on the reform of shoes, altering their design to meet the design of each foot rather than the sway of fashion. Getting outside for exercise and engaging in sport, competitive or otherwise, appealed to MacFadden. These would revitalize the spirit, almost as if they could build more energy than they required. He also urged that sunlight bathe the body as fully as possible to allow "sunrays an opportunity to revivify the body."[22] When he argued for the use of scant clothing at the beach, MacFadden violated social custom and prevailing thought. Yet these views were later to be taken as common sense. Still later, they became suspect due to fears of skin cancer. Common sense might no longer be common, and it might not even be sense. The question of whether MacFadden was a quack requires knowing when the question was asked.

In one important respect, MacFadden may even be considered a pioneer on behalf of new views about the body and its proper treatment. The unabashed love of his own body, which made MacFadden

more notorious than famous with his critics, was very much in tune
with new ideas about culture and popular behavior in twentieth-
century America. Less and less did it seem necessary to explain care
for the individual body by the gain society would reap from its health.
Ever more, it sufficed simply to say that individuals won enjoyment
from their bodies and experienced personal well-being. One might
still talk of winning protection against disease and a host of ailments, and one might still see widespread illness and debilitation as
a threat to society. Beneath it all, however, the pleasure of the individual gained importance as a critical standard of behavior and personal care.

During the first half of the twentieth century, a highly orchestrated
movement to improve the posture of America's young people developed, also linking concerns for the individual with care for the society
at large. The posture movement won substantial institutional support
from federal agencies and from the American Medical Association
(AMA). In fact, it was the AMA that in 1923 founded *Hygeia*, a journal that gave much space to medical discussion of posture. "Posture
workers" claimed that bad posture caused "organic problems such
as backache, vomiting, colitis, constipation, menstrual irregularity,
heart disease, tuberculosis and mental impairment." In addition, they
regarded bad posture as the visual symbol of an underlying moral
weakness and cultural decline.[23] Although the preachings of posture
workers were amply published in *Hygeia* and despite the advocates'
substantial presence at the White House Conference on Child Health
in 1932, their work lacked appropriate "scientific rigor"—they failed
to define good posture in ways that could allow comparison and independent verification of experimental results.[24] Nonetheless, the
posture workers had one quite important feature in their favor—the
great popular appeal of anything that smacked of a panacea. So
many ills and ailments could be remedied merely by sitting and standing "properly."

During the 1920s and 1930s—the heyday of publication concerning posture—*Hygeia* offered plays for classroom use, poems, photographs, and purportedly scientific articles. A matter that had once
seemed aesthetic and temperamental was thus transformed into an
issue of public health. The *American Physical Education Review* and *Research Quarterly* also devoted substantial space to the dangers of bad
posture. Here, too, the actual experimental evidence was scant, reflecting the continuing dominance of predetermined belief over dis-
passionately acquired data and inductive reasoning. Between 1923
and 1962, only 10 percent of the 108 papers on posture appearing in

the two journals even attempted to ground claims on experimentally acquired information. Nor was there much to be said for the three papers using experimentation to back up assertions of a positive correlation between bad posture and pathological effects. Several of the claims appear to have been largely psychological, having only the most tenuous possible tie to the specifics of posture and, for that matter, a tie that might have been either cause or effect if it existed at all. One researcher claimed that bad posture produced self-consciousness and timidity (as well as an array of physical problems such as heart disease and hearing defects), while another suggested that good posture led to capable scholarship.[25] Criteria were lacking, control groups were absent, but conclusions prospered nonetheless.

That the posture workers should have received cooperation from some popular and lay constituencies may not be surprising. But why they also gained support from professional quarters is quite another matter. The answer may have to do with the second of their judgments about bad posture—namely, that it was a visible, physical emblem of underlying failings in what can only be called temperament and character. In this respect, they echoed an older pattern of commitment, particularly a belief in absolute criteria for behavior that were, external to the individual and that had to be internalized by voluntary action and discipline. The "neutrality" of medicine as generally understood in the twentieth century aimed in a different direction, one that tended to discard the element of personal choice and commitment. "Absolute criteria," if they existed in "genuine" or "modern" medicine, had to do with narrowly defined physical and physiological specifics. The aspect of character fell out of favor. Still, in the earlier decades of the twentieth century, the residue of ways of thinking often ascribed to the nineteenth century remained considerable and powerful.

In fact, perhaps they are not best described as "nineteenth-century" ways at all but rather as dispositions and inclinations that may recur in any era, even if they did seem to dominate the attention of American social elites in the nineteenth century. This would help to explain how chiropractic experienced a parallel rise to eminence among the American public at much the same time as did the posture movement. Although it promised results as wide-ranging as did the posture movement with which it had a certain obvious kinship, chiropractic was nettlesome for the traditional medical professionals, whose organizational and disciplinary authority chiropractic challenged and upon whose economic interests they infringed. Moreover, traditional medical professionals were becoming ever more deeply

committed to specialization at precisely the time that the chiropractors reasserted a simple and single explanation for a constellation of
ills. Here, clearly, was a bastion of quackery—clearly, at least, from
the vantage of those who stood to lose fees and prestige if chiropractic
held sway. Yet its scientific basis was scarcely less firm than that of the
posture movement, which enjoyed substantial favor within the main-
line medical establishment.[26]

One of America's sharpest satirists, H. L. Mencken, saw chiropractic as a leap of faith. In his more biting remarks, Mencken approved
of chiropractors, suggesting that the inefficacy in their treatment favored a kind of "survival of the intelligent." To end the "coddling of
the half-witted," he asserted, "nothing operates more cheaply and
effectively than the prosperity of quacks." Mencken's underlying
criticism, however, resembled that which the medical establishment
lodged against the chiropractors. "What is needed," Mencken argued,
"is a scientific inquiry into the matter, under rigid test conditions. . . ."[27] Mencken lavished irony on those who trusted a "shaved
and fumigated longshoreman" to treat a diseased appendix by "balancing him on McBurney's spot and playing on his vertebrae as on a
concertina. . . ."[28] Yet in doing so he confirmed the growing bias that
conventionally educated Americans held in favor of specialization—a
trend that threatened to make virtually any regimen that offered
sweeping remedies seem close to quackery.

Something in the expansiveness of claims made for a regimen or a
cure defied—or at least inhibited—careful experiment and syllogistic
proof. Unlike specific measures that might be tested according to
established scientific procedures, a cure that claimed general and
sweeping impact was awash in a sea of variables, isolated from the rescue and social comfort that scientific testing might procure. Yet the
sweeping claims of cure-alls and quackery survived the lack of scientific verification, since failure could always be blamed on apostates
fallen from faith.

Such words are more than mere rhetorical flourishes. Physical regimens, much like religious creeds, have many purposes. By its very nature, scientific assessment focuses on one claim at a time. The true
believer may claim that his "physical faith," much like a religious one,
is only made to appear false when its tenets are taken out of context.
For those faithful to a physical regimen, each tenet can survive rigorous scrutiny by arguing that the value of each specific remedy or
routine comes only when practiced holistically. Poking at the skin of
belief may cause the believer some irritation, but its heart goes on
beating. In addition, the scientific assessment of schemes concerning

physical culture suffers from a special confusion as to their purpose. For example, the scientific appraisal of sport and its risks to the participant commonly presupposes that the purpose of sport is to enhance personal health. There is no reason why this should be so, and quite often it is not. When the purpose to which a regimen is put by its adherent is so little understood by the scientifically disposed investigator, the results of scientific study are likely to be accurate but quite irrelevant.

The confusion over motives showed itself unmistakably in the 1960s and after during the rise of interest in running and "jogging." The confusion was suggested by the very need to use two words—"running" and "jogging"—which some inaccurately thought to be synonyms. Interest in "jogging" grew directly from a doctor's prescription of aerobic exercise as a means of improving cardiovascular fitness. But running had appeal for many other people with quite different concerns. For example, Thaddeus Kostrubala proclaimed running a form of "Western Zen." Coupling physical, psychological, and spiritual benefits, Kostrubala wrote of a "refreshment of the soul" experienced "by those who practice meditation and by long-distance runners."[29] In *Holistic Running* (1978), Joel Henning claimed that running was "a form of worship, an attempt to find God, a means to the transcendant."[30] Henning offered a new clarification of health itself. "Holistic health," he noted, "means the integration of mind, body, and spirit for the attainment of whole health." In turn, "holistic running" was his way of "helping to integrate our physical and spiritual selves"—incorporating "aspects of exercise physiology along with Western religion, biochemistry, feedback, yoga, and Zen."[31]

The claims for running and, even more, the intense focus that some of its practitioners gave it brought on a sometimes playful reaction. Perhaps the most obvious and literal was *The Non-Runner's Book* by Vic Ziegel and Lewis Grossberger, a deliberate takeoff on an enormously popular book by runner and writer James F. Fixx.[32] Twitting people for taking their running too seriously, Ziegel and Grossberger kidded instead that "non-running is life itself," assuring the reader that doctors guarantee that one could go on "non-running" for years.[33] But the most prevalent reaction to writings that tapped running as a form of meditation were those that saw it almost exclusively as a means to improve cardiovascular fitness. Even Jim Fixx, the butt of much humor, produced a book centered on enhancing athletic performance by practical development of strength and skill. In *Maximum Sports Performance* (1985), Fixx cooperated with the Nike Sports Laboratory; and poetic flights in praise of running as a "lifestyle" were kept to a minimum.[34] So, too, *The Running Book* (1978), produced by the editors of *Consumer's Guide,* allowed that some runners claimed a psychological "high" from their activity but concentrated on practical, measurable cardiovascular benefits.[35] The pseudonymous "Leo Diporta" made an explicit link between Zen and running in the very title of his work *Zen Running* (1977).[36] But Jim Ferstle offered a simple and health-focused alternative in *Contemporary Jogging* (1978).[37] Which was fad, and which was healthful practice? Who was to judge? And by what standards? Clearly, different runners—or joggers—had many different purposes for doing what they did. For some it was sport, for others a form of competition, for still another group a means to health, and at least for some special groups a means of spiritual self-discovery. If the individual case was the true test, then what was the relevance of scientific study?[38]

Not all investigators miss this problem entirely. At the risk of substituting rhetoric for logic, some observers have often seen "madness in sport," as surely as there was a form of madness in Charles Guiteau. The sportsman has the advantage over the assassin, however, in that his pursuit pretends to the divine but makes no claim to begin there. Psychiatrists such as Arnold Beisser have begun to enumerate cases in which sport has become the refuge of obsessive and otherwise troubled personalities.[39] In such instances, sport loses its neutrality and, within the context of individual obsession and compulsiveness, becomes a manifestation of disease. Whether one may properly call sport a form of quackery when it is warped to the purposes of mental affliction, it is clearly not healthy in the common sense of the word. Still, the passionate commitment to sport shares with true madness an insistence upon personally generated criteria for respectability and success. So, too, they are alike in putting individual fulfillment over an externally developed standard of social benefit.

The final presumption that what is good for the individual and suits the individual's tastes and instincts must benefit society is perhaps the ultimate in presumptuousness. But it is an integral element in sport as it has been carried on, especially since the mid-twentieth century. With so high an emphasis on the individual as the unique point of reference and criterion, external standards fall to unimportance. External verification cannot be undertaken, since exploration of the internal mind and personality by the external examiner must always remain impeachable. Results thus can not be reproduced to the satisfaction of the tests of science, since one can never be sure whether they have been reproduced at all. And sport itself—

clearly a fad in some of its forms during certain eras—begins to look uncomfortably like a kind of quackery.

Notes

1. James C. Jackson, *The Sexual Organism and Its Healthful Management* (Boston: B. Leverett Emerson, 1861; reprint, New York: Arno Press, 1974), 124.

2. Ibid., 120–24, 125–27, passim.

3. For an insightful suggestion of the difference between "character" and "personality," see Warren I. Susman, "Personality and the Making of Twentieth-Century Culture," *Culture as History* (New York: Pantheon Books, 1984), 271–85.

4. On the impact of anesthesia in the medical world and on its encouragement of lay optimism, see Francis D. Moore, "Surgery," in John Z. Bowers and Elizabeth F. Purcell, eds., *Advances in American Medicine* (New York: Josiah Macy, Jr., Foundation, 1976) vol. 2, 619 ff.

5. One study suggesting the interest in making sport serve health is Roberta J. Park, "The Attitudes of Leading New England Transcendentalists toward Healthful Exercise, Active Recreation, and the Proper Care of the Body! 1830–1860," *Journal of Sport History* 4 (Spring 1977): 34–50.

6. A key statement of the "muscular Christian" view is Thomas Wentworth Higginson, "Saints, and Their Bodies," *Atlantic Monthly* 1 (March 1858): 582–85.

7. See Charles E. Rosenberg, *The Trial of the Assassin Guiteau, Psychiatry and Law in the Gilded Age* (Chicago: University of Chicago Press, 1968).

8. Concerning Guiteau's interest in schemes for his physical improvement, see Rosenberg. *The Trial of the Assassin Guiteau*, 16–17.

9. There is a special irony in this interest in phrenology, since phrenologists played some role at Guiteau's murder trial. By that time, however, Guiteau proclaimed himself uninterested in such physical measurements, claiming the "spiritology" and a man's spiritual dimensions were all that mattered. Since Guiteau asserted that his shooting of Garfield was done on direct orders from God, the precise shape of his own skull struck him as supreme irrelevance. Concerning phrenology, see John D. Davies, *Phrenology, Fad and Science: A 19th-Century Crusade* (New Haven: Yale University Press, 1955).

10. See Dudley Allen Sargent, *Physical Education* (Boston: Ginn, 1906) and Dudley Allen Sargent, *Dudley Allen Sargent: An Autobiography* (Philadelphia: Lea & Febiger, 1927).

11. Sargent, *Dudley Allen Sargent*, 33.

12. Ibid., 35–36.

13. See, for example, Horace Fletcher, *The A. B.-Z of Our Own Nutrition* (New York: Frederick A. Stokes, 1903).

14. See Harvey Levenstein, "The New England Kitchen and the Origins of Modern American Eating Habits," *American Quarterly* 32 (Fall 1980): 369–86.

15. For an example of Atwater's work, see W. O. Atwater, "The Chemistry of Foods and Nutrition," *Century* 34 (May 1887): 59–74; *Methods and Results of Investigations on the Chemistry and Economy of Food.* Bulletin 21, U.S. Department of Agriculture, Office of Experiment Stations, [mid-1880s].

16. See, for example, Bernarr MacFadden, *MacFadden's Encyclopedia of Physical Culture* (New York: Physical Culture Publishing Co., 1914); *Marriage: A Life-Long Honeymoon* (New York: Physical Culture Publishing Co., 1903); *Physical Culture Cook Book* (New York: MacFadden Publications, 1924); *The Power and Beauty of Superb Womanhood* (New York: Physical Culture Publishing Co., 1901). Also see Mary MacFadden and Emile Gauvreau, *Dumbbells and Carrot Strips: The Story of Bernarr MacFadden* (New York: Henry Holt and Co., 1953) and Clement Wood, *Bernarr MacFadden, A Study in Success* (New York: Beekman Publishers, 1974 [1929]).

17. Bernarr MacFadden, *The Physical Culture Cook Book* (New York: MacFadden Publications, 1924), 33.

18. Wood, *Bernarr MacFadden*, 64–65.

19. Ibid., 99.

20. Ibid., 98.

21. Ibid., 97.

22. Ibid., 216.

23. Andrew McClary, "What Is a Health Fad? The Posture Movement as an Example," *Journal of American Culture* 6.4 (Winter 1983): 50. Reputable physical educators also wrote for *Hygeia;* see R. Tait McKenzie, "Posture," *Hygeia* 7 (1929): 1092. Concerning the nature of a "health fad," see Louis Lasagna, "Clinical Analysis of Medical Fads," *New York Times Magazine* (June 24, 1962): 22; Marvin D. Dunnette, "Fads, Fashions, and Folderol in Psychology," *American Psychologist* 21.4 (April 1966): 443–52.

24. McClary, "What Is a Health Fad?" 51.

25. Ibid., 52.

26. It is also possible that the chiropractor's suspicion of synthesized chemicals contributed to his poor repute with a medical establishment that was eagerly advancing their use. The insistence on "natural" solutions, which became a part of chiropractic, in this way extended the tradition of which James C. Jackson was also a part.

27. See H. L. Mencken, "Chiropractic," in H. L. Mencken, *Prejudices, A Selection*, ed. James T. Farrell (New York: Vintage Books, 1947), 253. Far from limiting his criticism to quacks, Mencken had no high regard for the "Medical Trust," as he referred to the traditional medical establishment. However, it is all the more telling that he regarded them as capable of delivering on much that they promised, precisely because they conformed to the rules of scientific study and practice.

28. Mencken, "Chiropractic," 252.

29. Thaddeus Kostrubala, *The Joy of Running* (New York: Pocket Books, 1976), 111. Kostrubala himself is a medical doctor.

30. Joel Henning, *Holistic Running* (New York: New American Library, 1978), 20.

31. Henning, *Holistic Running*, 23.

32. Vic Ziegel and Lewis Grossberger, *The Non-Runner's Book* (New York: Collier Books, 1978).

33. Ibid., xi.

34. James F. Fixx., *Maximum Sports Performance,* with the Nike Sport Research Laboratory (New York: Random House, 1985). It was perhaps inevitable that critics would pounce on the circumstances of Fixx's death while running as a case against the activity that he had long advocated. However, such critics assumed that perpetual health was both the goal and the result of running, something that Fixx himself would not have claimed. In fact, even temporary physical health could not be assured by running or other forms of sport and exercise. It all depended on how the activity was pursued rather than just what the activity was.

35. Editors of *Consumer's Guide, The Running Book* (New York: Warner Books, 1978).

36. Leo Diporta [Leon Rappaport], *Zen Running* (New York: Everest House, 1977).

37. Jim Ferstle, *Contemporary Jogging* (Chicago: Contemporary Books, 1978).

38. Such concerns were repeated when Norman Cousins chose to use videocassettes of Marx Brothers comedies to overcome seemingly incurable illness for which his medical doctors had no remedy.

39. Arnold Beisser, *The Madness in Sports, Psychosocial Observations on Sport* (New York: Appleton-Century-Crofts, 1967).

9 *James C. Whorton*

Muscular Vegetarianism: The Debate over Diet and Athletic Performance in the Progressive Era

Milo of Croton, the ancient Greek wrestler who won the laurel wreath at seven consecutive Olympiads, is reputed to have built his prodigious strength with a daily training diet that included twenty pounds of meat as its *pièce de résistance*. The longevity and popularity of Milo legends (there is another that credits him with celebrating a victory by killing a bull with a single blow of his fist and eating the animal completely in one day) dramatize the continuing appeal of the assumption that exceptional performance is possible only for those athletes who consume liberal quantities of flesh food. The notion is deepseated, an intuitive response to the strength and ferocity of carnivorous animals, but its hold on the minds of competitors and fans alike has been loosened in recent years by a more sophisticated public awareness of the facts of nutrition, the resurgence of vegetarianism, and the success of vegetarian athletes such as Bill Walton. The resultant brouhaha over whether beansprouts are better than beefsteaks, however, is only a renewal of hostilities between vegetarian and meateating athletes. The issue was first joined (and contested with considerably more spirit than presently) during the closing years of the nineteenth century, just as American society's fascination with competitive athletics was first blossoming.[1]

Treatises on athletic training during the Progressive years gave a good deal of attention to diet. The rather spectacular growth of sophistication of biochemistry over the last quarter of the nineteenth century had generated almost unbounded confidence in a "chemical machine" model of human functioning. The machinery was complex, to be sure, but progress in nutrition theory suggested that the operating needs of the machine were quite simple and easily met.

Adequate protein was required for maintenance of the tissues (or parts of the machine), and carbohydrates and fats were needed as fuel for movement.[2]

Nutritionists were in fact quite smug about their understanding of the physiological roles of the major food groups, for they had recently corrected erroneous early attempts to define those roles. The trailblazer among the early metabolic theorists, the brilliant German organic chemist Justus von Liebig, had relied on educated speculation rather than experiment to formulate the first correlations of food composition with physiological use. His 1842 *Animal Chemistry*, the seminal work in modern biochemistry, separated food components into two classes: plastic (protein) and respiratory (fat and carbohydrate). The latter was presumed to supply, through molecular oxidation, all the heat needed to maintain body temperature. Plastic food, as the name implies, was regarded as the substance of growth and repair, *but* it was also supposed to be the source of all energy (Liebig called it "force" [*Kraft*]) used for muscular motion. In the Liebig scheme, therefore, there was an assumed direct proportion between the amount of muscular work accomplished and the quantity of protein oxidized; athletic effort demanded a high-protein diet.[3]

Liebig's facile system of nutrition was soon challenged, and several experiments carried out during the second half of the century disproved the notion that protein was the source of muscular energy. But though it was supplanted by carbohydrate as an energy source, protein continued to enjoy undeserved status for its plastic properties. The large quantities of protein consumed by athletes and heavy workers (who earned hearty appetites and found protein-rich foods to be especially palatable) were rationalized by the assumption that the protein appetite was a physiological craving representing the body's demand for repair of muscle worn down by exercise. The high protein diet of athletes, which was actually a custom, was thus accepted by nutrition scientists as a physical necessity. The very same dietitians who scoffed at Liebig for having recommended superfluous protein for energy, in the next breath recommended superfluous protein for tissue maintenance. Turn-of-the-century dietary allowances, based on surveys of actual consumption by healthy adults who could afford to eat as much as they wanted, proposed 118 to 127 grams of protein per day for average-sized sedentary males, and up to 150 grams per day for hard laborers (the present recommendation for a 70 kilogram man is 56 grams; athletes are advised to take somewhat more protein, but nothing like the 150 grams of 1900).[4]

Early twentieth-century studies of the diets of competing athletes revealed that the majority exceeded the most liberal standard. W. O. Atwater, America's premier nutritionist and a man who was adamant that a training diet should include "especially large amounts of protein," performed careful investigations of the food taken by the Yale and Harvard crews and found 150 to 170 grams of protein to be the daily average. Other inquiries showed college football players often consumed more than 200 grams per day, the University of California squad averaging a robustious 270 grams. Sandow, the most celebrated strongman of the day (he was a blockbuster attraction with Ziegfeld), ate nearly 250 grams of protein, and an English prize fighter approached 280 on his regimen of one pound of mutton three times daily, and a bit of bread and ale.[5]

The latter's predilection for animal protein was common. Training guides suggested that two kinds of meat be served at all three meals, supplemented with "a moderate quantity" of fruits and vegetables. Atwater calculated that generally more than two-thirds of the protein eaten by his rowers was taken in the form of meat products. Most training manuals, furthermore, made a point of advising that beef be served rare or "underdone," seemingly agreeing with the ancient vegetarian charge that carnivorous eating habits created an aggressive carnivorous behavior. According to one observer, meat was so rare at some training tables the athletes referred to it as "red rags." When the popular medical writer Woods Hutchinson taunted vegetarians for being repelled by "Meat! R-r-red meat, dr-r-r-ripping with b-l-lood, r-r-reeking of the shambles," he was playing on the primitive suspicion that one needs blood to make blood, and muscle to make muscle; a diet devoid of red rags could never build full manly strength and energy.[6]

Those presumptuous vegetarians who ignored this elemental precept had been butts of ridicule for years before Hutchinson's jibes. Vegetable or Pythagorean diet (named for Pythagoras, the ancient Greek vegetarian-natural philosopher) had been introduced to the United States by the Reverend William Metcalfe in 1817, but did not spread beyond the confines of his small sectarian Bible Christian Church until the 1830s. During that decade, however, Sylvester Graham and William Alcott, the leaders of the Jacksonian popular health reform movement, carried the Pythagorean message to a larger public audience and gave vegetarianism solid footing in American culture. Graham and Alcott were also significant for initiating the project of establishing a physiological rationale for the superiority of vegetable to ordinary diet. Their simplistic and premature interpretations of nascent biochemistry were founded upon the premise that flesh food is overly stimulating to physiological processes and thus erodes vital power.[7]

The principle implied a physical (athletic) advantage for Pythagoreans, and Graham, Alcott, and their comrades were not reticent about citing examples of vegetarian muscularity. Graham was awed by the ancient Roman legions who had conquered their world on rations of bread. Although he normally agreed with the time-honored vegetarian metaphysics, which made fleshless diet the precursor of a kindly and peaceful temperament, he celebrated those ancient soldiers "whose success depended . . . on bodily strength and personal prowess, in wielding warclubs and in grappling man with man in the fierce exercise of muscular power, and dashing each other furiously to the earth, mangled and crushed and killed." Alcott preferred modern examples and in his 1838 *Vegetable Diet* presented cases of numerous living vegetarians noteworthy for their physical preeminence, including the amazing Amos Townsend, a graminivorous bank cashier who could "dictate a letter, count money, and hold conversation with an individual, all at the same time, with no embarrassment."[8]

But while Alcott often ran the mile between his home and the post office and was a capable pedestrian, once walking seventy-eight miles in a bit over two days, he and his fellow health reformers rarely offered testimonials of genuine athletes. It was not until the final third of the century and the post-Civil War explosion of public interest in sports and games, that athleticism became a meaningful ideal for vegetarian propagandists. It was not, however, an easy ideal to promote, for "vegetarian athlete" seemed an obvious contradiction in terms to most people. Jacksonian vegetarians had already been subjected to much derisive commentary on their physical condition: "Emasculation is the first fruit of Grahamism," sneered one critic, while another laughed at Graham's "lean-visaged, cadaverous disciples," and a third described Alcott's followers as "gaunt, wry-faced, lantern-jawed, ghostly-looking invalids." And as vegetarians' athletic ambitions climbed during the second half of the century, so did the contempt with which they were showered by cynical meat eaters. That immensely popular philosopher of evolution Herbert Spencer tried vegetable diet for six months, but abandoned the experiment because it lowered his "energy of both body and mind." He afterwards dismissed vegetable-built muscles as "soft and flabby." The respected New York physician George Beard lamented the fate of a vegetarian hiker he had met, a young man of "pale and feminine features, tinged with an unnatural flush," whose attempt to maintain a mere twenty mile a day pace had killed him within a year.[9] And when London's Vegetarian Society announced the formation of an athletic and cycling club, flesh-eating sportsmen could scarce contain their merriment:

> we shall hear of the vegetarian "scorcher" [racing cyclist] and gymnast, of the athlete who is trained on artichokes, and the pacemaker who is built up with asparagus. It is a dangerous competition, into which the vegetarians are urged by overweening ambition. Evidently there are men amongst them who are not content with a spiritual mission, who say, "let us produce a record-breaking cyclist; let us have our own strong man; only by such prodigies can the world be converted." This challenge to the eater of beef must cause some misgiving amongst the orthodox. Suppose the vegetarian athlete should be tempted from the faith by the success of his carnivorous compeers? He may forget that it was vegetarianism he was appointed to vindicate, and not the egotism of his thews and sinews.[10]

But vegetarians did not forget their purpose, and so strong was their desire to vindicate their diet that carnivorous compeers were soon covered in their dust. In 1896, for example, the aptly named James Parsley led the Vegetarian Cycling Club to easy victory over two regular clubs. A week later, he won the most prestigious hill-climbing race in England, breaking the hill record by nearly a minute. Before the summer was out, Parsley had set a new fifty-mile record, as well as several records for shorter distances on a tandem and for London to Brighton and back on a tricycle. Other members of the club (numbering altogether about ninety, including thirteen ladies) also turned in remarkable performances, and none gave any evidence of being "soft and flabby." Their competitors were having to eat crow with their beef.[11]

American vegetarian cyclists were soon in hot pursuit of the English. Will Brown, who in the 1890s switched to vegetable diet to save himself from an early death from tuberculosis, gained so much strength in just three years that he bettered all records for the 2000-mile ride. And Margarita Gast established a women's record for 1000 miles on a diet of fruit, zwieback, raw potatoes, and, shockingly, "sometimes a little claret."[12]

Cycling, moreover, was only one sport in which vegetarians were trouncing the opposition. Long-distance walking races were also very popular in the 1890s and were regarded as an ultimate test of endurance. In the 1983 race from Berlin to Vienna, the first two competitors to cover the 372-mile course were vegetarians. They required 155 and 156 hours respectively; the next finisher, a meat eater, arrived 22 hours later. A 100-kilometer race held several years later in Germany also attracted much attention, for of the first fourteen

THE VEGETARIAN CYCLING CLUB.

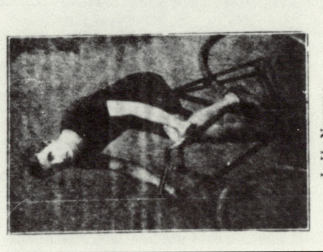

J. H. NICKELS.

(*100 miles on Bath Road, 5 hrs. 38 ms.*)

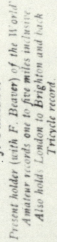

J. PARSLEY.

Present holder (with F. Beaver) of the World's Amateur records one to five miles inclusive. Also holds London to Brighton and back Tricycle record.

Figure 9.1 Late nineteenth-century British cycling champions, representatives of the Vegetarian Cycling Club, from Charles Forward, *Fifty Years of Food Reform* (London: Ideal, 1898), p. 145.

finishers, eleven were vegetarians. A similar outcome attended a 70-mile walking match in which contestants were required to complete the course within fourteen hours. Six of the eight vegetarian entrants met the standard, and the other two failed only for having gotten lost and travelled an extra five miles. Not a single flesh eater could meet the fourteen-hour limit, and only one finished the race.[13]

Runners throve on vegetarian diet, too. To consider only one example, Jonathan Barclay, secretary of the Scottish Vegetarian Society, in 1896 competed in twenty some races at distances from the half mile to ten miles, and won eleven while never finishing lower than third. (Some years later, in 1912, the vegetarian Kohlemainen became one of the first men to complete the marathon under 2:30.) Comparable records were compiled by vegetarian swimmers, tennis players, and other athletes, including the West Ham Vegetarian Society's undefeated tug-of-war team. So impressive did the vegetarian athletic record become that when Berlin's Wilhelm Caspari published his unprecedentedly thorough studies of vegetarianism and physiology (1905), he devoted a lengthy concluding section to the analysis of vegetarian athletic success. The focus of his discussion was the 1902 walking race from Dresden to Berlin, a contest that drew thirty-two competitors. Prior to the race, Caspari selected the leading vegetarian and flesh-eating contenders and subjected each to thorough physical evaluation. The vegetarian champion was a twenty-eight-year-old man who had adopted the vegetable diet eight years before and had since developed, in Caspari's judgment, a "physique like Sandow." He also had the highest oxygen capacity per kilogram of body weight that Caspari had yet measured. The vegetarian subject went on to capture the race handily, in record time (26 hours, 58 minutes for the 125-mile course), while the meat-eating co-favorite Caspari had tested failed to finish. Places two through five, incidentally, were also won by flesh abstainers.[14]

Caspari nevertheless refused to credit vegetable diet "in itself as decisive" for the humiliation of the carnivorous walkers. Since vegetarians were more self-conscious about health, he reasoned, they were more likely to live regular, hygienic lives year-round and particularly to refrain from the use of alcohol (the meat eater who had dropped out had refreshed himself during the race with wine). But the physical advantage from healthful living was minor, in Caspari's estimation, to the psychological advantage of vegetarians. Having already called attention to the importance of will power for the completion of feats of endurance, he now presented the vegetarian life as a daily training ground for perseverance and determination. Not only was the diet itself painful to adhere to, but the frequent social embarrassment accompanying refusal to eat meat demanded psychological firmness of practitioners. When to these considerations were added the regular necessity of defending unusual principles, one could easily see vegetarian strength of will becoming fanaticism. And it was this *Fanatismus,* Caspari insisted, that carried so many vegetarians to victory. Athletes on ordinary diet saw the contest solely as a sporting event, but vegetarians approached it as a struggle to justify their life ideals and demonstrate physical and moral superiority to their adversaries.[15]

The vegetarian's zeal for vindication, it might be argued, was even more important during training than in the competition itself. Any veteran of endurance contests knows that willpower may hold one up to the end, but by itself cannot produce respectable, let alone winning, times. Rigorous training is the difference between running well instead of merely finishing, and vegetarians undoubtedly benefitted from the relatively lenient attitudes toward training in the early 1900s. The training programs recommended for young and serious distance runners at that time, for example, were considerably less demanding than the schedules followed by thousands of middle-aged marathoners today. The vegetarian's desire to win for his philosophy was a spur that could goad him beyond the accepted boundaries of training, give him the fortitude to put in the extra miles at extra effort. The high oxygen consumption rate of the Dresden to Berlin winner suggests a rigorous training regimen.[16]

But stiffer training was perhaps not all. Despite Caspari's certainty that there was no *dietary* advantage to vegetarianism, there probably was. Numerous studies in recent years have documented the value of a high-carbohydrate diet for endurance performance. Athletes engaged in competition extended over several days (such as the distance walkers) are especially likely to benefit from the ability of a carbohydrate-heavy diet to restore depleted muscle glycogen to high levels after each day's contest. There surely was a significant difference in the carbohydrate content of the vegetarian athlete's training diet and that of the conventional athlete who followed the standard advice to maintain himself on a high-protein diet. Vegetarian temperance was an advantage, too. Athletes at the turn of the century made free use of alcohol as a stimulant. Several marathoners at the 1906 Olympics drank cognac during the competition to keep up their strength, and a walker in a 100-kilometer contest in Germany the same year was reported to have consumed twenty-two glasses of beer and half a bottle of wine. These dietary factors combined with more serious training and fanatical willpower to resist fatigue to give vegetarians the competitive edge needed to win.[17]

Pythagoreans were as awesome in the gymnasium as on the roads. During the first decade of this century there were several experimental comparisons of endurance in vegetarians and in flesh eaters, and in every instance the vegetarians won. The most thorough study was carried out by Irving Fisher, the respected Yale economist and a tireless (though not vegetarian) health reformer. Fisher collected fortyseven subjects whom he divided into three groups—Yale athletes trained on a full-flesh regimen, athletes who abstained from meat, and sedentary vegetarians (nurses and physicians from the Battle Creek [Michigan] Sanitarium). Each was tested to determine the maximum length of time he could hold his arms out horizontally and the maximum number of deep knee bends and leg raises he could perform. The final tally—"much to my surprise," Fisher avowed—was heavily in favor of the flesh abstainers. Only 2 of the 15 meat eaters, for example, were able to maintain the arm hold for more than 15 minutes; none achieved half an hour. Of the vegetarians, however, 22 (of 32) exceeded a quarter-hour, and 15 broke the 30-minute barrier. In fact 9 doubled that time, and 1 surpassed 3 hours. But the final touch to the carnivores' embarrassment was supplied by the six-year-old son of one of the Sanitarium volunteers, who, curiously imitating his father, "held his little arms out, and did not drop them until 43 minutes had elapsed."[18]

The meat eaters were similarly humiliated in the other tests, and the results could not, Fisher believed, be explained by Caspari's hypothesis. While a few of the vegetarians had exhibited some degree of "fanatical desire," it had not been evident in the majority. Most of the subjects were clearly moved by pure competitive drive, by the determination to break the records set by others, whatever their dietary persuasion. Fisher even warned his flesh eaters that their performances would be recorded as evidence of Yale athletic ability, confident that "Yale spirit" would prove "as great a stimulus as any 'vegetarian' spirit could possibly be." In one case, Fisher reported in a letter to his wife, he stood in front of a Yale track man and continually urged him to hold out his arms for the glory of his school; the spiritless lad gave out in less than ten minutes.[19]

Other factors—training, amount of sleep, work load, use of alcohol and tobacco, etc.—were considered, but Fisher could find nothing to reasonably account for the vegetarians' performance except diet. The similar studies noted above reached like conclusions, but they were not given serious attention by scientists, and the subject seems to have been pursued no further. Nutritionists had long before become jaded by vegetarian exaggerations, and neither Fisher nor his colleagues could be regarded as disinterested or accomplished physiologists. Their investigations are still occasionally cited in discussions of diet and fitness, but are dismissed as "dated" and not credible.[20]

Vegetarians of the Progressive era accepted and were heartened by those researches, however, and set forth elaborate physiological mechanisms to explain their superiority in experiment and in competition. The leading theoretician among their number was John Harvey Kellogg, director of the Battle Creek Sanitarium (and father of the pre-cooked breakfast cereal industry). Kellogg practiced vegetarianism at the "San," as his institution was familiarly known, and preached it in his countless books, lectures, and articles in his own popular health periodical *Good Health*. His case against meat eating was built from arguments taken from evolution (the human race had descended from frugivorous ancestors), bacteriology (meat was commonly contaminated with the germs of a host of diseases), and biochemistry (an animal's struggles before death, Kellogg asserted, produced "fatigue poisons" in its tissues, and these would be ingested by people who ate its flesh). Those last two areas were the source of yet another objection to meat, the menace of "autointoxication." The most villainous of all microbes, in his opinion, were the various species responsible for putrefaction, the decomposition of protein into a variety of compounds, some of which are extremely malodorous (e.g., indole, skatole) or toxic (e.g., neurine, putrescine). These putrefaction products are generally present in human feces as a result of the bacterial decomposition of residual dietary protein in the intestines, but are not absorbed in sufficient amount to be a health hazard. Nevertheless, their isolation in the 1880s and the demonstration of their toxicity when injected directly into the blood gave rise to an unfounded fear of autointoxication, or self-poisoning, from these "ptomaines." While medical leaders made a concerted effort to dispel this bugaboo, many physicians accepted it as a definite pathological entity into the 1920s. The recommended therapies included yogurt, whose fermentative bacilli would displace the putrefactive bacteria in the colon, and surgical shortening of the intestines. Kellogg's remedy was the elimination of meat from the diet. By his analysis, the ordinary diet was so high in protein as to greatly encourage the growth and activity of proteolytic (putrefactive) bacteria in the colon. As the microbes operated on undigested flesh food, the body would be "flooded with the most horrible and loathsome poisons" and brought to suffer headache, depression, skin problems, damage to the liver, kidneys, and blood vessels, and chronic fatigue (i.e., lack of strength and endurance), as well as other injuries totalling up to "enormous mischief." Anyone who read to the end of Kellogg's baleful list must have been ready to agree that "the marvel is not that human life is so short and so full of miseries, mental, moral, and physical, but that civilized human beings are able to live at all." It was certainly no marvel that flesh-eating athletes so often went down to defeat at the hands of vegetarians.[21]

But according to Alexander Haig, even vegetarians were far from realizing their full athletic powers. Haig was the expositor of the "uric-acid-free diet," a refined brand of vegetarianism that was promoted with special attention to athletic performance.[21] A London physician, he had discovered in the 1880s that elimination of animal food from his table brought relief from the migraine he had suffered for years. With further experimentation and reflection he arrived (through a process too intricate and esoteric to be recounted here) at the conviction that the cause of his headaches, and virtually every other ill known to humanity, was uric acid. That compound, the metabolic end product of the purines present in all meat, was already implicated in the ailments of gout and kidney and bladder stones. Haig proceeded to demonstrate to his own satisfaction, and that of many other biochemical novices in the medical profession, that uric acid deposits were also responsible for eczema, jaundice, gastritis, and even flatulence. Still more numerous were the problems associated with uric acid suspensions, or colloids, in the blood. This "uricacidemia" or "collaemia" was believed responsible for a pathological spectrum that ran from anemia to atherosclerosis, and included sub-maximal athletic performance.[22]

Haig had been a rower in college, in spite of his uricacidemia-induced headaches and was determined that athletes of the future should not suffer the deprivation he had. His contribution to that cause was *Diet and Food,* a book that went through six editions in the years from 1898 to 1906 and seems to have been as popular in America as in England. Its theory of strength and endurance, however, was outmoded even by Haig's quaint standards. The premise on which the entire book was built was the idea that the energy for muscular motion was derived from the oxidation of protein to urea. That idea, originally offered by Liebig half a century earlier, had long since been discredited and was no longer taken seriously—except by Haig. Yet he seems to have been unaware of his loneliness on this position, presenting the theory as if it were generally accepted, and even using his inimitable analytical skills to find a direct correlation between quantity of exercise and excreted urea. If the energy for exertion came from protein, Haig hypothesized, maximum strength and endurance required a free flow of protein-rich blood to the muscles. But vessels clogged with colloidal uric acid would not be able to supply a full complement of protein molecules to the tissues, nor to remove the waste of protein oxidation. The more uric acid food an individual consumed, therefore, the more physiological "friction" he would have and the lower would be his achievement in contests of endurance. That was undoubtedly why meat eaters usually succumbed to vegetarian rivals, but vegetarians, he continued, had no reason to rejoice. Their vessels too were contaminated, for beans, asparagus, and mushrooms contained purines and thus produced uric acid. Ordinary vegetarianism granted a relative advantage, but uric-acid-free vegetarianism was required for absolute superiority. Support for this point was provided by the history of Karl Mann, the vegetarian walker studied by Caspari at the Dresden to Berlin contest. Mann had been converted to vegetable diet in 1894, then switched to Haig's improved version in 1898. Within the year he won an important seventy-mile race, but it was the 1902 Dresden-Berlin triumph that catapulted him into the international spotlight. Haig rushed to Berlin immediately, personally examined Mann just a few days after the race, and was pleased (but hardly surprised) to find him free of the cardiac hypertrophy that was supposedly epidemic among carnivorous competitors. "Athlete's heart," he concluded, was still another uric acid ailment.[23]

The uric-acid-free (purine free) diet was limited to milk, cheese, some vegetables, fruits, nuts and—a unique position for a food reformer—white bread. Additional blandness was imposed by the prohibition of coffee, tea, and cocoa on the grounds that they contained methyl xanthines (it was later found that caffeine and similar compounds are not metabolized into uric acid). And any solace that at least alcoholic beverages were free of uric acid-producing substances was quickly squelched by Haig's promise that his diet removed any need for stimulation and thus destroyed the taste for strong drink. Hence even though the theory was widely circulated, and clearly captured the support of a number of physicians in the United States, there were probably few athletes who permanently converted to Haig's diet. One who did at least try it for a while was another major participant in the debate over nutrition and athletics. Eustace Miles's life was miserable for his first twenty-seven years. He did, to be sure, achieve a certain level of success as a classical honors coach at Cambridge and as a skilled tennis player, but he was often restless and depressed, slept poorly, suffered headaches, colds, constipation, and had a "great liking for any form of alcohol." About 1896, though, he chanced to encounter Haig's writings, took up the uric-acid-free diet, and before long found himself feeling and looking better. His muscular flexibility and endurance improved, and even his memory grew stronger. Not least important, his thirst for alcohol disappeared.[24]

Miles's alcohol-free, uric-acid-free regimen allowed him to become one of muscular vegetarianism's best advertisements. He captured the British national tennis championship in 1897, as well as a number of other major titles. By the time some of those victories were recorded, though, Miles was no longer an advocate of the Haig diet. He learned through experience that pulses—anathema to Haig—did not injure, but actually aided his vitality, and he soon ignored the uric acid theory's restrictions on certain vegetables. He became, in effect, an ordinary vegetarian, but he refused to be known by the name because he thought it had been sullied by mistaken practice. One of his many books, in fact, was dedicated wholly to the *Failures of Vegetarianism,* though those failures were hardly so numerous and complex as to require a separate volume. Most could be reduced to a simple ignorance of the nutritional needs of the body which, Miles believed, left too many vegetarians content with "an idiotic Potato-Cabbage Diet," woefully lacking in protein. His own diet, emphasizing legumes, grains, milk products, and high-protein meat substitutes, he preferred to call "Simpler Food."

> Choose the cheaper, Simpler Food
> cheese and Protene [meat substitute], milk (if good),
> Gluten, Hovis [a health bread], macaroni;
> oats and other grains, and honey;
> orange, apple, other fruits;
> vegetables, pulses, roots.[25]

This poetic doctrine was pushed in Miles's monthly *Healthward Ho!;* it was the teaching imparted to boarders at "The Old House," his health retreat in the English countryside with a "delightfully homelike atmosphere." One suspects that the same dogma was somehow served with the bread at his restaurant, which hosted more than a thousand diners daily and marked menu items to identify uric acid-containing dishes. (Apparently the quality of all the dishes was well above the vegetarian standard; American gastronome James Beard has cited Miles's restaurant as the only good vegetarian restaurant in his experience, and Miles himself rejected most vegetarians' meals as "execrably cooked.") But it was primarily through his actions on the court that Miles drew international attention to the possibility that the simple vegetable diet might improve one's playing skills, as well as overall health.[26]

The ranks of muscular vegetarians were enlarged still further by the addition of Russell Chittenden and Horace Fletcher. Although neither was a vegetarian in theory, both approached a meatless diet in practice and each espoused a doctrine that was most attractive to pure vegetarians. It was a doctrine that promised to free them from the criticism they had had to endure ever since the publication of Liebig's *Animal Chemistry*. That work's assignment of a major energy, as well as plastic, function to protein had forced vegetarians to scramble to justify their relatively low-protein diet. Some of the attempts to rationalize working power with a low-protein intake were embarrassing. The English Pythagorean John Smith, for example, struggled to prove that vegetarians manufactured much of their tissue protein from the nitrogen inhaled from the air—why else, he asked, would nature have put so much of that gas in the atmosphere? He also suspected atmospheric nitrogen might be swallowed with food and get into the blood from the stomach.[27]

As has been noted, Liebig's theory was soon repudiated, but the dietary protein recommendation remained high through the rest of the 1800s. It was finally challenged early in the twentieth century by Chittenden, professor of physiological chemistry at Yale and the ranking scientist in his field in the United States. Intrigued by several recent reports of individuals maintaining health on daily protein intakes as low as 15 to 30 grams, Chittenden brushed aside the warnings of physician friends and dropped his own protein consumption to 35 to 40 grams a day. And far from experiencing the predicted deterioration, he found himself suffering less from a rheumatic ailment of his knee, indigestion, and "sick headaches" and actually growing in strength and endurance (while losing about sixteen pounds weight). He was soon taking long daily rowing workouts, something that had been beyond his capacity when on the old diet.[28]

Convinced of the safety and efficacy of the low-protein regimen in his own case, Chittenden procured funds to support an elaborate study of the effects of low protein on sedentary workers (Yale professors), moderate workers (U.S. Army volunteers), and heavy workers (Yale athletes). Between autumn, 1903, and summer, 1904, each group lived, for periods ranging from five to eight months, on a diet containing less than half the orthodox protein recommendation. There was no medical evidence of decline in health among the participants, and their performance of calisthenic exercises and on strength-testing machines indicated a significant rise in strength over the course of the experiment. One of the athlete volunteers even won two national gymnastic championships while on the diet. Such results persuaded Chittenden that the average person consumed much more protein than his body needed, and that the excess was a burdensome tax which lowered physiological efficiency. The mechanism by which redundant protein inhibited strength and endurance could not yet be explained with certainty, but Chittenden was clearly quite comfortable in his own mind with the theory that the products of protein catabolism inhibit muscular function. He also feared these metabolites might injure the nervous system and was sure they must overload the liver and kidneys.[29]

Chittenden's data and interpretations were presented in 1904 in *Physiological Economy in Nutrition,* a hefty treatise that was perhaps the most talked about scientific publication of the Progressive era. Much of that talk was deprecatory, it becoming quickly apparent that one man's economy is another man's parsimony. The initial reaction of the majority of physiologists was that such limited protein ingestion must be eventually murderous; Chittenden's experiments simply had not been conducted long enough to allow the damage to become obvious. The supposed improvement in health that had been observed, if accepted at all, was attributed to the general temperance and regular schedule associated with the experiment. In the end, of course, the reevaluation of the protein requirement that was forced by Chittenden's experiments led to a steady lowering of the recommendation until today it is essentially the same as the figure he established.[30]

Vegetarians of the early 1900s predicted as much, for they had already learned through experience that massive protein consumption was unnecessary for health, and their athletic conquests suggested that it actually depressed physical functioning. Praise for Chittenden's work was thus obligatory in expositions of muscular vegetarianism, and even athletes who balked at giving up meat altogether were willing to reduce their protein intake to Chittenden levels. And there were other examples to encourage that reduction. The Swedish physiologist V. O. Sivén claimed to maintain himself on 25 to 30 grams of protein, and the Copenhagen physiologist Mikkel Hindhede lived on a largely potato diet containing only 15 to 20 grams of protein. But none of these, Chittenden included, gave such a dramatic demonstration of the compatibility of low protein with athletic excellence as did Horace Fletcher.[31]

Born in Massachusetts in 1849, Fletcher won local fame as an all-around athlete in his youth, then moved on to success as a San

Francisco businessman. Unfortunately, as his wealth increased, so did his waistline, until by the age of forty his once graceful five-foot seven-inch frame had swollen to an unwieldy 217 pounds. Overweight, dyspeptic, constantly plagued by "that tired feeling," and subject to frequent attacks of influenza, he came to feel like "a thing fit but to be thrown upon the scrap-heap." When his application for a life insurance policy was denied, Fletcher resolved to regain his health, and his transformation from *bon vivant* to health reformer began. Reading and self-experimentation led him, through too circuitous a route to be traced here, to the adoption of extremely thorough mastication of all food as *the* method of health recovery and maintenance. Once outfitted with an elaborate, if juvenile, theory, Fletcherism became a health fad that was popular into the 1910s and ultimately helped break Americans of their "gobble, gulp and go" table manners.[32]

The more immediate impact of Fletcherism, however, was to strengthen the case for the low-protein diet for athletes. Fletcher asserted that the extraordinary vitality that he recovered through careful chewing was due to his reduction of all food to a pulp that could be completely digested and absorbed, and thereby used much more efficiently by the body. As proof of his more thorough utilization of food, he unblushingly reported the remarkable decrease in defecation frequency and stool volume that he experienced after taking up conscientious mastication. But thorough chewing had also led him, for reasons of time, to eat considerably less food than before, including less protein. It was Fletcher's unusually low protein consumption, in fact, that inspired Chittenden to undertake his investigations.[33]

Chittenden was particularly struck by Fletcher's ability for rigorous exercise on such a limited diet, an ability its owner himself had discovered by accident. In 1899, just before his fiftieth birthday and after only a year of devoted mastication, Fletcher celebrated the Fourth of July with a bicycle ride. Losing himself in the fun of the sport, he cycled more than 100 miles before stopping and was astounded to find he was still not tired and did not suffer from muscle soreness the next day. Such a claim would ordinarily invite denunciation, except that in subsequent, documented trials he demonstrated an almost incredible power to move easily from long periods of inactivity to the performance of demanding feats of endurance. Four years later, to cite the most notable example, Fletcher was tested by William Anderson, M.D., director of the Yale gymnasium and a commanding figure in the period's physical education revival. Just two years earlier, Anderson had published in a popular magazine his views on "the making of a perfect man," in which he had insisted on the possibility of maintaining strength and endurance in advanced years. He must have felt fully vindicated as a prophet by the time Fletcher left his gymnasium. Putting the now fifty-four-year-old subject through four days of the Yale university crew exercises (Anderson regarded rowing and football as the most demanding and effective programs of physical conditioning), he was, as he modestly phrased it, "surprised." "Mr. Fletcher has taken these movements with an ease that is unlooked for. He gives evidence of no soreness or lameness and the large groups of muscles respond the second day without evidence of being poisoned by carbon dioxide. . . . Mr. Fletcher performs this work with greater ease and with fewer noticeable bad results than any man of his age and condition I have ever worked with."[34]

In another four years Anderson's surprise turned to amazement, for Fletcher came back for a second battery of tests and surpassed his previous performance. In one measurement of the endurance of his calf muscles, he actually doubled a Yale student record! (though Fletcher's record was soon broken by the famous pedestrian Karl Mann). Fletcher apparently had an exceptional natural athletic prowess, freely exercised in his youth, then submerged by middle-aged obesity. As the fat receded after careful mastication was adopted, however, his genius for endurance returned to the surface and, coupled with zeal for demonstrating the benefits of chewing, enabled him to shatter the conventions of physical training. Yet this explanation is still not entirely satisfying, and one eventually has to agree with vegetarian Kellogg that Fletcher was "a physiological puzzle."[35]

The puzzle was complicated by experiments with volunteer Fletcherizers that also indicated a gain in endurance through thorough mastication of a low-protein diet. Fisher, for example, recruited nine of his own students to test the effects of Fletcherism on endurance. Beginning in January, 1906, this "eating club" devoted nineteen weeks to "thorough mastication and implicit obedience to appetite." During the second half of the study the subjects were also actively encouraged to eat less protein, and as might by now be predicted, the subjects soon found themselves wanting less food and voiding less offensive feces. And they all the while grew in endurance. Tests requiring repetitive exercises, such as calf-raises, knee-bends, and dumbbell lifts, were administered at the beginning, middle, and end of the test. All but one of the volunteers improved drastically (from 50 to more than 200 percent) between January and June, and it seemed more than coincidence that the exception was the student who had failed to reduce his protein consumption until near the end of the experiment, and whose fecal improvement rating was one of the lowest. Fisher carefully analyzed the experiment to be certain the improvement could have only come from diet, and he concluded by giving roughly equal credit to Fletcher and Chittenden—chewing and low protein together built endurance.[36]

A lesser-known investigator, YMCA trainer Elmer Berry, announced similar findings three years later, while the issue of diet and athletics was made cloudier still by the claims of yet other special dieters, such as the apyrotrophes (as the proponents of eating only uncooked foods pretentiously called themselves). This essentially vegetarian system (though some practitioners ate oysters and steak tartare) also affected a healthier-than-thou attitude toward conventional dietetics, offering as its chief exhibit the record of apyrotropher Gilman Low, one of Sandow's rivals for weight-lifting supremacy.[37]

The feats of Low and Mann could not be denied, but they could be explained. The consensus among orthodox nutritionists was that while vegetarian, uric-acid-free, low-protein, and apyrotrophic dieters were "more than likely to be obsessed" with a complete program of temperate hygiene, "the heavy eater . . . , reveling in protein and total calories, is likely to be hygienically delinquent in many other ways and to flaunt and glory in his hygienic lawlessness." And even if sometimes lawless, carnivorous competitors were not always outclassed. Apologists for flesh food delighted in confounding vegetarians with such examples of meat-built stamina as Johnnie Hayes, the winner of the marathon at the 1908 Olympics. Hayes's workouts were punctuated by two meat meals daily, and he was confident that "plenty of meat such as steaks, chops and roast beef and lamb are beneficial while training."[38]

The controversy continued to be waged, but never advanced beyond the stage already outlined and was considerably more subdued after the 1910s. Those years witnessed a waning of enthusiasm for vegetarianism (and indeed of public interest in all radical health reform movements) that reflected the subsiding of the buoyant optimism that had so animated Progressive society in general. Extremist systems of personal improvement through hygiene are, after all, also optimistic and typically anticipate that mental and moral elevation will necessarily follow physical purification. They are actually hygienic ideologies that exist in a symbiotic relationship with their cultural *milieu*, both drawing from contemporary hopes for human betterment and feeding those hopes with specific recipes for perfection. Thus while hygienic ideologies have been a constant feature of American life since the early 1800s, they have naturally flourished in periods of general reformist ferment and social optimism, when an expanding public spirit has enlarged the constituency for perfectionist campaigns. The Progressive decades were in fact richer in unconventional systems of nutrition than any other period of American history, and each system presented its own plan for realizing the aspirations, and quelling the anxieties, that preoccupied society at large. Progressivism's commitment to renew the nation's vitality and remedy the abuses of unbridled industrialism, its Arcadian longing for a life more attuned with nature, its trust in the power of science, reverence for worldly success, and determination to direct evolution so as to reverse the trends towards "race suicide" all found ready expression in crusades for reformed personal hygiene. The Progressive gospel of "efficiency"—in business, government, or any public endeavor—was particularly amenable to hygienic interpretation. Initially a financial concept, efficiency was easily translated from fiscal to physical meaning by health accountants who analyzed body functions in terms of deposits of food and rest, and withdrawals of exertion and self-neglect. The quantity, and quality, of the deposits and withdrawals determined the degree of physiological wealth, and wise management yielded efficiency of operation—maximum production with minimum waste. And what was athletic success except a demonstration of physiological (and mental-moral) efficiency? Unconventional dietary schemes such as vegetarianism were inextricably entwined with Progressive social philosophy and public fascination with competitive sports.[39]

The fascination with athletics continued into the post-war years, but early century zeal for social reform gave way to the complacency of the "return to normalcy." Muscular vegetarianism inevitably suffered a decline as well. A sad sign of the changed times was Kellogg's venture at fielding a football team. In 1923 he opened Battle Creek College, a four-year program in physical education and home economics that soon enlarged its program to include a football squad. It was the director's hope that players nourished at a meatless training table would so overwhelm opponents as to win them, and the rest of the public, to vegetable diet. The team was disbanded after its inaugural season, though. The college administration's official reason was that the game was too violent, but the team's poor won-lost record was undoubtedly a consideration. It was not a shining denouement for muscular vegetarianism.[40]

Notes

1. H. A. Harris, "Nutrition and Physical Performance. The Diet of Greek Athletes," *Proceedings of the Nutrition Society* 25 (1966), 87–90, 89; J. D. Reed, "They Hunger for Success," *Sports Illustrated*, Feb. 28, 1977, 64–74.

2. For the evolution of nutrition to 1900, see Elmer McCollum, *A History of Nutrition* (Boston: Houghton Mifflin, 1957), 10–154.

3. Justus von Liebig, *Animal Chemistry, or Organic Chemistry in Its Application to Physiology and Pathology* (Cambridge, Mass.: John Owen, 1842), 10–92, 211–13.

4. McCollum, *History of Nutrition*, 192; Ruth Leverton, "Building Blocks and Stepping Stones in Protein Nutrition," *Journal of Nutrition* 91, supp. 1 (1967), 39–43; *Recommended Dietary Allowances* (Washington, D.C.: National Academy of Sciences, 1980), 46.

5. W. O. Atwater and A. P. Bryant, *Dietary Studies of University Boat Crews,* U.S. Department of Agriculture, Office of Experiment Stations, Bulletin no. 25 (Washington, D.C.: Government Printing Office, 1900), especially pp. 66–72; Russell Chittenden, *The Nutrition of Man* (New York: Stokes, 1907), 156.

6. Martin Holbrook, *Eating for Strength: or, Food and Diet in Their Relation to Health and Work* (New York: Holbrook, 1888), 149–54; Woods Hutchinson, *Instinct and Health* (New York: Dodd, Mead, 1909), 34.

7. James Whorton, " 'Tempest in a Flesh-Pot': The Formulation of a Physiological Rationale for Vegetarianism," *Journal of the History of Medicine* 32 (1977), 115–39.

8. Sylvester Graham, *Lectures on the Science of Human Life* (Boston: Marsh, Capen, Lyon and Webb, 1839), vol. 2, 188; William Alcott, *Vegetable Diet: As Sanctioned by Medical Men and by Experience in All Ages* (Boston: Marsh, Capen and Lyon, 1838), 75–76.

9. *American Vegetarian* 1 (1851), 141; "Dietetic Charlatanry; or the New Ethics of Eating," *New York Revue* 1 (1837), 339, 341; *Boston Medical and Surgical Journal* 19 (1838–39), 221; ibid. 14 (1836), 169; Herbert Spencer, *Education: Intellectual, Moral and Physical* (New York: Appleton, 1881), 57, 236; George Beard, *Eating and Drinking; a Popular Manual of Food and Diet in Health and Disease* (New York: Putnam, 1871), 91.

10. "The Vegetarian Creed," *Living Age* 216 (1898), 128.

11. Charles Forward, *Fifty Years of Food Reform* (London: Ideal, 1898), 154–57.

12. W. R. C. Latson, *Food Value of Meat* (New York: Health-Culture, 1900), 60–63.

13. Forward, *Fifty Years*, 156; Jacques Buttner, *A Fleshless Diet* (New York: Stokes, 1910), 163, 170–71; *Lancet* 1 (1893), 1396–97; John Harvey Kellogg, *Shall We Slay to Eat?* (Battle Creek, Mich.: Good Health, 1905), 106.

14. Forward, *Fifty Years*, 158–60; Jules Lefevre, *A Scientific Investigation into Vegetarianism* (London: Bale and Danielson, 1923), 162. Wilhelm Caspari,

"Physiologische Studien über Vegetarismus," *Pfluger's Archiv* 109 (1905), 473–595, 569–72 and 580–83 especially.

15. Caspari, "Physiologische Studien," 585.

16. Malcolm Ford, "Distance Running," *Outing* 18 (1891), 205–10; ibid., "Training," *Outing* 19 (1891–92), 421–24; Randolph Farles, "On Training in General," *Outing* 30 (1897), 177–82.

17. Ernst Jokl, "Notes on Doping," *Medicine and Sport* 1 (1968), 55–57. Also see J. B. Blake and R. C. Larrabee, "Observations upon Long-Distance Runners," *Boston Medical and Surgical Journal* 148 (1903), 195–206.

18. Irving Fisher, "The Influence of Flesh-Eating on Endurance," *Yale Medical Journal* 13 (1906–7), 205–21, 214.

19. Irving Fisher [Jr.], *My Father, Irving Fisher* (New York: Comet Press, 1956), 111.

20. Fisher, "The Influence," 219; McCollum, *History of Nutrition*, 198; Melvin Williams, *Nutritional Aspects of Human Physical and Athletic Performance* (Springfield, Ill.: Thomas, 1976), 303.

21. Richard Schwarz, *John Harvey Kellogg, M.D.* (Nashville: Southern Publishing Association, 1970); Kellogg, *The Itinerary of a Breakfast* (Battle Creek, Mich.: Good Health, 1919), 25, 36, 82; ibid., *Autointoxication or Intestinal Toxemia* (Battle Creek, Mich.: Good Health, 1919), 131.

22. Haig published numerous papers and several books presenting his theories on uric acid as a pathological agent. The most comprehensive is *Uric Acid as a Factor in the Causation of Disease* (London: Churchill, 1892).

23. Alexander Haig, *Diet and Food, Considered in Relation to Strength and Power of Endurance, Training and Athletics* (London: Churchill, 1902), 2–3, 6, 23, 34, 95; ibid., *Uric Acid as a Factor in the Causation of Disease*, 6th ed. (Philadelphia: Blakiston, 1905), 42–43, 99–103, 830–35.

24. Eustace Miles, *Muscle, Brain and Diet* (London: Swan Sonnenschein, 1900), 40–48.

25. Lefèvre, *Scientific Investigation*, 163; Miles, *Muscle*, 165, 227–29, 252–53, 334.

26. Eustace Miles and C. H. Collings, *The Uric Acid Fetish* (London: Miles, 1915), 268–69; Miles, *Self-Health as a Habit* (London: Miles, 1919), 11, 190.

27. John Smith, *Fruits and Farinacea: The Proper Food of Man* (New York: Fowler and Wells, 1854), 133–37.

28. Russell Chittenden, *Physiological Economy in Nutrition* (New York: Stokes, 1904), 4–17.

29. Ibid., 440, 455–70.

30. Virginia Schelar, "Protein Digestion, the Protein Requirement in Nutrition and Food Additives: The Contribution of Russell H. Chittenden," doctoral dissertation, University of Wisconsin, 1969; see pp. 202–38 for the reaction to Chittenden's protein recommendations.

31. V. O. Sivén, "Zur Kenntnis des Stoffwechsels beim erwachsenen Menschen, mit besonderer Berücksichtigung des Eiweissbedarfs," *Skandinavian*

Archives für Physiologic 11 (1901), 308–32; Mikkel Hindhede, *Eine Reform un-serer Ernährung* (Leipzig: Kohler, 1908).

32. James Whorton, "'Physiologic Optimism': Horace Fletcher and Hygienic Ideology in Progressive America," *Bulletin of the History of Medicine* 55 (1981), 59–87.

33. Horace Fletcher, *The A.B.-Z. of Our Own Nutrition* (New York: Stokes, 1903), 11; ibid., *The New Glutton* (New York: Stokes, 1903), 147–50; Chittenden, quoted by Hubert Vickery, "Biographical Memoir of Russell Henry Chittenden, 1856–1943," *National Academy of Science, Biographical Memoirs* 24 (1947), 59–104, 80–81.

34. Fletcher, *The New Glutton*, 84–100; William Anderson, "The Making of a Perfect Man," *Munsey's Magazine* 25 (1901), 94–104; Anderson quoted by Chittenden, "Physiological Economy in Nutrition," *Popular Science* 63 (1903), 123–31.

35. William Anderson, "Observations on the Results of Tests for Physical Endurance at the Yale Gymnasium," *New York Medical Journal* 86 (1907), 1009–13; Buttner, *A Fleshless Diet*, 163–64, 173; Kellogg quoted in Fletcher, *The New Glutton*, 58.

36. Irving Fisher, "The Effect of Diet on Endurance, Based on an Experiment with Nine Healthy Students at Yale University, January-June, 1906," *Transactions of the Connecticut Academy* 13 (1907), 1–46.

37. Elmer Berry, "The Effects of a High and Low Proteid Diet on Physical Efficiency," *American Physical Education Review* 14 (1909), 288–97; Eugene and Mallis Christian, *Uncooked Foods and How to Use Them* (New York: Health-Culture, 1904), 27.

38. Eugene Howe, "Diet and Endurance," *American Physical Education Review* 21 (1916), 490–502, p. 490; Hayes quoted by Berry, "The Effects", 294.

39. A detailed analysis of the evolution of health reform movements can be found in James C. Whorton, *Crusaders for Fitness: The History of American Health Reformers* (Princeton: Princeton University Press, 1982). For coverage of Progressivism, see Richard Hofstadter, *The Progressive Movement, 1900–1915* (Englewood Cliffs, N.J.: Prentice Hall, 1963); David Noble, *The Progressive Mind, 1890–1917* (Chicago: Rand McNally, 1970); Peter Schmitt, *Back to Nature: The Arcadian Myth in Urban America* (New York: Oxford University Press, 1969).

40. Schwarz, *John Harvey Kellogg*, 102.

10 *Terry Todd*

A History of the Use of Anabolic Steroids in Sport

The fact that athletes are now hormonally manipulating themselves in order to enhance their performance has aroused great concern among those who are close to athletics—especially since the media circus surrounding Ben Johnson's use of steroids for the 1988 Olympic Games in Seoul—because it is feared that these athletes may be doing irreparable harm to themselves as well as to "sport." As Peter Lawson of the *Manchester Guardian* put it, "Unless something is done soon, international sport will be a competition between circus freaks manipulated by international chemists."[1] Even so, the history of drug use by athletes has received little scholarly attention. Though there are now several popular treatments of the use of anabolic drugs by athletes, most notably Bob Goldman's *Death in the Locker Room,* William Taylor's *Hormonal Manipulation,* Melvin H. Williams's *Beyond Training, Drugs in Sport,* edited by D. R. Mottram, and Brian Hainline's *Drugs and the Athlete,* none of these books contain much discussion of the chronology of this phenomenon or, sad to say, much documentation.[2] What follows is an attempt to provide a chronology and, perhaps, an insight into this baleful aspect of modern sport.

Tam Thompson, a thirty-year-old graduate student in physical education, has competed in the sport of powerlifting since 1982 and admits having used anabolic steroids to improve her performance. Like many other athletes in an increasingly wide variety of sports, Tam felt that using anabolic steroids (synthetic derivatives of the male hormone, testosterone, which helps in the building of muscle size and strength) would give her a competitive edge. Before using steroids, Tam had never won a national title nor set any official records and she hoped steroids would allow her to catch the top women. In this quest she was ultimately unsuccessful. Five years ago, Tam decided to stop using drugs and the result was a significant drop in her level of strength.

The following interview, done in 1986, represents one of the first times a woman athlete has discussed her drug usage for the record.[3] Much of what Tam has to say may seem extraordinary to those who are removed from the world of competitive sports, but neither the amounts of drugs she took, her attitude toward those drugs, nor the side effects she experienced are atypical of what many observers now see regularly among men and women who use these substances. Tam's interest in, involvement with, and ultimate opposition to anabolic steroids began shortly after her first competition in powerlifting.

> I remember after my first powerlifting meet thinking, "I can't believe I finished sixth out of the nine women in my weight class. I know I'm stronger than they are." And so, instead of training harder or going to better techniques, I figured they were taking drugs and I would too. I'd catch up. "And besides," I told myself, "if I decide this is a bad thing, I can simply stop."
>
> The dealer was steering me. He told me, "Stay away from Dianabol and testosterone, they're not good for women." And, of course, that was tantalizing to me. I thought, "What is this? This is chauvinistic. Why can the men take these stronger drugs and not me?"
>
> I started on Anavar and decided it didn't work, so I switched to injections of Equipoise—you know, the new veterinary steroid everyone's using—and decadurabolin. Then I added some Dianabol on top—generally five to six a day, and then, when I was about five weeks out from the U.S. Women's Nationals I started a cycle of testosterone, too. I started off with one half cc a week, then one cc the next week, then to one and one-half, then two cc's, and finally the week before the meet, I took three cc's. I was pretty well tanked.
>
> And then three days before the meet I started taking shots of aqueous testosterone—the real nasty stuff that hurts when it goes in. I mean you put that thing in your hip and it feels like it's dripping all down the back of your hamstring. It makes the hamstrings cramp really bad. I took one cc in the morning and one cc at night for the first two days, then the day before the meet one cc in the morning and two cc's at night, and the morning of the meet I took two more cc's, and then three more right before the meet started. And during the meet I took some of those sublingual testosterones—I don't remember how many—and right before the deadlifts I took an injection of adrenalin backstage—about one-half cc, I guess.
>
> How did I feel? Like I was on the top of the world. Not high, just a very super feeling. I thought I could do anything . . .
>
> Unwanted side effects? I didn't really notice anything the first cycle. So I figured, "OK, we're safe, this isn't going to do anything to me." And it

didn't, not the first time. But the second cycle, my voice started getting lower, and I noticed these strange hairs showing up. I thought, "Well, that's no big deal. A hair here, a hair there. Big deal. I can live with it." Some of it was on my face, some on my chest. And the next cycle it got worse. But by then, I figured the damage had already been done, and I went ahead with the full cycle of steroids because I had a meet coming up. It's hard to explain to people that once you're on the drugs you lose sight of everything but winning. That's one thing they don't understand. I mean, I could look at myself, back then, and I could sort of see what was happening, but I didn't care. I don't feel that way now. I've been off the drugs for almost two years now, but I still have to shave every day.[4]

Tam admits that she was obsessive, even fanatical, in her approach to sport. But so, apparently, are thousands of other athletes in a variety of sports. Consider the comments of Harold Connally, gold medal winner in the hammer throw in the 1956 Olympic Games: "I think that any athlete should take any steps necessary, short of killing himself, to maximize his performance." Or consider a study done by Dr. Gabe Mirkin. He once asked more than 100 competitive runners if they would take a "magic pill" that guaranteed them an Olympic gold medal but would also kill them within the year and found, "to my amazement, more than one-half of the athletes responding stated they would take my magic pill." A comparable study involving lifters found similar results. And sports scientist Gideon Ariel admitted that if he had had to choose during his days as an Olympic discus thrower between an extra five inches in distance or an extra five years of life, he'd have chosen the distance.[5]

The use of ergogenic—performance-enhancing—drugs by athletes is certainly not a new phenomenon. What *is* new, and distressing to many who observe sport, is that these more recent additions to the athletes' bag of tricks—anabolic steroids—have the power to do more than simply enhance an athlete for a single, isolated athletic event. They can physically alter the athlete, sometimes permanently. Tam's use of steroids, for instance, left her with noticeable hair on her chest, enough facial hair to produce a beard and mustache, the beginnings of male pattern baldness, clitoral enlargement, and a significantly lowered voice. Whether she also suffered internal side effects is unclear. She did not get her drugs from a doctor and she had no tests made. But she knows, just as the many thousands of other athletes who regularly take steroids know, that liver dysfunction and an increased susceptibility to cancer, cardiovascular disease, prostatic enlargement and infertility are also all associated with the use of steroids.

Steroids also affect athletes psychologically. Some experts think, in fact, that the greatest benefit to athletes from steroids is not the fact that they allow the body to build more muscle, but that, as central nervous system stimulants, they make the athlete more aggressive about training and competition.[6] Many athletes would even argue, as Tam does, that the use of these drugs fundamentally changes who they are.

> There's not doubt in my mind that when I took the drugs I was no longer the same person I was before I took them. And I'm not simply talking about the facial hair and the lower voice. My personality completely changed. I trained harder. I wanted to win more. And I got much more aggressive. There was one woman at the nationals last year who looked at me the wrong way, so I invited her out in the hall.[7]

By anyone's lexicography, powerlifting is a minor sport. Though national and world championships are held, these contests are not part of the Olympic Games and they have recently attracted very little media attention, in part because of the ubiquitous drug use in the sport.[8] Nor is prize money offered in powerlifting; it is strictly an amateur affair and the greatest reward one can achieve is the holding of a world record or being named to a national team. Seen in this light, the risks Tam Thompson took seem astonishing. Yet she is certainly not unique. Nor is she without historical precedent.

Although anti-sports-doping laws were passed in 1965 in both France and Belgium, the International Olympic Committee defined "doping" in 1967 as the "use of substances or techniques in any form or quantity alien or unnatural to the body with the exclusive aim of obtaining an artificial or unfair increase of performance in competition."[9] Under this broad definition, even such regularly followed dietary practices as taking protein powder and vitamin therapy might count as "doping." In reality, though, what the IOC and the sports community consider "doping" or drug abuse is the use of substances and techniques that have to be either *administered* by physicians (such as "blood doping," when the athlete removes several pints of blood months before a competition, stores them until the day of the competition, and then reinjects them to increase endurance) or drugs that would normally be *prescribed* by physicians—amphetamines, sympathomimetic amines, narcotics, and steroids. (There are also other substances—such as alcohol and caffeine—on the IOC list, as well as a number of over-the-counter medications that contain minute amounts of amphetamines or other drugs banned by the IOC.) The IOC's thrust was, in 1967 and today, twofold. First, these substances and procedures were banned because they posed potential health threats to the athletes. Furthermore, they were banned because their use made competition unfair to the non-user.[10] By 1967, the IOC already had good reason for concern.

Throughout history, athletes have used a variety of substances in an attempt to get a competitive edge. The ancient Greeks, for instance, idolized for their athletic purity by such *fin de siècle* sports promoters as Pierre de Coubertin, the self-styled founder of the modern Olympic Games, were well-paid professionals who also tried a variety of "medical" measures to enhance their performances at Olympia.[11] The probable originators of the "high protein diet," for instance, were wrestlers from the classical period who often consumed as much as ten pounds of lamb a day, and there are reports from the third century A.D. that Greek athletes used certain types of hallucinogenic mushrooms to mentally prepare themselves.[12] Other reports indicate that Greek long-distance runners ate sesame seeds during races in the belief that the seeds would increase endurance.[13] It is also known that Nordic "Berserkers" thought they could increase their fighting strength twelvefold by eating *amanita muscaria,* a type of psychoactive mushroom.[14]

In the nineteenth century, as sports rose in prominence, there were many known reports of drug use. The first surfaced in Amsterdam in 1865, when several swimmers in a canal race were charged with "taking dope."[15] And as bicycle races swept into prominence in both Europe and America, experimentation with a variety of stimulants became common. Goldman reports that by 1869 cyclists were known to use "speed balls" of heroin and cocaine to increase endurance. And in 1886, as a result of such practices, a cyclist died, the first known drug-related death of an athlete.[16] Thomas Burk has also pointed out that the use of caffeine, alcohol, nitroglycerine, ethyl ether, strychnine, and opium was common among athletes in the late nineteenth century.[17]

The most famous early case of drug enhancement, however, occurred at the 1904 Olympic Games in St. Louis. The case is well known because at the conclusion of the marathon, the winner, America's Thomas Hicks, collapsed. During the investigation, Hicks's handlers, who had been allowed to accompany him throughout the course of the race in a motorcar, admitted they had given him repeated doses of strychnine and brandy to keep him on his feet. Even so, Hicks's medal was not taken away, and his joy at winning was expressed to reporters in a telling way when he finally revived: "I would rather have won this race than be president of the United States."[18]

Most of these early cases deal, of course, with stimulants, not muscle-building drugs such as anabolic steroids. But what these early reports do suggest, and why they are important to understanding the rapid growth of the use of anabolic steroids in the second half of the twentieth century, is that even in the so-called golden age of amateur sport, ethical considerations were often overridden by the desire for attainment. Pierre de Coubertin was just one of many in the nineteenth century to argue that sport should consist of contests between gentlemen and be untainted by any hint of "professionalism."[19] But what Coubertin and other sporting officials failed to fully understand was that money was not the only dangerous incentive for athletes. For some—for most athletes, in fact—the recognition and feelings of personal satisfaction they received from winning an event were sufficient in themselves to drive these athletes to extraordinary, often perilous, lengths. And as the twentieth century progressed, the old adage that, "It matters not whether you win or lose, but how you play the game," was less and less germane to what actually occurred on the playing fields. The attitude that now prevails is well summed up by Lou Simmons, a powerlifter and coach who opposes any controls on drug use in sport: "The psychology of a champion lifter is to reach the top *no matter what.* . . . if he doesn't take full advantage of everything at his (or her) grasp, it is his own fault."[20]

In any case, the record seems clear that had steroids, or testosterone, been available in the late nineteenth century, athletes and others would have used them. It was not until 1927, however, when Fred Koch, an organic chemist at the University of Chicago, and his graduate assistant, Lemuel Clyde McGee, were finally able to isolate a highly impure but nonetheless potent form of testosterone. Koch and McGee extracted the hormone by pulverizing several tons of bull testicles and then treating what was left with benzene and acetone to obtain their essence, an essence that had nearly miraculous properties. Capons, for instance, demonstrated masculine characteristics when administered the drug and later studies on hens and female calves confirmed the capacity of the extract to produce aggressive behavior.[21] But the expense and difficulty of the extraction process prohibited any widespread use of the substance and this precluded serious interest by the medical community. By 1935, however, several European physicians were also studying the hormone, and one of them, Yugoslavian chemist Leopold Ruzicka, came up with a process to alter the molecular structure of cholesterol and thus produce synthetic testosterone.[22]

According to science writer Paul de Kruif, there was a great interest in the new hormone throughout the remainder of the thirties since many people saw it as a potential fountain of youth. In *The Male Hormone* (1945), de Kruif describes many studies that used human subjects. He reports that scientists found that this new synthetic testosterone "did more than give [the subjects] more energy and a gain in weight. . . . It changed them, and fundamentally . . . after many months on testosterone, their chest and shoulder muscles grew much heavier and stronger. . . . in some mysterious manner, testosterone caused the human body to synthesize protein, it caused the human body to be able to build the very stuff of its own life."[23]

Much of the research involving testosterone and human subjects was done in Germany before World War II. Heinz Arandt recorded seventeen case studies of testosterone use, all of which showed positive results.[24] There is also evidence that the Germans continued their experimentation during the war, and even administered testosterone to some storm troopers to increase their aggressiveness. Dr. William Taylor has speculated that since Hitler had used the drug, it might have accounted for some of the mood swings and aggressiveness of the German Führer.[25]

In any case, *The Male Hormone* is full of praise for testosterone, since de Kruif saw in this new hormone a way to extend man's sexual life and increase his productivity. De Kruif himself experimented with the drug and argued that its use was no different than injections of insulin for diabetics. "I'm not ashamed that it's no longer made to its old degree by my own, aging body," he wrote. "It's chemical crutches. It's borrowed manhood. It's borrowed time. But just the same," he added, "it's what makes bulls bulls."[26] And in an observation made chilling by the passage of time, de Kruif speculates on the possible effects of testosterone on athletes: "We know how both the St. Louis Cardinals and the St. Louis Browns have won championships supercharged by vitamins. It would be interesting to watch the productive power of [a] . . . professional group [of athletes] that would try a systematic supercharge with testosterone."[27]

De Kruif would not have long to wait. At the 1952 Olympic Games in Helsinki, the Soviet Union did exceptionally well in the weight-lifting competition, despite having been ravaged by World War II, garnering seven medals—three gold, three silver, and one bronze. And in what may well have been the first public charge regarding the Soviets and drugs, the U.S. Olympic weight-lifting coach, Bob Hoffman, told the Associated Press, "I know they're taking that hormone stuff to increase their strength."[28]

As it turned out, Hoffman was right, and he soon had the proof. At the 1954 World Weight-Lifting Championships in Vienna, Hoffman was the U.S. team coach and the team physician was Dr. John Ziegler.

Ziegler carefully observed the Soviet team and suspected they were using testosterone, a suspicion that was later corroborated at a tavern by one of the Russian team physicians. Armed with this knowledge, Ziegler returned to the United States, acquired some testosterone and tested it on himself, on Bob Hoffman, and on several east coast weight-lifters, including Jim Park and Yaz Kuzahara.[29] Concerned about the side effects of testosterone, including prostatic problems and libido increase, Ziegler wanted a drug that would have the "anabolic" or muscle-building effects of testosterone without the "androgenic" effects (heightened aggression, hirsutism, increased libido, etc.). Then, in 1958, the Ciba pharmaceutical company released Dianabol (methandrostenalone), the first U.S. "anabolic steroid." The drug was not intended for use by athletes, of course, but was developed for burn patients and certain post-operative and geriatric cases.

Dr. Ziegler, however, had another agenda and what he did with Dianabol was critical in the spread of anabolic drugs in sport. With Hoffman's blessing, he convinced three members of Hoffman's York Barbell Club team to begin using Dianabol. In addition, Ziegler persuaded them to begin using—in secret—a new, little-known training program called "isometric contraction," which involved pulling or pushing against immovable resistance. Almost immediately, the three lifters began making unprecedented progress in strength and muscle size, and other lifters clamored to know why and how this progress had been effected. Then, as the lifters approached the world record level, Hoffman published a hyperbolic article in his widely read magazine, *Strength and Health,* entitled, "The Most Important Article I Ever Wrote."[30] And in a way it was, as it outlined the new training routine the three lifters were using but failed to mention the little pink pills. But the article only led to further speculation concerning the reason for the continued success of the three lifters, since the use of isometric contraction by his readers generally failed to produce significant improvement. Soon, however, the secret began to leak and it became known that the reason for the meteoric rise of the three York lifters, by now all national champions, was their use of Dianabol.[31]

And so, in a number of predictable ways, the news of steroids spread. The combination of a radically different exercise routine, an evangelical physician, an aggressive promoter with access to a national fitness magazine, and the startling progress being made by a few elite lifters, produced a climate of rising expectations in which strength athletes began a big arms race, fueled by an ever-expanding array of pharmaceuticals. This is not to say that any one of these four components was individually responsible for the increased use of drugs in sport—only that these components happened to exist at the same time and to interact in such a way as to produce the critical mass necessary for the strength-building drug scene to explode. Ziegler and Hoffman are now dead, the pace-setting lifters have all long since retired, and isometric contraction has acquired a patina similar to that of the bunny-hop and the Hula-Hoop, yet the many and various ergogenic kin of Dianabol continue to thrive.[32]

Evidence of this spread comes from the hammer thrower Harold Connally, who testified in 1973, at the U.S. Senate subcommittee hearings on drugs and athletics, that he had become "hooked" on steroids in 1964.[33] By the Mexico City Games in 1968, things had advanced to the point that Dr. Tom Waddell, who placed sixth in the decathlon that year, told the *New York Times* that he estimated a full third of the U.S. track and field team—not just the field event specialists—had used steroids at the pre-Olympic training camp held at Lake Tahoe.[34] This did not, of course, occur in a social and cultural vacuum.

The 1960s were a period of innovation and experimentation in nearly every aspect of American life. As a people we became fascinated with change and technology; science and progress received a special reverence in our lives, yet, at the same time, millions of young Americans turned to mood-altering drugs such as LSD and marijuana because they felt increasingly alienated from and dehumanized by our technological society. It now seems clear that it was the combination of these seemingly contradictory phenomena that helped further the drug revolution in athletics. The first phenomenon instilled in athletes who grew up in the sixties the belief that science could make their lives—their athletic quests—easier; the second phenomenon created a significant sub-culture within our society in which the use of illegal substances was not only permissible, but a hip badge of honor. As Ken Kesey said, you were either on the bus or off the bus.[35] Furthermore, as James Wright pointed out in *Anabolic Steroids and Sports*, by the sixties the average American home contained more than thirty different drugs, vitamins, and nostrums.[36]

Even so, most athletes in the sixties and early seventies were secretive about their use of anabolic steroids. But in 1971, American super-heavy-weight weight-lifting champion Ken Patera shattered the code of silence when he told reporters that he was anxious to meet the famous Russian super-heavy, Vasily Alexeev, in the 1972 Olympic Games. The previous year, at the World Championships, Alexeev had barely beaten Patera, but Patera now felt they were on a more equal footing: "Last year, the only difference between me and him was that

I couldn't afford his pharmacy bill. Now I can. When I hit Munich next year, I'll weigh in about 340, maybe 350. Then we'll see which are better—his steroids or mine."[37]

Patera's comments sent shock waves throughout the sporting media, although Patera maintained in a recent interview that he "didn't hear a peep out of anyone from the U.S. Olympic Committee."[38]

In the 1960s most of the attention on the question of drugs in athletics focused on the use of "hard drugs" such as amphetamines and heroin. A series of drug-related incidents had kept those particular drugs in the forefront of the public's consciousness since the Rome Olympics was marred by the death of Danish cyclist Knut Jensen, who had taken a "blood circulation stimulant."[39] There were other problems throughout the decade. Boxer Billy Bello died in 1963 of a heroin overdose while Britain's Tommy Simpson died in an amphetamine-related death in the 1967 *Tour de France*. Also in 1967, Dick Howard, a bronze medal winner at the Rome Olympics, died from an overdose of heroin. And then, in 1968, another cyclist, Yves Mottin, succumbed to amphetamine complications.[40]

Because of such problems, the IOC established a medical commission in 1967 and banned certain drugs. At the 1968 Games, however, drug testing was done only for research purposes and even then the "research" did not include anabolic steroids, since they were not yet on the IOC's banned substances list. The only meaningful testing done at the 1968 Games was, in fact, a chromosome check to determine whether all the female competitors were biologically women. The chromosome check was prompted in part by the fact that many female athletes had begun training with weights and thus projecting a more "masculine" image, an image that caused some sport officials to suspect that some of the competitors were not, in fact, women. In 1966, the International Amateur Athletic Federation instituted its first femininity screen, a gynecological inspection by a team of female physicians. Noticeable in their absence were the famous Russian sisters, Olympic gold medalists Tamara and Irina Press. In 1967, at the European Cup Track and Field Championships, the IAAF moved to the chromosome test as the IOC did for the 1968 Olympic Games. At the European Cup, Polish sprinter Eva Klubokowska became the first woman to fail the test.[41] Olympian Pat Connally reflected on the issue of sex testing in 1981: "The current situation [regarding steroids] in women's athletics is very disturbing. When I competed against the Press sisters from the Soviet Union, there were problems with sex tests and talk of men disguised as women. Now there are problems with steroids and we're back to the question of who's really a woman."[42]

Gender disputes aside, however, there were several reasons why the IOC failed to include anabolic steroids and testosterone among the banned substances at their 1967 meeting. The first was that throughout most of the sixties the use of anabolic steroids was still little known to most sports officials. The second, and perhaps more telling reason, was that there was then no way to test for the presence of such drugs. The IOC was also influenced by prevailing medical opinion, which maintained that these hormonal substances provided no athletic advantage. This opinion now seems astonishing, especially in light of the already widespread anecdotal evidence of the potency of anabolic steroids. In fairness, however, it should be added that little research attention had been given to the question of the use of the substance by athletes, since the drugs were not developed *for* athletes. The research that *was* done, such as a frequently cited UCLA study, found "that steroid administration in normal therapeutic doses is unlikely to increase muscle size or strength in healthy young men."[43] And even though subsequent research sometimes found otherwise and thus supported the overwhelming endorsements of the athletes, it was not until the early 1980s that the opinion of the medical community began to significantly change. A thorough discussion of the medical community's unwillingness to recognize the potential benefits of these drugs to athletes is beyond the scope of this study, but the feeling persists among athletes that one reason the medical community was so unwilling to admit the gains steroids could produce was that physicians hoped this non-admission would cause athletes to avoid such potentially harmful substances. This suspected strategy backfired, however, as it only caused athletes to distrust doctors and to turn, instead, to the black market for drugs and information.[44]

Fed by the powerful sports grapevine, the use of steroids burgeoned as more and more athletes began to train with weights and thus come into range of the siren song sung by competitive lifters and bodybuilders. So rapidly did the usage of anabolic steroids increase that in 1969 they moved squarely into the mainstream of America's sporting consciousness when *Sports Illustrated* writer Bil Gilbert published a three-part exposé entitled "Drugs in Sport." Gilbert charged that there were "some players on almost every NFL and AFL team that have taken the drugs." He quoted Ken Ferguson of Utah State, who went on to play pro football in Canada, as saying, ". . . anybody who has graduated from college to professional football in the last four years has used them."[45] Gilbert also pointed out that although rumors of both male and female use abounded, nothing was being done to stop the spread of such drugs. He correctly argued that the delaying of the decision to ban the drugs from sport was helping to promote their usage. As Dave Maggard, a high school coach and a former Olympic competitor, said, "I'd like to see the NCAA, the AAU and the U.S. Olympic Committee . . . go ahead and put us straight— tell us to either use the drugs, or don't. . . . It's this halfway stuff, the rumors, the idea that maybe you *have* to use them to be competitive that has made it such a mess."[46]

But still the use increased. At the 1972 Olympic Games in Munich, for instance, Jay Sylvester, then a member of the U.S. track and field team and now a faculty member at Brigham Young University, unofficially polled all the track and field contestants in Munich. He found that 68 percent had used some form of anabolic steroid in their preparation for the Games.[47]

In order for the drugs to be effectively banned, however, a viable test had to be found. Finally, in 1973, two reports in the *British Journal of Sports Medicine* suggested solutions to the problem of steroid testing. The first described a detection procedure utilizing radioimmunoassay, while the second advocated the use of gas chromatography and mass spectrometry.[48] The IOC decided to adopt both procedures in order to guarantee absolute accuracy. The only drawback to the new testing—a significant one—was that few laboratories in the world possessed all the equipment and computer data to do IOC-level testing. Even now, in 1987, there are only eight labs throughout the world with IOC approval. This shortage has made testing both expensive and administratively cumbersome.[49]

The new testing procedure was first used on a trial basis at the Commonwealth Games in Auckland, New Zealand, in February 1974. No sanctions were imposed and the participating athletes were not identified, but nine of the fifty-five samples tested contained steroids. In 1975, at the European Cup (track and field), sanctions were included and two athletes tested positive for steroids, were disqualified from the competition, and subsequently suspended by the international federation.[50] The first Olympic use of the new test came in 1976 at the Montreal Games, and only eight athletes out of 275 tested were found positive for anabolic steroids—seven weight-lifters and one woman discus thrower.[51]

It would be easy to assume from such a low percentage of steroid positives that the athletes had simply decided to come "clean" to the European Cup and the Games. Sadly, this was not the case. Despite the IOC's best intentions, they had left a way to get around the test because there were still some substances that enhanced athletic performance but for which the IOC had not developed a test. Ironically, the drug to which the athletes turned at the 1976 Games was the male hormone itself—testosterone—with all its potent side effects; it was the drug Dr. John Ziegler had abandoned in 1958 in favor of Dianabol. The most striking of those side effects are extreme aggressiveness and mood swings.

There is a long history of animal studies in which abnormally high serum testosterone levels or the use of anabolic-androgenic steroids have been associated with behavior that is either overly aggressive or violent. Also, when synthetic testosterone was used on human subjects in the 1930s, there were indications of its effect on behavior. Later studies suggested a positive relationship between levels of circulating testosterone in human subjects and certain types of either criminal or violent behavior. More recently, studies of steroid-using weight trainers have reported an increase in the aggressiveness of these athletes. And in an interview, Dr. William Taylor revealed that he had conducted a study involving 100 bodybuilders and other athletes who used steroids and that 90 of the 100 subjects admitted that while using steroids they had experienced episodes of behavior that were either uncharacteristically aggressive or actually violent.[52]

A more recent and widely publicized study of the relationship between the use of steroids and behavior was done by Drs. Harrison G. Pope and David L. Katz, both of whom are psychiatrists on the medical school faculty at Harvard University. Pope and Katz studied forty-one steroid-using athletes and found that nine subjects displayed a full affective syndrome while on steroids and that five experienced classic psychotic symptoms. None of these athletes had experienced such attitudes or symptoms before using steroids and none had family histories that would have predicted such changes. The subjects of the study also displayed an increased tendency toward violence and risk taking. One young man, for instance, was so convinced of his invulnerability that he arranged to be videotaped while he drove a car into a tree at a speed of forty miles per hour.[53]

Such behavior is often associated with psychological dependence, and a study by Charles Yesalis and associates concluded that adolescents who use steroids display this sort of habituation.[54] Although such side effects appear to be to some extent both individually variable and dose dependent, they can have devastating personal consequences, as the following set of separate, paired interviews makes clear. The man interviewed was a former all-pro lineman in the NFL.

Wife: He's so impatient when he's on steroids, so easily annoyed. He becomes vocal and hostile real fast and he was never that way before.

Husband: It definitely makes a person mean and aggressive. And I was always so easygoing. On the field I've tried to hurt people in ways I never did before.

Wife: His sexual habits really changed. On the testosterone he not only wanted to have sex more often, he was also much rougher. And his sleep patterns were completely different on the testosterone. The Dianabol changed him some, but on the testosterone he was always ready to start the day by five-thirty or six, no matter how late he'd turned in. In the old days he'd sleep till noon.

Husband: One of the bad things about the testosterone is that you never get much sleep. It just drives you so. With amphetamines the effect wears off after a game, but with the testosterone it's almost as if you're on speed all the time.

Wife: I don't think he'll ever be able to give it up. It cost him a wife who loved him and the chance to watch his two children grow up. There've been times when I felt he was almost suicidal. Sometimes, late at night, he'd tell me that he just couldn't help himself and that he couldn't stop using it because of the football, and then he'd cry.

Husband: A lot of guys can't handle it. I'm not sure I can. I remember a while back five of the guys on our team went on the juice at the same time. A year later four of them were divorced and one was separated. I've lost a lot of hair from using it, but I have to admit it's great for football. People in the game know that 50 percent of football is mental, and that's why the testosterone helps you so much. I lost my family, but I think I'm a better player now. Isn't that a hell of a trade-off?[55]

As for the original motivation amateur athletes had to use testosterone, further insight was provided in a 1982 interview with Professor Manfred Donike, head of the IOC-approved drug-testing laboratory in Cologne, West Germany: "The increase in testosterone is a direct consequence of the doping control for anabolic steroids. In former times, athletes . . . have to stop the use of the anabolic steroids at least three weeks before the event. So they have to substitute. And the agent of choice is testosterone—testosterone injections."[56] Donike, perhaps more than any other member of the IOC medical committee, was concerned about testosterone and its effect on sport. And so, as had been done earlier for anabolic steroids, Donike found a way to determine whether an athlete was using "exogenous" testosterone—testosterone from outside the body. It is important to note that the screening procedure for testosterone involves the use of a ratio of 6:1. In other words, for either a man or a woman to test positive for testosterone, he or she must possess, at the time of the testing, six times more testosterone than is considered "normal" for their respective sex. The 6:1 ratio was arbitrary, though one of the reasons given for its adoption was that it removed any possibility of a false positive. A negative aspect of the 6:1 ratio is that it leaves considerable room for cheating. In any case, after the U.S.-boycotted 1980 Olympics in Moscow, Donike performed unofficial testosterone screens on the urine samples that had been collected, and although not one positive test had turned up for anabolic steroids in the Games, he found that 20 percent of *all* the athletes—male and female—would have failed the 6:1 testosterone screen. This 20 percent included sixteen gold medalists.[57] Armed with this evidence, Donike was able to convince the IOC in 1982 to add testosterone to its list of banned substances.

The first official use of Donike's testosterone screen did not come about until the 1983 Pan American Games in Caracas, Venezuela. There, fifteen male athletes were found to be drug positive. Included in that fifteen were eleven weight lifters (some of whom were using testosterone), one cyclist, one fencer, one sprinter, and one shot-putter. While those figures are high, what raised the media's and the public's concern to even greater levels was the fact that twelve members of the U.S. track and field team simply packed their bags and flew home after the weight-lifting positives were announced. It was apparent by this time that the testing procedures Donike implemented in Caracas were more sophisticated than any ever administered to athletes. Not only could he test for testosterone, but he could detect further back in time the presence of anabolic substances. Several of the U.S. athletes, in fact, openly complained that they were being set up by the IOC as guinea pigs for the new procedures. Adding to the controversy as the Games continued was the fact that a large number of other athletes either withdrew with sudden "muscle pulls and injuries" or performed well below their previous bests in order to finish low and thus avoid being tested.[58]

The resulting furor further elevated the question of drugs and athletics. But Caracas was simply the largest in a series of major steroid scandals following Montreal. In 1979, for instance, the International Amateur Athletic Federation banned seven women track athletes: three Romanians, two Bulgarians, and two Soviets; and as a report in *Sports Illustrated* said, "Now even athletes with slight builds, such as middle-distance runners, believe steroids provide explosive power."[59] Though the women were supposed to be "banned for life," subsequent appeals allowed several of them to be back in action by the time of the Moscow Olympics. The earlier (1977) banning and early reinstatement of East German shot-putter Ilona Slupianek had aroused similar controversy, and this controversy intensified in 1980 when, after Slupianek won a gold medal in the Moscow Olympics, she was elected by a panel of international track and field experts as sportwoman of the year.[60]

Even with all these precedents, when the Pan American Games fiasco erupted, many U.S. journalists and commentators seemed shocked, and they focused on the fact that twelve members of the American team thought it best to leave Caracas without competing and being tested. Journalists also speculated about why the USOC had done virtually nothing up to that time to control the use of these substances. Furthermore, as the media's analysis continued over the next several weeks, Americans discovered that steroids and testosterone were not used only by Olympic athletes and weight lifters but by athletes in nearly every branch of professional sport. And as the journalists probed more deeply into America's sporting wound, they found that the USOC was not the only group of sports administrators who had chosen the "see no evil, hear no evil, speak no evil" approach to the problem. The NCAA was doing nothing about it either—nor were the NFL, the NBA, pro baseball, pro hockey, or even professional bodybuilding, a sport nearly synonymous with steroid use. And the journalists wondered why this was so. Why, they asked, had many European countries adopted rigorous testing programs while in America nothing was being done.[61]

Finally, after repeated questions from the press regarding drug testing, F. Donn Miller, then head of the USOC, announced that there would be testing at all the upcoming 1984 Olympic trials in various sports. According to a later report from Miller, however—issued *after* the Games—eighty-six of the tests performed during the pre-Olympic season in 1984 were positive. No sanctions were levied against any of the athletes, with the exception of two track athletes who were removed from the official U.S. team. This after-the-fact disclosure was apparently motivated at least in part by a desire on the part of the USOC not to lose face *before* the Los Angeles Games.[62] Even so, the penalty-free testing and the threat of real testing at the Games led many of the athletes, in their never-ending game of cat and mouse with the drug testers, to another way to beat the test—Human Growth Hormone (HGH), a hormone manufactured by the pituitary.[63]

HGH apparently made its debut in athletic circles around 1970 when an intrepid bodybuilder began experimenting with it. As this bodybuilder was unable to get *human* GH, he used GH from rhesus monkeys, which he hoped would also work on him, since it came from a fellow primate.[64] The primary reasons HGH was not used earlier by athletes seem to be that athletes either did not know about it or couldn't get their hands on it. Until 1985 HGH was produced only by extraction from the pituitaries of cadavers, and what was produced was limited in supply and very expensive. Now, however, biosynthetic versions of HGH are being marketed by Genentech and Eli Lilly and many people fear it may have an impact on the future of athletics as no test now exists that can effectively discover its use. Recently, the two most renowned sprinters in the world—Ben Johnson and Florence Griffith-Joyner—have been associated with HGH. In Johnson's case, sworn testimony during the official, post-Olympic Canadian inquiry into ergogenic drugs and sports revealed that Johnson had used HGH as well as steroids in his preparation for the Olympic Games in Seoul. But even though Johnson admitted he had used HGH, Florence Griffith-Joyner has denied the assertions of a fellow athlete and former national champion, Darrell Robinson, who told the West German magazine *Stern* and the television audience of NBC's "Today" show that he had been given $2000 by Griffith-Joyner in 1988 and asked to use the money to buy HGH for her so that she could use it in her training for the Seoul Games.[65]

Even though it is undetectable, however, it is doubtful that Growth Hormone would have achieved its recent popularity had it not been for Dr. Robert Kerr, a physician from San Gabriel, California, one of the few physicians to openly admit prescribing anabolic steroids and other drugs for athletes. In his book, *The Practical Use of Anabolic Steroids with Athletes,* Kerr equates this drug use to cosmetic surgery such as breast implants. He writes, "It really doesn't matter, the important factor is that they [the athletes] are going to take them anyway. If they are taking them anyway, then at least I can play a role in guiding them in the right direction. . . . If I should stop performing this work right now, who would my few thousand . . . patients go to for help, understanding and guidance?"[66] But Kerr was not the drug's only publicist. The authors of *The Underground Steroid Handbook,* in fact, wrote in a special issue on growth hormone: "Just why is it a desired drug? Not only does it make muscle cells grow bigger, but it makes the body grow *more* muscle cells. Tendons and ligaments get thicker, as do bones. Also, GH mobilizes stored fat, and if your body has plateaued on steroids, it can still respond to Growth Hormone. And, lastly, it is not detectable in drug tests used in international Olympic and powerlifting competitions."[67] In the first edition of the Handbook, the authors had concluded that HGH was the only drug that could "overcome bad genetics. . . . We LOVE the stuff."[68]

Such articles and interviews helped to create the attitude that pervades many of the books and pamphlets about steroids and HGH that are usually for sale at most bodybuilding and lifting contests. Essentially recipe books for drug users, these books explain how and when to use steroids, and what the latest wisdom is on beating the drug tests. At a recent powerlifting meet in Austin, Texas, for instance, a neophyte on the drug issue could have purchased, in addition to the above-mentioned publications, Fred Hatfield's *Anabolic Steroids: What Kind and How Many*, Boyer Coe's *Steroids: An Adjunctive Aid to Training*, Dan Duchaine's *Ultimate Muscle Mass*, Stan Morey's *Steroids: A Comprehensive and Factual Report*, or three publications put out by L&S Research: *Human Growth Hormone: Bodybuilding's Perfect Drug*, *Anabolic Steroids and Bodybuilding*, and *In Quest of Size: Anabolics and Other Ergogenic Aids*.[69] Besides telling the secrets of "proper" steroid use, some of these books contain another message; they argue for what Fred Hatfield has called a "new ethic."

> Many who hold to this [new] ethic recognize that science is ever advancing in technology and knowledge. . . . New ethic athletes are pioneers. . . . implicit in their philosophy is the notion that no amount of legislation has ever been able to halt the progress of science. As pioneers, these athletes carefully weigh the risk-to-benefit ratio and proceed with caution and with open minds. Can there be much wrong with getting bigger and/or stronger?

And, in a further discussion of his "new ethic," Hatfield states, "[drug use is unethical] by your moral code, but not by OURS!"[70]

Nor is Hatfield alone. In an anonymous interview in a leading bodybuilding magazine, one of the largest steroid dealers in the country explained his reasons for selling steroids: "Steroids are needed by people who wish to set themselves apart from the rest of our weakling society. . . . Steroid users aren't suicidal; they're adventurers who think for themselves and who want to accomplish something noble before they are buried and become worm food."[71] As can be imagined, such attitudes bode well for the continuation of a flourishing trade in black market steroids. No one really knows, of course, how large the black market is, but well-informed insiders know it is very large indeed.

An Ohio drug dealer who was arrested by FDA officials in 1985 consented to talk about the extent of the drug network in the United States. A former world champion with a good job, he began dealing steroids on the side during the late seventies. At first, it was simply a way for him to cover the expense of his own drug use; he saw himself as helping his fellow lifters. His insights into the extent of the drug traffic in athletics are important in understanding the size of the industry.

I can't be sure, of course, but I think there may be as many as 10 dealers in the U.S. who grossed at least $1,000,000 last year, and they'll net at least half of that. And some do more.

The way it works with the domestic stuff is that the big dealers either get it from drug manufacturing companies, from drug wholesale houses, from pharmacists, or from other big dealers and then sell it either to users or to local distributors. . . . Most of the main dealers have two or three hungry pharmacists in their pocket. You've got to realize that pharmacists can make more by spending a few hours a month ordering steroids for a big dealer than they can all the rest of the month running a drug store. Figure it out. They can get Dianabol, for instance, for around $7 a bottle, and it will sell on the street for $20 or $30 or even as much as $40 and $50 on the West Coast. I can get it for $11 a bottle, so you see there's a lot of money made as it changes hands. I believe there must be at least 200 pharmacists in the U.S. dealing steroids on the black market.

Another way the stuff gets on the market is through Mexico. My guess is that at least 100 guys go down regularly to buy drugs and then smuggle them across the Texas or California border. The Mexican connection is really valuable because of the devaluation of the peso. You can buy Primabolin down there for maybe 30 to 40 cents a unit and sell it up here for four dollars.

Most people don't understand how easy it is to buy steroids. All you have to do is to go into almost any gym in the U.S. and inside of a day you can score. Every gym has at least one dealer, and those thousands of small dealers usually get it from the big boys. The largest group of users would be bodybuilders, of course, and I don't mean competitive bodybuilders. I mean average guys who just wanted to be bigger and stronger as fast as they can. The last three or four years, the use of the stuff has just exploded and I'd bet there are over a million guys in the U.S. using steroids.[72]

One reason for the rapid growth of the black market during the early 1980s was the virtual impunity with which dealers could act. Tony Fitton, for instance, who was released in the fall of 1986 after serving nine months in the federal penal system for attempting to smuggle steroids across the Mexico-California border, was stopped by customs agents on at least two previous occasions and subsequently released without serving any jail time. In 1981, for example, he was stopped by the customs police at Atlanta International Airport with more than 200,000 doses of anabolic steroids in his luggage. He received a suspended sentence.[73] An interesting demonstration of the entrenchment of steroids in the administrative structure of the sport of powerlifting is the United States Powerlifting Federation's choice of Tony Fitton, shortly after his release from prison, as the official manager of the U.S. team for the 1987 Women's World Championships.[74]

Over the past four years, however, the attitude of state and federal officials has undergone a substantial change. Aware at last of the size and seriousness of the problem, various agencies have begun to act, as Fitton and others have learned to their sorrow. The mail-order steroid business has been hit especially hard as the following passage makes clear. It is from a current order form of a California concern known, with wonderful irony, as the John Ziegler Fan Club.

> These ordering instructions are current as of 2/2/86. Please follow these instructions exactly for your safety and ours. Do not write or speak on the phone the full name of the product, use only its assigned number code. Method of payment should be either cash or a totally blank POSTAL money order.
>
> You may or may not know that the federal government, particularly the FBI, has instigated a serious effort to WIPE OUT the black market steroid business. In the last month, major suppliers on both the east and west coasts have been put out of business. Why are we doing all this? The government can legally open mail. The FBI can legally, without a court order, tap a phone for 48 hours. We want to stay in business, and you won't believe how hard it's going to be to find anabolics in the future.[75]

In January of 1985, the Food and Drug Administration began to pay particular attention to the problem of black market steroids. The FDA asked the Department of Justice to coordinate a national investigation into the problem, and since that time these two agencies have worked with the U.S. Customs Service, the U.S. Postal Service, the Federal Bureau of Investigation, and various state and local agencies. The investigation has revealed that, although in the early days of black market steroid trafficking the sales were mostly made by athletes with no prior criminal record, the current situation features "(1) the wholesale smuggling of foreign, manufactured products into the United States; (2) the domestic, clandestine manufacture of counterfeit steroid products; and (3) the involvement of criminals."[76]

According to Department of Justice officials, there has been a steady increase over the past four years of counterfeit steroids on the black market. In that time period, thirty-five different counterfeit operations have been uncovered. And, although the majority of confiscations have occurred in California, the black marketing of steroids goes on in all sectors of the United States. As of April 25, 1989, the Department of Justice and the Food and Drug Administration had investigated 440 cases of illegal steroid distribution. The conservative estimate of the value of the confiscated steroids in those cases was $16 million.[77]

The first steroid dealer to receive much mainstream publicity was Charles J. Radler of Pittsburgh, who was arrested by Pennsylvania narcotics agents in July 1984. Radler's records indicated that, in the final nine months of 1983, he deposited more than $673,000 in four different bank accounts. Radler began small, but then he acquired a drug wholesaler's license, even though he had a police record as a heroin addict; soon he had eighteen employees, an office building, and a large account with United Parcel Service.[78]

In May 1987, the largest undercover investigation up to that time became known to the public when thirty-four people were named in a 110-count indictment, which included such charges as smuggling, tax fraud, and conspiracy. Those indicted included David Jenkins, member of the British team and winner of a silver medal in the mile relay in the 1972 Olympic Games; Pat Jacobs, former strength coach for the University of Miami; Mike McDonald, former world record holder in powerlifting; and Jerry Jones, former world powerlifting champion. Government officials have estimated that during 1986 and 1987 this particular steroid distribution ring sold approximately $4 million worth of steroids to approximately fifteen distributors in every section of the United States.[79]

Another well-known figure in the shady world of steroid indictments is Dan Duchaine, the California steroid "guru" who became famous through the success of his publication, the *Underground Steroid Handbook* and its subsequent "updates."[80] Duchaine, who has no formal training in science, became even more famous after his indictment on charges of defrauding the Federal Government and interstate selling of steroids. As of late 1989, he was still serving time in a California prison.[81]

Another way in which the federal government is cracking down on the indiscriminate use of anabolic steroids involves the FDA, as the following passage from an article in the *Medical Advertising News* explains.

> In its attempts to curtail the black market for anabolic steroids, the FDA recently tightened the approved uses of steroids. The regulatory agency removed all "possibly" or "probably" effective indications for which manufacturers could not provide efficacy proof. In March, the agency pulled off the market two anabolic steroids, methandrostenalone and methandriol, manufactured by 29 companies—most of them generic—because of the lack of proof of efficacy.[82]

Many people who observe the larger sporting world worry that such actions are too little and too late, that anabolic drugs have ruined sport. The main problem with these drugs is that not only do they vitiate fairness and pose potential harm to the health of athletes, but they rob the spectator as well. They require us to bring to the stadiums a new cynicism, a new rationale for the watching of sport. No longer is it possible to simply witness a world record and thrill at the marvelous achievement an athlete can produce through the combination of talent and will. Spectators now also ask, "Yes, but did he or she use drugs to set this record?" Florence Griffith-Joyner's marvelous performance in the Seoul Games, coming as it did after the announcement of Ben Johnson's positive test for steroids and amidst rumors about her own suspected use of these drugs, was met with an unusual amount of skepticism by many observers who would otherwise have felt only admiration and awe as she ran the 100 meters faster than Jesse Owens ran it to win at the 1936 Olympic Games. Ultimately, such speculation may turn spectators away from sport. The attraction of sport has always resided largely in the simple clarity of the struggle of man against man, woman against woman, actual against potential. Some sport scholars, such as John Hoberman, author of *Sport and Political Ideology,* fear that the most dramatic symbol of the technologizing of sport is a future in which handpicked, chemically manipulated athletes will compete against other handpicked, chemically manipulated athletes.[83] Whether we can find a mythology that allows us to be interested in such activity—let alone honor it— remains to be seen.

If the last five years are any indication, however, Hoberman and others have good reason to be concerned about the continuing spread of drugs—the continuing technologizing of sport. Consider these facts: (1) San Diego State University suspended its track and field program pending the investigation of steroid use among its athletes and coaching staff; (2) Baylor's head basketball coach resigned after a player went public with a tape he made while discussing steroids with the coach; (3) Vanderbilt University's strength coach and a local pharmacist were indicted for providing steroids to the Vandy players and for participating in a "steroid ring" that involved numerous other East Coast colleges; (4) a survey by a *Waco Times Herald* reporter revealed that steroid use existed at every school in the Southwestern conference; (5) Michael David Williams, a Maryland bodybuilder, went on a crime binge while on the top end of a long cycle of steroids, robbing six homes and burning three, yet was only required to undergo outpatient counseling after his attorney successfully argued that the steroids and testosterone had altered his personality and made him unable to fully understand the consequences of his actions; (6) five Canadian weight-lifters returning from the 1985 world championships in Moscow were stopped at the Montreal airport and found to be in possession of tens of thousands of doses of steroids purchased from the Soviet athletes for resale over here; (7) the two top super-heavyweight lifters in the world—Anatoly Pisarenko and Alexander Kurlovich—were stopped a year or so later in the same airport on their way to a Canadian competition and found to have over $10,000 worth of steroids in their luggage; (8) Dr. Walter Jekot, a physician who treats athletes on the West Coast, distributed printed announcements in at least one of his three offices offering free injections of steroids in exchange for the referral of new patients; and (9) in the 1986–1987 bowl season, Brian Bosworth and twenty other collegiate football players were banned by the NCAA from participation in post-season bowls after testing positive for anabolic steroids; (10) Keith Kephardt, strength coach at Texas A&M University and former strength coach at the University of South Carolina was indicted, along with three South Carolina assistant football coaches for providing steroids to college athletes. The indictment also indicated that the four coaches had used steroids themselves and that Kephart, who served as president of the National Strength and Conditioning Association in 1985–86, had imported steroids into South Carolina and dispensed them without a prescription; (11) a page one, "above the fold" report in the *New York Times* following the 1988 Olympic Games stated that "At least half of the 9000 athletes who competed at the Olympics in Seoul have used anabolic steroids in training to enhance their performances, according to estimates by medical and legal experts as well as traffickers in these substances. These experts also contend that the drug-testing programs of the International Olympic Committee and other sports associations have had no impact in reducing the use of such drugs"; (12) a national study published in 1988 found that 6.6 percent of high school senior boys use or have used anabolic steroids. In addition, there have been seven other studies of steroid use in high schools, most of which report a higher percentage of use; (13) according to a 1989 "60 Minutes" broadcast, $500 million worth of anabolic steroids were either manufactured or imported into this country last year, but only $10 million worth were prescribed by physicians; (14) following Ben Johnson's loss of his Olympic medal and world record at the Seoul Olympic Games, gym owners around the country reported that they received many hundreds of telephone calls from young men, impressed by Johnson's musculature and speed, who wanted to know how to get Stanazolol, the steroid that was found in Johnson's urine; (15) during the 1988 Olympic Games, the Bulgarian weight-lifting team, usually the best in the world, withdrew the rest of their lifters from competition after two of their first four Olympic gold medalists tested positive for a banned diuretic usually taken

in an attempt to conceal steroid use; (16) during the 1987 Pan American Games in Indianapolis, it was revealed that many athletes were
using Probenicid, a gout medication, to foil the steroid test and that
many had been successful in avoiding detection; (17) in March 1989,
Smena, a nationally distributed magazine in the Soviet Union struck
a blow for *glasnost* when it revealed that the Soviet sports federation had a secret, $2.5 million laboratory on a ship docked sixty kilo-
meters off the coast of Korea for the purpose of testing Soviet athletes
for banned substances immediately before their competition. Con-
firmation of this report is available from an interview the author
had with Angel Spassov, a national-level coach on the Bulgarian
weight-lifting team. Spassov reported that Anatoly Taranenko, the
premier superheavyweight weight-lifter in the world, was pulled out
of the Seoul Games by the Soviet officials after he registered a
testosterone-epitestosterone ratio of 5.75 to one. A six to one ratio (or
above) is required for a positive test, but the Soviet officials were
aware that the test results can vary enough so that Tarenenko might
have reached the six to one ratio and thus brought down onto the
heads of the Soviets an enormous public relations nightmare; (18)
in March 1990, Arnold Schwarzenegger, the recently appointed
chairman of the President's Council on Physical Fitness and Sports,
who had, by his own admission, used steroids to enhance his physical
development, sponsored the first drug-tested professional bodybuilding competition for men. Four of the twelve contestants failed,
including the winner, Shawn Ray, even though the International Federation of Bodybuilders asked for and received special dispensation
from the IOC to allow the contestants to send urine samples to the
IOC-approved Montreal lab before the event to determine whether
they would test positive. Apparently, not all of the contestants took
advantage of this unusual opportunity.[84] The problem is clearly not
going away.

What can be done? For one thing, testing, when properly administered, and with appropriate sanctions in place, makes a difference.
Studies have shown that when testing is done, performance levels
drop, thus making the competition fairer for non-users.[85] It is, however, no secret that just as Donike and the testers are searching for
greater accuracy, the athletes are searching for loopholes. Growth
hormone, for instance, will remain a problem until a test is developed
for it. Some experts recommend that all of these substances—
testosterone and its synthetic derivatives as well as HGH—be reclas-
sified by the Food and Drug Administration. As of April 1, 1990,
there was legislation before Congress making anabolic steroids a

Schedule Four controlled substance. Were these drugs to become "controlled" substances, it would be much harder for pharmacists to sell them indiscriminately and black marketeers would face stiffer penalties when caught. Legislation such as that recently passed by the California and Florida state legislatures will also have an impact since it makes the illicit sale of steroids a more serious offense. As of late 1989, twenty-six states either had passed similar laws or had them pending.[86]

But even if all fifty states were to pass such legislation, and all sporting bodies were to test with regularity, it is unlikely that athletics would return to relatively drug-free times. The new wave, the athletic avant-garde, is already looking into other techniques, such as the possible use of implants—electrodes and computer chips—inside the body. One researcher has already succeeded in producing an excess of natural testosterone in animals by implanting and stimulating electrodes in their brains. He told a reporter for *Women's Sports*, "If you're trying to develop superfolk, I can tell you for a fact that the way to do it is through substances in the brain. There are many proteins that can absolutely turn someone into a raging superstar if tapped appropriately."[87]

Finally, consider the fact that the same bodybuilder who first experimented with rhesus monkey Growth Hormone is now working with a team of Japanese scientists on the possibility of a computer chip implant that will control his hormonal secretions. He estimates that the project may cost him as much as $2 million, but he is now a wealthy man and he intends to go ahead with the project. He began his bodybuilding career as most young men do—with the simple desire to become a little stronger, a little healthier. But, as the philosopher George Santayana said, "Fanaticism consists in redoubling your efforts when you have forgotten your aim."[88]

Notes

1. "Drugs: The Use and Abuse," *Manchester Guardian*, 17 Sept. 1983, 18.

2. Bob Goldman, *Death in the Locker Room* (South Bend: Icarus Press, 1984); William N. Taylor, *Hormonal Manipulation: A New Era of Monstrous Athletes* (Jefferson, N.C.: McFarland and Co., 1985); Melvin H. Williams, *Beyond Training: How Athletes Enhance Performance Legally and Illegally* (Champaign, Ill.: Leisure Press, 1989); D. R. Mottram, ed., *Drugs in Sport* (Champaign, Ill.: Human Kinetics, 1988); and Gary Wadler and Brian Hainline, *Drugs and the Athlete* (New York: F. A. Davis Co., 1989).

3. Another woman who openly admits to steroid use is the bodybuilder "Pillow," who began an anti-steroid campaign in 1984. See Jan Todd, "Pillow Talks," *Strength Training for Beauty* 2 (Sept., 1985): 65–68.

4. Taped interview with powerlifter Tammy (Tam) Thompson, 15 April 1986. Tape on file at Todd-McLean Sports History Collection, the University of Texas, Austin, Texas.

5. Connally quoted in Jan Todd, "Former Powerlifter Calls for Steroid Curbs," *Austin American Statesman*, 13 Sept. 1983, 6; Mirkin in "High Risk Gamble to Obtain Winning Edge," *San Diego Union*, 13 July 1982, sec. C, 1; weightlifting study is from Goldman, *Death in the Locker Room*, 32; Ariel in Jan Todd, "Former Powerlifter Calls for Steroid Curbs," 6.

6. Terry Todd, "The Steroid Predicament," *Sports Illustrated* 59 (Aug. 1, 1983): 70–73.

7. Tam Thompson interview.

8. Both women's and men's powerlifting attracted a good deal of media attention in the latter part of the 1970s and early part of the 1980s. Both the national and world championships were regularly covered by CBS's "Sports Spectacular" and NBC's "Sports World," and several positive articles in *Sports Illustrated* and other mainstream publications appeared. However, as powerlifting became more closely identified as a sport that abused anabolic steroids—and, in particular, as many of the women who dominated the sport looked more androgynous and in some cases were growling and sprouting facial hair—the sport became harder to sell to the national networks. NBC announcer, Mike Adamlie, put this concern into words at the 1981 Women's World Championships, when he told Jan Todd, as head of the IPF Women's Committee, that powerlifting simply had to do something to clean up its image. According to Adamlie, his viewers might be interested in watching these women once—as he put it, just as people will pay to see the freaks in the sideshow—but he did not see them becoming interested in the sport or the women on a long-term basis.

9. A. H. Beckett and D. A. Cowan, "Misuse of Drugs in Sport," *British Journal of Sports Medicine* 12 (1979): 185, and Mauro DiPasquali, *Drug Use and Detection in Amateur Sports* (Warkworth, Ontario: M. G. D. Publishing, 1985) 3. "Doping" appeared in the English dictionary about 1889. Its origins are in South Africa where the word "dop" was used in the Kaffir dialect to describe a type of hard liquor used as a stimulant in religious ceremonies. The Boers apparently added the "e." By the latter part of the nineteenth century, the term had come to describe a mixture of opium and narcotics used as a stimulant in horse racing (see David P. Webster, *The Truth about Drugs*, circa 1973, privately published treatise in Todd-McLean Collection, 2).

10. Interview with Manfred Donike, head, IOC drug-testing committee, 1982. Notes on file at Todd-McLean Collection.

11. David C. Young, *The Olympic Myth of Greek Amateur Athletics* (Chicago: Ares Publishers, 1984), contains an excellent examination of the role of amateurism in the nineteenth century and its exploitation by Coubertin and others.

12. Thomas F. Burk, "Drug Use in Athletics," Symposium presented by the American Society for Pharmacology and Experimental Therapeutics at the Sixty-fourth Annual Meeting of the Federation of American Societies for Experimental Biology, Anaheim, California, April 15, 1980. Published in *Federation Proceedings* 40 (Oct. 1981): 2680.

13. "For Athletes, Drug Test Is an Easy Opponent," *Los Angeles Times*, 19 Jan. 1984, sec. 3, 14.

14. Ibid.

15. Webster, *The Truth*, 2.

16. Goldman, *Death,* ·26.

17. Burk, "Drug Use in Athletics," 2680.

18. David Wallechinsky, *The Complete Book of the Olympics* (New York: Penguin Books, 1984), 44–45.

19. Richard D. Mandell, "Stakes Too High for Olympians to Remain Amateurs," *New York Times,* 12 Feb. 1984.

20. Louis J. Simmons to Pat Malone, 17 Jan. 1981, personal letter. Simmons's letter was prompted by a drug use survey conducted by Malone among women powerlifters. Letter on file at Todd-McLean Collection. Simmons was subsequently arrested for selling steroids illegally.

21. Paul de Kruif, *The Male Hormone* (Garden City, N.Y.: Garden City Publishing, 1945), 67–70. For specific studies in this area see: L. C. McGee, "The Effect of the Injection of a Lipoid Fraction of Bull Testicle in Capons," *Proceedings of the Institute of Medicine* 6 (1927): 242; T. F. Gallagher and F. C. Koch, "The Testicular Hormone," *Journal of Biological Chemistry* 84 (1929): 495; F. C. Koch, "The Biochemistry and Physiological Significance of the Male Sex Hormones," *Journal of Urology* 35 (1936): 382; F. C. Koch, "Recent Advances in the Field of Androgens," *Cold Spring Harbor Symposia on Quantitative Biology* 5 (1937): 34; Allan T. Kenyon et al., "The Effect of Testosterone Propionate on Nitrogen, Electrolyte, Water and Energy Metabolism in Eunuchoidism," *Endocrinology* 23 (1938): 135; C. R. Moore, "Gonadotropic Substances and Male Hormone Effects in the Organism," *Journal of Urology* 42 (1939): 1251; J. Eidelsberg, M. Bruger, and M. Lipkin, "Some Metabolic Effects of Testosterone Implants," *Journal of Clinical Endocrinology* 2 (1942): 329; W. M. Kearns, "Testosterone Pellet Implantation in the Gelding," *Journal of the American Veterinary Medicine Association* 100 (1942): 197; See also, de Kruif, *The Male Hormone*, 229–31.

22. L. Ruzicka, A. Wettstein, and H. Kaegi, "Sexualhormone VIII Darstellung von Testosterone unter Anwendung gemischter Ester," *Helvetica Chimica Acta* 18 (1935): 1478. See also de Kruif, *The Male Hormone*, pp. 79.

23. De Kruif, *The Male Hormone*, 125–30, 152–56.

24. H. Arndt, "Zur Therapie extragenitaler Storungen mit Sexualhormonen," *Wiener Medizinische Wochenschrift* 89 (1939): 222.

25. William Taylor, "The Case against the Administration of HGH to Normal Children," presented at a symposium on *Ethical Issues in the Treatment of Children and Athletes with Human Growth Hormone,* University of Texas at

Austin, 26 April 1986. Taylor's information on Hitler came from: "Hitler's Final Days," *American Medical News*, 11 Oct. 1985, 1, 58–69.

26. De Kruif, *The Male Hormone*, 226.

27. Ibid.

28. "Easy Opponent," *Los Angeles Times*, 14.

29. Terry Todd, "The Steroid Predicament," *Sports Illustrated* 59 (1 August 1983): 64–69; interviews with Dr. John B. Ziegler, Jim Park, and Yaz Kuzahara, April 1983. Notes on file at Todd-McLean Collection.

30. Bob Hoffman, "The Most Important Article I Ever Wrote," *Strength and Health* 29 (Nov. 1961): 30–34.

31. Terry Todd, "The History of Resistance Exercise and Its Role in United States Education," (Ph.D. dissertation, University of Texas at Austin, 1966), 109–13.

32. Todd, "Predicament," *Sports Illustrated*, 66.

33. "Easy Opponent," *Los Angeles Times*, 15.

34. Tom Wolfe, *The Electric Kool-Aid Acid Test* (New York: Farrar-Strauss-Giroux, 1968), 29.

35. H. Wayne Morgan, *Drugs in America* (Syracuse: Syracuse University Press, 1981), 154–56.

36. James E. Wright, *Anabolic Steroids and Sports* (Natick Mass.: Sports Science Consultants, 1982), 2:119.

37. "Easy Opponent," *Los Angeles Times*, 15.

38. Telephone interview with Ken Patera, 16 May 1986.

39. Wallechinsky, *Olympics*, 207.

40. Ibid., 57, and Goldman, *Death*, 27–28.

41. "The Female Athlete and Her Problems," *San Francisco Chronicle*, 6 January 1981, 7.

42. Ibid.

43. Wright, *Anabolic*, 36.

44. Taylor, "The Case against the Administration of HGH."

45. Bil Gilbert, "Drugs in Sport: Problems in a Turned-On World," *Sports Illustrated* (23 June 1969): 71.

46. Bil Gilbert, "Drugs in Sport: Something Extra on the Ball," *Sports Illustrated* (30 June, 1969): 42.

47. Wright, *Anabolic*, 33.

48. Allan J. Ryan, "Anabolic Steroids Are Fool's Gold," Symposium presented by the American Society for Pharmacology and Experimental Therapeutics at the Sixty-fourth Annual Meeting of the Federation of American Societies for Experimental Biology, Anaheim, California, 15 April 1980. Published in *Federation Proceedings* 40 (October 1981): 2685.

49. Personal communication from Dr. Manfred Donike, head of the IOC drug-testing committee, April 1987.

50. Ryan, "Anabolic Steroids Are Fool's Gold," 2685–86.

51. Jerry Kirshenbaum, "Steroids: The Growing Menace," *Sports Illustrated* 51 (12 Nov. 1979): 33. Two of the weight lifters were Americans: Mark Cameron and Phil Grippaldi.

52. Telephone interview with Dr. William Taylor, Nov. 18, 1987. For information on animal studies see: W. C. Allee, N. C. Colia, and C. Z. Lutherman, "Modifications of the Social Order in Flocks of Hens by the Injection of Testosterone Propionate," *Physiol. Zoology* 12 (1939): 412–40; M. F. Buoissou and V. Gaudioso, "Effect of Early Androgen Treatment on Subsequent Social Behavior in Heifers," *Horm. Behav.* 16 (June 1982): 132–46; N. E. Van de Poll, F. de Jonge, and H. G. Van Oyen, "Failure to Find Sex Differences in Testosterone Activated Aggression in Two Strains of Rats," *Horm. Behav.* 15 (Mar. 1981): 94–105; N. E. Van de Poll, S. van Zanten, F. H. de Jonge, "Effects of Testosterone, Estrogen, and Dihydrotestosterone upon Aggressive and Sexual Behavior of Female Rats," *Horm. Behav.* 20 (Dec. 1986): 418–31; M. G. Bouissou, "Androgens, Aggressive Behavior and Social Relationships in Higher Mammals," *Horm. Res.* 18 (1983): 43–61; D. Zumpe and R. P. Michael, "Effects of Testosterone on the Behavior of Male Cynomolgus Monkeys," *Horm. Behav.* 19 (Sept. 1985): 166–77; H. D. Steklis, G. L. Brammer, and M. J. Raleigh, "Serum Testosterone, Male Dominance and Aggression in Captive Groups of Vervet Monkeys," *Horm. Behav.* 19 (June 1985): 154–63.

For information on testosterone use on humans, see: S. A. Vest and J. E. Howard, "Clinical Experiments with the Use of Male Sex Hormones," *Journal of Urology* 40 (Jan. 1938): 154. For information on circulating testosterone, see: H. Persky, K. D. Smith, and G. K. Basu, "Relation of Psychotic Measures of Aggression and Hostility to Testosterone Production in Man," *Psychosom. Med.* 33 (May-June 1971): 265–77; L. E. Kreuz and R. M. Rose, "Assessment of Aggressive Behavior and Plasma Testosterone in a Young Criminal Population," *Psychosom. Med.* 24 (July-Aug. 1972): 321–32; J. E. Ehrenkrants, E. Bliss, and M. H. Sheard, "Plasma Testosterone: Correlation with Aggressive Behavior and Social Dominance in Man," *Psychosom. Med.* 36 (Nov.-Dec. 1974): 469–75; C. H. Doering, H. K. Brodie, and H. C. Kraemer, "Negative Effect and Plasma Testosterone: A Longitudinal Human Study," *Psychosom. Med.* 37 (Nov.-Dec. 1975): 469–75; D. Olweus, A. Mattson, and D. Schalling, "Testosterone, Aggression, Physical and Personality Dimensions in Normal Adolescent Males," *Psychosom. Med.* 42 (March 1980): 253–69.

For aggression in steroid-using athletes see: R. H. Strauss, J. E. Wright, and G. A. Finerman, "Anabolic Steroid Use and Health Status among Forty-two Weight-Trained Male Athletes," *Medicine and Science in Sports and Exercise* 14 (February 1982): 119; D. R. Lamb, "Anabolic Steroids in Athletics: How Well Do They Work and How Dangerous Are They?" *American Journal of Sports Medicine* 12 (Jan.-Feb. 1984): 31–38; R. H. Strauss, M. T. Liggett, and R. R. Lanese, "Anabolic Steroid Use and Perceived Effects in Ten Weight-Trained Women Athletes," *Journal of the American Medical Association* 253 (May 1985): 2871–73; H. A. Haupt and G. D. Rovere, "Anabolic Steroids: A Review of the Literature," *American Journal of Sports Medicine* 12 (1984): 469–84.

53. H. G. Pope and D. L. Katz, "Affective and Psychotic Symptoms Associated with Anabolic Steroid Use," *American Journal of Psychiatry* 145 (April 1988): 487–89.

54. C. E. Yesalis, "Anabolic Steroid Use: Indication of Habituation among Adolescents," *Journal of Drug Education* 19 (1989): 113.

55. Todd, "Predicament," 71.

56. Transcript of interview with Dr. Manfred Donike, 6 February 1982, for *Sports Illustrated* Television, Ronox Productions, #06. On file at Todd-McLean Collection.

57. "Easy Opponent," *Los Angeles Times,* 15.

58. Craig Neff, "Caracas: A Scandal and a Warning," *Sports Illustrated* 59 (5 Sept. 1983): 18–19.

59. Kirshenbaum, "Menace," 33.

60. "Easy Opponent," *Los Angeles Times,* 15.

61. Todd, "Predicament," 73–77.

62. "U.S. Olympic Group to Weigh Drug Test Plan; 86 American Athletes Failed 1984 Screening," *Chronicle of Higher Education* (23 Jan. 1985): 3.

63. Children's pituitaries produce large amounts of this hormone to stimulate growth in height; at maturation, the production of HGH diminishes and vertical growth stops. Gigantism is caused by an overabundant supply of Growth Hormone during adolescence, while the condition known as acromegaly, which can cause horrific distortion of the face, feet, and hands, is primarily produced by an oversupply during adulthood.

64. Telephone interview with bodybuilder Peter Grymkowski, 9 May 1986.

65. *Austin American Statesman,* Sept. 21, 1989, C-1.

66. Robert Kerr, *The Practical Use of Anabolic Steroids with Athletes* (San Gabriel, Calif.: Robert Kerr Publishing, 1982), 2. Dr. Kerr is presently being sued by three ex-patients who believe that their steroid use contributed to and/or caused their afflictions. The three are: William Lumus, a recreational weight trainer who developed a carcinoma of the liver that required the removal of nearly 70 percent of that organ; Glenn Maur, a thirty-five-year-old former Mr. California who recently underwent quintuple bypass surgery and Dean Moore, a nineteen-year-old record-holding Olympic weight lifter who suffered a stroke that left him both physically and mentally impaired. Documentation on these cases is available at the Todd-McLean Collection.

67. *The Underground Steroid Handbook, Update #1* (Venice Beach, Calif.: OEM Publishing, 1982), 1.

68. *The Underground Steroid Handbook for Men and Women* (Venice Beach, Calif.: OEM Publishing, n.d.), 7. The full citation in *USH* is worthy of note: "Wow, is this great stuff! It is the best drug for permanent muscle gains. It is the basic pituitary hormone that makes your whole body grow. People who use it can expect to gain 30 to 40 pounds of muscle in ten weeks if they can eat around 10,000 calories per day. It is about $600–800 per 4 vials, and we think this to be another best buy. It has been very hard to get in the past as it was made from the pituitaries of rhesus monkeys and is illegal for general sale in the USA. It is now being made from 'smart' E-coli bacteria at Baylor Medical School in Texas. Usual dosage has been two units every three days. This is the only drug that can remedy bad genetics as it will make *anybody*

grow. A few side effects can occur, however. It may elongate your chin, feet and hands, but this is arrested with cessation of the drug. Diabetes in teen-agers is possible with it. It can also thicken your ribcage and wrists. Massive increases in weight over such a short period of time can, of course, give you heart problems. We have heard of a powerlifter getting a heart attack while on GH. GH use is the biggest gamble that an athlete can take, as the side effects are irreversible. Even with all that, we LOVE the stuff."

69. Frederick C. Hatfield, *Anabolic Steroids: What Kind and How Many* (Madison, Wis.: Fitness Systems, 1982); Boyer Coe and Stanley Morey, *Steroids: An Adjunctive Aid to Training* (Baton Rouge, La.: Boyer Coe Pub., 1979); Dan Duchaine, ed., *Ultimate Muscle Mass* (Venice Beach, Calif.: OEM Publishing, n.d.); Stanley W. Morey and Ken Passariello, *Steroids: A Comprehensive and Factual Report* (by the authors, 1982); Scott Chinery, *Human Growth Hormone: Bodybuilding's Perfect Drug* (Toms River, N.J.: L&S Research, 1983): idem, *Anabolic Steroids and Bodybuilding* (Toms River, N.J.: L&S Research, 1983); idem, *In Quest of Size: Anabolics and Other Ergogenic Aids* (Toms River, N.J.: L&S Research, n.d.).

70. Hatfield, *Anabolic Steroids*, 3.

71. Doug Nassif, "Steroid Underground," *Muscle and Fitness* 27 (Dec., 1983): 244.

72. Interview conducted by Terry Todd. Subject's name withheld by request. Transcript on file at Todd-McLean Collection.

73. Telephone interview with Clifford A. Stitcher, assistant district attorney, Jonesboro, Georgia, 2 July 1985. Notes on file at Todd-McLean Collection.

74. Fitton has continued to be involved with the coaching of the women's team for the United States Powerlifting Championships and was appointed team manager again in 1990.

75. Advertising flyer, "John Ziegler Fan Club," 2 February 1986. On file at Todd-McLean Collection.

76. United States General Accounting Office, *Drug Misuse: Anabolic Steroids and Human Growth Hormone* (Aug. 1989), 31 [Report to the Chairman, Committee on the Judiciary, U.S. Senate].

77. United States General Accounting Office, *Drug Misuse*, 31.

78. "A Business Built on Bulk," *Sports Illustrated* 62 (May 13, 1985): 56–57.

79. J. Eisendrath, "Confessions of a Steroid Smuggler," *Los Angeles Times Magazine* 4 (April 24, 1988): 8–10.

80. Following the publication of the original *Underground Steroid Handbook*, Duchaine published periodic "updates" as new drugs were developed and used experimentally by athletes. Like the original *Handbook*, these updates also included personal endorsements.

81. P. Alfano and M. Janofsky, "A 'Guru' Who Spreads the Gospel of Steroids," *New York Times*, November 19, 1988, 1.

82. Valerie DeBernadette and Terry Todd, "Anabolic Steroids: Black Market and Black Eye," *Medical Advertising News* 5 (15 June 1986): 5.

83. John M. Hoberman, "Sport and the Man Machine Synthesis," Unpublished Manuscript. (Apr. 1986) On file at Todd-McLean Collection.

84. "San Diego State Track Team Hit with Steroid Scandal," *Press-Telegram*, 26 Mar. 1986, 33; "Steroid Use Cloaked in Secrecy," *Dallas Morning News*, 23 Feb. 1985, C-1; "Vandy Players Used Steroids," *The Tennessean*, 9 Jan. 1985, B-1; "On Your Marks," *Track and Field News*, June 1985, 39; "Steroid Use on Trial," *New York Times*, 2 Apr. 1986, 14; "Canadians Busted for Steroids," *International Olympic Lifter* 8 (Aug. 84): 29; "Pisarenko and Kurlovich Nabbed for Steroid Smuggling," *International Olympic Lifter* 9 (Sept. 1984): 12–13; Flyer on Dr. Walter F. Jekot's stationary: "Bodybuilders—For each new patient you refer to our office you will receive one of the following: 1. Either six free Deca 50 mg. injections or three free Deca 100 mg. injections." Flyer on file at Todd McLean Collection; Craig Neff, "Bosworth Faces the Music," *Sports Illustrated* 66 (5 Jan. 1987): 20–25; *Austin American Statesman*, Apr. 20, 1989, F-11; P. Alfano and M. Janofsky, *New York Times*, Nov. 17, 1988, 1; U.S. General Accounting Office, *Drug Misuse*, 41; "60 Minutes," 10 Nov. 1989; S. Myslenski, "Pumping Drugs," *Chicago Tribune Magazine* (2 Jan. 1989): 7–9; *New York Times*, Sept. 24, 1988, 22; M. Janofsky, *New York Times*, Aug. 19, 1987, 28. Prior to the Seoul Games, Probenicid was added to the IOC's list of banned substances; *The Globe and Mail*, Mar. 25, 1989, 1, and interview with Bulgarian weight lifting coach Angel Spassov in Austin, Texas, March 18, 1990; telephone interview with Dr. Bob Goldman, supervisor of drug testing for the International Federation of Bodybuilding, April 1, 1990; see also Wendy Leigh, *Arnold: An Unauthorized Biography* (New York: Congdon and Weed, 1990), 146–47, for a discussion on Schwarzenegger's steroid use.

85. Interview with Professor Arnold Beckett of the IOC Drug Testing Laboratory at the University of London, January 1982.

86. United States General Accounting Office, *Drug Misuse*, 38.

87. Marjorie Shuer, "Steroids," *Women's Sports* 4 (Apr. 1982): 58.

88. George Santayana, *The Life of Reason* (New York: Scribners, 1905), 2:85.

Contributors

Jack W. Berryman, Ph.D., is associate professor in the Department of Medical History and Ethics at the University of Washington and teaches a course devoted to the "Rise and Development of Sports Medicine" in the School of Medicine. He was editor of the *Journal of Sport History* from 1974 to 1981 and is completing a book on the history of the American College of Sports Medicine.

John M. Hoberman received his Ph.D. in Scandinavian languages and literatures from the University of California at Berkeley and has taught courses on sports, politics, and the Olympic movement at Harvard University and the University of Texas at Austin, where he is associate professor of Germanic languages. He is the author of *Sport and Political Ideology* (1984), *The Olympic Crisis: Sport, Politics and the Moral Order* (1986), and is at work on a history of sport sciences.

Donald M. Mrozek, Ph.D., is professor of history at Kansas State University, where he has taught since completing his Ph.D. at Rutgers University in 1972. He is the author of *Sport and American Mentality* (1983), the editor of special issues of the *Journal of the West* focusing on sport, and the coeditor of the microfilm series *Sports Periodicals* (1977). He also researches and publishes in the field of American military history and defense policy.

Roberta J. Park, Ph.D., is professor of physical education and chair of the Department of Physical Education at the University of California. She has coedited, *Play, Games and Sport in Cultural Contexts* and *From "Fair Sex" to Feminism: Sport and the Socialization of Women in the Industrial and Post-Industrial Eras.* She is the regional editor (USA) for the

International Journal of the History of Sport, section editor for the *Research Quarterly for Exercise and Sport,* and a member of the Editorial Review Board of the *Journal of Sport History.*

Jan Todd, M.Ed., is a lecturer in the Department of Kinesiology and Health Education at the University of Texas at Austin. She coordinates the strength and conditioning programs of the department and serves as the chief archivist of the Todd-McLean Physical Culture Collection. She won the 1986 North American Society for Sport History's graduate student essay competition for her paper on Bernarr Macfadden. As an athlete, she held numerous world records in powerlifting and coauthored *Lift Your Way to Youthful Fitness* with Terry Todd. She also serves as coeditor of *Iron Game History,* a bimonthly journal devoted to the history of physical culture.

Terry Todd, Ph.D., is the Roy J. McLean Centennial Research Fellow in Sport History in the Department of Kinesiology and Health Education at the University of Texas at Austin. He is also the curator of the Todd-McLean Physical Culture Collection and teaches American studies. The author of five books and over three hundred articles in a variety of popular and scholarly journals, he was national champion in both powerlifting and weightlifting and has served as a color commentator covering these sports for CBS, NBC, ESPN, and BBC. He coedits *Iron Game History,* a bimonthly journal dealing with the history of physical culture.

Patricia Vertinsky, Ed.D., is professor of physical education, and associate dean of education at the University of British Columbia, Vancouver. Her particular research interest relates to the sociohistorical determinants of women's health and exercise behavior, especially the role played by the medical profession in articulating acceptable physical behavior for women. Her most recent book is *The Eternally Wounded Woman: Women, Exercise and Doctors in the Late Nineteenth Century* (1990).

James C. Whorton, Ph.D., is professor in the Department of Medical History and Ethics, University of Washington. He is the author of *Before Silent Spring: Pesticides and Public Health in Pre-DDT America* (1974), and *Crusaders for Fitness: The History of American Health Reformers* (1982). He is completing a book on the history of inner hygiene in British and American health culture.

Index

Books in the Series Sport and Society

A Sporting Time: New York City and the
Rise of Modern Athletics, 1820-70
Melvin L. Adelman

Sandlot Seasons: Sport in Black Pittsburgh
Rob Ruck

West Ham United: The Making of a Football Club
Charles Korr

Beyond the Ring: The Role of Boxing in
American Society
Jeffrey T. Sammons

John L. Sullivan and His America
Michael T. Isenberg

Television and National Sport:
The United States and Britain
Joan M. Chandler

The Creation of American Team Sports:
Baseball and Cricket, 1838-72
George B. Kirsch

City Games: The Evolution of American
Urban Society and the Rise of Sports
Steven A. Riess

The Brawn Drain: Foreign Student-
Athletes in American Universities
John Bale

The Business of Professional Sports
Edited by Paul D. Staudohar and James A. Mangan

Fritz Pollard: Pioneer in Racial Advancement
John M. Carroll

Go Big Red! The Story of a
Nebraska Football Player
George Mills

Sport and Exercise Science: Essays in the
History of Sports Medicine
*Edited by Jack W. Berryman and
Roberta J. Park*

Reprint Editions

The Nazi Olympics
Richard D. Mandell

Sports in the Western World,
Second Edition
William J. Baker